The Freudian Paradigm: Psychoanalysis and Scientific Thought

The Freudian Paradigm: Psychoanalysis and Scientific Thought

Md. Mujeeb-ur-Rahman, Ph.D.,
editor

nh
Nelson-Hall
Chicago

Library of Congress Cataloging in Publication Data
Main entry under title:

The Freudian paradigm.

    CONTENTS: Freud and the structure of scientific
revolutions: Md. Mujeeb-ur-Rahman The Freudian
paradigm. Ramzy, I. From Aristotle to Freud.
Walker, N. D. A new Copernicus? Shakow, D. and
Rapaport, D. Darwin and Freud. Kazin, A. The
Freudian revolution analyzed. [etc.]
    Bibliography: p.
    Includes index.
    1. Psychoanalysis. 2. Freud, Sigmund, 1856-1939.
I. Md. Mujeeb-ur-Rahman [DNLM: 1. Psychoanalysis.
WZ100   F889]

ISBN 0-911012-89-3 (cloth)
ISBN 0-88229-461-X (paper)
Library of Congress Catalog Card No. 73-89486

For
Frank A. Logan
and
All those whom he best represents:

the skeptical psychologist in general, and
the "hard-headed" experimental psychologist
in particular.

In the hope that these essays will pave the
way for a healthy dialogue.

Moi, je ne suis pas un Freudiste.
(S. Freud, in a conversation with Theodor Reik.
Quoted in "Listening with the Third Ear.")

Looking back, then, over the patchwork of my
life's labours, I can say that I have made many
beginnings and thrown out many suggestions.
Something will come of them in the future,
though I cannot myself tell whether it will be
much or little. I can, however, express the hope
that I have opened up a pathway for an important
advance in our knowledge.*

It may be asked whether and how far I am myself
convinced of the truth of the hypotheses that have
been set out in these pages. My answer would be
that I am not convinced myself and that I do not
seek to persuade other people to believe in them.
Or, more precisely, that I do not know how far I
believe in them.**

*S. Freud, from *An Autobiographical Study*, W.W. Norton, New York, 1963.
**S. Freud, from *Beyond the pleasure Principle*, Liveright, New York, 1970.

Contents

Contributing Authors   *xi*

Acknowledgments   *xix*

Preface   *xxi*

FREUD AND THE STRUCTURE OF SCIENTIFIC REVOLUTIONS

Md. Mujeeb-ur-Rahman
1. The Freudian Paradigm   *3*

Ishak Ramzy
2. From Aristotle to Freud: A Few Notes   *21*
on the Roots of Psychoanalysis

Nigel D. Walker
3. A New Copernicus?   *35*

David Shakow and David Rapaport
4. Darwin and Freud: *43*
A Comparison of Receptions

Alfred Kazin
5. The Freudian Revolution Analyzed   *65*

FREUD AND THE MODERN PHILOSOPHY OF SCIENCE

Abraham Kaplan
6. Freud and Modern Philosophy   *75*

Philipp Frank
7. Psychoanalysis and Logical Positivism   *101*

Else Frenkel-Brunswik
8. Meaning of Psychoanalytic Concepts and   *107*
Confirmation of Psychoanalytic Theories

Leonard Horwitz
9.   Theory Construction and Validation   123
in Psychoanalysis

Robert Waelder
10.   The Validation of Psychoanalytic   147
Interpretations and Theories

Heinz Hartmann
11.   Comments on the Scientific   169
Aspects of Psychoanalysis

Wesley C. Salmon
12.   Psychoanalytic Theory and Evidence   187

Gail Kennedy
13.   Psychoanalysis: Protoscience   201
and Metapsychology

FREUD AND THE SCIENCE OF PSYCHOLOGY

Junius F. Brown
14.   The Position of Psychoanalysis   213
in the Science of Psychology

Ernest R. Hilgard
15.   The Scientific Status   229
of Psychoanalysis

Lawrence S. Kubie
16.   Pavlov, Freud and Soviet Psychiatry   247

David C. McClelland
17.   Freud and Hull: 257
Pioneers in Scientific Psychology

David Shakow
18.   Psychoanalysis and American Psychology   269

George S. Kline
19.   Orientations from Psychoanalysis   295

Heinz Hartmann
20.   Psychoanalysis as a Scientific Theory   317

Jacob A. Arlow
21.   Psychoanalysis as Scientific Method   345

Gardner Murphy
22. Psychoanalysis as a Unified Science   *355*

James A.C. Brown
23. Assessments and Applications   *365*

David Shakow and David Rapaport
24. Conclusions   *391*

Contributing Authors

JACOB A. ARLOW received his M.D. from New York University in 1936. He has been associated as a neuropsychiatrist with the U.S. Public Health Service, King's County Hospital in Brooklyn, Montefiore Hospital in Bronx and the New York Psychiatric Institute. He is a member of the Psychiatric Association, Psychosomatic Society, Psychoanalytic Association (of which he was also president), and the International Psychoanalytic Association. He is currently a practising psychiatrist and Clinical Professor of Psychiatry at the State University of New York, Downstate Medical Center.

JAMES A.C. BROWN took a degree in Medicine at the Edinburgh University. During the Second World War he served as a specialist in psychiatry in the Middle East. After the war he joined a large industrial concern and on the basis of his experience there for seven years wrote *The Social Psychology of Industry* (1954). Later he became deputy director of the Institute of Social Psychiatry in London. He wrote several books on psychology and psychiatry, among them *The Distressed Mind, The Evolution of Society, Freud and the Post-Freudians* (1961), and *Techniques of Persuasion: From Propaganda to Brainwashing* (1963). He died in 1964.

JUNIUS F. BROWN received his Ph.D. from Yale University in 1929. He taught at the universities of Colorado and Kansas prior to assuming the position of Chief Psychologist at the Menninger Clinic in 1939. His contributions ranged widely over several areas in psychology including experimental and mathematical psychology, abnormal and social psychology, and human perception and motivation. He is the author of the widely cited book *Psychology and the Social Order* (1936) and *The Psychodynamics of Abnormal Behavior* (1940).

PHILIPP FRANK received his doctorate in Physics at the University of Vienna in 1907. In 1912 he succeeded Einstein as Professor of Theoretical Physics at the German University of Prague, where he stayed until 1939. In 1939 he came to Harvard as visiting lecturer and later established permanent residence in the United States. As a visiting professor he taught at several universities including City College of New York, Brown, Purdue, Brandeis, and M.I.T. He was a member of the Vienna Circle, founder and first president of the Institute for the Unity of Science. He also served as the associate editor of the International Encyclopedia of Unified Science, which was devoted to a conception of science that both integrated human knowledge and worked against over-specialization. He was regarded as one of the world's leading authorities in physics and philosophy, and his many works which enriched the philosophy of science include *The Theory of Knowledge and Modern Physics, Modern Science and Its Philosophy, The End of Mechanistic Physics, Between Physics and Philosophy, Relativity—a Richer Truth.* His close personal and scientific contact with Einstein was summed up in his authoritative biography *Einstein—His Life and Times.* Dr. Frank died in 1966 at the age of eighty-two.

ELSE FRENKEL-BRUNSWIK received her Ph.D. from the University of Vienna in 1930. She taught in Vienna until 1938 when she came to the United States and obtained a research associateship and lectureship in Psychology at the Institute of Child Welfare in California. She also held the Social Science Research Council fellowship and a fellowship at the Institute for Advanced Study in Behavioral Sciences at Stanford. She was a fellow of the American Psychological Association and a member of the American Philosophical Society. In addition to her many contributions in the areas of personality, motivation, child, adolescent and social psychology, she was the co-author of *The Authoritarian Personality* (1950). She has also been a professor of psychology at Berkeley University.

HEINZ HARTMANN obtained his M.D. from the University of Vienna Medical School in 1920. He then worked in the Psychiatric and Neurological University Clinics in Vienna under Dr. Wagner von Jaureg. He came to the United States in 1941, and was director of the treatment center of the New York Psychoanalytic Institute for several years. He was president of both the New York Psychoanalytic Society and the International Psychoanalytic Association. As a leader of "ego psychology" he made significant contributions to the growth and development of psychoanalysis. He was co-founder and editor of *The Psychoanalytic Study of the Child*. Several papers that he wrote since 1924 were published in his book *Essays on Ego Psychology* (1964). A collection of essays in his honor by his colleagues and former pupils appeared in a volume entitled *Psychoanalysis: A General Psychology* (1968). Dr. Hartmann died in 1970 at the age of seventy-five.

ERNEST R. HILGARD received his Ph.D. from Yale University in 1930 and taught there until 1933. He then moved to Stanford where he has been since, except for a short break for service in Washington during the Second World War. He has held the fellowship of the Center for Advanced Studies in the Behavioral Sciences and has served on the boards or committees of several national bodies including the Social Science division of the National Research Council and the U.S. Public Health Service. He is a member of the National Academy of Sciences, the American Academy of Arts and Sciences, and the American Psychological Association (of which he was also president). He is a recipient of the Warren Medal and the APA award for distinguished scientific contribution. He has contributed extensively in the areas of learning and motivation in animals and men, and hypnosis. He is the author of three preeminent textbooks, *Conditioning and Learning*, with D. G. Marquis (1940), revised by G. Kimble (1961), *Theories of Learning* (1948), revised edition, with G. H. Bower (1966), *Introduction to Psychology* (1953), revised edition, with R. C. Atkinson (1967). His research in hypnosis was published in *Hypnotic Susceptibility* (1965). Currently he is emeritus professor in psychology at Stanford.

LEONARD HORWITZ took his Ph.D. from New York University in 1951. He is a member of the American Psychological Association and a diplomate (in Clinical Psychology) of the American Board of Professional Psychologists. He has numerous publications in the areas of psychotherapy, group therapy, and psychoanalysis. Since 1969 he has been director of the Group Psychotherapy Service at the Menninger Foundation.

ABRAHAM KAPLAN obtained his Ph.D. in philosophy from the University of California in 1942. He has been on the faculties of Harvard, Columbia, University of Michigan, Brandeis Institute, and Hebrew Union College in Los Angeles. For several years he has also been a consultant to the Rand Corporation. He is a member of the American

Philosophical Association (also former president of its Pacific division), Association of Jewish Philosophy and Academy of Psychoanalysis. In addition to other distinctions he has been the recipient of the Guggenheim and Rockefeller fellowships and a fellowship at the Center for Advanced Study in the Behavioral Sciences. He has written several articles in professional journals and is the author of *The New World of Philosophy* (1962) and *The Conduct of Inquiry* (1964). At present he is professor of philosophy at the University of Haifa in Israel.

ALFRED KAZIN obtained his M.A. from Columbia University in 1938. He has taught at Harvard, Princeton, University of California, New York University, New School for Social Research, Amherst College and was Fulbright Lecturer at Cambridge University in 1952. Since 1963 he has been a distinguished professor of English at the State University of New York at Stony Brook. He is a member of the American Academy of Arts and Sciences and the National Institute of Arts and Letters. He has also held Guggenheim and Rockefeller fellowships. His many writings include *On Native Grounds (1942), A Walker in the City (1951), The Inmost Leaf* (1955). He has edited books on Blake, Scott Fitzgerald, Dreiser, Melville, Emerson, and Nathaniel Hawthorne.

GAIL KENNEDY obtained his Ph.D. from Columbia University in 1928. He taught at Columbia University, New School for Social Research, Bennington College, and Amherst College. He was professor of philosophy at Amherst College from 1939 until his death in 1972 at the age of seventy-one. He was a member of the American Philosophical Association and contributed a number of articles to professional journals. Books he wrote, co-authored, or edited include *Bacon, Hobbes and Locke, Selected Writings* (1937), *Democracy and the Gospel of Wealth* (1949), *Pragmatism and American Culture* (1950), *The Classic American Philosophers* (1951), *'Education for Democracy* (1952), *Evolution and Religion* (1957), *The American Pragmatists: Selected Writings* (1960). At his death, Dr. Kennedy was working on the papers of John Dewey, the American philosopher.

GEORGE S. KLEIN took his Ph.D. in psychology from Columbia University in 1942. He taught at the Menninger Foundation graduate school in psychology, was an associate psychologist at the Menninger Clinic, and also served as a consultant to the Austen Riggs Center in Massachusetts. He is a member of the American Psychological Association and the American Association for the Advancement of Science. He was editor of *Psychological Issues* and has contributed extensively in the areas of personality, cognition, and motivation. He is the author of *Perception, Motives and Personality* (1970). Currently he is professor of psychology and director of the clinical laboratory at New York University.

LAWRENCE S. KUBIE received his M.D. from Johns Hopkins University in 1921. He was associated with the faculties of several medical schools including the College of Physicians and Surgeons, Columbia University, Yale Medical School, and the Jefferson Medical College. He also served on the staffs of many hospitals including the Neurological Institute of New York, Mount Sinai Hospital, and the Sheppard Enoch Pratt Hospital in Maryland, and was director of research and training at the N.Y. Psychoanalytic Institute. He was a member of the American Medical Association, Neurological Association, Psychiatric Association, Psychoanalytic Association, and the Psychosomatic Society (he also held presidential positions in the latter two). In addition to his many contributions in the area of neuropathology, etiology of neuroses, and practical and theoretical aspects of psychoanalysis, he was the editor-in-chief of the *Journal of Nervous and Mental Diseases* and the author of *Neurotic Distortion of the Creative Process* (1958). At his death in 1973, Dr. Kubie was professor emeritus in psychiatry at Johns Hopkins University.

DAVID C. McCLELLAND took his Ph.D. in psychology from Yale in 1941. He taught at Wesleyan University for several years before he moved to Harvard in 1956 as professor of psychology and chairman of the Department of Social Relations. He is a fellow of the American Psychological Association and the American Academy of Arts and Sciences. He has held a Guggenheim fellowship, acted as deputy director of the behavioral sciences division of the Ford Foundation, and served on the training grants committee of the National Institute of Mental Health. He has made significant contributions in the areas of personality, human motivation, and imagination. He is the author of *The Achieving Society* (1961) and *The Roots of Consciousness* (1964). Currently he distributes his time between teaching at Harvard and traveling to different parts of the world in connection with his research on achievement motivation.

MD. MUJEEB-UR-RAHMAN took his Ph.D. in psychology from the University of New Mexico in 1970. He was lecturer in psychology at Osmania University (India) and came to the United States for his doctoral work on a Fulbright scholarship. He has also been visiting assistant professor at the University of New Mexico and St. Francis Xavier University in Nova Scotia (Canada), and consultant to the Stanford Research Institute. He is a member of the American Psychological Association, the Canadian Psychological Association, the American Association for the Advancement of Science and the Sigmund Freud Society in Vienna. His research interests are in the areas of motivation (curiosity), cognition, psychoanalytic theory, and philosophy of science. Currently he is assistant professor of psychology at the University of Prince Edward Island (Canada).

GARDNER MURPHY received his Ph.D. in psychology from Columbia University in 1923 and remained with its faculty until 1940 when he moved to the City College of New York as professor and chairman of the department. In 1952 he was invited to the Menninger Foundation in Kansas where he became the director of research on perceptual learning; the results of this research were published in *Development of the Perceptual World* (with C. M. Solley) in 1960. His experiences as a consultant for UNESCO in India are summed up in his book *In the Minds of Men* (1953). He is a fellow of the American Psychological Association, its past president, and a recipient of its Gold Medal Award. He has made significant contributions in the areas of psychology of personality, perception, social behavior, and parapsychology. He is the author of *Experimental Social Psychology* with his wife, Lois Murphy, *Personality: A Biosocial Approach to Origins and Structure* (1947), *Human Potentialities* (1958) and *The Challenge of Psychical Research (1961)*.

ISHAK RAMZY received his Ph.D. from the University of London in 1948. He is a member of the American Psychological Association and has made contributions in the areas of personality and psychopathology. Since 1958 he has been at the Menninger Foundation as a training and supervisory psychoanalyst.

DAVID RAPAPORT received his Ph.D. from the University of Budapest in 1938. He was general director of research at the Menninger Foundation and also served as clinical professor of psychology at the foundation's School of Psychology. Until his untimely death in 1960 at the age of forty-nine, he served as research associate and senior staff member at the Austen Riggs Center in Massachusetts. His contributions to the systematizing of psychoanalytic theory earned for him a distinguished place in "ego psychology." Among a few of his contributions are *Emotion and Memory* (1942), *Organization and*

Pathology of Thought (1951), *The Development and Concepts of Psychoanalytic Ego Psychology* (1955). He was also the co-author of *The Influence of Freud on American Psychology* (1964).

WESLEY C. SALMON obtained his Ph.D. in philosophy from the University of California in 1950. Since then he has taught at Northwestern and Brown universities. Currently he is a member of the editorial board of *Philosophy of Science,* a member of the U.S. National Committee of the International Union for History and Philosophy of Science. He has written many articles on logic and the philosophy of science and is the author of the book, *The Foundations of Scientific Inference (1966).*

DAVID SHAKOW took his Ph.D. at Harvard University in 1942. For several years he was director of psychological research at Worcester State Hospital. As professor of psychology, he taught at the University of Illinois Medical School and the University of Chicago. Since 1954 he has been chief of the psychology laboratory at the National Institute of Mental Health. He also served as consultant to the Veterans Administration and the U.S. Public Health Service. He is a fellow of the American Psychological Association, Orthopsychiatric Association, and the Psychosomatic Society. In 1959 he received the Distinguished Contribution to Clinical Psychology Award. He has several publications in the areas of experimental psychopathology and the psychology of schizophrenia. He is also the co-author of *The Influence of Freud on American Psychology* (1964).

ROBERT WAELDER received his Ph.D. from the University of Vienna in 1922. He taught at the psychoanalytic institutes of Vienna, Boston, Philadelphia, and New York, and at Bryn Mawr College. He was also training and supervisory analyst at the Philadelphia Association for Psychoanalysis and the New York Psychoanalytic Institute. He was a fellow of the American Association for the Advancement of Science and the Orthopsychiatric Association, and a member of the American Psychological Association and the Psychoanalytic Association. His important contributions were in the areas of psychoanalytic theory, psychoanalysis, social science and history, psychological aspects of war and peace, totalitarianism. He is the author of *Basic Theory of Psychoanalysis* (1960).

NIGEL D. WALKER received his Ph.D. from Edinburgh University in 1954 and the D. Litt. from Oxford University in 1970. He was reader in criminology and professorial fellow at Nuffield College, Oxford, until 1973, when he moved to the University of Cambridge as Wolfson professor of criminology. He is a member of the Royal Society of Medicine and the British Society of Criminology, and has served on the Advisory Council on Penal System and the Advisory Council on Probation and After-care. He has contributed several articles to journals in criminology and the philosophy of science. He is the author of *A Short Hisotry of Psychotherapy* (1957), *Crime and Punishment in Britain* (1965), *Crime and Insanity in England*, 2 vols. (1968, 1972), and *Sentencing in a Rational Society* (1969).

Acknowledgments

Many thanks are due to all the authors who granted me permission to include their enduring contributions to the science of psychoanalysis in the present collection. In addition, I am also very grateful to their publishers for permission to reprint the material. A special word of thanks is due to the Nelson-Hall Company and its editors, Mr. William C. Steubing and Mr. Elbert P. Epler, for making the publication of this book possible. I am quite sure that their judgment will be amply rewarded.

The quotations from Sigmund Freud at the beginning of the first and third sections are reprinted with the permission of W.W. Norton and Company, New York. The Freud quotation at the beginning of the second section is reprinted by permission of Basic Books, Inc., Publishers, New York, by arrangement with The Hogarth Press Ltd. and The Institute of Psycho-Analysis, London. Quoted material in the first reading is reprinted by permission of the copyright owners.

At this end, I am very thankful to Miss Linda Murphy, Sherlyn Bevan, Heather Birt and Anne McLennan for their painstaking work in helping with the preparation and organization of the manuscript to the point where the publishers could take over. Grateful acknowledgments are also due to my colleagues at the University of Prince Edward Island, for providing a continuous source of moral support, interest, and help in various phases of organizing the present work. A delightful evening spent in discussing the project with Dr. Ronald H. Forgus of Lake Forest College provided a booster dose of moral support which had the effect of raising the level of my spirits in both mind and body!

Most important of all, and certainly more than I can possibly express, is my gratitude to Dr. Ralph D. Norman of the University of New Mexico. His sincere and critical appreciation, encouragement, and interest in my initial attempts to make a case for Freudian theory played a very important part in bolstering my morale. The first article in this book is a revised version of a paper I presented* in one of the many stimulating seminars he held on personality theory. Another source of inspiration was the challenge provided in the person of Dr. Frank A. Logan, chairman of the Department of Psychology at the University of New Mexico. In a sense, this collection of essays is an attempt to meet the challenge of a skeptical psychologist more than halfway—on the same ground and by the same ground rules. Even the remote possibility of gaining one such man's mind and heart for psychoanalysis was, I thought, worth the effort! The same sentiments apply in the case of Professor Julian Jaynes of Princeton University. In the many interesting conversations I have had with him, I have expressed my earnest desire that he give himself just one more chance; if this series of essays does not make a Freudian out of him, I am afraid nothing ever will!

Finally, in keeping with Freud's reality principle, I must acknowledge the role of my 'libidinally cathected objects.' Two screaming kids, Gina and Moiz, joined occasionally by a wife, Asifa, provide quite a formidable combination as far as stimulation for work is concerned—but then 'nirvana' can hardly be the lot of a family man!

*In September, 1967.

Preface

Freud's theories have always been a subject of considerable debate and dispute. Nevertheless, there is general agreement that his thinking has had a widespread effect on psychological research and a very significant influence on inquiry in a variety of fields ranging from anthropology and literature to mythology and religion.

Yet, academic psychology has continued to be reticent in acknowledging the Freudian paradigm. Experimental psychologists (to whom this book is dedicated) in particular have been in the forefront of those who have reached the verdict that Freud's theory is inaccessible to conventional tests of 'proof' and 'disproof,' and hence unscientific. That the 'case against psychoanalysis' is not closed is attested by some recent works which include a comprehensive account of all the attempts to 'check up on Freud,' and thus separate 'fact from fiction.' Supporting such attempts are some recent, as well as not so recent, methodological and philosophical analyses by authors who have examined the pros and cons of the Freudian model within the context of the modern philosophy of science.

It is my contention that the Freudian paradigm is consistent with the modern philosophy of science—both critical and postcritical (a la Polanyi). Experimental psychologists, in their efforts to be objective, have continued to subscribe to an 'operational approach' put forward by the physicist P. W. Bridgman over half a century ago; since then so qualified by the author himself as to accommodate the more subjective phenomena heretofore considered as inaccessible to the scientific method. It was primarily on the grounds of its nonobjective (which meant nonoperational) nature that psychoanalytic theory was refused, and continues to be refused, a fair hearing in scientific circles. Although one may always retort with a question like "What exactly constitutes objectivity?" it is possible now to question even the necessity and feasibility of the so-called operational approach in the science of psychology. This approach in its strict sense has been outmoded even in the physical sciences and is no longer regarded as the sine qua non of scientific methodology.

Indifference to such changes in scientific and philosophical thought has posed the chief obstacle for the academic-experimental psychologist in the full acknowledgment of the paradigmatic nature of the Freudian system; the many valuable findings and concepts of Freud, therefore, do not receive an adequate share of his attention. Indeed, it is also a fact that quite a few of the ideas and concepts proposed by Freud have found their way into the mainstream of academic psychology under various guises; yet, 'old wine in new bottles' soon comes to look and taste different with the result that the 'old brewer' gets no acknowledgment! Adding to the confusion and reinforcing the continued indifference are the many books on the relationship between psychoanalysis, scientific method, and philosophy which present many divergent and even diametrically opposed points of view. Thus, they leave unclarified the place of the Freudian model in the science of psychology as it is conceived today in the light of changes in the philosophy of science.

The major reason for organizing the present series of essays is to establish sufficient grounds for a healthy dialogue between 'objective' psychology and 'subjective' psychoanalysis. In emphasizing the scientific underpinnings of psychoanalysis, the essays provide not only the possibility of enhancing communication between the two camps, but also of the ultimate integration of the best in the objective experimental tradition of Pavlov with the best in the clinical tradition of Freud.*

The book is divided into three parts: The first part, "Freud and the Structure of Scientific Revolutions," draws some interesting parallels between the Freudian revolution and other revolutions in science due to men like Copernicus, Darwin, and Einstein. The second part, "Freud and the Modern Philosophy of Science," analyzes the scientific meaning, possible approaches to validation, and the criteria of evidence of psychoanalytic hypotheses. The third part, "Freud and the Science of Psychology," examines the place of psychoanalysis (theory, method, and body of knowledge) in the context of the modern science of psychology.

Perhaps the only unique feature of this book is its emphasis on reflecting a consistent point of view. All the available books of readings present the reader with conflicting and contradictory viewpoints; a few extremely negative views then serve to reinforce such readers (including psychologists) who have always approached the subject with a closed mind. The present book is an attempt to correct this state of affairs by providing for the reader essays by different authors who, in spite of the diverse angles from which they have approached the matter, share a common belief that much can be said for the psychoanalytic approach and a great deal justified scientifically, All the authors whose essays have been selected possess an expertise in the philosophy of science and/or a deep knowledge and familiarity with the work of Freud. This makes the present book one of the most comprehensive single sources of comments on conceptual issues, controversies, and implications of Freudian theory. In contrast to those books that include such essays that highlight the negative aspects (and many a time unjustifiably so), the present book will serve to reflect the fact that equally respectable opinion and highly cogent arguments are available to make a reasonably strong case for psychoanalysis.

---

*That Pavlov himself was so disposed (having been greatly influenced by Freud) should provide some stimulus for thought to academic psychologists with a behavioristic-experimental orientation. [See Epilogue to L. Kubie's article "Pavlov, Freud, and Soviet Psychiatry," pp. 253-254 in this volume.]

FREUD
and the Structure
of Scientific Revolutions

Psychoanalysis, in my opinion, is incapable of creating a *Weltanschauung* of its own. It does not need one; it is a part of science and can adhere to the scientific *Weltanschauung*. This, however, scarcely deserves such a grandiloquent title, for it is not all-comprehensive, it is too incomplete and makes no claim to being self-contained and to the construction of systems. Scientific thought is still very young among human beings; there are too many of the great problems which it has not yet been able to solve. A *Weltanschauung* erected upon science has, apart from its emphasis on the real external world, mainly negative traits, such as submission to the truth and rejection of illusions. Any of our fellowmen who is dissatisfied with this state of things, who calls for more than this for his momentary consolation, may look for it where he can find it. We shall not grudge it him, we cannot help him, but nor can we on his account think differently.

S. *Freud,*
New Introductory Lectures on Psychoanalysis*

*New York, Norton Press, 1933, pp. 181–182.

The Freudian Paradigm

Mujeeb-ur-Rahman

The entry into Freud cannot avoid being a plunge into a
strange world and a strange language . . . a diagnostic
language of formidable technicality.

Norman Brown
Life Against Death

Attempts have been made from time to time to make "the house that
Freud built" an inhabitable place for all self-respecting, scientifically
minded psychologists. However, many a "case against psychoanalysis,"
even when conducted by a biased jury, has only returned the rather mild
Scottish verdict—"not proven," a verdict equally applicable even to
some of the most respectable scientific theories. The many brilliant
attempts by those who have taken up the case for the defense have not
been able to make more than a dent on the closed minds of hardheaded
academic-experimental psychologists. Why then another attempt to
break into the stronghold of objective psychology? Only the hope that
the several arguments that have been pulled together here, some for the
first time in such a context, may summate to reach at least the threshold
of a fair hearing. Once psychoanalytic theory is seen as sharing some of
the basic characteristics of theory in such a hard core science as physics,
traditional resistance may give way to acceptance with a clear
"objective" conscience.

The thesis supported in this paper, then, is that with regard to the
nature and essentials of theory construction, psychoanalytic theory is
comparable to some of the best forms of theory in science. Such a

comparison will also reveal some highly suggestive conceptual and philosophical parallels between Freud's psychoanalytic theory and Einstein's theory of relativity.

Before proceeding to an examination of its scientific status, I will make a few introductory comments on the nature of psychoanalytic theory[1] in order to provide a perspective on the subject under discussion. To state the obvious first, psychoanalytic theory is a complex system of inferential statements based on observations made in the interpersonal clinical situation. The processes inferred have been so related as to form an internally consistent model of the human personality.

Certain difficulties encountered by psychoanalytic theory seem to arise from the very nature of the theoretical task. Theories are ways of formulating our experience into coherent and meaningful patterns and represent the symbolic expression of the relations existing in the world of "facts." However, the "verbal net" of our language is not fine enough to catch all the "small fish" of human experience, nor is its logic always the logic of psychological processes. Thus in attempting to get at the logic of nonverbal processes of feeling and emotions, psychoanalytic formulations often appear nonlogical or downright contradictory. Even novelists in trying to portray the dynamic forces underlying human behavior seem to be up against this kind of difficulty. As Koestler (11) put it, "it is difficult and frustrating to write consciously on the unconscious, rationally on the irrational" (11a). Such is the predicament, then, in which psychoanalytic theory finds itself.

Nevertheless, the theory of Freud constitutes a bold attempt to order and organize the complexities of behavior and experience by codifying the empirical relationships into theoretical constructs which, when combined into propositions, allow for deductive inferences to specific events. Such shortcomings as are generally pointed out in this connection are bound to exist in any scientific theory. This, however, does not justify an overthrow of the theory as such—unless we are ready to throw out "the baby of fruitful hypothetical constructs with the bathwater of transcendent speculations" (4a).

The Scientific Status
of Psychoanalytic Theory

In spite of repeated questioning and criticism, frank recognition of the scientific nature of psychoanalysis has not been found wanting. Thus with reference to the scientific method in Freudian theory, Brown

---

1. The terms "Freudian theory" and "psychoanalytic theory" have been used interchangeably.

(2) remarks that "Freud alone amongst the founders of the analytic and dynamic schools understood and made thorough use of the scientific method in his investigations. Freud's approach was as logical and his findings as carefully tested as Pavlov's, but he was able to deal successfully with phenomena inaccessible to Pavlov: for in spite of denials, the fact remains that the foundations of his method—psychic determinism and the relentless logic of free-association—are scientific and are so over a wider area of experience than anything before or since" (2).

How then are we to account for the unacceptability of large portions of Freudian theory on supposedly scientific grounds? Ego-resistance, often invoked by psychoanalysts, is rather difficult to establish. Anticipating the discussion to follow, we may state that the single greatest source of confusion has been the failure on the part of the critics to maintain, or even recognize, the valid distinction between theory construction and theory validation. The claim that psychoanalytic theory is comparable to any scientific theory can be justified only in the context of the former. Grounds for validation are not equally strong but do not constitute any overwhelming problem. These two problems will be discussed separately, although they are so intertwined that some degree of overlap is unavoidable.

THE PROBLEM OF THEORY CONSTRUCTION

Operationism and the "Creation" of Concepts. Although almost superfluous, it would still be worthwhile to begin with the most general aim of scientific activity. Freud (7a), like all empiricists, considered that the aim of scientific thought was "to arrive at a correspondence with reality," i.e., "with what exists outside of us, and independently of us." It is "this correspondence with the real external world we call the truth." Truth is, therefore, dependent on experience. Scientific theories and laws are thus established by inference on a "trial and error" basis—with the data of observation serving as the major criteria for the confirmation of any theoretical system. However, this does not mean that theory construction should continuously "stick" to the ground. Feigl (4a) points out that Einstein has repeatedly stressed that "the formation of scientific theory is a matter of free construction, a matter of casting a net of concepts and laws, tied only in a relatively small number of points to the ground of experience." In a similar vein, Freud (8a) observes that the processes which psychology deals with are "in themselves just as unknowable as those dealt with by other sciences, by chemistry or physics for example; but it is possible to follow over long and unbroken stretches their mutual relations and interdependences, in short to gain what is known as an understanding of the sphere of natural phenomena in question. . . . This cannot be effected without forming fresh hypotheses and creating fresh concepts."

This problem of the creation of fresh concepts, however, leads us straight into the face of another widely respected trend in modern objective psychology—namely "operationism." Operationism requires that theoretical constructs be anchored to the data of observation and points towards the need for careful definitions of the operations performed by the observing scientist. Such a strategy has been found useful by all scientists and has formed the modus operandi of those working in the empirical tradition. However, like many other trends in science, the pendulum of operationism seems to have swung a bit too far—thus requiring confirmation in terms of the concrete performable operations as a necessary condition for the scientific significance and meaningfulness of a hypothesis or a proposition. The restrictiveness of such a doctrine must be quite obvious; questions that pertain to subjective experiences, not operationally definable, must be regarded as pseudo-problems. However, as Feigl (4b) has noted, such an "ultraoperationism" is anachronistic in psychology; and although the operational analysis of terms seems to have got its original impetus from a consideration of procedures in the theory of relativity, a strictly operational theory seems to be impossible even in physics. Thus a recent analysis shows that the quantum theory of Dirac (one of the founders of quantum mechanics) "presupposes a particle analogy which is not directly given in experimental data, and thus does not meet the rigorous requirements of operationism" (22). Wolman (22) also points out that operationism seems to have naively believed that "the observations of the actions or operations of the observer are more truthful than the observations of all other things" (22b).

Even before operationism came into vogue, Freud had offered an analysis of the operations involved in the creation of fresh concepts which still seems a more mature and realistic approach to scientific theory construction than a naive operationism. Pointing out the common fallacy of "clear definitions to begin with," Freud says that "the view is often defended that sciences should be built upon clear and sharply defined basic concepts. In actual fact, no science, not even the most exact, begins with such definitions. The true beginning of scientific activity consists rather in describing phenomena and then in proceeding to group, classify and correlate them." He goes on to point out that the application of abstract ideas to the observational material cannot be avoided even at the stage of description. So that ideas that will later become the basal concepts of science must at first necessarily possess some measure of uncertainty—without any clear limitation of their content. Such ideas, he says, gain meaning by constant references to the material of observation from which they have been inferred—but which are in point of fact subject to them. Thus the abstract ideas are actually "in the nature of conventions," determined, however, by their relation to the empirical material. And furthermore, the increase in the clarity of these concepts comes only from investigation, which leads to a modification of concepts such that they become more widely applicable yet at the same time remain logically consistent. Freud maintains that at this stage "it may be possible to immure them in definitions." He adds, however, that the progress of science "demands a certain elasticity even in these definitions." Physics, he says, "furnishes an excellent illustration of the way in which even 'basic concepts' that have been established in the form of definitions are constantly being altered in their content" (6).

With reference to shift in meanings, MacCorquodale and Meehl (13) point out that such Freudian terms as libido, censor, or superego, which were introduced originally as intervening variables (or as conventionalized designations for a class of observable properties), are in course of time shifted towards becoming hypothetical constructs. Hence "what began as a name for an intervening variable is finally a name for 'something' which has a host of causal properties" (13a). They note that "by this device there is subtly achieved a transition from admissible intervening variables to inadmissible hypothetical constructs. These hypothetical constructs unlike intervening variables are inadmissible because they require the existence of entities which cannot be seriously believed because of other knowledge," admitting, however, that "if such criteria were applied a large and useful part of modern science would have to be abandoned" (13b).

Disagreeing with this analysis, Frenkel-Brunswik (5) maintains that "statements containing intervening variables are by no means exhaustible by statements concerning their observational basis," supporting her position by reference to Carnap and Hempel who made it clear that "sentences containing disposition terms cannot be fully translatable into sentences about observables. Since all conditions and manners in which latent tendencies become manifest, cannot be specified, disposition statements involve 'open' terms and require an infinite series of conditions in order to be tested" (5a). Most Freudian concepts like id, ego, and superego are thus theoretical abstractions, which primarily give generic names to several categories of psychological phenomena, endowed with hypothetical functions or dispositions. The approach that Freud adopted, therefore, seems to be quite consistent with the modern philosophy of science. Thus it is precisely the "fictitious concepts rather than those fully definable by observables that seem to enable science to proceed to explanation and prediction" (5b). Einstein (3a) himself was quite aware of the fact that "every theory is speculative," noting that "when the basic concepts of a theory are comparatively close to experience . . . , its speculative character is not so easily discernible." On the other hand, if "a theory is such as to require the applications of complicated logical processes in order to reach conclusions from the premises that can be confronted with observation, everybody becomes conscious of the speculative nature of the theory." Einstein concludes by pointing out that "in such a case an almost irresistible feeling of aversion arises in people who are inexperienced in epistemological analysis and who are unaware of the precarious nature of theoretical thinking." The speculative nature of psychoanalytic theory must be all the more aversive dealing as it does with matters of human behavior and personality, about which there is no dearth of philosophical vantage points and assumptions.

The Logic and Limitations of Measurement. In striving towards the ideal of natural sciences, to which it has constantly looked for its methodology and justification, objective psychology has found it necessary to espouse operationism. However, two other principles, namely the principles of indeterminism and the relativity of measurement, which have had a greater impact on the science of physics, seem to have been entirely overlooked by psychology. Shuey (19) notes the serious implications that these two principles had for psychology. With reference to the principle of indeterminism (the impossibility of ascertaining both the position and velocity of the particle at the same time) he points out that since at a certain level of investigation measurement and prediction become incompatible, the increase in the accuracy and precision of instruments actually leads to the paradoxical situation that with an increase in the knowledge of one goes a further decrease in the knowledge of the other. He concludes with the observation that "the cruder the instruments the more accurately both velocity and position can be studied at the same time," which, he says, probably explains the reason why "earlier experiments in a field have often shown an accuracy that is amazing to later workers in the field who use far finer instruments" (19a). This could well be the reason why the crude and "nonmetrical" instrument of psychoanalysis—namely free-association—seems to have worked so well in the relatively more accurate overall understanding of the human personality.

The second principle referred to by Shuey concerns the relativity of measurement. It has been found in physics that when a system is measured, "the measuring instrument must conform with the system, i.e., a system in motion when measured by a motionless instrument will give a different result than when the instrument is moving at the same rate as the system measured" (19b). Pointing out that psychologists have been laboring on the refinement of instruments and the elaboration and standardization of tests, Shuey remarks that "they have not only been using static measurements on a dynamic system but they have been attempting prediction of life activities from these measurements" (19b). Another serious problem with measurement in psychology seems to be that no matter how accurate it is, the constantly changing nature of the organism prevents it from being used another time. On the grounds that a measuring instrument must conform with the system being measured, a fine case may be made for the scientific validity of the free-association method used in psychoanalytic investigations. Free-association may well be regarded as an instrument that "moves" at the same rate as the system being studied, thus making it a model case of the use of a "dynamic instrument" on a dynamic system.

Thus in spite of the "fineness" of static measurements, psychology, if it is to be consistent in striving towards its ideal of natural sciences, will have to consider seriously the whole problem of measurement—both in regards to its relativity to the system being measured and its relation to prediction in cases where more than one variable has to be measured at the same time. Shuey sums up the argument by pointing out that "the idea that measurements are not yet fine enough for prediction is erroneous since with an increase in their fineness will go a decrease in the ability to predict. This peculiar situation arose in physics and it is now facing the psychologists with the same paradoxical force. . . . The long dream of psychologists to perfect instruments of measurement as fine as those of natural sciences has finally led to an increased ignorance of the very thing they wanted to know" (19c).

The essential reason why psychoanalysis has added to our knowledge of human behavior seems clearly due to the fact of its having developed its own unique method for the exploration of the total personality in terms of innumerable variables involved in interpersonal relations. As Frendel-Brunswik (5) observes, "regardless of how imperfect psychoanalytic theory may be in its formal structure, it has no rival among psychological theories as far as the range of both its evidence and its explanatory power is concerned" (5b).

Metaphors and Models. Objections concerning the scientific nature of psychoanalysis also stem from the use that the theory makes of supposedly "unrealistic" analogies and models. Thus MacCorquodale and Meehl (13), in making the distinction between hypothetical constructs and intervening variables, maintain that no principle used in psychological theory be contradictory to established generalizations in other sciences. Using Freud's quasi-hydraulic theory of libido they point out that "the central nervous system does not in fact contain pipes or tubes with fluid in them, and there are no known properties of nervous tissue to which the hydraulic properties of the libido could correspond" (13b). Admitting that such a term may be legitimately used as a generic name for a class of empirical events or properties or as an intervening variable, they note, however, that the allied sciences of anatomy and physiology impose restrictions on its being used as a hypothetical construct. Hence they conclude that "this part of the theory about 'inner events' is likely to remain metaphorical" (13b). However, Mandler and Kessen (14) consider this a bad example, commenting that "this reinterpretative device misses the function of explanatory systems," going on to observe that "Freud's theory has as its range of intent certain responses of human beings, e.g., reports of fantasies and dreams, sexual behavior, etc. If the libido explanation leads to testable and confirmed statements about such behavior, then it has met the central requirements of a good theory. If it achieves this function at a very high level then discussions of the 'reality' of the libido in pipes becomes as irrelevant as discussions of the 'reality' of the electrons in orbits" (14). This would mean that a theory which could make confirmed predictions and which can be used as a basis for the design of informative research could be regarded as a good theory, "regardless of whether or not it is possible to reinterpret its premises into statements consistent with current physiological theory" (14). Feigl (4), taking a middle of the road position, maintains that analogical models of the Freudian type "will from now on have to be appraised in terms of the isomorphism they attain with the corresponding structures and processes certified by the physiological approach" (4b). However, he admits that "there is no question that the mythological as well as the hydraulic models of psychoanalysis have been immensely heuristic devices."

It must be pointed out at this stage that the so-called hydraulic model of libido functioning does seem to have found an isomorphism with neural functioning identified by recent neurophysiological research. The present evidence in neurophysiology overwhelmingly favors the hypothesis that the transmission of information along synapses of nerve cells is chemical in nature at least for the mammalian nervous system. Thus R. F. Thompson (20) states that "it is presumed that Ach (acetylcholine) is present in nerve cells in bound form (i.e., in association with other substances) and when released or utilized changes to free or unbound form. Thus at the neuro-muscular junction it crosses the synaptic space as free Ach and combines with chemical substances on the nerve fibers to produce activation of the fiber" (20). He then goes on to point out that "there is evidence that bound Ach may be manufactured in the cell bodies at least in spinal-motor neurons (which send axons to form the neuro-muscular junctions) and then *flows* down the axon to be released at the terminals" (20). Apart from Ach, a variety of other substances (e.g., noradrenalin and others as yet unidentified) may well play important roles in synaptic transmission and other aspects of neural functioning.

Thus, although Freud himself was convinced that new physicochemical discoveries would make the whole libido theory obsolete, the present state of neurophysiological theory seems to be pointing in the other direction. The "damming up of the libido" may actually turn out to be more than just another Freudian metaphor!

Mentalistic Versus S-R Psychoanalysis. Although the analogical procedure may not be very suitable for purposes of ultimately proving a scientific hypothesis, it could be argued that mentalistic analogies do have an important function in psychology. As Frendel-Brunswik (5) points out, "the assumption of the dynamisms of the 'inner man' to which behaviorist critics of psychoanalysis . . . have objected, actually tend to increase the parsimony of scientific description of behavior patterns" (5c). Although the translation of psychoanalytic concepts into S-R terms does seem to have been useful in certain cases, it also seems to involve definite limitations. Since psychoanalysis lays emphasis on the investigation of internal causes, it includes subjective experience and the differential meanings of external events for different individuals. In fact Freud admitted that he had gained an understanding of hysteria only on giving up the search for external causes when he realized that what the patients had felt as having really occurred was equally significant. It was the concept of "hysterical fantasies" which led to the comprehension of the structure of the neurosis. Frenkel-Brunswik, therefore, feels that "since the relationship of these fantasies to external factors is most complex and ambiguous, it seems heuristically fruitful to assume the internal mechanisms postulated by psychoanalysis, leaving their full operational specification for a later time" (5d). Such assumptions, she says, "do not carry us outside the bounds of natural science."

With reference to the question of the correspondence of psychosocial phenomena to external reality, Brown (2) notes that "myths, fairy tales, literature, political and religious beliefs, or art, become scientifically meaningful to the psychologist precisely to the degree that they do *not* correspond with the facts of external reality, and from this there follows the converse proposition that to the extent they do so correspond they are none of the psychologists' business" (2). The S-R approach which goes about the business of finding such correspondences with external events may in the case of many psychological phenomena find itself in a blind alley. Thus, in spite of the fruitfulness of the approach to construct a "behavioristic psychoanalysis," such an approach must be seriously limited if only because of the wide gap that the unconscious creates between the stimulus and the response, making "psychic reality" outweigh external reality.

THE PROBLEM OF VALIDATION

The Question of Experimental Evidence. Although the experimental method offers a definite advantage with regard to variations and control of data, several empirical sciences, including biology and astronomy, make wide use of observation. Besides, as Sears (18) has pointed out, the methodological difficulty arises from the subjective character of the psychoanalytic system which does not permit being submitted to conventional scientific tests of proof and disproof. In addition to this, Sears also laid his finger on what may be the most significant drawback for experimentation with psychoanalytic hypotheses when he observed that "psychoanalysis deals heavily in the more potent emotions and motives, and if society is hard put to control sex, aggression, anxiety, unreason etc., it is little wonder that the experimentalist shies away from unleashing them in the laboratory" (18). Psychoanalysis then may never become an experimental science because of the difficulty of experimenting on the various subtle and complex phenomena of human life. However, to disregard psychoanalysis as a science on the ground that it does not admit of experimental proof would be as justified as disregarding astronomy. For as Freud himself had once remarked, "experimentation with the heavenly bodies is after all exceedingly difficult" (7b).

However, in spite of the great difficulties involved in experimentation, several attempts have been made in this direction and have provided some support for certain Freudian propositions (18). It would, however, be profitable to exercise a great deal of discretion in accepting either positive or negative evidence from experimentation. Experimental evidence can never confirm or disprove the theory itself, but only the empirical propositions derived from the theory. Besides, verification is a matter of degree and sources of error may escape identification. However, the greater the number of objective, carefully planned and controlled experiments the greater would be the support lent to the theory. Failure to obtain observational support for a hypothesis would still not constitute disproof since a great number of Freudian findings are related to unconscious and unobservable processes, and translation of these into empirically testable hyptheses needs to be preceded by more precise definitions of the theoretical constructs involved.

At this point, it is worth taking note of an interesting problem in theoretical physics. As G. Thomson (21) states, "it is not surprising that for most purposes Newton and Einstein give the same result. Only three effects, all small, are known which can distinguish them . . . but the effects are so small that percentage errors are considerable and the agreement not very precise" (21a) except in one case, which Thomson regards as the least decisive test and also alternatively accountable in terms of Newton's theory. However, in spite of this, Thomson noted "few doubt that Einstein's theory is superior to Newton's in accuracy, though very much harder to use" (21a). This does suggest that experimental evidence alone hardly seems the sole arbiter for the acceptance of a theory even in the most hard core science of physics.

Due to the wide gap between observations and its basic conceptions, the experimental verification of psychoanalytic propositions seems to require a special ingenuity which, as Frenkel-Brunswik pointed out (5a), is also required by modern physics in verifying its theories and is a result of the greater abstractness of its concepts. Psychoanalysis thus seems to "share with modern physics" the fact that its propositions cannot easily be submitted to "more direct and obvious types of confirmation" (5e). Frenkel-Brunswik (5e) concludes that "in each case the highly interpretive statements involved do not carry the rules of their confirmation as obviously with themselves as do the more descriptive statements" (5e), and further adds that "by involving concepts more removed from immediate data, psychoanalysis has lengthened the chains of intellectual and experimental work that connect the principles with the observational protocols" (5a). In this connection, Einstein (3a) has observed that "more and more, as the depth of our knowledge increases, we must give up this advantage [closeness to experience] in our quest for logical simplicity and uniformity in the foundations of physical theory," pointing out that "general relativity has gone further than previous physical theories in relinquishing closeness to experience of fundamental concepts in order to attain logical simplicity." Therefore, Einstein admits, "in the generalized theory the procedure of deriving from the premises of the theory conclusions that can be confronted with empirical data is so difficult that so far no such result had been obtained." There seems hardly more reason to expect that the empirical validation of psychoanalytic theory is any less difficult or that such results as have been obtained be more conclusive from the start.

The "Interpretive Laboratory." One method of verification of hypotheses developed in the clinical situation comes from the method of "internal consistency" (8b). This method involves the continuous and repeated crosschecking of inferences drawn from evidence based on the many different aspects of the behavior of the individual—from free-association to the transference phenomena—until the many facts and inferences fall into a coherent and meaningful pattern. Considering that the psychoanalytic method involves work over the case material for long periods of time, it seems to afford full opportunity for repeated checking of hypotheses before arriving at correct interpretations. This is in marked contrast to the fact that "the subject in a typical psychological experiment performed under controlled conditions is observed and tested only one or two hours on the average" (8b). In this connection, Hendrick (10) correctly notes that "the analytic situation is itself a special laboratory where all simple and complex relationships between the patient and the other human beings, past and present, are reduced to the standard conditions of the interactions of two persons during the analytic interview" (10).

In regards to the matter of prediction of an individual's future behavior, Freud was convinced that given the present state and symptoms of an individual, it was possible for psychoanalysis to work backwards and trace out the determining conditions. However, he admitted that given those conditions alone it would never have been possible to predict the present outcome. This seems to reflect well the fact that the Freudian concept of "psychic determinism" goes beyond the simple one-to-one relationship between cause and effect and regards each mental event as being "overdetermined"—being as Brown (2) notes, "a final common path of many forces, whether constitutional, developmental or environmental." This fact seems to underlie the many complexities involved in experimental tests of psychoanalytic theory and may also provide the basis for psychology's own "indeterminancy principle." For in any complex system—such as the human organism or community—so many things must be known in order to make a specific prediction that by the time all the relevant information is obtained it is already out of date. Moreover, the very consequences of studying the variables must disturb the status quo of the system. So that prediction of any specific future behavioral state would have to be ruled out in favor of, at best, a close approximation. In view of the existence of such a "prediction barrier," Freud's stand on the impossibility of such predictions is fully vindicated. However, since such an "indeterminism" is methodological in nature, the implication drawn here (from the concept of "overdetermination") would still not be inconsistent with Freud's strict theoretical adherence to the principle of "psychic determinism."

With regard to Freudian theory, Brown (2) has, therefore, correctly observed that it "does not represent a limited theory of the type beloved by experimental scientists . . . which deal mathematically with the relationships between a small number of data within a narrow range of observation," (2b) but that it "is a hypothesis covering a wide range of facts with correspondingly less overall accuracy in matters of detail." In this respect, he says, it may be regarded as being "comparable in form to Newton's hypotheses which made an imaginative leap into space on the basis of a few observations of the behavior of falling objects on earth— although fortunately for Newton nobody was foolish enough to complain that he had not tested out his hypothesis on the extragalactic nebulae." He concludes by saying that "Newton's and Freud's propositions are inadequate to explain every phenomenon which is why they are described as hypotheses" but, he notes, "Freud still awaits his Einstein" (2c).

FREUD AND EINSTEIN: PARALLEL REVOLUTIONS

Considering the nature of the so-called revolutions in human thought it would seem that the essence of science lies not in the discovery of new facts but in the discovering of new ways of thinking about them. The gap between the pre-Freudian and the Freudian way of thinking is very wide indeed. As Mace observed, "Little is gained by trying to place Freud's system against the background of its antecedent" (2d). However, the transition from pre-Freudian to Freudian psychology is certainly as abrupt, if not more so, as any transition in the history of scientific thought. Freud's method of approaching psychological problems revolutionized psychology, and "transformed it from an academic and wholly static discipline into a science rooted in biology but spreading outwards into sociology, describing behavior in dynamic goal-directed terms" (2e).

Thus psychology after Freud may be compared to physics after Einstein in that both revolutions have not only introduced totally new ways of thinking but have also made an enduring contribution to philosophical thought and awareness.

New Ways of Thinking

First, the introduction of the unconscious dimension with its mode of operation was as great a leap in psychological thought as was the linking of the time dimension to that of space in the field of theoretical physics. To the more or less logical and time-bound dimension of consciousness was added the dimension of a timeless and alogical unconscious. The existence and recognition of the "unconscious before Freud" is also paralleled by the existence in scientific thought of the concept of "time" before Einstein. However, the revolutionary nature of both the psychoanalytic and relativity theories lay not simply in establishing the significant connections that had not existed before but also in their very conceptualization of these phenomena. The "conscious-unconscious" notion has since proved as decisive for psychology as the "space-time" notion has for physics.

Secondly, relativity theory has resulted from a shift in conceptualization that also finds its parallel in psychoanalysis. A significant contribution of relativity theory is attributed to "visual thinking" which, as Koestler (11) suggests, seems to have enabled Einstein "to escape the snares of verbal thought" and "to brave the apparent logical contradiction that 'at the same time' for A may mean 'at different times' for B. This apparent contradiction derived from the axiom of absolute time which had been built into the codes of 'rational' (meaning post-Newtonian) thinking about the physical world" (11b). Furthermore, as Russell (16) has observed, a very significant fact in the development of modern physics was in regarding "force" not in tactual or physical but in visual terms. So that bodies do not behave in certain ways because of some physical force from some other distant body, but because of the circumstances of the immediate field of "space-time" which surrounds it. Russell concludes that "as science has advanced it has seemed more and more that 'sight' is less misleading than 'touch' as a source of fundamental notions of matter" (16a).

In psychology such a shift in the way of looking made its appearance with psychoanalysis and has also proved of great significance in the development of psychology. Although constituting an affront to rational thinking, the "mentalistic" or "animistic" vocabulary of psychoanalysis formed almost a counterpart to the "pictural vocabulary" which modern physics recognized as legitimate in the earlier stages of conceptualization. From the earlier conceptions of the operations of the mind (or the brain at the other extreme of explanation) in accordance with the laws of association, psychoanalysis shifted the focus on to psychological systems or organizations within the personality and in communication with each other. Freud's constructs introduced the ability to describe the psychological processes in their constantly shifting mutual relationships within the dynamic organization of personality. Due to such constantly shifting relationships between psychological processes, it may never be possible to cast the psychoanalytical theory into static mathematical equations, but this by itself would not detract from its value as a scientific theory. In this context it would be appropriate to quote Russell, who noted that "Physics is mathematical not because we know so much about the physical world, but because we know so little; it is only its mathematical properties that we can discover" (17b). It seems to be true, therefore, that theoretical physics is no longer concerned with things or "reality" as such, but with the mathematical relations between abstractions. The "maturity" of a science then cannot be correlated, as is often thought, with the extent to which it is mathematical—if science is to be regarded as the means to the understanding of "reality."

The Enduring Contribution

Finally, both revolutions in human thought have certain characteristics in them which are of a permanent nature. According to Bridgman (1), this permanent contribution of the relativity theory is to be found in an improved understanding of our mental relations to nature and that this attitude which rests on the "permanent basis of the character of our minds," he says, "shall not be subject to future change." Thus, "another change in attitude such as that due to Einstein shall be forever impossible" (1).

Psychoanalysis too has made a permanent contribution to our "mental relations to nature," and has also provided an insight into the character of the human mind. Although our views of personality will always be subject to future change as we gain more knowledge, what will not be the subject of future change is that part of our knowledge from psychoanalysis which rests on this "permanent foundation of the character of our minds." This idea is very succinctly paraphrased by Langer (12) in the following words: "The great contribution of Freud to the philosophy of mind has been the realization that human behavior is not only a food-getting strategy, but is also a language; that every *move* is at the same time a *gesture*. Symbolization is both an end and an instrument" (12).

This form of approach has led to the most profound and illuminating interpretation of human experience in the whole history of scientific thought. However, the full potential in the 'Freudian revolution' still remains to be tapped. Nelson (15) considering the possibility that "the impact of Freud will in the end prove to be more decisive and far-reaching than the discoveries of Planck and Einstein," feels that "the new forms of awareness growing out of Freud's work may come to serve as a more authentic symbol of our consciousness and the quality of our deepest experience than the uncertain fruits of the fission of the atom and the new charting of the cosmos" (15). Thus in psychology too another change such as that due to Freud may be forever impossible.

A Concluding Note

For those committed to the task of building on the foundations laid down by Freud, the following reflection by Einstein (3b) provides a final, and consoling, parallel:

> Experience alone can decide on truth. Yet we have achieved something if we have succeeded in formulating a meaningful and precise question. Affirmation or refutation will not be easy in spite of an abundance of known facts. The derivation, from the equations, of conclusions which can be confronted with experience will require painstaking efforts and probably new mathematical methods.

There is no reason, then, to suppose that the empirical validation of psychoanalytic propositions, which deal with the complexities of human behavior, could be anything less than a Herculean task

Finally, it must be admitted that theoretical analysis or academic discussion alone can never be convincing unless the "game" of psychoanalysis is played according to its rules. To quote Freud's own words of warning:

> The teachings of psychoanalysis are based on an incalculable number of observations and experience, and no one who has not repeated those observations upon himself or upon others is in a position to arrive at an independent judgement of it. (8c)

This should not be construed as a solipsistic position; the final test of truth is always experience.

References

1. BRIDGMAN, P. W. "The Logic of Modern Physics," in H. Feigl and M. Brodbeck (Eds.), *Readings in the Philosophy of Science*. New York: Appleton-Century-Crofts, 1953. p. 34.
2. BROWN, J.A.C. *Freud and the Post-Freudians*. London: Pelican Books, 1961. pp. a) 195 b) 187 c) 196 d) vii e) 2.
3. EINSTEIN, A. "On the Generalized Theory . . . of Gravitation," reprint from *Scientific American*, Freeman and Co., April 1950. pp. a) 5 b) 7.
4. FEIGL, H. "Principles and Problems of Theory Construction in Psychology," in W. Dennis (ed.), *Current Trends in Psychological Theory*. Pittsburgh: University of Pittsburgh Press, 1951. pp. a) 203 b) 206.
5. FRENKEL-BRUNSWIK, E. "Meaning of Psychoanalytic Concepts and Confirmation of Psychoanalytical Theories," in M. Levitt (ed.), *Readings in Psychoanalytic Psychology*. New York: Appleton-Century-Crofts, 1959. pp. a) 37 b) 30 c) 35 d) 35–36 e) 38.

6. FREUD, S. "Instincts and their Vissicitudes" (1915), *Collected Papers*. London: Hogarth Press, vol. 4, 1925. pp. 60–83. pp. 60–61.

7. FREUD, S. *New Introductory Lectures on Psychoanalysis*. New York: Norton, 1933. pp. a) 170 b) 22.

8. FREUD, S. *An Outline of Psychoanalysis*. New York: Norton, 1949. pp. a) 35–36 b) 54 c) 9.

9. HALL, C. S., and LINDZEY, G. *Theories of Personality*. New York: John Wiley and Sons, Inc., 1970. p. 54.

10. HENDRICK, I. *Facts and Theories of Psychoanalysis*. New York: Dell Publishing Co. (Laurel Edition), 1966. p. 261.

11. KOESTLER, A. *The Act of Creation*. New York: Dell Publishing Co., 1964. pp. a) 207 b) 183.

12. LANGER, S. *Philosophy in a New Key*. New York: Mentor Books, 1942. p. 53.

13. MACCORQUODALE, K., and MEEHL, P. E. "On a Distinction Between Hypothetical Constructs and Intervening Variables," *Psychological Review*, 55, 1948. pp. 95–107. a) 105 b) 106.

14. MANDLER, G., and KESSEN, W. *The Language of Psychology*. New York: John Wiley and Sons, Inc., 1959. p. 268.

15. NELSON, B. "Preface," in B. Nelson (ed.), *Freud and the 20th Century*. New York: Meridian Books, 1957. p. 9.

16. RUSSELL, B. *The ABC of Relativity*. New York: Mentor Books, 1958. p.12

17. _____. *An Outline of Philosophy*. London: George Allen and Unwin, 1910. p. 163.

18. SEARS, R. R. "Experimental Analysis of Psychoanalytic Phenomena," in J. McV. Hunt (ed.), *Personality and the Behavior Disorders*. New York: Ronald, 1944. p. 306.

19. SHUEY, H. "Recent Trends in Science and the Development of Modern Typology," *Psychological Review*, 41, 1934, pp. 207–235. pp. a) 213 b) 214 c) 215–216.

20. THOMPSON, R. F. *Foundation of Physiological Psychology*. New York: Harper and Row, 1967. p. 122.

21. THOMSON, G. *The Inspiration of Science*. New York: Anchor Books, Doubleday, 1961. pp. 88–89.

22. WOLMAN, B. B. *Contemporary Theories and Systems in Psychology*. New York: Harper, 1960. p. 507.

2

From Aristotle to Freud: A Few Notes on the Roots of Psychoanalysis*

Ishak Ramzy

It was not a psychoanalyst who once announced as his well-considered judgment: "In my opinion Freud has, quite unquestionably, done more for the advancement of our understanding of human nature than any other man since Aristotle" (9). It was William McDougall, the founder of a well-known system and school of psychology. In spite of his continuous criticisms of Freud over a number of years, he did not fail to admit the true greatness of the founder of psychoanalysis and said that he singled it out as the object of his critical attack because he considered "Freud's system the most deserving of honest criticism, to have the essential formulations of truth which are lacking in most other contemporary systems" (10).

Neither was it a psychoanalyst who said that, "Freud was the actual discoverer of new territory. . . . Freud is, for all his empirical pretensions, primarily a constructor of logical systems, a man whose approach to irrational problems is that of an extreme rationalist. Freud smashed into the barricades of science as a revolutionist, but his revolution will no doubt become incorporated in the deeper and more constant stream of evolution" (11). This sour opponent of psychoanalysis, Müller-Freienfels, being the good scholar and careful historian of psychology that he was, could not but admit the everlasting importance and truth he saw in the major chapter of psychology, which Freud contributed.

*Reprinted with permission from the *Bulletin of the Menninger Clinic*, Vol. 20, pp. 112-123. Copyright 1956 by the Menninger Foundation.

It was a psychoanalyst, however, Kurt Eissler (4), who said, "Freud's technique of free association and his conception of the laws underlying this process are not a foreign body in the development of psychology, but a logical link between the old psychology of the associationists and modern psychology. Whereas modern psychologists usually reject the psychology of the 18th and 19th century *in toto*. Freud succeeded in synthesizing the early psychological theories with modern discoveries into a new system of the total personality. It is almost always overlooked that Freud rescued the work of those great philosophers who laid the foundation of present day psychology, that he was not only a great revolutionary, but a great conserver in psychology. Anyone who rejects entirely the so-called free association technique is ignorant of the very basis upon which psychology of the last three hundred years has rested."

Contrary to the general impression, psychoanalysts have on the whole been averse to entering into controversies, and they are still reluctant to make the necessary contact with other systems of science and human knowledge. They had their hands full from the very beginning and their sight engrossed by the many unexplored territories of the human mind. Besides, there was ample obstruction raised against their endeavors by the pundits of formal knowledge in academic circles.

When Putnam suggested that it would be important to study the relations of psychoanalysis to wider philosophical concepts, Ferenczi (5) wrote in 1911 that this idea seemed to be "particularly dangerous to psychoanalysis, which has not yet properly cleared up all the interconnections even within its own field. Surely an off-season, like that in which game may not be shot, should be granted to a young science such as psychoanalysis, and a substantial delay should elapse before it is approached with the armament of metaphysics. The longer one postpones system-building and contents oneself with collecting facts and establishing their interconnections, the greater is the prospect of making fresh discoveries. . . ."

And thus for more than half a century psychoanalysts continued to explore the unconscious and went on gathering masses of data about the working of the human mind. A generation went by and another generation and another following the same tradition of confining themselves to their subject, a tradition not only set by the master but also imposed by the rigorous requirements of their training and their daily tasks. Their conferences and journals are mainly interested in facts, though, of course, they do deal at times with general problems of the methodology of their science, its forerunners, or its ramifications and connections with other disciplines.

Psychoanalytic textbooks, however simple, elaborate, or encyclopedic still fall short of any acceptable standard of systematic coherence or logical structure. The problem seems to stem not only from the intricacy and complexity of the subject matter; from its elusiveness and the difficulties of putting its elements into words and terms; from the admitted existence of fine and strong links between the various aspects of the mind; and from the impossibility of singling out any one aspect or function without doing violence to it as well as to the rest, but also from the basic foundations of the whole edifice being submerged and overlooked when the sight is focused on the upper and newer layers of the structure. This very often leads to unwarranted so-called deviations, superfluous, assumed innovations or eulogies, apologies and controversies.

As often happens in the intellectual experience of any analyst, one can, whenever bewildered or despondent, go back to Freud's works where one will always be rewarded by a refreshing, reassuring breeze which can fill the sails anew. Anyone who has a nodding acquaintance with the history of human thought cannot fail to recognize time and again in its totality or in its details, how much Freud's work embodies in form and in content the main features of the Western attempts to understand human nature and the human mind.

Such a recognition and such an implicit basic pride and confidence in the roots of psychoanalytic theory were implied in the contributions of the earlier workers. But fashions of thinking and expression changed, as did the fashions of education and academic background. This, together with the ambivalent attitude of other systems and the popularization of psychoanalysis, seem to have obscured the clarity and definiteness of those roots out of which the theory of the new science budded and flourished.

The understandable keen interest of psychoanalysts in direct clinical work, and the increasing demand for their clinical services do not explain, however, their limited interest in the origins of their own science. Nothing helps more than a good method, and nothing works better—as is known—than a good clear theory. If it is said that history is neither method nor theory, it is also said that the history of science is science itself.

The delay and neglect in studying the historical foundations of psychoanalysis may be due to Freud himself who gave only the scantiest information about the origins of his thinking. But the work of Bernfeld (1, 2) and Zilboorg (12), together with the outstanding biography by Jones (8) and the publication of Freud's letters (7) provide initial material for a closer study of the basic roots of psychoanalysis. As Jones says: "It is the rarest event—if it ever happens at all—for an original idea to be purely spontaneous in origin, with no precursors of any kind. One reason why the present book is being written is in the hope of elucidating something of the processes in Freud's mind and the experiences in his life, that culminated in his discoveries. . . ."

I

Using only the documented landmarks in Freud's academic background, one can begin with what he said was the determining coincidence for the choice of his career, ". . . the theories of Darwin, which were then of topical interest, strongly attracted me, for they held out hopes of an extraordinary advance in our understanding of the world, and it was hearing Goethe's beautiful essay on Nature read aloud at a popular lecture by Professor Carl Bruhl just before I left school that decided me to become a medical student" (6).

Freud's basic curiosity, his known habits of work and meticulous ways of searching for the origins of things most probably led him to delve further and deeper into the sources that inspired Goethe's essay. More so, the intellectual atmosphere at that period was saturated with the teachings and theories of "the philosophy of nature." This *Naturphilosophie* was the doctrine developed by the German philosopher Schelling (1775–1854), hailed by his contemporaries as a personality of the true romantic type. Schelling, the son of a learned orientalist and minister, combined the study of theology with physical science. He was one of those people who live out their genius with all its power and daring; he came in direct contact with many of the outstanding thinkers of his time. With Goethe, in particular, Schelling was on good terms, but with Fichte and Hegel he had much friction. After a turbulent personal life, which would be a fertile topic of study for psychoanalysts, Schelling settled down in Munich around the middle of the 19th century. Interestingly enough, his best known work, *Aphorisms on Naturphilosophie,* was first published in the *Jahrbücher der Medizin als Wissenschaft.*

Schelling's thinking is notoriously complex, and at times very intricate and shrouded in mystic veils. It is dominated by the idea of liberation of the individual and his fusion with the universe through reason and love. He considered that Spinoza's pantheistic views were the nearest precursors to his own. In Spinoza, the doctrine of man, his conduct and place in the universe evolve around the idea of the individual, the organism, where soul and body are only two aspects of the one being. For him God is an infinitely absolute substance constituted of an infinite number of attributes each expressing an eternal, infinite essence. Simply put, the pantheist advocates that God is Nature and its laws.

Along that line of approach, but with an added blend of idealism and mysticism, Schelling sought for a reconciliatory basis behind all the eternal conflicts, polarities, theses and antitheses of existence. He assumed that the uniting basis which underlies all the differences and conflicts in the universe is an absolute undifferentiated self-equivalence. Thus, mind and body are only manifestations, forms or consequences of the absolute which sustains all differences. And the ultimate ground of reality is the absolute Reason. But Schelling attempted later to give this absolute a character which he derived from the philosophies of both Spinoza and Plato. He thus advocated that things either physical or mental have an actual being. They exist not merely as topical consequences of the absolute, but have a stubbornness of existence in themselves. He went on to conceive of the will as something beyond reason and thought.

Fascinated by the "Philosophy of Nature," the young Freud entered medical school, not so much with the ultimate aim of practicing medicine, but because it was the best place to satisfy his interest in the study of the sciences of nature. It is significant that most of his eminent teachers were physicians whose main vocation was research, and that most of them, though qualified, had never treated a patient but confined themselves to unraveling the mysteries of the human organism in health and sickness.

At the medical school, Freud followed a group of courses which may now seem strange in its array, but is of utmost importance in understanding not only his tendencies but also the influences he came under. His studies ranged from physics, physiology, and zoology, to philosophy and logic. And it was at the Brücke Institute, where Freud spent six important years of his intellectual development, besides his other acquisitions during that period, which most probably provided him with the basic elements of his theories that culminated later in his discovery of psychoanalysis.

Brücke, according to Freud, was the teacher who influenced him more than any other man in his life. As we are confining ourselves, in this paper, to tracing intellectual and educational influences, it may suffice to single out just two important currents that characterized the approach of Brücke and his group.

It was around the last quarter of the 19th century that the prestige of biology reached its height, especially under the influence of Darwin's work and the theories of evolution. Darwin became as much a source of disturbance and excitement for the 19th century as Galileo or Newton was for the 17th. Although the doctrine that the different forms of life had a common ancestry was as old as the Greek thinkers themselves, Darwin provided masses of evidence which gave the theory enough force to have it accepted by any average educated person of his time. It is significant that one of the optional courses Freud attended when he joined the University was a course on "Biology and Darwinism."

The publication of Darwin's *Origin of Species* in 1859, was not only a major fruit of the inductive method in science, but it was also the beginning of a trend which reached far and wide. After the battle that raged about it, it established a new mode of thought which had come to stay. Some of its important results should be mentioned here. After Darwin no intelligent scientist could ignore that fact that in every subject the genesis, as well as the actual form of the product, must be considered. In studying living organisms many organs and functions are found to exist together for no particular reason in the present; lower levels of organization still exist when higher forms such as intelligence have already developed, and useless organs or functions remain to challenge anyone who claims that everything was created by one decisive original act.

If Darwin thus gave a sustained impulse to the study of origins and a genetic point of view, there is another side of his theory which, though more disputed, left its indelible impact on many a thinker and scientist. This was his attempt to formulate the motive force of evolution to fit his theory regarding the struggle for existence and the survival of the fittest. Animals and plants multiply very fast, and many of them perish. Sheer luck admittedly interferes, but there is another more important course which determines which will survive. In any given environment members of the same species compete for survival, and it is the one best adapted to its surroundings which has the best chance of living and of multiplying through its offspring. Each generation thus carries the most helpful characteristic of survival, and this, so Darwin thought, could explain the long chain of development from the primitive forms of life to the human species itself.

As a consequence, the interest of many scientists not only focused on the study of animals and children, on the physical and nonphysical functions common to them and to the human adult, but also on such problems as heredity, instinct, emotions, individual differences and intelligence.

This evolutionistic orientation was not the only or the main trend of Brücke, the teacher whom Freud adored and respected. Brücke was the leader, in Vienna, of physical physiology and the ambassador of the influential German school of Helmholtz of whom Freud said, "He is one of my idols."

Helmholtz was the leader of an outstanding group of the students of Johannes Müller, one of the greatest scientists of the 19th century, and the first man to hold a chair of physiology in the world at the University of Berlin. Partly under the influence of the "Philosophy of Nature" and Schelling's "speculative physics," and mainly in revolt against it, and also against vitalism which was the main belief of their master, Müller's bright pupils united to overthrow anything that smacked of mysticism, emotionalism or vitalism, and made the resolution expressed by Raymond DuBois in 1842. "Brücke and I pledged a solemn oath to put in power this truth: No other forces than the common physical chemical ones are active within the organism . . ." Helmholtz himself, adopting the inductive and mathematical methods of Müller, made many outstanding and theoretical contributions in physics, physiology and psychology, amongst which are his experiments on reaction time and his studies on hearing and vision. It is well to remember that it was Helmholtz who revived and popularized the principle of conservation of energy that says, "the sum of forces remains constant in every isolated system," and that whatever form these forces may take, light, heat, electricity, etc., further knowledge would lead to reducing them all to two, namely, attraction and repulsion— a principle which would seem very familiar to any psychoanalyst, whatever terms he might use to describe the basic human feelings.

Brücke kept his pledge. With his impressive uncompromising character, and an unswerving trust in scientific methodology, he established the name and tradition of his Vienna Institute upon the belief in physical physiology. He set himself to prove with the help of a few gifted pupils, the assertion that, "No other forces than the common physical and chemical ones are active within the organism." When, some thirty years later, he published his lectures, he mentioned that the definition of physiology he had used was, "It is the science of organisms as such which differ from dead material entities, *i.e.*, machines, in possessing the faculty of assimilation. But they are all phenomena of the physical world: systems of atoms, moved by forces, according to the principle of conservation of energy." Jones (8), who provided a description of Brücke's "Lectures," pertinently observed, "The spirit and content of these lectures correspond closely with the words Freud used in 1926, to characterize psychoanalysis in its dynamic aspect: The forces assist or inhibit one another, combine with one another, enter into compromises with one another. . . ."

Whatever may be the details of Freud's work under Brücke, and whatever assignments he conscientiously concentrated upon during that period; whether it was Freud's first research on the existence of testes in the eel which had puzzled people since the time of Aristotle, or his later work on the histology of the nerve cells, enough is now known to establish the importance of this stage in Freud's development. Thanks to Bernfeld and Jones, basic information has been unearthed to affirm that in spite of the revolutionary features of psychoanalysis, its core is a continuation of the work Freud did at Brücke's Institute. The later Freudian theories derive their roots from this work not only in fundamentals but also in detail. The impact of these intensive six years cannot be over-emphasized, nor has it yet been well studied. If we have come to know something of what Freud acquired in content, we should not underestimate what was acquired in form. He lived among a group whose belief in science, whose integrity, dedication, self-sacrifice and denial in the search for truth characterized each one of them in his own way. And it was in this atmosphere that Freud matured those qualities which made up the warp and woof of his private and professional personality.

II

There was another influence, though, which has been so far unduly neglected and even intentionally underestimated. This was Freud's familiarity with Aristotle's theories and his logic. Freud not only joined Franz Brentano's course on philosophy, for three years, but later added his course on Aristotle's logic. For some reason Bernfeld throws doubts on Freud's own account of his being a pupil of Brentano, and without any explicit or tenable explanation he goes on to say that "one is inclined to think of Brentano and Freud as almost diametrical opposites." However, he comes by later and admits that "this does not exclude the possibility that Freud was impressed by some of Brentano's polemics and statements . . . Preserved them in his preconscious and that they influenced his thoughts twenty years later" (2).

Franz Brentano (1838-1917) was a Dominican trained for the priesthood and well versed in philosophy, especially Aristotle's doctrines. His first paper was on the various meanings of Being in Aristotle, which became one of his life-long interests. Among the positions he held was a professorship at Vienna for six years from 1874 to 1880. Brentano had trouble with the church when he stood out strongly against the dogma of the infallibility of the Pope. He wrote so bravely and forcibly that he became the intellectual leader of the liberals within and without the church, a matter which ultimately led to his resigning the professorship and to his giving up his ecclesiastical affiliation and clerical status.

Brentano's major contribution was a first volume (the second came out some thirty years later) which he published in 1874, under the title of *Psychology from the Empirical Standpoint*. In this book, his best known work, Brentano attempted to build up a theory of psychology based on experience, not on experiment. He believed that psychology is a science, but tried to refute the rigid methodologies of physiological psychology which were being propounded by such of his contemporaries as Helmholtz, Fechner, or Wundt.

In spite of a life partly consumed by spiritual or ideological conflicts and partly weighed down by many professional difficulties and personal misfortunes, Brentano was acknowledged as a distinguished forerunner of several schools of psychology such as that of Stumpf or of the Gestalt. Edwin Boring (3) says, "His influence is to be explained in part by his personality, in part by the remarkably effective and trenchant character of the little writing that he produced, and in part by the historical accident that it was he who deflected the light of Aristotle into the realm of modern psychology."

According to Brentano, mental phenomena have an immanent objectivity, they are *acts*. But these acts are not self-contained, the act depends on an extrinsic object. Thus, hearing is a psychical act which implies an object, *viz.* the sound heard. Physical phenomena are different, they are complete within themselves and do not refer to any extrinsic objects. In this manner there is as much difference between psychology and physics as there is between act and object. But they are also related inasmuch as it is to the physical objects that the mental acts refer. When one sees a color, the act of seeing in itself is a mental process, but it contains the sensation of color which is a physical phenomenon. Brentano classified mental acts into three basic groups; the acts of ideating, the acts of judging and, interestingly enough, a third group of *loving* and *hating*, which cover the various shades of affects, emotions and conations.

This is a very concise account of the work of Brentano whom Freud listened to in two of his most successful courses. It is of great importance to know that attendance at philosophy courses had ceased to be an obligatory requirement of medical students when Freud joined Vienna University. Whatever may be the details of these courses, it can be safely assumed that they centered around the Aristotelian doctrines and theories.

Aristotle's influence, enormous as it was in many fields, was greatest of all in logic. To him we are indebted for the rules that should be adopted to organize good presentation and argument; he was the inventor of formal logic which deals with reasoning as such, irrespective of its content. His works on logic contained in what is known as the *Organon* (the instrument) have such chapters as "the Categories" or the theory of logical terms, "On Interpretation," or the theory of propositions, "The Prior Analytics" or the theory of syllogism in general, "The

Posterior Analytics" or the theory of proof, "The Topics" or the theory of dialectic and probable reasoning, and so forth. Even Aristotle's opponents admit that his work on formal logic, on fallacies and deductive thinking are both important and admirable.

Anyone who reads Freud, without knowing anything of the historical facts of his connections, cannot fail to be struck by his impeccable lucidity. His well built arguments, his long breath in following a proposition to the end, the absence of any fallacy in his long chains of inference, are bound to be accepted by any reader who is logical enough to understand what Freud is trying to present. If any of his theories are unacceptable, this is not due to the way he argued it, but to the premises he started with; but this is another matter that lies in another side of logic and scientific methodology which will be touched on later.

It is naturally beyond the scope of this paper, if it is ever possible in any short communication, to describe even the most salient features of Aristotle. It was said that for more than twenty centuries Aristotle held the world a slave; and it is admitted, even by his adversaries that it was two thousand years before the world produced any thinker who could be regarded as approximately his equal. His teacher, Plato, used to call him The Intellect; the Arabs referred to him as the First Master, and his authority in nearly every branch of human knowledge remained over the centuries almost as unquestioned as that of the church. Out of his system a few points should be mentioned, though, because of their probable influence in germinating Freud's initial hypotheses.

In general, it should be kept in mind that in contrast to his teacher, Plato, Aristotle represents the realistic, rational, scientific, logical approach to the problems of the universe and of man. Aristotle believed that things appear to us as they are, that the human mind is constructed in such a way as to supply us with a valid picture of the external world. Truth is not outside our universe, it is under our eyes. The first instance of science is experience; it is the observation and study of natural phenomena. Aristotle's belief in the efficiency and supremacy of reason led him to conceive that the only happy way of existence is that of thought. Even his God was the supreme Reason, eternal Thought thinking itself.

The central idea in the Aristotelian system is that Being is only that of the individual. But the individual is composed of matter and form. It is by virtue of the form that matter becomes a definite thing. Movement, change or evolution is the passage from one state to another, from the possible to the real, from matter to form, from potentiality to actuality. Other causes besides the material and the formal are needed to achieve change; these are the efficient and the final causes. But these can be included in the formal cause which makes an actuality out of pure matter, which is only the potentiality. Needless to say, these terms are not used in the everyday sense of matter or shape. A simple example is a statue: Marble is matter, the chisel and work of the sculptor is the efficient cause, his goal is the final cause and what the statue represents is its formal cause. This is, obviously, plain common sense—a thing exists as some content bound within certain limits.

Nature always follows a course that ascends from lower levels of existence to higher ones. Even mineral has a form, because pure potentiality does not exist in fact. But the inorganic is the matter of the living. A plant contains all the qualities of inorganic matter, but in the organization of its elements, a new form is achieved—life. The animal, in addition to a vegetative life, possesses sensitivity and movement. At the top of the scale comes man who has, in addition to the vegetative and animal properties, reason and thinking. Man is truly man when he accomplishes the human act par excellence; not life, which we have in common with animals, but thought, the property of man alone. Perfect happiness is thus the unhindered exercise of reason and thought. It is beyond the lowlier needs of the animal or vegetative components in the human being, although it does not cancel them out.

Whenever students of Freud find it hard to follow one part or the other of his theories, it would probably be of help to go back to some of Aristotle's doctrines. The libido theory and the supremacy of genitality could perhaps be more easily understood if one recalls Aristotle's view that the higher levels of organization contain the lower levels and something more. Instead of wasting energy on endless superfluous controversies such as those connected with heredity and environment, constitutional or cultural factors, it is fruitful to remember that Freud—time and again—pointed out that things are over-determined and that he specifically mentioned the complementary series in the causation of symptoms. For Freud, as for Aristotle, everything has to have matter and form. Early traumata without later precipitating factors would not bring about a neurosis, neither would a constitutional makeup without an unfortunate life experience. If we are puzzled when Freud says that the death instinct is mute, we should remember that Aristotle had said that when we are, there is no death; and when dead we are not.

III

But it would be a grave mistake to infer from the many instances where the influence of Aristotle can be detected in Freud that psychoanalysis was a by-product of the Peripatetic school or, for that matter, any other doctrine or group of philosophical doctrines. That is because Freud, aware of his speculative tendencies, firmly and ruthlessly tried to check them by adhering to modern scientific methodology and following its basic rule of drawing conclusions only after ample data had been carefully gathered and inspected. For years it was under the microscope, on slides and in test tubes that he searched for answers to the questions that occupied his mind. It was along this line of intensive, meticulous, persistent work that he was trained before he set himself the task of trying to understand the riddles of human behavior and to unravel its motives and determinants.

Another fortunate coincidence occurred during that period to complement Freud's scientific way of reasoning. In 1879, he was asked, through the recommendation of Brentano, to translate some of J. S. Mill's essays. Whether Freud accepted this task to pass time or to earn a little money, as Jones suggests, it is warranted, knowing Freud's erudition and curiosity, to suppose that he did not stop with the mere drudgery of translation. One might safely speculate that he read such views of Mill as those on utilitarianism, association or his book, *System of Logic,* which was the most important formulation of modern scientific methodology since Bacon's *Novum Organum* which in its turn complemented Aristotle's *Organon.* It is also intriguing that one of Mill's essays, translated by Freud, dealt with Plato's theory of reminiscence, the revival of memories, long standing, but forgotten, in the mind.

It will be noticed that we have not mentioned in the foregoing account some other traceable links between Freud's theories and several other thinkers such as Schopenhauer, Herbart, or Fechner. These were intentionally overlooked not only because of the boundaries of this paper, but also because in the presence of giants, human beings, whatever stature they may have, can hardly attract the attention of the observer.

Historical facts and chronological order do not justify any undue emphasis on the influence of a Herbart or a Fechner in Freudian psychology, True, Freud might have studied, during his last year at the gymnasium, Lindner's handbook on psychology, which was avowedly based on the Herbartian system. However, one can hardly infer from this probability that Freud gained much from this book at that stage in his development. Not only was he disinclined all through his life to read, let alone absorb, books on psychology, but in his school days he had not yet decided on a career. He was still playing with the phantasy of being a lawyer or a politician. Even if Freud, later on, had become acquainted with Herbart's views, either directly or through Meynert's lectures on psychiatry, there is enough disparity between the basic principles of Freud's psychology and that of Herbart to outshadow their similarities. What similarities there may be are due to Freud's familiarity with the original earlier sources, which were the forerunners of such concepts as that of the unconscious, association, or pleasure.

When the works of Freud have been more fully studied, and when more historical investigation has been undertaken on his readings or his library, it may become more evident how much he has derived from the thinkers who preceded him across the ages. The incompatible array which he picked from, not only shows his outstanding reach and explains much of the complexity in his theories, but it also demonstrates what a daring intellectual attempt he made to put together such a large assortment of contradictory views about the human nature and the human mind.

His work becomes more impressive when we realize that he did not adopt the easy way of building up a theory through speculation. True, he used an armchair, as many thinkers do. But he used it to listen, to observe and collect more and more information that would sustain or refute ideas that he might have stored in his memory from his precursors. Fully aware of the requirements of modern scientific method, morally and intellectually equipped for it and trained to follow it, he started with certain ideas as hypotheses to be checked and verified in order to build up a theory. This was and still is the method for dealing with every psychoanalytic case.

That psychoanalysis also proved to be of help to certain individuals in their emotional distress does not mean that it will survive only as long as it is useful or popular. Sometime in the unforeseeable future, a shorter or a non-psychological therapy may be discovered, as Freud himself said. But the basic concepts of psychoanalysis are probably destined to remain the core of any psychology of the human mind at any time and in any place.

REFERENCES

1. BERNFELD, SIEGFRIED: Freud's Earliest Theories and the School of Helmholtz. *Psa. Quart.*13;341–362, 1944.
2. _____; Freud's Scientific Beginnings. *Amer. Imago* 6:162–196, 1949.
3. BORING, EDWIN: *History of Experimental Psychology.* New York, Appleton-Century-Crofts, 1950.
4. EISSLER, K. R.: The Attitude of Neurologists, Psychiatrists and Psychologists Towards Psychoanalysis. *Psa. Quart.* 10:297–319, 1941.
5. FERENCZI, SANDOR: *Final Contributions to the Problems and Methods of Psychoanalysis.* New York, Basic Books, 1955.

6. FREUD, SIGMUND: *An Autobiographical Study.* London, Hogarth, 1935.
7. _____; *The Origins of Psychoanalysis—Letters to Wilhelm Fliess 1887-1902.* Marie Bonaparte, Anna Freud, Ernst Kris, eds. New York, Basic Books, 1954.
8. JONES, ERNEST: *Sigmund Freud, Life and Work,* Vol. I. London, Hogarth, 1953.
9. MCDOUGALL, WILLIAM: *Outline of Abnormal Psychology.* New York, Scribners, 1926.
10. _____; *Psychoanalysis and Social Psychology.* London, Methuen, 1936.
11. MÜLLER-FREIENFELS, RICHARD: *The Evolution of Modern Psychology.* W. B. Wolfe, tr. New York, Yale University, 1935.
12. ZILBOORG, GREGORY: Some Sidelights on Free Association. *Int. J. Psa.* 33:489-495, 1952.

3

A New Copernicus?*

Nigel D. Walker

The century that follows a man's birth is usually long enough to let him find his proper place in history. In Freud's case it is a little too short. The science of the mind is still a battle-field for rival empires of faiths, ideologies and academic theories; and a battle-field is no place for a monument until the fighting is over. What is more, one of the exceptional things about him was that most of his original thinking was done after his fortieth year, at a time of life when most men, whether they know it or not, are being carried forward by the intellectual momentum which they acquired in their twenties or thirties. Freud continued to produce new ideas until his seventies—some would say until his eighties. As a result, we are still too close to him to plan the scale of his monument.

Another difficult question to answer is "What should be inscribed on the monument?" With what victories should he be credited? Freud was not always modest in speaking about his contribution. He once referred to himself as the Copernicus of the mind, and on another occasion compared himself to Darwin . But his achievement is not so easily defined as that of the great astronomer or biologist. His own followers, when they try to articulate on the subject, tend to be incoherent through enthusiasm or mysticism, while his enemies owe him more than they dare admit.

.*Reprinted from *Freud and the 20th Century*, edited by Benjamin Nelson, by permission of author and editor. Copyright ©1957 by The World Publishing Company.

For example, he did not discover, or "invent," the unconscious. Herbart and Eduard von Hartmann did that. What he did discover—and here "discover" and "invent" mean the same thing—was a technique for alleviating certain kinds of disorder by making the patient talk. Mesmer, Charcot and Bernheim had shown how certain disorders could be alleviated if the physician talked to the patient; theirs was the technique of hypnotism and suggestion. Freud, who had studied under Charcot and Bernheim but was not a particularly successful hypnotist, achieved more permanent results than they did by making the patient talk to the physician: this was the psychoanalytic technique.

In some cases this technique worked only if the patient could be brought to talk about incidents which he could not normally remember, or about desires and feelings which he could not admit, even to himself. Freud found it easier to picture the state of affairs in his patients' minds if he visualized them as consisting not only of a conscious, introspectible mind but also of an unintrospectible, unconscious one. In doing this he made use of Herbartian psychology which he had learned at his Vienna school. The importance of this step was threefold. It was the first real use of the academic science of psychology in a therapeutic technique; hitherto psychologists had made their "discoveries" in their armchairs or their laboratories, and had neither helped nor been helped by the hospitals and clinics. Secondly, the technique itself was important because its very nature made it necessary to think of the mind in a new way. Hitherto it had been possible to conceive it as consisting simply of conscious processes—to see it in a two-dimemsional way. It was like the discovery of perspective by the early Italian painters.

But its real importance lay in the fact that it provided Freud with a method of making use of the close connection which he had observed between the experiences of the infant and the disorders of the adult. He was not of course the first person to discover that the child is father to the man. What he did discover was how. to lessen the effects of childhood upon the mental health of the adult. His method was to treat the long-past experiences and emotions as if they were still present in the adult; and the concept of the unconscious was the only thing that made this possible. It enabled both analyst and patient to think of these experiences as being preserved underneath the latter's conscious thoughts. By inducing his patients to think in this way he made it easier for them to revive these experiences. I do not mean that he regarded the unconscious as simply a useful fiction; he believed in its reality. But whether he was right or wrong in this, its therapeutic value is beyond doubt.

Nor was Freud the first to make the distinction between what he called the "ego" and the "id"—between that collection of organized, more or less conscious and more or less consistent bunch of principles and prejudices that we loosely call the "self" and the unorganized, inconsistent, sometimes unrecognized and often anti-social needs and emotions with which our bodies are endowed. A good deal of the credit for this distinction, as Freud acknowledged, must go to the unpopular Nietzsche, and some of it to a little-known doctor called Groddeck. What Freud did, and what no psychologist, philosopher or psychiatrist had hitherto done, was to weld together all these notions—the unconscious, the ego, the id and one or two additions of his own, such as the superego—and make of them a diagram of the mind that was of practical value for therapeutic purposes. The history of psychology is full of psychological systems; every well-known name belongs to someone who drew a new diagram of our mental processes. Some of these were extremely useful for explaining and systematizing the phenomena studied in the laboratory; some of them even made our everyday behavior seem plausible. But when it came to sorting out the tangle of the disordered mind they proved useless, and the psychiatrist had to rely on trial and error with drugs and shocks and knives. Freud's diagram looked rather different from those of the laboratories; to some people it appeared gross and overcomplicated. But the technicians who used it in tinkering with the mechanism seemed to get results.

Freud's own explanation of the success of his technique was not necessarily the right one. Even his own latter-day followers think that he attributed too much virtue to the catharsis of the past, and not enough to the patient's relationship to the analyst—in technical terms, the "transference". But most psychiatric techniques—even such drastic ones as prefrontal leucotomy—have been introduced with even less idea of why they worked; and this has not prevented them from working, although it has made the task of improving them a slow and empirical one.

Like many great clinicians, Freud was an observant natural historian of man as an animal. As a clinician, he found that a large number of his patients suffered from some disturbance of normal sexual function. As a natural historian (and a father) he observed what had previously been revealed only to anthropologists and nursemaids— namely, sexual behavior among the young of the human species, who had hitherto been regarded as sexless by all right-thinking people. As a psychologist he therefore saw in the sexual instinct the physiological power-source for many adult drives. He was not the first psychologist to emphasize the importance of man's sexual behavior to an understanding of his whole complex personality. The Frenchman Charcot, although careful in his public utterances, had privately stressed this to the young doctors who understudied him in the Salpetriere, among them Freud.

Meanwhile a contemporary of Freud, an Australian doctor called Havelock Ellis, was beginning the first volumes of his enormous *Studies in the Psychology of Sex*. Freud himself, although he began by attributing most neurotic disorders to disturbance of the sexual function, soon saw that this was much too simple to fit the facts, which pointed also to the importance of the other natural functions of the infant—feeding and excreting. As time went on his explanations were more and more frequently couched in terms not of sex but of a psychic force called the *libido,* which, coupled with the instinct of aggression, underlay the apparently diverse forms of human conduct.

Now that we have survived the initial shock to our prudery and pomposity, we can see his notions not as a far-fetched piece of foreign dirty-mindedness, but as an attempt to reduce to the smallest possible number the principles underlying the multifarious pursuits of man. Although William of Occam was the first to put it into words, this has always been the aim of science—to explain with the minimum number of entities. This is what the physicists since Democritus have been trying to do for matter—to reduce it to the minimum number of homogeneous particles.

Many Freudian concepts—such as repression or the wish-fulfilment function of dreams—are such common intellectual coinage nowadays that they need no explanation or comment. What is not so commonly recognized is that underlying them is a startling anticipation of one of the most recently developed sciences—cybernetics. War-time advances in methods of designing automatic gun-aimers, electronic computers and other self-correcting devices have shown how the principle of homeostasis can be used to explain many of the more complex ways in which the human nervous system operates. A homeostatic device is one which automatically corrects or compensates for any deviation from a predetermined set of values—whether this is a temperature as in the case of a thermostat, or a height and compass bearing, as with an automatic pilot. Fifty years ago Freud saw that this principle could be used to explain the way in which human beings reacted to stimuli. At first sight they seemed to seek certain stimuli (such as food) and avoid others (for instance dangerous animals). Freud saw that it was possible to regard all reactions of this kind not as being of two kinds— positive and negative—but as consisting entirely of one kind—negative, that is avoidance, reactions. Even when we appear to be seeking the stimulus as we do with food when we are hungry, it is possible to regard this as the avoidance of the pricks of hunger. This point of view made it possible for him to interpret all the reactions of the human central nervous system as designed to protect it from stimuli. The infant cries to protect itself from hunger. In the same way, he thought, the central nervous system tries to protect itself from certain of its own processes which threaten it with distress, and this kind of avoidance reaction is called "repression." In the same way, too, when the nervous system is asleep it tries to protect itself from stimuli that threaten to awake it, and thus creates dreams which disguise the stimulus or delude the dreamer into thinking he has dealt with the stimulus. The hungry man dreams he is eating, and does not awake. This is what Freud called the wish-fulfilment function of the dream.

This explanation of phenomena such as dreams and repression led Freud to define the central nervous system as a mechanism of which the function is to reduce stimulation to its lowest possible level. This is of course a completely materialistic definition, and perhaps even more depressing and derogatory of human dignity than most materialism. But if you can overlook this for the moment, it is possible to see in it that profound kind of simplicity that characterized such great scientific thinking as, for example, Newton's Laws of Motion. Like Newton's Laws, Freud's definition is a little too simple to fit all the phenomena; but that is another story. The point is that this hardly recognized theoretical formulation of Freud's would have been a natural accompaniment to the development of cybernetics in the nineteen-forties: but Freud formulated it in 1915. This is, of course, of no more than historical interest, for the idea was not taken up and investigated, and it was left to the mechanically-minded neurologists and cyberneticists to rediscover it on their own.

It will be obvious that I am not concerned, except indirectly, with the practical therapeutic aspects of the technique which Freud evolved. Nor shall I try to deal with his excursions (and those of his enthusiastic followers) into the fields of anthropology and literature. Like many a recreational outing, these were not complete successes, but I do not think anyone will maintain that they were altogether unilluminating.

What I am trying to decide is whether the comparison of Freud to Copernicus and Darwin is justified.

Almost all scientific advances are of three kinds. They may be technical; a method may be discovered of doing some hitherto impossible thing, or of doing an old thing in a new and better way. They may be what are nicknamed "natural history" discoveries—that is, observations of a new phenomenon, or more accurate descriptions of one that is already known. Thirdly, they may be theoretical—a neater equation to describe magnetic phenomena, or an extension of Boyle's Law so as to include the behavior of gases at particularly low temperatures. This sort of advance going on all the time, and every few years, in some field or other, a sufficiently important one occurs to become headline news.

There is, however, a fourth kind of advance which is not nearly so familiar. Indeed in any single science it probably occurs only once in two or three hundred years. It consists of a thorough revolution in the way in which that particular science looks at its subject. Take the case of chemistry. By the end of the eighteenth century there had been a good deal of accurate observation, with precise measurements, of the ways in which various elements combined with each other or behaved under changes of temperature. These were in themselves scientific advances of the kind I have labelled "technical" or "natural history." There were also quite a number of explanatory theories of very limited utility, including the notorious phlogiston theory of combustion. In 1803, however, Dalton showed how the laws which explained these phenomena could be simplified by the assumption of the atomic structure of matter. This assumption did not make the observations of his predecessors any truer than they had always been; but without it very few of the subsequent observations and technical advances of the nineteenth and twentieth centuries would have taken place. Its original simplicity has now become complicated again by the assumption of a variety of subatomic entities; but it was the revolutionary step in chemical thinking which turned chemistry into a science.

Consider, too, one of the men with whom Freud compared himself—Copernicus. As every schoolboy knows, the Ptolemaic conception of a geocentric universe was the official theory of occidental astronomy until the enormous simplification made possible by Copernicus' heliocentric assumption was appreciated. Like Dalton, Copernicus was not the first to make his revolutionary suggestion; he was anticipated by the Pythagoreans just as Dalton was by the Epicureans. Copercicus' theory, like Dalton's, did not go all the way; he did not, for example, realize that the earth's orbit was an ellipse and not a perfect circle. Some of his reasons for arriving at his theory were extremely unsound. Yet without it modern astronomy would not have been a possibility.

As there is no handy name for conceptual advances of this kind, I do not see why we should not call them "Copernican." Other Copernican thinkers—for they are molders of thought rather than discoverers of fact—were Newton, Einstein and that other figure with whom Freud compared himself, Darwin. I do not want to suggest that such a revolution is entirely the work of one man, or that a Copernican notion springs fully grown from his head without warning. Most of those I have mentioned owed a great deal to the work of their predecessors and even of their contemporaries, although Copernicus himself is probably an exception. If any of the Copernicans had been prevented by some accident from putting forward his idea, someone else would have been bound to do so, sooner or later. But none of these reservations lessens the achievement of these men or their entitlement to a special place in the history of their science.

Was Freud a Copernican? I find this a difficult question to answer. His influence on twentieth-century thinking about the mind has certainly been immense. What is more, it has been achieved almost entirely through his own writings, and owes little to his followers. As I said at the beginning, we are too close to his influence to assess it impartially. But I should like to offer a guess at what people will say about him a hundred years from now. By that time he will no longer be regarded as the "discoverer" of the unconscious of the ego and the id. His attempt to derive all instinctive behaviours from two basic drives will be of purely historical interest. So will his homeostatic account of the central nervous system, since it was forgotten and the principle rediscovered in a more precise form by the neurologists of the nineteen-forties.

He will be remembered for his achievement in selecting from among the techniques for treating disorders of the mind, and from among the psychological systems of the academic psychologists, the only pair that would form a working team. This synthesis was of course partly due to a lucky combination of circumstances. A free-thinking Jew learns Herbartian psychology in the sixth form at a Vienna school. After becoming a neurologist and discovering the limitations of physical methods of treatment he studies the hypnotic techniques of the Paris school. Not being a particularly good hypnotist, he tries to achieve similar results by other means. Result—psychoanalysis.

It was this synthesis that transformed the treatment of mental disorders from a semi-religious, semi-empirical study into a systematic technique with rules and reasons. What Freud thought of, therefore, as a scientific revolution in our conception of the mind was rather a technical advance which, by its spectacular nature, popularized the three-dimensional conception already suggested by nineteenth-century German thinkers. In much the same way the circumnavigation of the globe did more to convince people of the earth's roundness than all the geographers' arguments. In comparing Freud to Magellan rather than Copernicus I am not devaluing his achievement. Technicians such as Watt and Marconi probably had a greater effect upon the next generations' way of life than Newton or Dalton. It is true that the number of patients treated by psychoanalysis or derivative methods is a negligible fraction of twentieth-century mankind, so that its direct effect has been less tangible than that of the steam-engine or the wireless set. But its indirect effects upon our approach to problems connected with the mind, whether therapeutic, legal or educational, has exceeded even the hopes of its discoverer.

4

Darwin and Freud:
A Comparison of Receptions*

David Shakow
David Rapaport

THE THREE HISTORICAL BLOWS

On at least three different occasions[1] Freud implied a similarity between himself, Copernicus, and Darwin. His comparison was not actually a personal one; rather, he compared psychoanalysis with the Copernican and Darwinian theories.[2] When Abraham commented on the apparent personalness of one of these passages (Freud, 1917), Freud replied: "You are right in saying that the enumeration in my last paper may give the impression of claiming a place beside Copernicus and

---

*Reprinted from *The Influence of Freud on American Psychology* by David Shakow and David Rapaport, by permission of International Universities Press, Inc. Copyright© 1964 by International Universities Press, Inc.

1. *Introductory Lectures on Psycho-Analysis* (1916-1917, pp. 284-285), "A Difficulty in the Path of Psycho-Analysis" (1917, pp. 139-144 [originally written for the outstanding general Hungarian periodical, *Nyugat*]), "The Resistances to Psycho-Analysis" (1925a, p. 221).

2. It is true that upon occasion Freud did make a direct comparison of himself with historical figures. One such comparison was with Columbus, whom he considered an important explorer-discoverer, but not a great man (Jones, 1955, p. 415). Barzun's (1958, pp. 85-86) view of Darwin is of interest in this connection. He holds that Darwin ". . . does not belong with the great thinkers of mankind. He belongs rather with those others— men of action and feeling and unconscious power—whom Hegel termed world-historical characters because the world after them is not as it was before." Himmelfarb (1959, p. 164) expresses a similar view. Darwin, she thinks, might very appropriately have said of himself what Freud said of himself in a letter to Fliess: ". . . I am not really a man of science, not an observer, not an experimenter, and not a thinker. I am nothing but by temperament a *conquistador* . . ." (Himmelfarb quotes this letter from Jones' biography [Jones, 1953, p. 348]. It has not been included in the volume containing the Fliess letters.) Simon (1957) offers justification for Freud's identification of himself with Oedipus, Hannibal, La Salle, and particularly with Moses.

Darwin. But I didn't want to give up the interesting train of thought on that account, and so at least put Schopenhauer in the foreground" (Jones, 1955, p. 226).

Not only Freud, but also his biographer, Ernest Jones, seems to have been somewhat sensitive about this comparison. In 1956, Nigel Walker published an article entitled "Freud and Copernicus" in *The Listener*.[3] Although some exceptions may be taken to Walker's article on certain grounds,[4] the resulting exchange between Jones and Walker is a significant illustration of Jones' attitude. In this article Walker referred to Freud's comparison of himself with Copernicus and Darwin, but concluded that Freud more closely resembled Captain Cook (changed to "Magellan" in the reprinted version). For this, Jones took Walker to task: ". . . nothing would ["could" in original version] have been more unlike Freud" (Nelson, 1957, p. 287). This sensitivity of Freud and Jones is rather difficult to understand, considering Freud's repeated juxtaposition, if not complete identification, of psychoanalysis with the other two historical developments. Modesty of both author and biographer perhaps forbade their pointing to the amount of objective justification for the comparison.[5] As Heidbreder (1940) said in her obituary of Freud, and as so many others have repeated since, the comparison with Copernicus and Darwin has "become inevitable."[6]

In both *Introductory Lectures on Psycho-Analysis* and "A Difficulty in the Path of Psycho-Analysis" Freud made the comparison of psychoanalysis with Copernican and Darwinian theory in terms of the three historical blows which human narcissism has had to undergo: the *cosmological* blow administered by Copernicus, the *biological* blow administered by Darwin and his group, and the *psychological* blow administered by psychoanalysis. These blows jolted respectively man's

3. Reprinted, with minor changes, as "A New Copernicus?" (Walker, 1957).

4. For instance, Walker's emphasis on the special importance of Herbartian psychology in Freud's background. See Kris' comment about Freud and Herbart (in Freud, 1887–1902, p. 47).

5. Although Freud perhaps never thought about himself as a genius, emphasizing instead the importance of his discoveries, Jones' reaction to Walker is rather belied by what he says about Freud in various other places. For instance, in the third volume of the biography (1957, p. 304), he says he "bestowed on Freud the title of the Darwin of the Mind." See also Jones (1955, especially Part III) and particularly his *Centenary Addresses* (1956).

6. For example, E. D. Adrian (1954), in his Presidential Address to the British Association for the Advancement of Science on "Science and Human Nature," has briefly made this comparison. Alex Comfort (1960) has compared Darwin and Freud, calling for more interrelationships between Darwinians and Freudians—a suggestion which deserves strong support. Erikson (1956a) has sensitively compared Darwin's and Freud's problems in their respective fields of biological and individual prehistory and very briefly touched on the differing implications of each.

geocentrism, anthropocentrism, and egocentrism.[7] Freud himself considered the blow to the ego's mastery of its own mind as the "most wounding blow" of the three.[8]

A detailed comparison of the effects of all three major historical contributions is beyond our scope. However, the major aspects of the impacts of the differing but related Darwinian and Freudian theories can, we believe, serve as an effective introduction to some of the problems we shall be facing in the attempt to trace Freud's influence on psychology. This comparison seems particularly appropriate during this centennial period, when there is so much discussion concerning Darwin's influence.

RECEPTION OF THE THEORIES

A dependable evaluation of the effects of the respective blows is particularly difficult to make because of the chronological relationship of Darwin and Freud, who came within only half a century of one another. Our main concern is not, of course, the relative importance of the two theories[9] or the relative greatness of the two men. Rather, we are interested in comparing the *responses* to these two revolutionary theories in their respective historical situations.

To begin with, was there a difference in the length of time it took for each of these theories to be accepted? To say *when* a theory is "accepted" is, of course, most difficult. Perhaps the best we can do is to define as the time of acceptance the periods when the fundamental ideas seem to have passed through the usual initial period of marked opposition and to have become part of the general culture.

---

7. Closely associated with Darwin's disturbance of anthropocentrism is the little-noted but important contribution Alfred Russel Wallace made to the weakening of the intimately related ethnocentrism (see Eiseley, 1959, p. 303 ff.). See also Fenichel's (1946) comments on the narcissistic blow. Actually there is need for a re-examination of the whole problem of "blows," both those considered here and the most recent "galactic" blow which has such far-reaching implications for man (Shapeley, 1958).

8. "In the course of centuries the *naive* self-love of men has had to submit to two major blows at the hands of science. . . . This is associated in our minds with the name of Copernicus, though something similar had already been asserted by Alexandrian science. The second blow fell when biological research destroyed man's supposedly privileged place in creation and proved his descent from the animal kingdom and his ineradicable animal nature. This revaluation has been accomplished in our own days by Darwin, Wallace and their predecessors, though not without the most violent contemporary opposition. But human megalomania will have suffered its third and most wounding blow from the psychological research of the present time which seeks to prove to the ego that it is not even master in its own house, but must content itself with scanty information of what is going on unconsciously in its mind" (Freud, 1916-1917, pp. 284-285).

9. "Freud's effect is, however, still too recent to compare with Darwin's. For that we must wait fifty years" (Boring, 1950b, p. 743).

In both cases, approximately one generation appears to have been sufficient to make each theory a recognizable, even prominent, part of the culture.[10] Of the two theories, however, evolutionary ways of thinking have undoubtedly taken a greater hold and become a more intimate part of the culture and of man's concept of himself than have psychoanalytic ways of thinking.[11] Why is this so? The difference, we believe, cannot be accounted for merely by the four decades' seniority of the former. We must look to other factors also. From the first, Freudism seems to have met with greater opposition than did Darwinism. Let us therefore examine in some detail the nature of the differences in their reception.

Reception of On the Origin of the Species

How was the *Origin* received? As in the case of any scientific idea, certain groups were instrumental in determining its acceptance. Here four groups were involved: (1) those in the immediately concerned scientific disciplines, persons for whom evolutionary doctrines had direct professional significance—the life-scientists, such as geologists and paleontologists; (2) those in other academic fields and sciences; (3) clergymen; (4) educated laymen.

Among those immediately concerned, the reaction to Darwin's theory was on the whole favorable.[12] Especially important support came from Darwin's four "lieutenants": Hooker, the director of Kew Gardens; Lyell, the father of modern geology (with some residual resistance); Gray, the Harvard botanist; and Huxley. And naturally there was Wallace, who shared the honors of the 1858 presentation to the Linnean

---

10. Not that opposition did not persist considerably beyond a generation, even with respect to the essential aspects of the theories. Isolated opposition to Darwinism existed even two generations later—witness the Scopes trial in the United States and Sir Ambrose Fleming in England. The Scopes trial took place in the summer of 1925. According to Keith, Sir Ambrose Fleming's attack came on January 14, 1935 in a presidential address before the Victoria Institute and Philosophical Society of Great Britain (see p. 19). "In this he maintained that the account of the creation of man given in the book of Genesis is literally true, and that the 'evolutionary theory is totally at variance with the scriptural teaching as to man's original perfection'" (Keith, 1935, p. 51). Sir Ambrose was a F.R.S., a fellow of the University College, London, and a world authority on electrical engineering.

Opposition to psychoanalysis, both in the culture at large and in professional circles, still exists in even more widespread form at the present time—again several generations later. Dallenbach (1955) and Gengerelli (1957), for instance, are quite recent examples of this opposition among psychologists.

Copernicus met religious objection almost immediately (particularly from the Protestants; for example, Luther, Calvin and Melanchthon), although it is of interest to note that he himself did not believe that his views conflicted with the Bible. But recognition of how radical his ideas actually were did not occur for at least a generation. It was only after two generations, with Giordano Bruno's emphasis on the plurality of

Society. Other prominent persons reacted favorably: Carpenter, the physiologist; Ramsay, the geologist; Chambers, the geologist and publisher; and Galton. Some equally prominent persons were, of course, not favorably disposed. Agassiz was the most outstanding of this group which included Richard Owen, the "greatest anatomist of his time," Mivart, the Roman Catholic biologist, and Whewell (see Ellegard, 1958, Chapter 9), the leading philosopher of science.

In other parts of the academic community, the negative attitude of Herschel, the mathematician, was balanced by the positive attitude of Sir John Lubbock, the astronomer and mathematician. The attacks on the theory by physicists, however, particularly by Lord Kelvin (the greatest physicist of the nineteenth century) were especially troubling. These attacks, based on the then reasonable physical theories of the relative recency of the earth's origins, resulted in a brief period of anti-Darwinian feeling (see Eiseley, 1959, p. 233 ff.).

The most vehement opposition to the *Origin* came from the clergy. To them the book became a kind of anti-Bible, probably because it epitomized the issues in the long-standing battle between religion and science dating from Copernican times. Darwinism became the symbol of the growing secularization of society and the undermining of religious institutions.[13] A few clergymen, like the Reverend Charles Kingsley of *Water Babies* fame, accepted the revolutionary doctrine quite calmly. The great majority, however, including the Reverend Adam Sedgwick,

---

worlds and the infinite universe implied by the theory, that the Copernican view became the center of real controversy (see Butterfield, 1949, pp. 48-50; Wightman, 1953, p. 49). Copernicus' work was banned by the Catholic Church until 1822 (Schwartz and Bishop, 1958, p. 219). For a more detailed discussion, see Kuhn (1957), *The Copernican Revolution.*

See Freud's discussion of the acceptance of new ideas in *Moses and Monotheism* (1939, pp. 103-104). Darlington (1959a) and Himmelfarb (1959, p. 292) point out that the general aspects of Darwinian ideas actually triumphed within a decade.

11. See Sir Julian Huxley (1960) for a description of the vicissitudes of Darwinian theory, with its many very high ups and few downs.

12. Some question may be raised, as it has been by several persons, about beginning an assessment of the response to Darwin's views with the publication of the *Origin*. For there was much initial opposition from a number of his associates, even his "lieutenants." This was dispelled in the period prior to 1859 by considerable correspondence and personal discussion. However, since our concern is with the response in the culture as a whole, it seems reasonable to adopt as our starting point the date when Darwin finally decided to reveal his views publicly.

13. J. Pelikan (1960, p. 246) says: "Seldom in the history of the Christian church have theologians reacted as violently to a non-theological book as they did to Charles Darwin's *Origin of Species.*" See also C. C. Gillespie (1951), John C. Greene (1959a), Ruth Moore (1957, Chapter VI), Dillenberger (1960), and Ellegard (1958, especially Chapters 5 and 8).

Darwin's old geology teacher, raised a storm of protest. The clergy also received reinforcements from a "religious phalanx" among scientists and physicians. In 1865 this phalanx founded the Victoria Institute, " to investigate fully and impartially the most important questions of Philosophy and Science, but more especially those that bear upon the great truths revealed in Holy Scripture, with the view of defending these truths against the opposition of Science; falsely so called'" (quoted by Ellegard [1958, p. 104] from the Victoria Institute *Journal*).

Against this opposition, Huxley, in England, and Haeckel, even more spiritedly, in Germany, provided a most outspoken and ultimately successful defense (see A. D. White, 1896, especially pp. 70-71, 245). Even in 1860, in the celebrated collision between Huxley and Bishop Wilberforce—perhaps the most vocal opponent of the *Origin* in the early days after publication—Huxley emerged the winner (Irvine, 1955, pp. 5-7; see also R. Moore, 1957, pp. 110-123).

Among laymen, early acceptance of Darwin's views seems to have been quite positively correlated with educational level and degree of general liberalism (Ellegard, 1958, pp. 33-35). Barzun (1958, p. 33) points out that during the middle of the Victorian era, "press and public were in the right mood for the close and protracted discussion of ideas." We know that science figured prominently in the later nineteenth century school curriculum and enjoyed prestige among educated laymen. With the increasing acceptance of Darwinism by the scientific group, and the clergy's diminishing status and reduced opposition to Darwinism, the natural result was a gradual acceptance of Darwinian ideas by the layman.

Reception Of Freud's Ideas

Let us now turn to the reception of Freud's ideas. In Freud's case it is rather difficult to select a particular year to focus on. Rather, it seems most appropriate to take the decade from 1895 to 1905, in the middle of which appeared *The Interpretation of Dreams* (1900a). This period also included the appearance of important series of Freud's papers and presentations: in May of 1896 he gave an address to the Society of Psychiatry and Neurology in Vienna on the etiology of hysteria, and in 1898 published his paper on "Sexuality in the Aetiology of the Neuroses," which included the first mention of infantile sexualtiy. This is also the period of *The Psychopathology of Everyday Life* (1901), *Jokes and Their Relation to the Unconscious* (1905a), and *Three Essays on the Theory of Sexuality* (1905b). With *The Interpretation of Dreams*, these works helped to establish the image of Freudian thinking.

In the reception of Freud's thought, the relevant groups, parallel to those examined for Darwin, were: (1) the professionals and scientists most directly involved—psychiatrists, neurologists, and psychologists; (2) members of the other branches of the medical profession and academic disciplines; (3) the clergy; (4) educated laymen.

The contrast with the Darwinian situation shows up most strikingly in the reactions of the primary groups involved—psychiatrists, neurologists, and psychologists. Almost all the leading figures in these professions are to be found among the opponents. A list of those who expressed vehement opposition to Freudian ideas at various times during the early period, up to about 1910, is actually a "Who's Who" of psychiatry and neurology. In the Germanic countries the array is stellar: Aschaffenburg, Bumke, Forster, Heilbronner, Isserlin, Jaspers, Kraepelin, Moll, Oppenheim, Sommer, Spielmeyer, Vogt, Weygandt, and Ziehen, to mention the most prominent.[14] On the American scene, somewhat later, were Collins, Dercum, Sachs, Sidis, and Starr,[15] and on the French scene, Dubois. From psychology, Wilhelm Stern may be mentioned here merely as an example, since we shall be examining the situation in this field in detail later.[16]

The reactions of persons in other branches of medicine and science[17] to Freud's ideas were equally negative, as was to be expected from persons in fields that were little touched by the new theories. For in respect to psychoanalysis they were essentially laymen who, because of professional identification, tended to accept the guidance of their more involved colleagues. Jones' chapter on "Opposition" in the second volume (1955) of his biography provides one picture of the hostile reception of Freud by the professional world, particularly in the Germanic countries and in America.[18]

What about the clergy, from whom the main attack on Darwin had come? In Freud's case, the reaction of the clergy was much less evident.

14. It is possible that a good deal of the reaction of these persons was based on their essentially antipsychotherapeutic "organic" approach to psychopathology. However, a review of the content of their opinions, so frequently vituperative, leaves the impression that much more than a reaction to psychotherapy was involved. Their arguments seem largely directed at the sex aspect of Freud's theories.

15. Two Americans whose views were not quite so strong were S. Weir Mitchell and Southard. An example of Weir Mitchell's reaction to Freud is found in Earnest (1950, pp. 180–181). Southard's predominantly negative views of Freud are discussed by F. P. Gay (1938, pp. 194–201).

16. See Jones (1955, pp. 107–126) for some details.

17. See Freud's (1913, p. 182) point about biology, also see (1913, p. 166).

18. See Bry and Rifkin (1962) who present a somewhat different picture in their analysis of the reception of Freud's discussion of male hysteria and the reviews in journals of *The Interpretation of Dreams*. Although this is a helpful corrective effort, a much more inclusive analysis of the contemporary response is still needed.

To some extent, the difference may have arisen from the fact that, although "morality" was deeply involved in Freudism, and its moral implications were as great as or even greater than Darwinism's,[19] it did not, as had Darwinism, make a direct attack on such concrete religious tenets as the creation. It could therefore not so easily be taken as a symbol of the increasing secularization of society. Then, too, the relative absence of material on the attitude of the clergy may in part be the result of a difference in the cultural context in which Darwin and Freud developed their ideas. A greater interrelationship seems to have existed between religion and science in Darwin's Britain, as reflected, for instance, in the parson-naturalists of that country, than in the Germanic countries of Freud's time. Darwinism itself must certainly have made a significant contribution to the change in the tenor of the times. It may be that there was a lack of interest in the opinion of the clergy because of the lower status they held in the culture by the end of the century. And it may be that, as Jones says, "Freud lived in a period of time when the *odium theologicum* had been replaced by the *odium sexicum* and not yet by the *odium politicum*" (1955, p. 108).[20]

The strong opposition to Freudism by professional colleagues militated against its acceptance by the educated layman. Opposition among laymen was also aroused because the perversions and distortions of Freudian ideas which rapidly became current were antithetical to dominant public attitudes. It was only the next generation which found these distorted views not incompatible with other radicalisms they were accepting. Indeed, as we shall have occasion to review later, an important role was played by the educated layman in the eventual acceptance of Freud's views.

Thus we find that whereas Darwin had to contend primarily with the clergy while having strong support from other groups, particularly from his colleagues, Freud encountered opposition from almost all groups, especially from his colleagues.

Those who were drawn to psychoanalysis were almost exclusively in the group who eventually became psychoanalysts. They were mostly youngish, relatively unknown persons coming from nonacademic and even nonmedical fields, frequently from the humanities. With rare exceptions they were Jews, who lived their professional lives under many handicaps, and who had relatively little power and prestige. Later a few outstanding persons, largely from the Zurich group, became

19. See Brierley (1934-1947), Erikson (1950, 1961), Flugel (1945), and Hartmann (1960), who consider the "moral" aspects of psychoanalysis.

20. See Rieff (1959, p. 272), who quite flatly says that the attachment of clerics to Freud is misplaced.

associated with Freud. But the support of Jung and Bleuler, the most prominent of these, did not last.

FACTORS CONTRIBUTING TO RECEPTION

Why did these marked differences in the reception of Darwinism and Freudism exist? Among the multiplicity of probable contributing factors, some appear intrinsic to the theories and others more accessory in nature, though it is often difficult to define the forces at work as clearly belonging to one or the other of these categories.

Intrinsic Factors

Perhaps the most important of the intrinsic factors was the degree to which each theory threatened to disturb man's concept of himself. As psychologists, we agree with Freud's own view that psychoanalytic theory offers a more immediate and deeper threat to fundamental narcissism,[21] for it contains potentially anxiety-arousing elements less manifest in Darwinian theory. One can perhaps "take," and live quite comfortably with, the general and rather impersonal idea of a genetic descent from animals, an idea that does not necessarily carry negative implications about man's present status. It is much more difficult, however, to deal with an idea which focuses on the omnipresent existence of the animal within oneself. Actually this idea is a natural extrapolation of Darwinian doctrine, but not one that had been emphasized in the earlier period. The dethronement of rational control which accompanied Freud's central emphasis on the unconscious made his theory especially hard to take. The shock engendered by this view was apparently so great that even among persons in the psychological professions the response aroused was highly emotional.

Still another source of anxiety stemmed from Freud's minimization of the difference between the normal and abnormal. Almost from the very first Freud argued that the distinctions between normal and abnormal were not qualitatively great. While one of his earliest and most important formulations of this view is in *The Interpretation of Dreams* (1900a, pp. 603-608), it is perhaps more simply expressed in a paper published in 1937: "But such a normal ego is, like normality in general, an ideal fiction. The abnormal ego . . . is unfortunately no fiction. Now every normal person is only approximately normal: his ego resembles that of the psychotic in one point or another, in a greater or

21. No matter that the immediate and obvious outburst was probably against a theory based on a dirty subject—sex—put forth by a Jew, and therefore not being worthy of serious consideration. But perhaps the projection involved in this superficial "scapegoating" hid not only the fact that one was interested in sex, but also the awareness of how deep the interest was, and to what "untouchable" persons it was directed.

lesser degree, and its distance from one end of the scale and proximity to the other may provisionally serve as a measure of what we have indefinitely spoken of as 'modification of the ego' " (1937, p. 337).[22]

We have presented a psychologist's view of the relative disturbance to man's concept of himself made by these two revolutionary theories. Might not the biologist see the issues differently? Although we know of no direct attempt at comparison by a member of this discipline, the opinions of some biologists on the disturbing effect of Darwin's impact indicate that they indeed might. For instance, Simpson (1960), in his characteristically lucid and forthright address at the 1959 meeting of the American Association for the Advancement of Science, said:

> The influence of Darwin . . . has literally led us into a different world . . . Perception of the truth of evolution was an enormous stride from superstition to a rational universe.
> . . . According to the higher superstition, man is something quite distinct from nature. He stands apart from all other creatures; his kinship is supernatural, not natural.
> Another subtler and even more deeply warping concept of the higher superstition was that the world was created for man. Other organisms had no separate purpose in the scheme of creation. Whether noxious or useful, they were to be seriously considered only in their relationship to the supreme creation, the image of God.
> Those elements of the higher superstition dominated European thought before publication of *The Origin of Species*. . .
> A world in which man must rely on himself, in which he is not the darling of the gods but only another, albeit extraordinary, aspect of nature, is by no means congenial to the immature or the wishful thinkers. That is plainly a major reason why even now, a hundred years after *The Origin of Species*, most people have not really entered the world into which Darwin led—alas!—only a minority of us. Life may conceivably be happier for some people in the older worlds of superstition. It is possible that some children are made happy by a belief in Santa Claus, but adults should prefer to live in a world of reality and reason.[23]

And in a personal communication of April 11, 1960, he adds: "Except for what I have said about the impact of Darwin in that article, I doubt if I can be of real help in your comparative assessment of the influence of Darwin and Freud. . . . I feel that the Darwinian influence has been probably less superficially obvious and yet more profoundly disturbing and important."

Eiseley (1959, p. 257) states the same view of the Darwinian revolution somewhat differently: "It is my genuine belief that no greater

---

22. See Shakow (1960b) for a discussion of some present-day reverberations of this threat, as represented in the concern with "positive mental health."

23. Some psychoanalytically oriented persons hold that for many it is through the kind of self-examination suggested by Freud that such a goal may be achieved.

act of the human intellect, no greater gesture of humility on the part of man has been or will be made in the long history of science."

Viewing the issue as a whole, however, a different conclusion seems not unreasonable. It would seem relatively easy to live with the blow to man's collective pride at no longer being the darling of God, and even to suffer the violation of many of one's traditional religious beliefs—for these are distant issues, impinging relatively little upon daily life. Granting the validity of Eiseley's evaluation, we might wonder whether the self-sacrifice involved is not compensated for by the warm glow of humility to which one is entitled as an acceptor of the Darwinian view. Further, and perhaps more importantly, no immediate implications for *conduct* are attached to accepting Darwin's views. They can therefore be more readily tolerated.[24]

Even if one overcomes the blow to human pride coming from Freud's reduction of the importance of reason and his minimization of the difference of normal man from both the animal and the psychotic, implications for conduct remain to be dealt with. It is easy to derive an invitation to sexual and other licenses from Freudian theory. For, instead of being recognized as the potential liberator of man from the tyranny of the unconscious, Freud was seen as a seducer of man, as one who encouraged man to give free rein to animal desires. Freud's arguments for the existence of the unconscious and his detailed description of its characteristics were widely interpreted as open advocacy of the direct satisfaction of the wishes which were uncovered. The strong moral aspect of psychoanalysis with its motto "Where id was, there shall ego be" (Freud, 1932, p. 112) was overlooked by both professional opponents and the public.[25] Barzun (1958, pp. 353–354) puts the case

24. A letter from Mrs. Carlyle to Mrs. Russell, January 28, 1860, on this subject is relevant: "Even when Darwin, in a book that all the scientific world is in ecstasy over, proved the other day that we are all come from shell-fish, it didn't move me to the slightest curiosity whether we are or are not. I did not feel that the slightest light could be thrown on my practical life for me, by having it ever so logically made out that my first ancestor, millions of ages back, had been or even had not been, an oyster" (Froude, 1883, pp. 119–120).

25. Not until a somewhat later period (about 1910) did the outstanding proponents of the adaptive (in the sense of improvement) and moral aspects of psychoanalysis begin to become prominent, and even then there was some opposition from the more conventional Freudians, who were perhaps afraid that this emphasis might divert attention from the central issues. These proponents were Putnam (1915) in America, and Pfister (1913; also see 1923) and Silberer (Freud, 1900a, pp. 523–524; Freud, 1922, p. 216) on the European scene. For a description of some aspects of this development in America, see Matthews (1955, Chapter VI).

Nathan G. Hale (personal communication, April 16, 1963) believes that "there is a distinctively American interpretation of psychoanalysis—optimistic, simplified, eclectic, far more 'environmentalist' than Freud himself." This is in some ways corroborated by Putnam's views. Although this particular trend was probably most characteristic of the United States, it also existed elsewhere.

succinctly: "Freud's thought is a good example of the way in which work devoted to freeing man from thralldom through the use of intelligence has been blindly misinterpreted as proving the necessary slavery of man to 'unconscious urges,' and the advisability of giving loose rein to them because they were scientifically there."[26] It was in this way that Freudism gradually took on, for much of the culture, the meaning of "libertinism," and such an interpretation of Freudian theory presumably afforded the grounds for satisfaction at a concrete animal level. The acceptor thus faced a temptation to indulgence—a temptation which could arouse anxieties of a quite different character and intensity from those connected with the Darwinian view.

A different intrinsic reason for the dissimilar reception of Darwin's and Freud's ideas lies in the relative completeness and systematization of the early presentations of their respective arguments. In both these respects Darwin certainly had the advantage, despite Freud's greater skill as a writer.[27] It seems, however, that each spent a similar amount of time—a period of twenty to twenty-five years—on the development of his theories before presenting them in systematic form.

Darwin began his formulations during his fifty-seven-month voyage on the *Beagle* in the years 1831-1836. Actually his report on this voyage, published in 1839, contained many of the elements which were later included in the *Origin*. The year 1837 marks the beginning of the period of approximately two decades in which Darwin "never ceased working" on facts in preparation for *On the Origin of the Species*. This period includes the various publications relating to his voyage—the narrative, his writings on the mammalia and the fossil mammalia, coral

26. Saul Rosenzweig (1935) earlier pointed out this fact in a rather obscure journal, *The Modern Thinker*.

27. See Barzun (1958, pp. 74-75). Also see T. H. Huxley's (L. Huxley, 1900, p. 190) letter to Foster, February 14, 1888, on Darwin: "I have been reading the *Origin* slowly again for the nth time, with the view of picking out the essentials of the argument, for the obituary notice. Nothing entertains me more than to hear people call it easy reading.

"Exposition was not Darwin's *forte*—and his English is sometimes wonderful."

Those in a position to judge apparently have a high opinion of Freud as a writer, or at least as a stylist. In this connection, it is significant that Freud in 1930 won the Goethe Prize for Literature. Einstein wrote to Freud in 1939: "I quite specially admire your achievement [*Moses and Monotheism*], as I do with all your writings, from a literary point of view. I do not know any contemporary who has presented his subject in the German language in such a masterly fashion" (Jones, 1957, p. 243). Hyman's most interesting book, *The Tangled Bank* (1962), discusses Freud's rich use of metaphors—"the language of ideas." See also Jones (1955, pp. 400-402).

Both Darwin and Freud were, however, apparently guilty of what Freud exaggeratedly called "*Schlamperei*" ["sloppiness"], but which was really ambiguity. Barzun (1958, p. 74), however, makes a case for the virtue of this quality in the presentation of new ideas.

reefs, and volcanic islands, the *Geological Observations on South America*—the two monographs on barnacles, as well as several other monographs, and of course the writing of the *Origin* itself.

As nearly as one can tell, Freud's thinking along the lines which led to the psychoanalytic formulations started at the earliest about 1882 when Freud discussed Breuer's case of Anna O. with him.[28] At that time he began to use the term "unconscious," to which he gave increased emphasis in 1893 when the case was published. During this same period (1885-1886) he went to Paris to work with Charcot. It was during this decade that the major part of his shift from neurology to psychology occurred (Freud, 1886).

Yet, as we have indicated, despite the similar time span, the initial presentations of the two theories were strikingly dissimilar both in completeness and systematic formulation. The *Origin* reflects a tremendous piling up of evidence from a great variety of sources, presented in a form generally acceptable to science.[29] In contrast, we find in Freud a relatively unsystematic succession of papers and the *Interpretation*, which volume came some eighteen years after Freud first began to think psychoanalytically. This volume does, of course, contain a surprisingly complete presentation of his theory and a striking mass of observations were in a form science found easily acceptable.

The differing receptions of the two theories must also have resulted from dissimilarities in the subject matter, from their different methods of investigation, and from the contrasting nature of the evidence they provide.[30] However, a not inconsiderable part of the respective receptions may be attributed to less fundamental factors.

28. See Strachey's Introduction (Breuer and Freud, 1893-1895, p. xi).

29. As Simpson (1960) points out, and as others have pointed out before him, the "organization, understanding and conviction" with which Darwin presented his argument in the *Origin* were enough to change Huxley from an antievolutionist to an evolutionist.

30. See Freud's statement to Marie Bonaparte: "Mental events seem to be immeasurable . . ." (Jones, 1955, p. 419). In the discussion of one of his early case histories Freud said:

"I have not always been a psychotherapist. Like other neuropathologists, I was trained to employ local diagnoses and electro-prognosis, and it still strikes me myself as strange that the case histories I write should read like short stories and that, as one might say, they lack the serious stamp of science. I must console myself with the reflection that the nature of the subject is evidently responsible for this, rather than any preference of my own. The fact is that local diagnosis and electrical reactions lead nowhere in the study of hysteria, whereas a detailed description of mental processes such as we are accustomed to find in the works of imaginative writers enables me, with the use of a few psychological formulas, to obtain at least some kind of insight into the course of that affection" (Breuer and Freud, 1893-1895, pp. 160-161).

Extrinsic Factors

Extrinsic reasons are frequently no less important in their effect on the acceptance of ideas than those we have labeled "intrinsic" (see Barber, 1961). In the cases we are considering, the way in which the ground was laid for acceptance was of considerable importance.

Before publishing the *Origin* Darwin carried on an extensive correspondence with scientists, particularly outstanding biologists, and other significant persons. The relationships established through these contacts helped to insure a favorable reception for the *Origin* when it appeared. Darwin also made the *Origin* more palatable by avoiding a discussion of the application of the laws of evolution to man. He did not deal with this topic at length until twelve years later, in *The Descent of Man*, by which time his propositions had been generally accepted. In the first edition of the *Origin*, Darwin merely included one sentence toward the close of the last chapter suggesting that "light will be thrown on the origin of man and his history." (In later editions of the *Origin* he added the word "much" before "light.") He inserted the statement so that "no honourable man should accuse me of concealing my views" (F. Darwin, 1887, p. 76; see also F. Darwin, 1950, p. 61). His essential conservatism thus led to a gradual presentation of his views, a presentation which in effect made acceptance of his doctrine easier. Some have held, however, that this method was solely due to his desire to have the evidence sufficiently massive and complete. Schwalbe (1909, p. 114) believes that Darwin's characteristic delaying of publication for years until he had carefully weighed all aspects of his subject—his extreme scientific conscience—restrained him from challenging the world in 1859 with a book fully setting forth the theory of the descent of man. It is possible, however, that he realized he was offering a sufficiently radical pill in his *Origin* to make it unwise at that time to develop further the theory of the descent of man. Darwin characteristically avoided controversy and, as Irvine has put it, ". . . practiced the British art of reticent and unprovocative statement" (Irvine, 1955, p. 102). This showed up particularly in his lack of response to the Butler attacks (pp. 220-223).[31]

The problem of the "nature of the evidence" still plagues psychology today. In the natural sciences the evidence can be marshaled in such a way that "everyone"—participant or nonparticipant—can follow the general argument. Many psychological data, on the other hand, are relatively so subtle and so dependent upon the observer as a participant that it remains difficult to convey them to the nonparticipant. This is especially true since most nonparticipants consider themselves "psychologists" as well.

31. See Willey (1960, pp. 18-31). Darlington (1959b), a kind of "debunker" of Darwin, interprets Darwin's "flexible strategy" as "slippery" (p. 60), and uses such terms as "intellectual opportunism" (p. 63).

Freud's activities in comparable circumstances were quite different. No matter how much he himself may have wished otherwise, there was no parallel correspondence with outstanding members of his profession to prepare the ground. His voluminous correspondence does not appear to have been productive along this particular line. For instance, the Fliess letters represent correspondence with a person who for many reasons was most unlikely to be influential. Beyond this, Freud's letters seem largely limited to the psychoanalytic group and to some literary persons, again not persons likely to have the kind of influence necessary to aid in the acceptance of his ideas. This seems a reasonable conclusion to draw from the relevant material in the second volume of Jones' biography. In the Preface to this volume Jones refers to some five thousand of Freud's letters to which he had access for the writing of the biography. Among the letters that Jones cites, one finds no evidence of the kind of correspondence we have described in the case of Darwin. The selection of letters published by Freud's son (E. L. Freud, 1960) does not alter this conclusion.

Although Freud was much more direct about the presentation of his ideas, he followed Darwin's pattern in relation to controversy and the reply to criticism (e.g., Jones, 1955, pp. 112, 120–121, 426).

A more subtle extrinsic factor affecting initial acceptance resided in Darwin's social and scientific status as compared to Freud's. In the first we are dealing with a Darwin married to a Wedgwood, both belonging to a close, economically independent, intellectual elite. Add to this Darwin's own high scientific standing, as well as his family's, and imposing bases for recognition are provided. In the case of Freud, however, we are dealing with a person having no family or economic status,[32] and belonging to a rejected minority group. And for Freud there was no scientific standing. In considerable part this was because he lacked the conventional entrée in his culture to intellectual status—a "Herr-Professorship."[33]

Another, more complex, factor was predominantly extrinsic, although it also included intrinsic aspects. It is to be found in the cultural context in which each of the theories was presented. At the time of the publication of Darwin's *Origin*, some aspects of the general culture were favorable and some unfavorable to the kind of thesis he

32. There is no evidence of high Jewish intellectual accomplishment in his family background (see Jones, 1953, Chapter 1; Aron, 1956). But even if there had been such accomplishment, it would not have been an aid to the kind of intellectual status which Freud was seeking.

33. See Hughes (1958, p. 50 ff.) on the status of German professors in the 1890's. Also see Freud (1887–1902, p. 11).

proposed (see Carter, 1957). Favorable to the theory were the widespread interest in the study of nature, the rather vague evolutionary notions already current,[34] and the harmony of the theory with the strongly competitive *laissez-faire* economics of the period. Unfavorable were sentimental reactions to various aspects of the theory: to the emphasis on competition, to the contradiction of the story of creation in a time of considerable religious revival—especially in Protestant England—to the hint of physical animal ancestry contained in the theory, and to the extension to biology of materialistic views, views which had heretofore been limited to the physical, nonliving world.

Of course we could say in a general way that Freud had the inestimably great advantage of being able to build upon the revolution which Darwin had already wrought and which, as we have suggested, already carried in part the seeds of the Freudian concept of the animal in man.[35] For did it not naturally follow that if man were really part of the animal series, he should also have animal psychological characteristics and be subject to instinctual domination? In this connection William Morton Wheeler's (1921) reaction to psychoanalysis, which we shall discuss at length later, is particularly relevant. An additional favorable factor was that at the time Freud put forth his ideas, there was already an interest in the unconscious and a growing respect for the importance of psychology and psychiatry as fields of inquiry and endeavor.

Unfavorable was the Victorianism of the period, characterized by smug satisfaction with middle-of-the-road positions (see Brinton, 1959, p. 350) which naturally found intolerable such extreme opinions as Freud's. Probably most unfavorable was the factor that Hughes points out (1958, pp. 3–66): Freud presented his ideas in a period in which mechanism, naturalism, and positivism were dominant in the context of a "self-satisfied cult of material progress" (p. 41). The nineteenth century versions of these attitudes were a "travestied form" of the eighteenth century tradition of enlightenment, which had combined a "flexible use of the concept of reason, and . . . [a] sympathetic understanding for 'sensibility' and 'the passions'" (p. 27). Only in the narrow sense of "intellectual" as defined during the late nineteenth century

34. See J. C. Greene (1959b), who traces the rise of evolutionary views of nature in the eighteenth and nineteenth centuries, culminating in Darwin's two major works.

35. An attempt to trace Darwin's influence on Freud, as well as a detailed comparison of the personalities of the two men, would be illuminating for the further understanding of their methods of work and the dissemination of their ideas. In the present context, however, these tasks would take us too far afield. See Brosin (1960) for some discussion of the latter topic.

could Freud, with Durkheim, Weber,[36] Croce, and others, be considered one of the prominent "anti-intellectual" forces. In spirit, Freud's ideas were actually much nearer those of the eighteenth century.[37] Trilling (1955) and Bruner (1956) have pointed out the "Romantic" streak in Freud, the details of which we shall examine later.

SUMMARY

To summarize then, without regard for the relative importance of these two revolutionary upheavals in the history of ideas: an examination of the reception given them leads to the conclusion that the Freudian innovation had a more difficult time in being accepted. The blow was harder to tolerate, the argument was presented less effectively, the ground for acceptance was laid less adequately, the cultural climate was less receptive, and the standing of Freud and his supporters in the community was much lower than that of Darwin and his. With this appreciation of the complex factors involved in the initial reaction to Freud, let us now go on to a detailed consideration of the ways in which Freudian theory made its impact on the psychological scene.

REFERENCES

ADRIAN, E. D. (1954), Science and Human Nature. Supplement to *Nature*, 174:433–437.

ARON, W. (1956), Fartzachenungen vegen upshtam fun Sigmund Freud

36. Frenkel-Brunswik (1954, pp. 332–335) has made an interesting comparison of Freud with Weber and Durkheim. She points out that although Weber and Durkheim have been accused of rationalism, both actually saw the foundations of society as fundamentally based on nonrational moral qualities. "Freud, on the other hand, has been criticized for having given too much prominence to the irrational, while in fact his one hope is the overcoming of the irrational in a society built on reason" (p. 333).

37. Kaufman (1960, p. 309) says: ". . . [Freud] is probably the greatest among Nietzsche's heirs, a man who followed in the footsteps of Goethe, Heine, and Nietzsche by attempting to deepen and enrich the attitudes of the Enlightenment with the insights of romanticism. For Freud tried to bridge the gap between the German romantics' profound preoccupation with the irrational, on the one hand, and the Western faith in liberty, equality, and fraternity, and in science as an instrument to their realization, on the other." Trilling (1957, p. 39) makes a similar point in his discussion of "Freud and Literature." "If Freud discovered the darkness for science he never endorsed it. On the contrary, his rationalism supports all the ideas of the Enlightenment that deny validity to myth or religion: he holds to a simple materialism, to a simple determinism, to a rather limited sort of epistemology." "Validity" must, of course, be taken in the sense in which Trilling means it in this context. According to Peter Gay (1954, p. 379), Freud "was the greatest child of the Enlightenment which our century has known . . ."

This is not to deny that Freud had something of a credulous streak which was evidenced

un vegen zein yidishkeit. (Notes on Sigmund Freud's Ancestry and Jewish Contacts). *Yivo Bleter*, 40:166–174.

BARZUN, J. (1958), *Darwin, Marx, Wagner: Critique of a Heritage*, 2nd ed. Garden City, N.Y.: Doubleday.

BORING, E. G. (1950b), *History of Experimental Psychology*, 2nd ed. New York: Appleton-Century-Crofts.

BREUER, J. & FREUD, S. (1893-1895), Studies on Hysteria. *Standard Edition*, Vol. 2. London: Hogarth Press, 1955.

BRIERLEY, M. (1934-1947), *Trends in Psychoanalysis*. London: Hogarth Press, 1951.

BRINTON, C. (1959), *A History of Western Morals*. New York: Harcourt, Brace.

BROSIN, H. W. (1960), Evolution and Understanding Diseases of the Mind. In *Evolution After Darwin*. Vol. 2: The Evolution of Man, ed. S. Tax. Chicago: University of Chicago Press, pp. 373–422.

BRUNER, J. S. (1956), Freud and the Image of Man. *Amer. Psychologist*, 11:463–466.

BRY, I., & RIFKIN, A. H. (1962), Freud and the History of Ideas: Primary Sources, 1886-1910. In *Science and Psychoanalysis*. Vol. 5: Psychoanalytic Education, ed. J. H. Masserman. New York: Grune & Stratton, pp. 6–36.

BUTTERFIELD, H. (1949), *The Origins of Modern Science*. London: G. Bell, 1950.

CARTER, G.S. (1957), *A Hundred Years of Evolution*. London: Sidgwick & Jackson.

CASSIRER, E. (1955), *The Philosophy of the Enlightenment*. Boston: Beacon Press.

COMFORT, A. (1960), Darwin and Freud. *Lancet*, Vol. 2 for 1960:107–111.

DALLENBACH, K. M. (1955), Phrenology Versus Psychoanalysis. *Amer. J. Psychol.*, 68:511–525.

DARLINGTON, C. D. (1959a), The Origin of Darwinism. *Sci. Amer.*, 200:60–66.

DARWIN, F., ed. (1887), *The Life and Letters of Charles Darwin*, Vol. 1. New York: Appleton.

———— ed. (1950), *Charles Darwin's Autobiography*. New York: Schuman.

EARNEST, E. (1950), *S. Weir Mitchell*. Philadelphia: University of Pennsylvania Press.

EISELEY, L. (1959), *Darwin's Century*. London: Victor Gollancz.

---

in his interest in Lamarckism and the occult (Jones, 1957, pp. 310-311, 375-407). However, he seems to have kept such notions in a distinct compartment, well separated from his real work.

See Cassirer (1955, pp. 104-108), P. Gay (1954, especially p. 379), Freud (1927).

ELLEGARD, A. (1958), *Darwin and the General Reader*. Göteborgs: Göteburgs Universitets Arsskrift.
ERIKSON, E. H. (1950), Growth and Crises of the Healthy Personality. In "Identity and the Life Cycle." *Psychological Issues*, 1(1):50-100. New York: International Universities Press, 1959.
———— (1956a), The First Psychoanalyst: Crisis and Discovery. *The Yale Review*, 46:40-62.
———— (1961), The Roots of Virtue. In *The Humanist Frame*, ed. J. Huxley. New York: Harper, pp. 145-165.
FLUGEL, J. C. (1945), *Man, Morals and Society*. London: Penguin Books, 1955.
FRENKEL-BRUNSWIK, E. (1954), Psychoanalysis and the Unity of Science. *Proc. Amer. Acad. Arts and Sciences*, 80:271-347.
FREUD, E. L., ed. (1960), *Letters of Sigmund Freud*. New York: Basic Books.
FREUD, S. (1886), Report on My Studies in Paris and Berlin. *Int. J. Psycho-Anal.*, 37:2-7, 1956.
———— (1887-1902), *The Origins of Psycho-Analysis: Letters to Wilhelm Fliess, Drafts and Notes, 1887-1902*. London: Imago, 1954.
———— (1896), The Aetiology of Hysteria. *Standard Edition*, 3:187-221. London: Hogarth Press, 1962.
———— (1898), Sexuality in the Aetiology of the Neuroses. *Standard Edition*, 3:259-285. London: Hogarth Press, 1962.
———— (1900a), The Interpretation of Dreams. *Standard Edition*, 4 & 5. London: Hogarth Press, 1953.
———— (1901), The Psychopathology of Everyday Life. *Standard Edition*, 6. London: Hogarth Press, 1960.
———— (1905a), Jokes and Their Relation to the Unconscious. *Standard Edition*, 8. London: Hogarth Press, 1960.
———— (1905b), Three Essays on the Theory of Sexuality. *Standard Edition*, 7:125-245. London: Hogarth Press, 1953.
———— (1913), The Claims of Psycho-Analysis to Scientific Interest. *Standard Edition*, 13:163-190. London: Hogarth Press, 1955.
———— (1916-1917 [1915-1917]), Introductory Lectures on Psycho-Analysis. *Standard Edition*, 15 & 16. London: Hogarth Press, 1963.
———— (1917), A Difficulty in the Path of Psycho-Analysis. *Standard Edition*, 17:135-144. London: Hogarth Press, 1955.
———— (1922), Dreams and Telepathy. *Standard Edition*, 18:195-220. London: Hogarth Press, 1955.
———— (1925a [1924]), The Resistances to Psycho-Analysis. *Standard Edition*, 19:211-224. London: Hogarth Press, 1961.
———— (1927), The Future of an Illusion. *Standard Edition*, 21:1-56. London: Hogarth Press, 1961.

——— (1932), *New Introductory Lectures on Psycho-Analysis.* New York: Norton, 1933.

———(1937), Analysis Terminable and Interminable. *Collected Papers,* 5:316-357. London: Hogarth Press, 1950.

——— (1939 [1937-1939]), *Moses and Monotheism.* New York: Knopf.

GAY, F. P. (1938), *The Open Mind: Elmer Ernest Southard, 1876-1920.* Chicago: Normandie House.

GAY, P. (1954), The Enlightenment in the History of Political Theory. *Pol. Sci. Quart.,* 69:374-389.

GENGERELLI, J. A. (1957), The Limitations of Psychoanalysis—2. Dogma or Discipline? *Sat. Rev.,* March 23:9-11, 40.

GREENE, J. C. (1959b), *The Death of Adam.* New York: New American Library (Mentor Books), 1961.

HARTMANN, H. (1960), *Psychoanalysis and Moral Values.* New York: International Universities Press.

HIMMELFARB, G. (1959), *Darwin and the Darwinian Revolution.* Garden City, N.Y.: Doubleday.

HUGHES, H. S. (1958), *Consciousness and Society.* New York: Knopf.

HUXLEY, J. (1960), The Emergence of Darwinism. In *Evolution After Darwin.* Vol. 1: The Evolution of Life, ed. S. Tax. Chicago: University of Chicago Press, pp. 1-21.

HUXLEY, L. (1900), *Life and Letters of Thomas Henry Huxley,* Vol. 2. London: Macmillan.

HYMAN, S. E. (1962), *The Tangled Bank.* New York: Atheneum.

IRVINE, W. (1955), *Apes, Angels, and Victorians.* New York: McGraw-Hill.

JONES, E. (1953), *The Life and Work of Sigmund Freud.* Vol. 1: The Formative Years and the Great Discoveries, 1856-1900. New York: Basic Books.

——— (1955), *The Life and Work of Sigmund Freud.* Vol. 2: Years of Maturity, 1901-1919. New York: Basic Books.

——— (1956), *Sigmund Freud: Four Centenary Addresses.* New York: Basic Books.

——— (1957), *The Life and Work of Sigmund Freud.* Vol. 3: The Last Phase, 1919-1939. New York: Basic Books.

KAUFMAN, W. (1960), *From Shakespeare to Existentialism.* Garden City, N.Y.: Doubleday (Anchor Books).

KEITH, A. (1935), Darwinism and Its Critics. *The Modern Thinker,* 6:51-61.

KUHN, T.S. (1957), *The Copernican Revolution.* Cambridge, Mass: Harvard University Press.

MATTHEWS, F. H., Jr. (1955), Freud Comes to America: The Influence of

Freudian Ideas on American Thought, 1909-1917. Unpublished master's thesis. University of California.

NELSON, B., ed. (1957), *Freud and the 20th Century*. New York: Meridian Books.

PFISTER, O. (1913), *The Psychoanalytic Method*. New York: Moffat, Yard, 1917.

PUTNAM, J. J. (1915), *Human Motives*. Boston: Little, Brown.

RIEFF, P. (1959), *Freud: The Mind of the Moralist*. New York: Viking Press.

ROSENZWEIG, S. (1935), Freud Versus the Libertine. *The Modern Thinker*, 6(3):13-19.

SCHWALBE, G. (1909), "The Descent of Man." In *Darwin and Modern Science*, ed. A. C. Seward, Cambridge: University Press, pp. 112-136.

SCHWARTZ, G., & BISHOP, P. W. (1958), *Moments of Discovery*. Vol. 1: The Origins of Science. New York: Basic Books.

SHAKOW, D. (1960b), Psicopatologia y Psicologia: Nota Sobre Tendencias. *Rev.*

SHAPLEY, H. (1958), *Of Stars and Men*. Boston: Beacon Press.

SILBERER, H. (1912), Uber die Symbolbidung. *Jahrb. Psychoanal. Psychopathol. Forsch.*, 3:661-723. Translated in part as On Symbol-Formation. In Rapaport, ed. (1951), pp. 208-233.

SIMON, E. (1957), Sigmund Freud, the Jew. In *Year Book II:* Publication of the Leo Baeck Institute of Jews from Germany. London: East and West Library, pp. 270-305.

SIMPSON G. G. (1960), The World into Which Darwin Led Us. *Science*, 131:966-974.

TRILLING, L. (1955), *Freud and the Crisis of Our Culture*. Boston: Beacon Press.

———— (1957), *The Liberal Imagination*. Garden City, N.Y.: Doubleday (Anchor Books).

WALKER, N. (1957), A New Copernicus? In Nelson, ed. (1957), pp. 22-30.

WHEELER, W. M. (1921), On Instincts. *J. Abn. Psychol.*, 15:295-318.

———— (1923), The Dry-Rot of Our Academic Biology. *Science*, 57:61-71.

WHITE A. D. (1896), *A History of the Warfare of Science with Theology in Christendom*, 2 Vols. New York: Appleton.

WRIGHTMAN, W. P. E. (1953), *The Growth of Scientific Ideas*. New Haven: Yale University Press.

WILLEY, B. (1960), *Darwin and Butler: Two Versions of Evolution*. New York: Harcourt, Brace.

5

The Freudian Revolution Analyzed[*]

Alfred Kazin

It is hard to believe that Sigmund Freud was born over a century ago. Although Freud has long been a household name (and, in fact, dominates many a household one could mention), his theories still seem too "advanced," they touch too bluntly on the most intimate side of human relations, for us to picture Freud himself coming out of a world that in all other respects now seems so quaint.

Although Freud has influenced even people who have never heard of him, not all his theories have been accepted even by his most orthodox followers, while a great many of his essential ideas are rejected even by many psychoanalysts. In one sense Freud himself is still battling for recognition, for because of the tabooed nature of the materials in which he worked and the unusually speculative quality of his mind, Freud still seems to many people more an irritant than a classic.

On the other hand, Freud's influence, which started from the growing skepticism about civilization and morality after the First World War, is now beyond description. Freudianism gave sanction to the increasing exasperation with public standards as opposed to private feelings; it upheld the truths of human nature as against the hypocrises and cruelties of conventional morality; it stressed the enormous role that sex plays in man's imaginative life, in his relations to his parents, in the symbolism of language.

[*]Reprinted from *Freud and the 20th Century*, edited by Benjamin Nelson, by permission of author and editor. Copyright© 1957 by The World Publishing Company.

It is impossible to think of the greatest names in modern literature and art—Thomas Mann, James Joyce, Franz Kafka, T. S. Eliot, Ernest Hemingway, William Faulkner, Pablo Picasso, Paul Klee—without realizing our debt to Freud's exploration of dreams, myths, symbols and the imaginative profundity of man's inner life. Even those who believe that original sin is a safer guide to the nature of man than any other can find support in Freud's gloomy doubts about man's capacity for progress. For quite other reasons, Freud has found followers, even among Catholic psychiatrists, who believe that Freud offers a believable explanation of neurosis and a possible cure, and so leaves the sufferer cured to practice his faith in a rational way.

Many psychologists who disagree with Freud's own materialism have gratefully adopted many of Freud's diagnoses, and although he himself was chary about the psychoanalytical technique in serious mental illness, more and more psychiatrists now follow his technique, or some adaptation of it. For no other system of thought in modern times, except the great religions, has been adopted by so many people as a systematic interpretation of individual behavior. Consequently, to those who have no other belief, Freudianism sometimes serves as a philosophy of life.

Freud, a tough old humanist with a profoundly skeptical mind, would have been shocked or amused by the degree to which everything is sometimes explained by "Freudian" doctrines. He offered us not something that applies dogmatically to all occasions, but something useful, a principle of inquiry into those unconscious forces that are constantly pulling people apart, both in themselves and from each other.

Freud's extraordinary achievement was to show us, in scientific terms, the primacy of natural desire, the secret wishes we proclaim in our dreams, the mixture of love and shame and jealousy in our relations to our parents, the child as father to the man, the deeply buried instincts that make us natural beings and that go back to the forgotten struggles of the human race. Until Freud, novelists and dramatists had never dared to think that science would back up their belief that personal passion is a stronger force in people's lives than socially accepted morality. Thanks to Freud, these insights now form a widely shared body of knowledge.

In short, Freud had the ability, such as is given to very few individuals, to introduce a wholly new factor into human knowledge; to impress it upon people's minds as something for which there was evidence. He revealed a part of reality that many people before him had guessed at, but which no one before him was able to describe as systematically and convincingly as he did. In the same way that one associates the discovery of certain fundamentals with Copernicus, Newton, Darwin, Einstein, so one identifies many of one's deepest motivations with Freud. His name is no longer the name of a man; like "Darwin," it is now synonymous with a part of nature.

This is the very greatest kind of influence that a man can have. It means that people use his name to signify something in the world of nature which, they believe, actually exists. A man's name has become identical with a phenomenon in nature, with a cause in nature, with a "reality" that we accept—even when we don't want to accept it. Every hour of every day now, and especially in America, there are people who cannot forget a name, or make a slip of the tongue, or feel depressed; who cannot begin a love affair, or end a marriage, without wondering what the "Freudian" reason may be.

No one can count the number of people who now think of any crisis as a personal failure, and who turn to a psychoanalyst or to a psychoanalytical literature for an explanation of their suffering where once they would have turned to a minister or to the Bible for consolation. Freudian terms are now part of our thought. There are innumerable people who will never admit that they believe a word of his writings, who nevertheless, "unconsciously," as they would say, have learned to look for "motivations," to detect "compensations," to withhold a purely moralistic judgment in favor of individual understanding, to prize sexual satisfaction as a key to individual happiness, and to characterize people by the depth and urgency of their passions rather than by the nobility of their professions.

For much of this "Freudian" revolution, Freud himself is not responsible. And in evaluating the general effect of Freud's doctrines on the modern scene, especially in America, it is important to distinguish between the hard, biological, fundamentally classical thought of Freud, who was a determinist, a pessimist, and a genius, from the thousands of little cultural symptoms and "psychological" theories, the pretensions and self-indulgences, which are often found these days in the prosperous middle-class culture that has responded most enthusiastically to Freud.

There is, for example, the increasing tendency to think that all problems are "psychological," to ignore the real conflicts in society that underlie politics and to interpret politicians and candidates—especially those you don't like—in terms of "sexual" motives. There is the cunning use of "Freudian" terms in advertising, which has gone so far that nowadays there's a pretty clear suggestion that the girl comes with the car. There are all the psychologists who study "motivations," and sometimes invent them, so as to get you to buy two boxes of cereal where one would have done before.

There are the horrendous movies and slick plays which not only evade the writer's need to explain characters honestly, but, by attributing to everybody what one can only call the Freudian nightmare, have imposed upon a credulous public the belief that it may not be art but that it is "true"—that is, sex—and so must be taken seriously. And, since this is endless but had better stop somewhere, there are all the people who have confused their "urges" with art, have learned in all moral crises to blame their upbringing rather than themselves, and tend to worship the psychoanalyst as God.

The worst of the "Freudian revolution" is the increasing tendency to attribute all criticism of our society to personal "sickness." The rebel is looked on as neurotic rather than someone making a valid protest. Orthodox Freudians tend to support the status quo as a matter of course and to blame the individual for departing from it. Freud himself never made such a mistake, and no one would have been able to convince him that the Viennese world around him was "normal."

The identification of a military group, or a class, or a culture, with an absolute to which we must all be adjusted at any price is a dangerous trend. And the worst of it is that to many people psychoanalysts now signify "authority," so that people believe them on any and all subjects.

On the other hand, the greatest and most beautiful effect of Freudianism is the increasing awareness of childhood as the most important single influence on personal development. This profound cherishing of childhood has opened up wholly new relationships between husbands and wives, as well as between parents and children, and it represents—though often absurdly overanxious—a peculiar new tenderness in modern life. Similarly, though Freud's psychology is weakest on women, there can be no doubt that, again in America, the increasing acknowledgment of the importance of sexual satisfaction has given to women an increasing sense of their individual dignity and their specific needs.

But the greatest revolution of all, and one that really explains the overwhelming success of Freudianism in America, lies in the general insistence on individual fulfillment, satisfaction and happiness. Odd as it may seem to us, who take our striving toward these things for granted, the insistence on personal happiness represents the most revolutionary force in modern times. And it is precisely because our own tradition works toward individual self-realization, because private happiness does seem to us to be both an important ideal and a practical goal, that Freudianism has found so many recruits in this country.

Freud himself made his initial effect in the most traditional, the most rational, the most human kind of way; he wrote books; he presented evidence; he made claims and gave proofs. People read and believed. Many more did not read, and most of those who read Freud's first great work, *The Interpretation of Dreams,* did not believe any of it. But, after all, very few books ever have a decisive effect on the world. In Freud's case, what counts is that some of the people who read were so stirred that they went on to change other minds.

The only kind of change in life which means anything—because it transforms everything in its path—is that which changes people's thinking, their deepest convictions, that which makes them see the world in a different way. This does not happen often, and it is the effect of Freud's books and clinical papers, radiating from a small circle of fellow-doctors in Vienna, that made Freud's influence so impressive. Only the power of truth can explain it. For everything was against him.

He was a Jew in the obsessively anti-Semitic culture of Imperial Austria. He was working with names for things—id, libido, superego, Oedipus, complex, infantile sexuality—that required a special effort, a "suspension of disbelief," as Coleridge would have said, to believe in. Freud insisted that he had not looked for this kind of material.

He had been an extraordinarily able neurologist, was the greatest authority in Europe on children's paralyses, had independently discovered the anesthetic properties of cocaine, but in his usual fashion had impatiently gone on to other experiments before he could get independent credit for his discovery. Far from being flighty in scientific matters, he had been thoroughly trained by the prevailing school of physiology to think of the body as a machine, and in his own thinking he was a rigorous, old-fashioned rationalist whose only religion was science itself.

Freud even claimed that the evidence for his theories had been forced on him. But this was not quite true, either. Even when we remember Freud's rigid scientific training and his own utter honesty, it has to be made clear—not as a criticism of his method but as a characterization of his genius—that Freud was a "plunger," a highly speculative mind. It was the extraordinary combination of patience and daring, of method and radically new insight, that made him great.

Though his old teacher and colleague, Joseph Breuer, came upon the famous example of hysteria in a woman which was the first clinical source for the book they wrote together—*Studies on Hysteria,* which is technically the first document in psychoanalysis—Breuer soon took alarm from the dangerously "sexual" interest of the material and withdrew. Freud went on; working alone, he pieced together, in his own thinking, the whole set of sexual motivations that no one else had faced so bluntly or had systematized so closely into a whole new field of active cause-and-effect in the inner life of human beings.

It was this kind of comprehensive insight, backed up on the one hand by the utmost boldness in thinking out his material to its logical conclusion, and on the other by an extraordinary literary gift for persuading readers of the reality of what he was writing about, that led to Freud's effect on so many intellectuals, starting in the exciting years just before the first World War.

Freud's work appealed to the increasing regard for individual experience that is one of the great themes of modern literature and art. The sensitiveness to each individual as a significant register of the consciousness in general, the artistic interest in carrying human consciousness to its farthest limits—it was this essential side of modern art that Freud's researches encouraged and deepened. He brought, as it were, the authority of science to the inner prompting of art, and thus helped writers and artists to feel that their interest in myths, in symbols, in dreams was on the side of "reality," of science, itself, when it shows the fabulousness of the natural world.

Even if we regret, as we must, the fact that Freud's influence has been identified with a great many shallow and commercially slick ideas, the fact remains that if Freud's ideas appealed generally to the inwardness which is so important to modern writers and artists, it was because Freud thoroughly won his case against many aggressive but less intelligent opponents.

The people whose lives were changed by such masterpieces as *The Interpretation of Dreams, The Psychopathology of Everyday Life, Three Contributions to the Theory of Sex, Totem and Taboo,* were honestly convinced that Freud spoke the truth. They saw in Freud that passionate conviction of the reality of his theories that is the very stamp of genius, and as they read, they were prepared to give up other convictions—a sacrifice that caused some of them the deepest anguish, but which their conviction of Freud's utter truthfulness and objectivity made necessary.

Now, if we look back for a moment, the impact of these theories seems all the more remarkable in view of the natural human tendency to suspect, to limit and to derogate sexual experience. What Freud proclaimed above all else was that "nature," which is nearest to us in the erotic side of man, and which culture and society are always pushing away as unworthy of man's "higher" nature, has constantly to be brought back into man's awareness. Freud saw in man's sexual instinct a force of profound natural urgency, a whole system of energies, which could be repressed and forgotten and pushed back into the unconscious-ness only at the cost of unnecessary strain and even of self-destructiveness.

Yet far from preaching "sexuality" itself at any cost, Freud admitted that "civilization" requires the repression or at least the adaptation of sexuality. Civilization as we know it, Freud said, had been built up on man's heroic sacrifice of instinct. Only, Freud issued the warning that more and more men would resent this sacrifice, would wonder if civilization was worth the price. And how profoundly right he was in this can be seen not only in the Nazi madness that drove him as an old man out of Vienna, that almost cost him his life, but in the increasing disdain for culture, in the secret lawlessness that has become, under the conformist surface, a sign of increasing personal irritation and rebelli-ousness in our society. More and more, the sexual freedom of our time seems to be a way of mentally getting even, of confused protest, and not the pagan enjoyment of instinct that writers like D. H. Lawrence upheld against Freud's gloomy forebodings.

For Freud the continuous sacrifice of "nature" that is demanded by "civilization" meant that it was only through rationality and conscious awareness that maturity could be achieved. Far from counseling license, his most famous formula became—"Where id was, ego shall be"—the id representing the unconscious, the ego our dominant and purposive sense of ourselves. However, consciousness meant for Freud an unyield-ing insistence on the importance of sexuality. And it was just on this issue that, even before the first World War, his movement broke apart.

Jung went astray, as Freud thought, because he was lulled by the "mystical" side of religion; Adler, through his insistence that not sex but power feelings were primary. Later, Harry Stack Sullivan and Erich Fromm tended to emphasize, as against sex, the importance of personal relatedness to others, and nowadays many psychoanalysts tend to value religion much more highly than Freud ever could. But the root of the dissidence was always Freud's forthright insistence on the importance of sexuality and his old-fashioned, mid-nineteenth-century positivism. For Freud always emphasized the organic and the physical rather than the social and the "cultural."

In fact, it is now possible to say that it is precisely Freud's old-fashioned scientific rationalism, his need to think of man as a physical being rather than a "psychological" one, that explains the primacy of Freud's discoveries. Psychoanalysis, especially in America, has become more interested in making cures than in making discoveries, and it is significant that there has been very little original thought in the field since Freud.

Freudianism has become a big business, and a very smooth one. The modern Freudian analyst, who is over-busy and who rather complacently uses his theory to explain everything, stands in rather sad contrast to that extraordinary thinker, Sigmund Freud.

Perhaps it is because Freud was born a century ago that he had the old-fashioned belief that nothing—not even a lot of patients—is so important as carrying your ideas beyond the point at which everybody already agrees with you. Nowadays everybody is something of a Freudian, and to many Freudians, the truth is in their keeping, the system is complete. But what mattered most to Freud was relentlessly carrying on the revolution of human thought.

FREUD
and the Modern
Philosophy of Science

Psychoanalysis is not, like philosophies, a system starting out from a few sharply defined basic concepts seeking to grasp the whole universe with the help of these, and, once it is completed, having no room for fresh discoveries or better understanding. On the contrary, it keeps close to facts in its field of study, seeks to solve the immediate problems of observation, gropes its way forward by the help of experience, is always incomplete and always ready to correct or modify its theories. There is no incongruity (anymore than in the case of physics or chemistry) if its most general concepts lack clarity, and if its basic postulates are provisional, it leaves their more precise definition to the results of future work.

S. Freud
*Collected Papers**

* London: Basic Press, 1950, vol. 5, pp. 129–130.

6

Freud and Modern Philosophy*

Abraham Kaplan

Whatever else psychoanalysis has been called, nobody, I think, has accused it of being a philosophy. However much it may be given to speculation, in a sense in which this is contrasted with hard-core scientific inquiry, it aims at an understanding of human behavior in a scientific spirit. Yet both its subject matter and its insights are so closely involved in the characteristic concerns of philosophy that it is not unreasonable to talk of a Freudian outlook on life. This is why I venture to include a discussion of psychoanalysis among conventionally recognized philosophies. But there is another and more important reason.

Philosophy is culture become self-conscious; the business of philosophy is to rationalize revolutions in culture. The practices of religion, politics, art, and science may be carried on with greater or lesser awareness of their presuppositions and principles. To bring them into awareness is to begin to philosophize about them; the end of philosophy is to make them intelligible and acceptable. From time to time, in one or another area of culture, changes occur too great and sudden to be assimilated to established patterns of understanding and action. These are the cultural revolutions.

Now the products of every revolution—in science, art, or whatever—are hard to understand, for understanding is by way of the concepts and categories of the old dispensation. So these revolutions

*Reprinted from *Freud and the 20th Century*, edited by Benjamin Nelson, by permission of author and editor. Copyright© 1957 by the World Publishing Company.

provide a challenge for philosophy—as Greek geometry did for Plato, modern physics for Descartes and Locke, the Reformation for Kant, and Darwinism for Bergson and Dewey. Such a revolution was brought about by Sigmund Freud. The juxtaposition of Freud and philosophy in this essay does not mark a historical connection, therefore, but one which may yet become a matter of history. My aim here is to assess only the implications, not the influence, of Freudian thought on the main lines of contemporary philosophy—in epistemology, esthetics, ethics, social philosophy, and philosophy of religion.

First, epistemology. The goal of epistemology is to provide a theory of knowledge which accounts for the origin, content, and validity of knowledge, in whatever forms it occurs. This aim has traditionally been conceived as a matter of logic rather than psychology, of abstract norms rather than concrete facts. But between the conception and the creation of such a logic falls the shadow of a presupposed psychology. Whether based upon the psychology or only commingled with it, every episte-mology is shaped by underlying conceptions of the mind and conduct of which cognition is a product. Thus, Locke and Hume theorized about knowledge in the perspectives of associationist psychology, as in our own day Russell made use of behaviorism, Dewey of a functionalist psychology, and the phenomenologists of Gestalt. An epistemology which takes account of the depth psychology of Freud and his successors is yet to be written.

Psychoanalysis shares with philosophy the point of view which poses the problem of the theory of knowledge: a distrust of what people think they know. Much of what presents itself as known is projected onto the object from the depths of subjectivity. But an important element even of what is sound in knowledge is contributed by the knower. Freud provides an empirical refutation of Locke's *tabula rasa* and Baconian induction. His account of the growth and development of the reality-testing functions of the ego renders absurdly superficial any conception of knowledge as resulting from the cumulative force of objective facts acting on an empty mind. Knowledge grows by what it feeds on: not "pure" sensation but experiences made significant by present needs and learned patterns of behavior for their future satisfac-tion. What Nietzsche called the dogma of immaculate perception must now be recognized as psychological heresy. The difference between what is "observed" and what is "inferred" or "explained" is no longer a matter of abstract logic but of the concreta of personality and culture.

That knowledge is impossible without a significant contribution from the knowing mind was, of course, already explicit in Kant. But in the place of Kant's pure Reason with its transcendental categories Freud puts a mind with a determinate history, rooted in the biology of the organism and flowering in the sublimations of culture. Dewey has observed that the classical empiricists were empirical about everything save the concept of "experience" itself, making of it an all-embracing abstraction which miraculously gives birth to both knowledge and existence. But experience is something that happens, an event among other natural events, different for the infant and the mature adult, for the psychotic, the neurotic, and the mind that knows itself, varying in all of these with the constraints imposed by nature and society.

And if empiricists have been unempirical about "experience," rationalists have been equally guilty of irrationality in their conception of "reason." Epistemologies of this type made the senses suspect but accepted intellect without question. Knowledge was held to be genuine and compelling in proportion to the workings of reason in its production. For psychoanalysis, both as clinical practice and as theory, the misuse of reason is as characteristic of the human animal as is its proper employment. Far from being the avenue to truth, reason may serve as a powerful defense against the recognition of truth, masking anxiety by a quest for certainty, perpetuating illusion by elaborate rationalization. Both Hume and Spinoza saw in reason the slave of the passions. It was left to Freud to document this insight with detailed clinical observations. But Hume's scepticism condemned reason to cognitive impotence, while Spinoza's rationalism made it the sole source of truth. Both misconceived the workings of reason by setting it against emotion in its very nature. Not "reason" and "emotion" but rational and irrational emotion are the elements which enter into cognition. Freud's psychology calls for a more subtle appraisal than epistemology has yet made of the passion for truth.

It calls also for a re-examination of the range of cognitive experience. Contemporary analytic philosophy is inclined to restrict knowledge to the highest psychic levels, to what is fully conscious and wholly controlled by logic and the reality principle. In this conception, the paradigm of knowledge is science, but science rationally reconstructed as a product of pure intellectuality. Imagination is denied epistemic significance, and its work is identified as "poetry." Thus scientism peoples the mind with the children of light and children of darkness, and considers only the first to be wise in their generation.

Romanticism acknowledged this image of the poet as being, like the lunatic and the lover, a creature of the night. But the philosophers of romanticism insisted on the epistemic importance of the mytho-poeic faculty. Though he be of imagination all compact, the poet nevertheless arrives at truth. Poetry is not merely a matter of clothing with feeling a nakedly prosaic cognition. Truth is the very stuff of poetry; fact and fancy are but one. Such a romantic epistemology obviously courts the danger of obscurantism. When the literateur preempts the domain of truth, both science and letters are likely to suffer.

Yet the problem for epistemology is a real one. An adequate theory of knowledge must be comprehensive enough to do justice to the whole range of cognitive experience—in art and religion, in myth and mysticism, as well as in science. The faculty of imagination which Kant bequeathed to romanticism was, he said, "an art concealed in the depths of the human soul, which nature is unlikely ever to lay open to our gaze." Freud's theory of symbolism and of the workings of fantasy brings this "art" within the purview of science. And in doing so, it provides a challenge for philosophy.

As yet, philosophy has responded to this challenge only by reinstating, in a more subtle form, the classical doctrine of "two truths." What the medievals distinguished as the domains of philosophy and theology, and the moderns as the realms of reason and faith, is formulated today in the dualism of "referential" and "emotive" meaning. Knowledge is in these terms narrowly conceived as "referential" only; and the content of art, religion, and morality excluded from the province of epistemology as non-cognitive. But recognition of unconscious processes allows us to trace the affects with which symbols are charged to underlying cognitions, and to see these, in turn, as canalizations of impulse. The possibility thus emerges of a new epistemology, which neither limits reason to make room for faith nor emasculates it to counter the threats against its potency.

Even as an instrument of knowledge, to say nothing of its role in conduct, reason becomes effective only when it draws upon energies not themselves abstractly intellectual and shapes materials not of its own substance. Psychoanalytic therapy, as well as theory, makes central such an employment of reason, called "insight." It has a quality of irresistible immediacy which contrasts with the psychic distance of the purely discursive intellect. Modern philosophy has also distinguished two modes of cognition: James, between "knowledge by acquaintance" and "knowledge about"; Russell, between "acquaintance" and "knowledge by description"; Bergson, between "intuition" and "intellect." But in all of these, reason reaches out in vain for direct experience, and the deliverances of sense or intuition become ineffable. Bergson's romantic pragmatism, indeed, defines metaphysics, the area of what is truly cognitive, as the science which dispenses with symbols; and the early Wittgenstein's logical positivism terminates in the silence of the mystic.

Freud thus poses for epistemology the romantic's problem while suggesting a solution for it within the realist's framework. Knowledge is not the product of Augustine's light of grace, nor yet does it presuppose Santayana's animal faith. It can be accounted for without appeal either to the supernatural or to the subhuman. The resources of the human mind itself will suffice, but only if the mind is seen in its full depth and complexity.

It is in esthetics that Freud's thought has probably had the greatest, if not the most direct, influence on academic philosophy. But some of the implications of psychoanalysis for esthetics appear to me to have been often misconceived. And others have scarcely yet established themselves in philosophizing about the arts.

Freud gives art, like mind, a concrete history in the human organism. Art owes its origin neither to the artistic "soul" nor to a transcendent form of Beauty. Dewey's insistence on the continuity of art with non-esthetic experience, on bringing "ethereal things" into connection with "the live creature," accords wholly with Freud's perspectives. Psychoanalysis is at odds with the idealistic esthetics which conceives of a work of art as an ideal essence produced and contemplated by a correspondingly abstract Mind. Art is created and enjoyed by real people in their concrete individuality, with biological needs and socialized aspirations, acting on materials subject to physical constraints.

To such a naturalistic esthetics Freud makes an important though as yet sketchy contribution: his analysis of creativity provides a beginning for the serious task of dissipating the mystique of inspiration. The Muses are no more than a myth—and no less. That inspiration is as fundamental to art as are the skills of craftsmanship is unexceptionable. But the truism does not imply for the well of inspiration a source outside the psychic life of the artist, only outside his conscious life. The discovery of the unconscious brings within the domain of nature and science much of what traditional esthetics assigned to a transcendent metaphysics.

That psychoanalysis finds the same "primary process" at the core both of the dream and of art has led some to a wholly mistaken identification of art and dream. But surrealism and dada, and the "theories" they have generated, are no closer to Freud than is the purest classicism. For fantasy becomes art only when it is externalized and controlled by the responsible, realistic, and logical ego. The same "primary process" is at work also in the production of science, philosophy, and even mathematics—in short, wherever creative imagination must submit its work to the scrutiny of the critical faculties. The artistry lies in the care and judgment with which the critical task is performed, as much as in the richness of the creative materials available for criticism.

Without both, the work is either as formless and unintelligible as the so-called art of the insane, or as mechanical and superficial as the formulas of the skillful hack.

Because the process of creative imagination issues in symbols while the symptoms of neurosis are also symbolic, many literary critics and others have concluded that art is the product of neurosis. The depth meanings of art have been construed out of hand as latent meanings born of the artist's illness. But I cannot see that this conclusion is in any way warranted by psychoanalytic theory. That theory, to be sure, was developed largely from a study of psychopathology. On the contrary, Freud's theory of neurosis sees illness as impeding the creative impulse. The energies of the neurotic are deflected from realistic problems to cope with inner conflict. If he is unable to master his own emotions he cannot control the affect with which the symbols of his art are to be charged. If he does not understand himself, he cannot attain that understanding of the human condition which his art is to communicate. True, great works of art have been created by neurotic artists. But their achievement testifies to the force of genius triumphing over disease; not to a reward for the endurance of pain and suffering.

Indeed, psychoanalytic theory not only contradicts the conclusion that art springs from neurosis, but even contributes insights into the origin of this mistaken belief. It is not that art is thought to be the reward of neurosis but that neurosis is viewed as a punishment for art. The artist is guilty of the sin of *hubris*, taking unto himself the prerogatives of the divine. The arrogance of his passion to create makes him rival the Creator. What God hath put together he tears asunder, to remold it in his own image, nearer to *his* heart's desire. If his efforts succeed, it is only with God's help; inspiration is the touch of God's hand by which the artist becomes empowered to create. But to look upon God's glory is to be smitten with blindness; and he that wrestles with the angel of the Lord becomes lame. The myth of the blind artist long antedates Freud; but it need not long survive him.

For the blindness of the artist symbolizes only the inwardness of his vision. In enjoying access to his own unconscious he can make manifest to others their common humanity. This approach to art preserves the core of truth in the conception of art as self-expression, while freeing that conception from the infantilisms of romantic individualism. Not Narcissus but Pygmalion is the true artist. He is in love, not with his own image, but with a creation having a form, movement, and substance—in a word, a life—of its own. Only in these terms can art come to have importance for anyone other than the artist and his psychoanalyst. Throughout human history art has developed in intimate association with the most basic concerns of culture—in the institutions of religion, war, food-gathering, the family, and community life. The dehumanization to which art has been subjected in our own time—not least by artists themselves—cannot be made the basis for esthetics. By implication, if not in explicit detail, Freud allows to art a role far more important than a passing time for the onlooker. Art brings to artist and audience alike a pulsing awareness both of human desires and of the realities which frustrate and fulfill them.

It is in this sense that art is the fulfillment of a wish: it creates a microcosm in which everything has significance, everything is of value. And it does so by an objective transformation of materials which everyday experience finds recalcitrant. The masterpiece is the work of one who has mastered his materials, forcing them to yield to his will, and who has mastered his impulses, to accord with the real possibilities lying before him. Art is the triumph of the pleasure principle and the reality principle acting in concert. The former lies at the root of Plato's esthetics, for whom the form of Beauty and of the Good are one. The latter is the insight contained in Nietzsche's analysis of art as an expression of the will to power. For contemporary philosophy, Freud poses the challenge of providing an esthetics which does equal justice to both inspiration and skill, inner idea and outer expression, latent content and manifest form—in short, to both wish and reality.

And Freud suggests also the unifying conception which binds together these two moments of the esthetic; it is the symbol. Art as symbol is the distinctive contribution of modern esthetics, from Croce onward. The work of art does not answer to a mysterious "sense of form" nor yet merely to the desire for the delectation of sense: it *makes* sense. Yet its meanings are not to be literalized; the most abstract shapes and sounds can be as rich in content as the most faithful representations. Art, whatever its medium, depends on what is symbolically expressed, not on what is literally represented. An esthetic response to a work is a re-creation of the symbol, an imaginative interpretation in which the audience shares with the artist the shifts in psychic level and in psychic distance through which the work was created. Here, as Croce saw, all the resources of linguistics—or as we would say today, of semantics—can be brought to bear on the problems of esthetics. And the resources of psychoanalysis as well.

Ethics as a branch of philosophy is an abstract theory, not to be confused with the morality embodied in concrete behavior. It is a theory *about* such behavior, which attempts to lay bare the presuppositions and principles of moral conduct. Freud's thought has important bearings on both ethics and morals.

A perennial concern of traditional ethics was the problem of free will. The determinism presupposed and discovered by science was thought to be incompatible with the genuine acts of choice required by morality. Metaphysicians ranged themselves into two camps, one excluding man from the domain of science, the other excluding objective morality from the domain of action. Kant's resolution of the issue culminates the classical development: free will falls outside the realm of scientific reality, but is a necessary postulate for the kingdom of ends to which man by his moral nature owes allegiance. Freud's conception of human freedom bypasses these metaphysical controversies altogether.

As a scientist, Freud adheres unswervingly to a deterministic viewpoint. Indeed, the determinism espoused by scientific philosophies in the past went far beyond the actual scientific achievements of their day. Psychoanalysis contributed significantly to an experiential basis for the speculative conviction that causal law was as much at work in the realm of the spirit as in the rest of nature. Not just significant choices, but even the apparently meaningless, trivial, and "accidental" features of psychic life were brought by Freud into determinate connection with events of personal history. There is method in all madness, a meaning derived from causal connection with earlier patterns of impulse and action. The position Spinoza was brought to by his rationalism Freud arrived at empirically: what we call uncaused marks only our ignorance of causes.

But freedom, as Spinoza also insisted, can rest only on knowledge, not on ignorance. Slavery to an unknown master is slavery still; and not to know even that we are in bondage is only to deepen it. Metaphysical free will either puts ethics into irreconcilable conflict with science or can only identify freedom with an illusion. Either we must believe that the human psyche is too subtle to be caught in the coarse net of scientific causality, or else we must analyze freedom in terms of causal agency, not in contradistinction to it.

Such a causal analysis of freedom is at the core of the psychoanalytic theory of its own therapeutic method and aim. Its method is self-knowledge, its aim is self-mastery. Man is free when his choices are the product of full awareness of operative needs and actual constraints. Such needs and constraints, so far as they lie in the self, owe their being to a history of fulfillments and frustrations. But it is a history buried in the unconscious, and what irrationalities it engenders remain invulnerable behind masks of rationality. To remove their masks is not thereby to destroy them but only to reveal them for what they are. To know what he truly wants and what he can truly have—this truth does not make man free, but makes freedom possible. Self-mastery is not antecedently guaranteed, but is something to be achieved.

This conception of freedom accords well with the Stoic's formula of "recognition of necessity," Spinoza's "determination by Reason," and Dewey's "reflective choice." For such perspectives Freud provides a greater purchase on the concreta of human behavior. Whether and how far man is free need no longer remain a matter for dialectical dispute; it is to be settled by the empirical study of man. And in the course of such study, what freedom we find may be broadened in scope and strengthened in action. Psychoanalysis allots man less freedom than he thought was his, but makes possible more freedom than in fact he had.

Deterministic freedom, however, seems incompatible with moral responsibility. How can we hold a man responsible for what he "could not help doing"? But the question is ill-conceived. Responsibility is not retrospective but prospective. The question to be asked is rather, "Will he act differently for being held responsible?" Causally, the entire prehistory of the universe is "responsible" for every event; ethically, he alone is responsible who can respond to the duties the event calls forth. It is being *held* responsible which is primary; "responsibility" is but a name for that quality of character of which duty takes hold.

What psychoanalysis brings to this viewpoint is the insight that only the self can hold itself morally responsible. Obligations can only be accepted, not imposed. This, indeed, is what binds freedom and responsibility together. So long as a man's duty has another's voice, he is not yet free, and *therefore* not yet responsible. Here again Freud and Kant are at one. Kant's principle of the autonomy of the will is precisely that the moral law is given to the self *by* the self. But Kant grounds his principle on the pure rationality of an abstract noumenal self, while it is, alas, the all too human phenomenal self which appears on the scene of action. From Plato to the utilitarians morality appealed to "reason"; Freud addresses himself to the problem of the conditions under which the appeal can be made effective.

What is at issue is the conception of the relations between the self which promulgates the moral law, the self which assumes the moral obligations so defined, and the self whose impulses defy those obligations. Traditional ethics was unaware of the depth and complexity of these relations. It failed to recognize that moral integrity—the integration of these diverse selves, indeed, their very acknowledgment—cannot be presupposed. Rationality lies in the realistic unification of this diversity; it is not itself the moral agent which ethics postulates. That morality rests on the injunction "Know thyself" has been acknowledged since Socrates. But only since Freud has ethics been in a position to follow out its implications.

And if the appeal to reason requires revaluation, even more is this true of the appeal to conscience. Freud shares Kant's awe and wonder at the starry heavens above; but as for the moral law within, here, Freud says, God has been guilty of "an uneven and careless piece of work." The critique of conscience as the ground of morality is perhaps the most notable contribution of psychoanalysis to ethics. This critique is not simply a matter of tracing the development of a moral sense to the introjection of parental standards. To disregard conscience because of its origins is to be guilty of the most arrant genetic fallacy. The rational ego also has its history; it does not thereby stand condemned. Such reductionism is a recurrent charge against Freud. In my opinion it is a charge which finds its target only in the vulgarizations of psychoanalytic theory.

What Freud contributes to the critique of conscience is a recognition of its destructive potentialities. A man may be driven by duty as much as by desire, be in bondage to his "principles" as much as to his passions. And under such compulsion he is likely to bring others to perdition and not only himself; more blood has been shed by moral zeal than in the pursuit of pleasure. When the self is brutalized, brutality to others follows quickly. If a man is his own first victim, he is seldom the last.

Thus, while traditional ethics was content to castigate the passions, Freud invites the attention of the moral philosopher to the immoralities hidden in the castigation itself. Ethics must follow psychology in its exploration of the dark regions that lie beyond the pleasure principle.

All this is not to say that established morality must now go by the board. Psychoanalysis has often been attacked—and not alone by the Pharisees—for weakening moral principles. In part this stems from the detachment of the analyst, as theorist and in therapy. The amorality of objective inquiry is mistaken for the immorality of tacit approval. And the therapeutic aim of achieving "normality" is misconceived as a substitute for moral standards, rather than as a condition for the relevance of moral categories. But only those of little faith fear the outcome of an objective appraisal of their values. Freud is continuing the classical philosophic tradition in holding with Socrates that a life which cannot withstand examination is not worth living.

In part, the fears for morality also stem from another vulgarization of Freud, that the aim of analysis is to encourage the libido to express itself in libertinism. In fact, analysis aims at the resolution of unconscious conflict; and it is explicit in the theory that such conflict is not resolved by supporting one side or the other. Freud does, indeed, criticize conventional morality—and even more, conventional moralization—as futile and dishonest. For the moralizer relies heavily on repression, anxiety, guilt, and the magic of the word, rather than on mature moral insight and conviction. Though it may deplore the sickness, philosophy can only be grateful for the diagnosis: the prevailing moral code is largely a tyranny tempered by hypocrisy.

In short, Freud offers for philosophical consideration a perspective in which morality is seen to be no less complex than is the moral agent himself. Various ethical theories have focused on one or another element of this complexity—as, say, Kant did on the superego, Nietzsche on the id, and Dewey on the ego. But no ethical theory can be adequate which does not do justice to all these elements, in their relations to one another and to the cultures which provide both setting and significance for moral action. The primary task for a philosophical ethics, as for psychoanalysis, is to understand morality before judging it. Thirty years ago Santayana, writing of the modern conflict of ideals, observed that the "age of controversy" is past, and has been succeeded by the "age of interpretation." In this transition Freud has played a significant role. But it is in the nature of things that we should be better aware of what has already been lost than of what is yet to be won.

Social thought is shaped by its conception of the individual as well as of society. Accordingly, psychoanalytic psychology has profound implications for social science and social philosophy.

As a scientist, Freud posits a human nature sufficiently stable and invariant to make possible scientific generalization beyond individual case histories. Some such posit is presupposed in every study of man, and indeed in every science for its own subject matter. The kind of order and regularity Newton discerned in the physical world Kant thought Rousseau discovered beneath the varying forms of human personality. Contemporary philosophy can find in Freud a more empirical basis for the belief in such regularity.

Now the "deeply concealed essence of man" of which Kant speaks in this connection need not be understood in Aristotelian terms as a fixed and immutable "nature." Psychoanalysis postulates constancy, not fixity—a regularity of pattern, not recurrence of the elements composing the pattern from case to case. For Freud the constancy of human nature is biologically based. But this basis does not preclude—on the contrary, it produces—enormous variation in actual conduct. The plasticity of impulse and the range of its socially conditioned expressions is central to psychoanalytic theory. What is insisted upon is only that the variability is not endless. It occurs within limits, and it is these, rather than a fixed "essence," that make for discernible regularities.

To be sure, the location of the limits cannot be prejudged, but is itself the object of scientific inquiry. Undoubtedly some social philosophers have drawn them too narrowly, in order to rationalize a status quo as all that is humanly possible. But because "human nature" has been ideologically appealed to in defense of privilege, it does not follow that such a concept can be given no scientific standing.

How human nature is conceived obviously affects the formation of broad social policy. In particular, social philosophy has been especially influenced by a belief in a native moral disposition, good or bad. Classically, this belief is embodied in the fiction of the "state of nature"—man considered apart from the institutions of social control. For Locke it was a state of "good-nature"; for Hobbes, life without agencies of socialization would be "nasty, brutish, and short." On this issue Freud stands squarely with Hobbes: the belief in the innate goodness of man he regards as "disastrous." The fictitious "state of nature" can be given empirical anchorage in childhood, if anywhere. And the picture of an innocent childhood corrupted by society is a romanticist myth. Its being so is not simply a matter of infantile sexuality. Far more to the point in psychoanalytic theory are the aggressive impulses which from the outset play so important a role in patterning behavior.

But neither does Freud endorse the myth of the innate depravity of man. The condition of childhood departs from Hobbes' "war of each against all" because as yet the "each" is unformed—the self becomes socialized in the very process of its growth and maturation. And while it is true that Freud reveals the evil impulses in human nature, it is no less true—though less widely remarked upon—that he also reveals the powerful forces within the personality making for their censorship, suppression, or sublimation. In short, human nature for Freud is morally neutral. It is rich in potentialities for good and evil alike. Which is actualized, and to what degree, is not predestined, but depends—within limits—on the wisdom with which society nurtures its human resources.

Such wisdom can be grounded only in knowledge: rational social policy must be based upon the achievement of empirical social science. And social science, for Freud, is nothing other than the study of human nature. Social phenomena are paralleled in individual history, and can be explained by reference to that history. The culture pattern of taboo he interprets in terms of a compulsion neurosis; war, in terms of individual aggression; religion, by reference to father-fixation. The thesis of Plato and Hobbes that the state is "the individual writ large" Freud generalizes to all social institutions. The several social sciences are not autonomous but are all reducible to psychology.

Many critics of Freud have addressed themselves to this generalization, and with some justice. Inferences based on dynamic insights and checked by clinical observations are here too often replaced by sheer speculation, warranted only by extended analogies. Yet even here Freud's scientific genius did not entirely desert him. For indeed, the various social sciences cannot easily be distinguished from one another save, perhaps, as several points of anchorage to which the study of man moors floating anxieties about its scientific status. No institution—political, economic, or "social"—can be understood wholly in its own terms. This does not presuppose an organismic philosophy of culture, but marks only the recognition of empirical interconnections and dependencies among elements which have been abstracted to start with from what is given as unitary.

And what is given are the actions of concrete individuals; it is these on which all the abstractions of social science are ultimately grounded, and to which all observation in social science is at last directed. Empiricism is committed to individualism—as a methodology not as a social philosophy. It is the rationalists like Hegel who gave primacy to the group over its members, to wholes over parts, to History over discrete events. In Freud's perspective, Marx has not stood Hegel back on his feet at all: to account for individual behavior in terms of social classes and social forces is exactly to reverse the order of explanation. It is for this reason that psychoanalysis is often so much more sympathetic to literature than to contemporary "scientific" sociology. Because the novelist, at any rate, presents determinate individuals, and may do so with a consummate sense of psychological realities. It is the student of "movements," "forces," "classes," and "institutions" who runs the risk of writing fiction.

Yet the individual may in turn be analyzed socially: not even psychology is autonomous. And such a social analysis is explicit in Freud's own psychology, though its methodological implications are not explicitly assessed. For repression is imposed by man; and surely Freud yields to no one in the importance he assigns to the role of the family as a determinant of the character and action of its individual members. Psychoanalysis thus not only accommodates but requires the distinctively social processes insisted on by Durkheim and Weber. The methodologist is here confronted with a tangle of important questions concerning the interrelations among the human sciences.

But social philosophy is concerned with more than the methodology of social science. It aims at nothing less than an interpretation and appraisal of culture as a whole. Here again Freud raises possibilities for the replacement of speculative by empirical considerations. For to deal with the nature of culture as such is not necessarily to make of it a transcendent reality, but only to detach what is essential in it from the accidents of time and circumstance. But the essence of a thing is only the shadow it casts in the light of some purpose or other; the accidental is what our interests make irrelevant. Social philosophy is interested in social policy. For the philosopher, the essence of culture includes whatever bears upon the realization of human values.

In its full generality, this interest lies beyond the scope of psychoanalytic theory. Yet so far as it goes, that theory has a claim on philosophic attention. For it holds that inner conflict is a product of society as such and not of historical accident. Repression and a heightened sense of guilt is for Freud the price of civilization itself. It is on this basis that he condemns as futile both the cynical denunciations of "modern culture" and the romantic efforts to escape from it. What differentiates man from other species is precisely his capacity for culture, which is to say, his capacity for neurosis. Man is not the rational animal but the repressed animal, and repression and socialization are the same reality viewed from within and without. As in so much nineteenth-century thought, here conflict becomes the creative principle. The competition of species, the opposition of thesis and antithesis, and the class struggle are now joined by the antagonisms of id and superego and Eros and Thanatos as providing the dynamics of progress and growth. Through the workings of culture, libido is sublimated into social benevolence, aggression into mastery over nature. And in this transformation culture itself is created.

In his conception of man's place in nature, at bottom Freud belongs to the Age of Enlightenment. But in his view of man's relation to man his sober empiricism sometimes gives way to the dialectic of Romanticism. Freud says somewhere that he proposes to replace metaphysics by metapsychology. For philosophy this may not be an altogether favorable exchange. But the offer must be carefully weighed.

Man's place in nature—this is the preoccupation of the religious philosophies; and it is here that Freud's naturalistic temper is most marked. There is no need to make room for faith conceived as a relation to the supernatural. Lacking an object, faith is not a relation at all, but a condition in the faithful. The psychological understanding of religious belief is to replace the logical analysis of religious truth. Not the semantics but the pragmatics of theology is the proper province of the philosophy of religion.

Freud agrees with James in discerning certain uniformities beneath the variety of religious experience, but differs from him in their interpretation. For Freud they are traceable, not to the presumed identity of the object experienced, but to the shared humanity of the experiencing subjects. The genesis of religious belief is, in Ernest Jones' phrase, the dramatization on a cosmic plane of the child's relations to his parents. Infantile dependency is a crosscultural invariant under changing patterns of family relationships; and it is this invariant which is abstracted and projected as universal religious truth. The force of this analysis cannot be met by the easy charge of a genetic fallacy. It is not a question of the genesis of religious belief but of its latent content. Genetic propositions are instruments for interpretation, not premises for demonstrative syllogisms. Freud suggests more than once that scientific interests originate in curiosity about the facts of life; science is not thereby reduced to a state of mind. For science is a matter precisely of curiosity about the *facts;* the scientific interest can develop only with the maturity of a mind capable of sustaining the weight of the reality principle. The question is whether religious belief similarly accords with the norms of maturity. However that question be answered in its generality, religious philosophy cannot overlook the elements of infantilism so often expressed in what is conventionally identified as the religious life.

The psychoanalytic condemnation of religious belief properly extends only so far as faith substitutes for psychotherapy. The peace of mind or soul recurrently promised is not the peace which passeth understanding but one which can very well be understood in psychoanalytic terms. It is the rootless security found in an external source of morality and personal integrity. Such a sense of security is without ground either in a real self or in an external reality. In Freud's perspectives, it is the outlook of a child for whom the world is still a nursery. James' "will to believe" is the imperious claim of a neurotic dependency for its own preservation in the face of what James himself called the robust sense of reality.

Such a condemnation is shared, I am convinced, by the religious spirit. A faith justified by psychological rewards is subtly dependent on a sickness of soul, in which prayer can be only petition, worship only the awe of omnipotence. Not: to be loved though unworthy, but: to find the world worthy of our love—this is surely the religious quest. Security, integrity, and self-respect are its conditions, not its promise.

The mysticism which is the core of the religious experience is thus, to my mind, untouched by Freud's corrosive analysis of its external corruption. Of Bergson's two sources of the religious life, psychoanalysis challenges only the Law, not the Prophets. Perhaps it points to the need even for purification of prophecy—as speaking, not for the god, but out of the fullness of an encompassing self. Such an experience of boundless identification, what Freud calls the "oceanic feeling," he relates to early stages of ego development. Whether such an account of its genesis also exhausts its content remains problematic. What is beyond doubt is that the philosophy of religion cannot adequately deal with the problem without the fullest exploitation of psychoanalytic insights.

I cannot conclude this survey of the significance of Freud for philosophy without brief attention to Freud's own philosophy—the *Weltanschauung* grounded in character and temperament, more or less independent of the formulas in which academic philosophy finds expression.

From this standpoint, Freud is a rationalist, following in the Jewish tradition of Maimonides, Spinoza, and Einstein, closer perhaps to the intellectualism of the first than to the rational mysticism of the other two. With Spinoza's "intellectual love of God" Freud shares the attitude, if not the object. Reason itself is for him emotionally charged, and from its own nature, he is convinced, must give the emotions the place they are entitled to. His best hope for the future is that "the intellect—the scientific spirit, reason—should in time establish a dictatorship over the human mind." On his banner is inscribed "Where id was, there shall ego be."

This rational ideal Freud holds out for everyone, not just for Plato's caste of intellectuals. Its attainment is a mark of maturity rather than of philosophical achievement. In an era when political suppression from without reinforces the psychic repression within, Freud remains confident that the voice of intellect, though it speak softly, will persist till it is heard, and heard by all.

Such a conviction is scarcely the credo of the pessimism with which he has been charged. Freud is not so much a pessimist as a realist, possibly the most thoroughgoing realist in Western thought. The noblest enterprise of philosophic antiquity Kant saw in the attempt to distinguish appearance from reality. At bottom, this remains the philosophical task. Freud was occupied with its most basic part: to dispel man's illusions about himself. The rejection of his work he traces to the blow which he delivered to human pride, like those struck by

Copernicus and Darwin; and indeed, in that achievement he himself takes pardonable pride.

What is remarkable is that he dispelled illusion without falling into cynicism or groping for new illusions to replace the old. In his own words, he bows to the reproach that he has no consolation to offer. But he is not himself inconsolable; he remains always a yea-sayer to life. The apostle of reason among contemporary academic philosophers is unquestionably Bertrand Russell, whose *Free Man's Worship* hurls defiance at a universe to which human meaning and value is foreign. Freud's rationalism is more resigned: his aim is only "to transform neurotic despair into the general unhappiness which is the usual lot of mankind."

Whether such an appraisal is true of the human condition or only of the life of man in the century since Freud's birth, it is surely impossible to say now. But if in time to come man is secure in a freer, more creative, and more rational existence, not just philosophy and psychology, but human culture as a whole, will owe a debt to Freud's achievement.

QUESTIONS

How can psychoanalysis claim any scientific status if it always explains away any facts that count against it?

It does certainly seem as if psychoanalysis is impervious to any criticism based on contrary evidence. Objections to the theory are explained as manifesting "resistance" to disclosure of the contents of the objector's own unconscious, and the more vigorous the objections the more insistent the psychoanalyst is on this interpretation. Behavior exactly contrary to what the theory calls for—like a son's active dislike of his mother instead of an Oedipal attachment to her—is explained as a "reaction-formation," a disguise of the true feeling, or else as showing only that the feeling must be ambivalent, combining both love and hate. A dream putting the dreamer in a painful or embarrassing situation is still claimed to be a wish-fulfillment, only the wish is to punish or humiliate oneself. And so on.

In this way it appears that the claims of psychoanalysis can never be falsified. If the evidence is favorable, good; and if it is unfavorable, it is interpreted to mean its opposite—good once more. But a proposition which is proved true no matter what happens has no content. As Karl Popper has especially emphasized, the content of a scientific statement consists essentially in what it excludes, in the things which it says do not happen. A statement that excludes nothing tells us nothing, for it does not narrow our expectations: as far as such a statement is concerned, anything at all might happen. And in that case, the statement may just as well be ignored, from a scientific point of view. (Of course, I exclude mathematics, which also cannot be falsified by any experience, but which serves in quite a different way, as an instrument for extracting the content of empirical statements which *can* be refuted by the evidence.)

In my opinion, however, the logic of the situation with regard to psychoanalysis is quite different. Its interpretations do not convert things to their opposites except in a special sense which still allows the theory to be falsified. Specifically, logicians distinguish two sorts of "opposites"—contradictories and contraries. Two propositions are *contradictories* of one another if, whenever either of them is true, the other must be false, and vice versa. They are *contraries* if they cannot both be true, but might both be false. The contradictory of "white" is "not white": everything must be one or the other. But "black" is only the contrary of "white": many things are neither one nor the other, but gray or purple. Now, it is only the transformation of unfavorable evidence to its contradictory which makes it favorable; transformed to its contrary, it may be just as unfavorable as before.

The propositions of psychoanalysis often have the form that something is either white or black, where the black is interpreted, say, as a reaction-formation against the white. But this could very well be false, if the real color were an intermediate shade or some other hue altogether. The theory of the Oedipus complex is not falsified, it may be, by the case of a son who hates his mother; but it would be falsified if he had no particularly strong feelings about her one way or the other, if she played no significant role in his emotional life. It seems strange to say that the atheist who spits at the church door is testifying to his faith; but after all, he could just pass it by. There is plenty of room for falsification of psychoanalytic hypotheses. The point is that all observations in science need interpretation before they become data for or against some hypothesis. So long as the interpretation leaves open the possibility that the data may be less favorable to the hypothesis than to its contradictory, the logical requirement of which we have been speaking is met.

Of course, the question whether the data do in fact support psychoanalytic hypotheses is an entirely different matter. It can only be decided by empirical considerations, not by purely logical ones. You are entirely free to repudiate Freud's claims; but I do not think you are free to appeal to logic alone to justify your repudiation.

Is the implication of psychoanalysis for the theory of knowledge that the difference between fact and fantasy depends, after all, on who is differentiating them?

Definitely not. It is true, I think, that a certain psychological relativism has sprung up which often appeals to psychoanalysis for justification; but I believe that this is a mistake. While much of what we think we see is a projection from our own psyche, in ways that psychoanalysis has elaborated, this does not destroy altogether the objectivity of our perceptions. Psychosis is not just a matter of cultural definition, and even neurosis is more than just a deviation from a social norm. Mental illness expresses itself, and may even consist essentially, in a failure to deal appropriately with the reality situation. What is "appropriate" may vary from person to person and group to group; but the reality is not subject to the same sort of variance. The neurotic is not just out of tune with his society, but with himself, and therefore fails, in the world as it is, to achieve even his own ends. In the psychotic it is precisely the reality-testing functions of the ego that are severely impaired or destroyed.

What psychoanalysis implies for epistemology in this connection is the enormous importance in knowledge of meanings, the interpretations made by the knower of the materials of perception. As pragmatists, too, have ceaselessly emphasized, the facts of experience are not "data"—what is given—but rather what is taken: a "fact" is etymologically something made. The perceptual experience from which knowledge issues is more like reading the expression in a face than it is like solving a cryptogram or a crossword puzzle. What is at work is not a process of sheer ratiocination, but processes of identification, introjection, projection, and other such mechanisms, largely unconscious and preconscious. The model of the knowing mind as a computing machine equipped with sensory receptors will serve at best only for a correspondingly eviscerated model of knowledge. It is human beings that know, and their full humanity—with its hopes, fears, desires, and hates—permeates the whole of knowledge, in both substance and form. No other conception, it seems to me, can make sense of the actual history of science. If the psychology of the human mind is to be dismissed by epistemologists as a corruption of its logic, we shall have to conclude that the only true scientist is, say, a fully automatic anti-aircraft battery, which locates targets and computes trajectories with perfect rationality. But it has no imagination, so that its hypotheses, however verified by its hits, never rise to the level of a scientific theory.

None of this should obscure the fact that, though it is we who make interpretations, it is not within our power to make them fit, save by altering them in accord with objective requirements. The symptoms of a neurosis have a meaning, and in terms of that meaning the neurotic behavior solves certain problems for the personality. But the solution is an inadequate one, from the very nature of the case. It is inadequate, first of all, because it takes the symbol for the reality itself, so that the needs which pose the problem are only symbolically satisfied, but not really: a starving man may dream of food, but he cannot feed on dreams. And it is inadequate, secondly, because it can satisfy some needs only by thwarting others—conflict remains at the core of every neurosis. The objective conditions which must be met by rational behavior are as fundamental for psychoanalysis as are the elements of subjectivity which make for irrationality. It is only when our preoccupation with the role of fantasy in psychoanalytic theory causes us to overlook the equally basic role of fact that we imagine that the theory leads to subjectivism. But in that case, the mistake is ours, not Freud's.

In the psychoanalytic approach to art, isn't the meaning to be found in a work of art a matter of subjective interpretation?

Psychoanalysis does emphasize the importance of imagination in the response to a work of art, as well as in its creation. What is called for on the part of the reader or viewer is a creative interpretation, not a predetermined assignment of meanings on the principle of a dictionary or code book. The response to a work of art, if it is to constitute an esthetic experience, cannot be a purely intellectual reconstruction of a fixed content which the art object unambiguously conveys. On the contrary, it must be in some measure a re-creation of the artist's achievement, sharing with him something of the process of inspiration by which it was produced. The reader of a poem must become in the reading something of a poet himself, or he will get the message but not the poetry. In this sense art does call for an investment of subjectivity: a work of art speaks only to those who make it their own.

There is, therefore, a certain ambiguity in every work of art, for if its content were unequivocally predetermined it could not provide an occasion for an imaginative and creative response. Such ambiguity—or richness of meaning, if you prefer—has been central in the ideas of many art critics and estheticians, and is not just postulated to fit the requirements of psychoanalytic theory. It is this that gives point to the question just posed. Modern psychologists have developed a number of projective tests in which the response that is made to highly indeterminate stimuli reveals something about the mind or personality of the respondent. What he sees is a projection from within, not a reflection of what is objectively present. But a work of art is not a Rorschach ink blot. The problem is to distinguish imaginative responses grounded in esthetic sensitivity from purely projective interpretations that are largely irrelevant to the work of art itself.

I believe that such a distinction can be made, though I freely admit that in particular cases it may not be all easy. If interpretations, whether of art or of any symbol, cannot be made on a dictionary principle, with a code book providing a mechanical translation of manifest meanings into latent content, it does not follow that in that case anything goes. There are still standards to be met for an interpretation to be something more than projective. There may be knowledge about the artist (or the patient, as the case may be) which gives more weight to one interpretation rather than another—biography may not be decisive, but it is surely not always irrelevant. There is the natural expressiveness of materials or subject matters, as well as the workings of conventions in an artistic tradition or a whole culture. Interpretations will differ in the comprehensiveness of what they take into account and also in the coherence which they can give to the various elements of manifest meaning. And a concatenation of evidence derived from a variety of sources—myth, folklore, ritual, dreams, and so on—may give to an interpretation a weight much greater than any single line of inference could provide.

Ultimately, however, the justification for any particular interpretation lies in what is to be done with it when it has been made: to enhance an esthetic experience, promote therapy, or open new lines of scientific inquiry. Whether or how well an interpretation will serve the purpose, whatever it is, is surely not just a matter of the interpreter's think-so. Here as elsewhere, objective constraints can be recognized in the gap that lies between a wish and its fulfillment. In closing the gap, we transcend subjectivity.

What room does the Freudian ethic have for any standards beyond those actually prevailing in society?

It is curious that psychoanalysis has been attacked, in terms of its bearings on morality, both for libertinism and for conventionality. On the one hand, there are objections that it gives sexuality altogether too much importance, making for a self-indulgence which weakens the moral fiber, if it is not downright immoral. On the other hand, there are objections that the outcome of psychoanalytic therapy is only to "adjust" the individual to a society whose moral achievement, whatever its standards, may leave a great deal to be desired. Both these sorts of objections, I think, come to the same thing: they suppose that psychoanalysis identifies the normative with what is normal, and so encourages and even justifies the immorality that is already so widespread in our culture. It aims at making the neurotic, who is abnormally conventional, normally unconventional—that is, no better than he should be, which is to say, as bad as the rest.

I think that this objection is sound in itself, but I believe it to be misdirected. There can be no question that the mere fact that a certain behavior pattern is widespread does not in itself make it right. Reviewers of Kinsey have often pointed out—but apparently, not often enough— that even if ninety-percent of the population suffered from a cold every winter, it would not thereby cease to be an illness. The normality which enters into the therapeutic goal just cannot be interpreted in a statistical sense, or at least, not in the simple and direct fashion that has become so common. Similarly, if adjustment is a passive conformity to prevailing practices, the adjusted individual has in effect abandoned moral aspiration. For his morality cannot rise any higher than its source—an inevitably corrupt society. Where all is rotten, it is a man's duty to say so. Peer Gynt was the great apostle of adjustment, in the hall of the Mountain King as in the madhouse; and in the end, he had no self left to adjust.

But psychoanalysis, in my opinion, is not committed to any specific moral doctrine, conventional or otherwise. Its aim is to make the individual capable of morality—that is, capable of free and responsible choice; but it does not predetermine what the choice is to be. I am not unaware of the difficulty, in psychoanalytic practice, of avoiding the imposition of the therapist's own values on the patient. This is not the only branch of medicine in which the cure involves a risk of infection with a new disease. But to acknowledge danger is not the same as predicting disaster; on the contrary, the more we are aware of the risk, the more we can do to minimize it. In fact, the psychoanalyst cannot ignore the risk in the converse direction—he himself may be unduly influenced by those he is treating: counter-transference may be as morally corrosive for the therapist as transference sometimes is for the patient.

Thus psychoanalysis, insofar as it succeeds in acting on its own principles, produces neither conformists nor rebels. Whether a man keeps a wife or a mistress, writes poetry or advertising copy, votes with the party or espouses anarchism, is in itself of no significance for his mental health. Psychoanalysis will wean him away from conventional patterns of behavior if in his psyche they are infantilisms which call, indeed, for weaning. Unconventional behavior will give way to more "normal" patterns if it is rooted in adolescent rebelliousness rather than expressing mature choice. Either pattern can be strengthened as the personality achieves more integration and awareness. The process of education in general does not consist in replacing one set of beliefs by another, but rather in transforming our reasons for believing. Cured of his neurosis, a man may espouse the same values as before; only now, he knows what he is doing, he is prepared to accept the consequences, and above all, he accepts himself as the man he now knows himself to be. Adjustment, in short, means the resolution of inner conflict and not the surrender to the demands of society, whatever the morality which those demands express.

I must add, however, that psychoanalysis does not leave the content of morality as completely undetermined as all this might suggest. For its therapeutic goal is not limited to the capacity for free and responsible choice; it consists also in the capacity for love and for work. More accurately, its theory is that these capacities are interdependent. No one can love another who hates himself, nor be creative in a life of self-destruction. The war within, like all others, replaces freedom by compulsion, and awareness by strategic deception. In the continuing neurotic conflict the victorious end never comes to justify these means: the emergency measures adopted in crisis become a way of life. Psychoanalysis is committed to a repudiation of this politics of personality, and thereby commits itself to the positive values in freedom and creativity. There is no doubt of the moral relevance of these ideas. But at the level of abstraction at which they function in the theory, they leave open an enormous range of possibilities for specific moral choice.

What justification can there be for applying a psychology of the individual to social issues?

Of course, the easy answer is that society consists of individuals, so that applying psychoanalysis to, say, politics is like using atomic physics to explain the behavior of the stars. In point of fact, political psychology is at least as old as .Machiavelli; in our times, Graham Wallis, H. D. Lasswell, and Erich Fromm, among many others, have made significant contributions, in my opinion, by focusing on the role of human nature in politics. Parties and governments are made up of men, after all, who cannot abandon their humanity as easily as their political principles. Much of political life is, in Lasswell's phrase, the displacement of private affects onto public objects.

Yet groups of men can behave in ways that are unknown to its members—sometimes, indeed, being downright inhuman. Bodies may remain motionless even though the atoms swarming within them rush about at breath-taking speeds. The transformation of individual to social psychology requires great care, and probably more knowledge of both individual and society than anyone can yet lay claim to. I cannot see, for instance, that a premise which endows each citizen with an aggressive instinct warrants the conclusion that wars among states are inevitable. Citizens also have sexual impulses, but I am not aware of a corresponding passion for world union. William James once urged the cultivation of what he called a moral equivalent of war, a discharge of hostilities in relatively nondestructive channels. No doubt, many worthy ends are served by the Olympic Games; but I beg leave to doubt whether an American victory over the Soviet track or swimming team will lessen the chances of conflict between us on land or sea.

The problem can be brought to focus, I think, by considering in what sense, if any, we can attribute to societies traits and behavior patterns which apply literally to individuals. So far as I can see, there are three possibilities. One is statistical: to say that a society is neurotic, for instance, might mean that some significant number of individuals in the society are neurotic. There are no particular difficulties here, but on the other hand, the question remains unanswered how groups and institutions are affected by having members with a certain individual psychology. A second approach is analogical: here to say that a society is neurotic is to imply that the behavior of the society as such—not necessarily the behavior of the individuals in it—exhibits the irrationalities and other failings characteristic of a neurotic personality. On this basis, whatever we have learned about the neurotic personality has an immediate relevance to social problems. Unfortunately, the ground for the analogy seems to be extremely shaky. What similarities are being assumed, and what evidence supports the assumption? Can a society be neurotic without an unconscious? Is it economic interest that serves in place of the libido? Is there an ego with defense mechanisms, and a symbolism at work in symptom formation? I am aware that any analogy can be pressed to absurdity, but there are surely some that need not be pushed very far.

There is a third approach, neither statistical nor analogical but causative. To say that a society is neurotic may mean that institutions and practices characteristic of the society contribute significantly to the development of neurosis in its individuals, and that their behavior, in turn, reinforces those very practices. A society which ceaselessly stimulates sexuality while condemning its gratification, that rewards competitiveness while extolling benevolence, that values ends for which it denies the means—such a society might be expected to generate conflicts, guilt, and anxiety in its members. And we can also expect that they, in turn, will seek out and support those institutional patterns which answer to their neurotic needs. I believe that Freud's social psychology can be reconstructed in some such framework as this, rather than analogically. The problem is how to carry out the reconstruction in a way which benefits both from the empirical soundness of the statistical approach and the speculative richness of the analogical one.

Here the social philosopher must wait upon the achievement of the social scientist. But there is one point on which I must insist. In my opinion, the Freudian outlook is not as gloomy as has often been made out. There are those who see the individual and society as caught up in a vicious circle: a sick society cannot nurture the growth of a healthy personality, nor can sick minds create and sustain healthy institutions. But we need only read the circle in reverse, and it is no longer vicious. Mature individuals, rational and realistic, can make some contribution to social sanity; and as social patterns improve, we can look to the growth of freer and more creative personalities. Which end of the stick you pick up—the individual or social institutions—doesn't much matter, if only you take hold, and lay it on. It may be that we do not have enough time or enough strength to ward off the madness that threatens. But we would be mad to quit before we have really begun.

7

Psychoanalysis and Logical Positivism*

Philipp Frank

If we want to understand thoroughly the status of psychoanalysis within the general body of scientific knowledge, we are bound to direct our attention to those theories of knowledge which have formulated the strictest criteria of admission into the realm of legitimate science.

Since the second quarter of our twentieth century the principal advocate of strict criteria for admission has been the school of Logical Positivism which originated from the "Vienna Circle" (1920-1935).

Obviously it would be difficult to prove that the theories of Freud or Jung could satisfy the criteria of acceptance advanced by Logical Positivism and shaped according to the model of mathematical physics. However, it is a matter of fact that among the founders of Logical Positivism, the members of the Vienna Circle, there have been quite a few scientists who exhibited a certain sympathy with the teachings of psychoanalysis. There was certainly no great inclination to pass a harsh judgment upon the discrepancy between the Freudian doctrine and the strict criteria of acceptance applied to general theories. Rarely were the psychoanalytic doctrines called "meaningless" or "tautological," as representatives of Logical Positivism have often and gladly branded the doctrines of "school philosophy" like Platonism, Thomism or even Kantianism. Otto Neurath, who was one of the leading members of the Vienna Circle and one of the strictest judges on "unscientific" and

*Reprinted by permission of the New York University Press from *Psychoanalysis, Scientific Method and Philosophy*, edited by Sidney Hook. Copyright © 1959 by New York University.

"meaningless" statements, said repeatedly about psychoanalytical theories that they revealed connections between a great range of new and surprising observed facts; hence one should not discourage this kind of research, although it is far from being logically and semantically satisfactory. This has also been the opinion of Rudolf Carnap and other positivists.

It is certainly a fact that the roots of psychoanalysis and of Logical Positivism grew up in one and the same soil, the intellectual and social climate of Vienna before and after the first World War. It is also a fact that among the workers in psychoanalysis there was a considerable group who attempted to keep contact with the Vienna Circle. We have only to mention Heinz Hartmann, who has been instrumental in keeping psychoanalysis close to scientific methods.

In order to understand this situation we have to glance at the original view of the Vienna Circle on science. This view has sometimes been obscured by a crust of technicalities, and it is certainly good occasionally to give a hard look at the core.

According to the usage of terms in modern science, a theory is "scientifically confirmed" if, first, all facts which are derived from the theory are in agreement with actual observation, and, secondly, if there is a great number of observable facts which *can* be derived from the theory. The latter criterion is to be taken with a grain of salt. The doctrine of Logical Positivism has always and precisely emphasized the point that from the theory itself observable facts can be derived only indirectly. The theory itself is a system of axioms (e.g., the axioms of Euclidean geometry); the axioms are not statements about observable phenomena, but they state relations between abstract concepts (or symbols) like "point," "straight line," "length," "congruence," etc. In order to derive observable facts from a theory we have to connect these abstract concepts with actual observations. The term "length," for example, has to be connected with an operation by which we can actually measure the length of a body. These connecting propositions have been introduced under different names: "rules of coordination," "operational definitions," "semantical rules," "epistemic correlations," etc. These propositions contain the description of actually observable facts and are formulated partly in the language of our everyday life.

It is easy to see that the operations which define "length" or "temperature" (let alone the operations which define "energy" or similar concepts) can be carried out only under particularly "smooth" conditions. There must not be abrupt spatial or temporal changes in temperature or density of matter. Hence, concepts like "energy" or "temperature" have certainly no general meaning; they can only be applied under smooth conditions. This very important point has been made repeatedly by P. W. Bridgman, most elaborately in his book on the *Foundations of Thermodynamics.*

If we say, for example, that the law of inertia or the law of the conservation of energy is confirmed by science, we mean only that there are in nature frequently conditions which can be regarded as smooth and can be, therefore, described by those laws. We must always have in mind that the facts of human behavior which are treated by psychology or sociology can hardly be described as smooth conditions.

It is well known that a sophisticated and somewhat malicious critic of physical science could easily uphold the proposition that the law of conservation of energy is confirmed by science not generally but only under certain restricted conditions. One could even uphold the statement that this law is in general meaningless or even tautological. Such an argument has been made by men like H. Poincaré and P. Duhem; it has been used (or misused) to prove that the general laws of traditional science are not better confirmed than the principles of theology. These authors claim that the general principles of science (inertia, conservation, etc.) are nothing but disguised definitions of terms like "rectilinear motion," "uniform motion," "energy," etc. This interpretation has been widely used as a proof of the inability of science to establish the "truth" of its general statements.

Logical Positivism accepted Poincaré's doctrine that a system of axiomatic principles can neither be confirmed nor refuted by actual sense observations. A system of axioms can be tested only if operational definitions are added. The statement "A system of axioms is confirmed by observations" means exactly: We can find convenient operational definitions which convert by their additions the system of axioms into a system of propositions that actually agree with observable facts. Since the term "convenient" has a purely pragmatic meaning, the expression "confirmation of a theory by observation or experiment" is pragmatic too. We can say that one theory is more practical or convenient than another one, but it does not make scientific sense to say that one theory is completely confirmed or completely refuted. J. B. Conant says in his book *Science and Common Sense,* commenting on the phlogiston theory in chemistry, that a theory was never refuted by a single experiment or observation, but only replaced by a new theory.

Hence, the truth of Freudian or similar theories must not be understood otherwise than pragmatically. It may be convenient or not to accept them.

But the convenience of a theory like psychoanalysis depends upon a great many factors, among which agreement with observations is only one. We have always to consider the agreement with the experience of everyday life, with the general philosophy of the period, the fitness to support some ways of life, some political, moral, and religious creeds.

There has been frequently a dilemma: Should we cover rather interesting new "facts" (direct observations) by a system which is too loosely knit to satisfy these criteria of Logical Positivism? Or should we keep strictly to these criteria and exclude some stimulating new facts from systematic treatment?

If we were to formulate this dilemma in an exaggerated way, we would say: We have a choice between a perfectly logical system which covers only a small number of observed facts and a system which covers a great realm of facts but is in some respects rather vague.

The general doctrine of the Vienna Circle does not solve this dilemma but recommends a compromise which depends upon the merits of any special case. It depends upon whether one believes that a theory like that of psychoanalysis provides important practical help in life or not.

The fundamental approach of the Vienna Circle to science was essentially pragmatic.

It is formulated well in Bridgman's statement that a theory is a "program of action." There have been brilliant men in the Vienna Circle who have developed the logical and semantic components to a high degree of perfection. Philosophers and scientists have been impressed by these successes so frequently and intensively that they have disregarded altogether the pragmatic component. However, leading authors of the Circle like Rudolf Carnap and Charles Morris have always stressed the indivisible trinity of the logical, the semantic, and the pragmatic components.

In order to understand well the attitude of the Vienna Circle towards psychoanalysis it is helpful to remember its attitude towards Marxism. Research on the connection between history and economic conditions has been generally encouraged as useful, and "historical materialism" has been regarded with an attitude of approval, while "dialectical materialism" has been mostly disapproved as a typically metaphysical doctrine.

There were even scientists in the Vienna Circle who manifested some interest in parapsychological research (such as on extrasensory perception) because they believed that there is a certain (even if small) probability that by this research new phenomena may be discovered. This line was pursued even by some strict mathematicians and logicians.

According to Logical Positivism, the system of axioms and the system of observed facts are, in principle, two independent systems which have their own lives. They are connected only by operational definitions. They form together a confirmed scientific theory if they have some points of contact where their agreement can be found. The more points of contact, the better. However, how many points of contact have to exist in a theory cannot be derived by any logical argument; it is a question of convenience and practice. It has been a main thesis of Positivism, from Auguste Comte to the Vienna Circle, that the axiomatic system by itself, as an isolated system, does not tell us any "instrinsic truth" about the real world.

From all these remarks it becomes clear that in terms of the general principles of Logical Positivism there is no reason for disliking psychoanalytical theories. It is a question to be determined by actual research, by observations and logical chains, whether theories such as Freud's should be approved by Logical Positivists.

8

Meaning of Psychoanalytic Concepts and Confirmation of Psychoanalytic Theories*

Else Frenkel-Brunswik

Freud's ideas in the sphere of personality at first aroused a clamor of protest that has never entirely subsided. Once the initial shock ensuing from Freud's discoveries had been overcome, however, the scrutinies of the system appear to be concerned more with its formal or methodological characteristics than with its content. Thus we hear of the alleged subjectivism or animism of psychoanalysis, of its confusion of hypotheses and facts, or of the nonverifiability of its hypotheses.

Many of the objections against psychoanalysis have their origin in an overly narrow interpretation of scientific empiricism or of operationism, and generally in a vaguely antitheoretical attitude. Since it is the physical sciences that are usually taken as the ideal model of scientific theory construction and of operational procedure, certain fundamental changes in the conception of theoretical structure that have taken place in the field of physics itself must be taken into consideration. Philipp Frank[1] points out that the earlier ultrapositivistic requirement, accord-

1. Frank, P. Modern Science and Its Philosophy, Cambridge, Harvard University Press, 1941.

*Reprinted by permission of the American Association for the Advancement of Science from *Scientific Monthly*, 79, 293-300, November 1954.

ing to which all principles of physics should be formulated by using only observable qualities, has been broadened to include indirection; Einstein[2] speaks of "the everwidening logical gap" between observation and basic concepts or laws. According to Hempel,[3] it is precisely the "fictitious concepts rather than those fully definable by observables" that enable science to proceed to explanation and prediction.

A comparison between the situation in physics and in psychoanalysis is certainly not in all respects justified. However, modern physics and psychoanalysis have in common a turning-away from the natural to a fictitious language. And the common result of this policy is that a wider and simpler network of interrelationships within observable data is ultimately being achieved. The fact that theoretical constructs, such as unconsciousness, id, superego, or repression, refer only indirectly, and not completely at that, to observable data must therefore not be made the basis of an objection against psychoanalysis as such. It may be helpful in the early stages of discovery to designate certain patterns of behavior in terms of the special and relatively fixed classifications listed. Today many of the earlier statements of psychoanalysis may be reformulated in terms of behavioral patterns in such a manner that the facets of behavior connected with the more genuinely biological and instinctual processes—the id—are differentiated from those that are the result of cultural and parental commands and taboos—the superego.

Whereas in Europe the most important function of logical positivism was to stress the necessity of relating existing theories to empirical data, in this country, and especially in the case of the social sciences, its major function seems to be the advocacy of the formation of, and a tolerance for, theory per se.

With regard to the definition of basic concepts, some critics of psychoanalysis have objected to an alleged lack of sophistication in Freud concerning the philosophy of science and to his tendency to reify his concepts. Actually Freud, in contrast to some of his followers, was keenly aware of logical and epistemological problems. Definitions in science, he maintains,

> . . . are in the nature of conventions; although everything depends on their being chosen in no arbitrary manner, but determined by the important relations they have to the empirical material—relations that

2. Einstein, A. The Philosophy of Bertrand Russell, Edited by P. A. Schilpp, Library of Living Philosophers, Evanston, Ill., Northwestern University Press, 1944, Vol. 5, p. 289.

3. Hempel, C. G. Fundamentals of concept formation in empirical science, International Encyclopedia of Unified Sciences, Chicago, University of Chicago Press, 1952, Vol. 2, No. 7.

we seem to divine before we can clearly recognize and demonstrate them. . . . Progressively we must modify these concepts so that they become widely applicable and at the same time consistent logically. Then, indeed, it may be time to immure them in definitions. . . . The science of physics furnishes an excellent illustration of the way in which even those "basic concepts" that are firmly established in the form of definitions are constantly being altered in their content[4]

Most clinical descriptions found in Freud employ the inferential construct of the *unconscious*. Freud considers the assumption of unconsciousness as necessary because the data of consciousness are "exceedingly defective."[5] Conscious acts alone do not enable us to account for certain aspects of slips of tongue and of other parapraxes, of dreams, of mental symptoms or obsessions in the sick, let alone the sudden inspirations of healthy persons. In carrying us, as Freud says, "beyond the limitations of direct experience," the assumption of unconscious acts makes the disconnected and unintelligible conscious acts fall into a demonstrable connection.

From the standpoint of the logic of science, unconscious tendencies are a special case of latent or dispositional characteristics. They are comparable to such physical characteristics as magnetism—provided that we do not insist on assigning them to the mind in a metaphysical sense. Such composite terms as "unconscious hostility" or "dependency" describe a disposition to display aggression or dependence under specified conditions, for example, in therapy. In his definition of behavior, Carnap[6] has expressly included "dispositions to behavior which may not be manifest in a given special case." We therefore must agree with Freud that it is the very assumption of unconscious processes that enables psychoanalysis to take its place as "a natural science like any other."[7] He goes on to explain that these processes are "in themselves just as unknowable as those dealt with by other sciences such as physics and chemistry." And he remains in the spirit of the natural sciences when he stresses that "it is possible to establish the laws which those processes obey and to follow over long and unbroken stretches their mutual relation and interdependences.[8]

4. Freud, S. Instincts and their vicissitudes (1915), Collected Papers, London, Hogarth Press, 1925, Vol. 4, pp. 60–83.

5. Freud, S. A note on the unconscious in psychoanalysis (1912), Collected Papers, London, Hogarth Press, 1925, Vol. 4, pp. 22–29.

6. Carnap, R. Testability and meaning, Phil. of Science, 3:420, 1936; 4:2, 1937.

7. Freud, S. An Outline of Psychoanalysis (1940), J. Strachey, Translator, New York, W. W. Norton & Co., Inc., 1949.

8. *Ibid.*, p. 36.

Originally the concepts of conscious and unconscious signify particular *systems* possessed of certain dynamic characteristics, calling for a specification of their relationships within the over-all formal model. When dreams or subsequent free associations are used, this is done for the establishment of intermediate links that can be inserted in the gap between the two systems and that help to recover the latent material in a process of interpretation. Obviously to avoid confusion concerning mentalistic reification, Freud suggests "employing for the recognized mental systems certain arbitrarily chosen names." But since he cannot ignore consciousness as the common point of departure, he proposes to use the abbreviation Cs (for consciousness) and Ucs (for the unconscious) when the two words are used in the systematic sense.

Only in Freud's later writings does the term "unconscious" take on a distinct reference to mental qualities. One of the chief reasons for this shift was the empirical realization that not only the id but also the superego is in part unconscious. In effect this merely underscores the increasing emphasis on the system-character of Freud's basic concepts and the decreasing emphasis on the more introspectionistic distinction between conscious and unconscious.

Freud readily acknowledges that a "rough correlation of . . . the mental apparatus to anatomy . . . exists." If so far every attempt to establish a localization of his constructs has miscarried, the present imperfect state of the biological sciences must be held responsible. Siegfried Bernfeld[9] has amply pointed out the influence of Helmholtz's physicalism and of the principle of conservation of energy on Freud. But it must be stressed that while, at the beginning, Freud was intensely dominated by neurophysiological thinking, the decisive progress in psychoanalysis did not occur until after he had freed himself from the search for such analogies and turned to more openly psychological models.

In defending the complexities of his approach, Freud stresses that there is no obligation to achieve, at our very first attempt, a theory that "commends itself by its simplicity, in which all is plain sailing." Freud argues that we must defend complexities of the theory itself so long as we find that they fit in with the results of observation; yet we must not abandon our expectation of being guided, in the end, by those very complexities to the recognition of "a state of affairs that is at once simple in itself and at the same time answers to all the complications of reality."[10] If we note a similarity of tone with logical empiricism, we

9. Bernfeld, S. Freud's earliest theories and the school of Helmholtz, Psychoanalyt. Quart., 13:341, 1944.

10. Freud, S. The unconscious (1915), Collected Papers, London, Hogarth Press, 1925, Vol. 4, pp. 98–136 (p. 122).

must not forget the fascination that in turn psychoanalysis has had for many of the logical empiricists; they have seen the genius of Freud at a time when most psychologists and psychiatrists were still deeply resistant.

Next to the concept of the unconscious, it is that of *instinct* which has been objected to most vigorously in the face of claims of psychoanalysis for consideration as a science. The psychoanalytic concept of instinct is complicated by the assumption of far-reaching transformations and disguises, particularly of the sex instinct. In reality, some parts of Freudian instinct theory, notably the theory of infantile sexuality and of the psychosexual stages of development, belong to the most lucid and most powerfully executed portions of the psychoanalytic system. As in the case of the unconscious, Freud pursues an essentially operational course in defining the instincts. He does so in pointing to the capacity of the instincts to "act vicariously for one another" and to readily change their objects. The mechanisms of repression, of reversal into the opposite, and of sublimation are some of the more striking examples of this variability. It may well be argued that the explanatory value of the concept of instinct lies precisely in this emphasis on variability. Only in the case of an assumed one-to-one correspondence between instinct and manifest behavior would the concept of instinct become circular or superfluous as an unnecessary duplication of behavior. Freud's concept of instinct is a truly explanatory, inferential construct imbued with some degree of independence. He avoided unnecessary duplication by fully considering the functional ambiguities inherent in the relationships between drives and the behavior rather than by directly projecting behavioral trends back into the subjects.

The mixture of pioneering gusto with an understanding for ultimate logical requirements, which is so characteristic of Freud, is revealed when he speaks of the "superb indefiniteness" of the concept of instinct. He goes on to claim for the instincts "the same value as approximations as belongs to the corresponding intellectual scaffolding found in other natural sciences." We must expect them to "remain for a considerable time no less indeterminate than those of the older sciences (force, mass, attraction, etc.)."[11]

Freud ascribes some of the difficulties in his speculations about the instincts—speculations that he likes to call his mythology—to our being obligated to operate with "metaphorical expressions peculiar to psychology." We must add in his behalf that, for the type of problems with which psychoanalysis deals, the mentalistic—introspectionist or

11. Freud, S. An Outline of Psychoanalysis (1940), J. Strachey, Translator, New York, W. W. Norton & Co., Inc., 1949, p. 36.

animistic—vocabulary constitutes the precise counterpart to what Frank[12] calls the "pictural" vocabulary, and that, in turn, this latter vocabulary is recognized in physics as a legitimate or at least tolerable ingredient of the earlier stages of concept formation. Whereas the analogical procedure may not be suited for purposes of ultimately proving a scientific hypothesis, it may well be argued that the function of mentalistic analogies is more important in psychology than it is in physics.

One of the most bewildering aspects of psychoanalytic theory is the turning away from the obvious face-value picture of personality as it derives from introspection or from the direct, *phenotypical* observation of external behavior segments. An example is in the reinterpretation of overt friendliness as a sign of underlying hostility, or of extreme tidiness as a sign of preoccupation with dirt. The discrepancy disappears with the specification of a set of fixed or variable operational conditions that determine when overt behavior is to be interpreted as genuine and when as manifesting some heterogeneous latent factor.

Since scientific inference concerning central processes—that is, the assumption of internal states on the basis of external evidence—cannot be defended unless it is based on a wide variety of circumstantial evidence,[13] central inference can be said not to have been legitimately attempted before psychoanalysis. It can be shown that, on the negative side of the ledger, psychoanalysis, especially in its beginnings, has comparatively de-emphasized both the surface manifestations in their specific identity and—what is more—the so-called distal achievements of behavior. These latter results of behavior in turn play the dominant role in Darwin's thinking and in such neobehaviorist systems as that of Tolman.[14] The regrouping of manifest observable facts as undertaken by Freud centers about sameness of *need*—that is, sameness of internal cause or dynamism—while in the case of Tolman it centers about sameness of *effect* and, as we may add, in the case of Egon Brunswik's theory of perceptual thing-constancy[15] it centers about sameness of *external object*.

By virtue of this inherent incompleteness, psychoanalysis did not altogether manage to avoid the pitfalls of motivational relativism and of a genetic dissolution of overt adjustment values. This one-sidedness has,

12. Frank, P. Modern Science.

13. Frenkel-Brunswik, E. Psychoanalysis and personality research, J. Abnorm. & Social Psychol., 35:176, 1940.

14. Tolman, E. C. Purposive Behavior in Animals and Men, New York, The Century Co., 1932.

15. Brunswik, E. Wahrnehmung und Gegenstandswelt, Vienna, Euticke, 1934.

to a certain extent, been remedied in the more recent turning of psychoanalysis from an almost exclusive emphasis on the id and on motivation to an increased concern with the ego—that is, with reality-oriented behavior, and with adjustment in general. Even so, psychoanalytic expansion in this direction has been more programmatic than real, and there are a number of problems that can be solved only by an explicit integration of psychoanalysis with psychology proper and with sociology. The conceptual tools of psychoanalysis just are not sufficient to explain fully rational and social behavior.[16] In fact, if we were to deny this, we would obscure the essential theoretical contribution of Freud, which is his discovery of motivational dynamics.

In the context of adjustment problems, Freud tends to view character structure from a merely defensive point of view—that is, in terms of protecting oneself from internal threats rather than in terms of external task orientation—and social influences are seen as a series of traumata that bring to a halt or discontinue instinctual gratification and expression. While providing an understanding of an important aspect of the individual's attitude toward society, this view does not do justice to all the satisfactions gained from moving along constructive social avenues.

With all this said it must be granted that so far as motivation per se is concerned, psychoanalysis has achieved a legitimate reconstruction of objective causes rather than a mere pseudo-explanation in terms of subjectively experienced motives, as such critics as Toulmin[17] and Flew[18] would have it. Far from identifying the introspectively reported motive and the objective explanation, the major merit of psychoanalysis is to have differentiated the two and unmasked and discredited as to their explanatory value the subjective experiences of motivation. The phenotypical, manifest characteristics are taken to provide only the indirect cues for inferences concerning the latent, genotypical forces of motivation. It is of comparatively lesser significance that in the majority of cases it is verbal behavior such as dreams, free associations, and the like, rather than overt motor behavior proper, that psychoanalysis takes as the manifest basis for drive interpretations. This does not mean, however, that psychoanalysis is introspectionistic. As everyone knows, it is precisely through psychoanalysis that we have learned to doubt the face value of introspection.

It must further be pointed out that the assumption of the dynamisms of the *inner man*, to which such behaviorist critics of psychoanaly-

16. Frenkel-Brunswik, E. Psychoanalysis and personality research.
17. Toulmin, S. Analysis, 9:13, 1948.
18. Flew, A. Analysis, 10:8, 1949.

sis as Skinner[19] have objected, can be shown to increase the parsimony of the scientific description of behavior patterns. A translation of the psychoanalytic concepts into the terminology of the classical behaviorist's so-called stimulus-response approach, useful as it may be in certain contexts, has its difficulties and limitations. As we have seen, the major emphasis of psychoanalysis is on the discovery of internal causes; these include, in the language of psychoanalysis, *subjective fantasies* and generally the differential meanings an external event may acquire for various individuals. Freud began to make progress in his understanding of hysteria only after he had given up the idea of a simple external causation. Freud points out that only after the hypothetical factor of the hysterical phantasies had been introduced did the structure of the neurosis and its relationship to the patient "become conspicuous." Since the relationship of these phantasies to external factors is most complex and ambiguous, it seems heuristically fruitful to assume the internal mechanisms postulated by psychoanalysis, leaving their full operational specifications for a later time. Contrary to Skinner, I believe that such assumptions do not carry us outside the "bounds of natural science." But I do agree with Skinner on the point that any "looking inside the organism for an explanation of behavior" can easily lead to a neglect of some of the environmental factors, and readily acknowledge that it has done so in the case of psychoanalysis.

Even more crucial is the fact that the hypothetical extrapolations from overt behavior help to select the most relevant, though often less conspicuous, aspects of behavior which otherwise would be lost in the practically infinite range of possible observation. The relatively great explanatory and predictive value of hypotheses dealing with underlying motivation can be demonstrated statistically by means of multiple correlation.[20] It is without doubt based on the fact that the selectivity just referred to enters crucially into the formation of these hypotheses. We may add that, from the standpoint of logical analysis, there is no alternative but to be behavioristic in any psychological endeavor; neither the so-called subjective phantasies in which psychoanalysis is interested, nor introspective events of any kind in others, can be constituted except by inference from the manifest physical observation of organisms.

In the process of theory-construction, Freud is generally quite careful in attempting to distinguish what we now call the *postulatory*

19. Skinner, B. F. Science and Human Behavior, New York, The Macmillan Co., 1953.

20. Frenkel-Brunswik, E. Motivation and behavior, Genet. Psychol. Monogr., 1942.

from what we now call the *operational* elements of the theory, at the same time allowing their interplay as he moves along. However, his system would benefit from greater formalization and especially also from a more systematic differentiation between basic assumptions and their derivations. For example, a combination of the assumptions of infantile sexuality and of repression may be able to cover many of the more specific theorems in psychoanalysis.

Feigl[21] places psychoanalysis at the third of the four levels of explanation he distinguishes, thus grouping it together with the relatively descriptive behavior theories of Tolman and Hull. To me it seems that at least a certain group of psychoanalytic concepts, including that of the unconscious, goes beyond this level of involving what Reichenbach[22] calls *surplus meaning*. In terms of a distinction recently injected into psychological theory by MacCorquodale and Meehl,[23] this latter group of concepts would seem to be "hypothetical constructs," in contradistinction to the "intervening variables" which are thought of as resting exclusively on the values of a specified set of empirically observed data. In their own rather sketchy analysis, the last-named authors point out that such terms as *libido, censorship,* or *superego* were, in psychoanalysis, originally introduced as intervening variables—that is, as conventionalized designations of observable properties—but that there frequently was an unnoticed shift toward hypothetical constructs.

In their arguments, the authors tend to overlook the fact that statements containing intervening variables are by no means exhaustible by statements concerning their observational basis. Both Carnap[24] and Hempel[25] have made it clear that sentences containing disposition terms cannot be fully translated into sentences about observables. Since we cannot specify all conditions and manners in which latent tendencies become manifest, dispositional statements involve *open* terms and require an infinite series of conditions in order to be tested.

The distinction between intervening variables and hypothetical constructs may, in my opinion, nonetheless be retained as a gradual one involving different degrees of indirectness of evidence or different kinds of surplus meaning. Possible relationships to the distinction made by Carnap and Hempel between postulatory theoretical constructs and

21. Feigl, H. Readings in Philosophical Analysis, Edited by H. Feigl & W. Sellars, New York, Appleton-Century-Crofts, Inc., 1949.

22. Reichenbach, H. Experience and Prediction, University of Chicago Press, 1938.

23. MacCorquedale, K., and Meehl, P. On a distinction between hypothetical constructs and intervening variables, Psychol. Rev., 55:95, 1948.

24. Carnap, R. Testability and meaning.

25. Hempel, C. G. Fundamentals of concept formation.

concepts more directly reducible to observation could be pointed out. Guided by some relatively fragmentary initial empirical observations, Freud seems to have proceeded rather directly to the building of a hypothetical theoretical structure, with empirical interpretation lagging somewhat behind; in the definition of such theoretical constructs as superego, ego, and id, the major emphasis is on their structural relationships to one another rather than on their relationships to observation. His frequent oscillation between hypothetical constructs and intervening variables has afforded some protection against both a too narrow operationalism and the dangers of meaningless generalization.

Considering now briefly the attempts at confirmation of psychoanalytic hypotheses, it must be pointed out that, by involving concepts more removed from the immediate data, psychoanalysis has lengthened the chains of intellectual and experimental work that connect the principles with the observational protocols. We may recall here the statement of Frank[26] that modern physics requires special ingenuity in verifying its theories and that this fact is a result of the greater abstractness of concepts. Traditional Newtonian physics could easily be verified by observation, since it was a direct formulation of everyday experience, obvious and plausible to common sense, whereas in Einstein's general theory of relativity "the description of the operations by which the quantities involved could be measured becomes a serious and complex task. It becomes an essential part of the theory."[27]

Psychoanalysis shares with modern physics the fact that its statements do not lend themselves to the most direct and obvious types of confirmation. In each case, the highly interpretive statements involved do not carry the rules of their confirmation as obviously with themselves as do more descriptive statements. In reviewing the extensive literature on objective studies of psychoanalytic hypotheses,[28][29] one is impressed by the fact that the more descriptive types of hypotheses involved in the theory of *fixation* and *regression* proved to be more readily accessible to experimental confirmation than the more explanatory ones on *repression, projection,* and *reaction-formation.* This may indeed be due to the fact that the latter derive from the more inferential and abstract parts of psychoanalytic theory. Complex conditions, such as those involved in the analysis of transference, are required before that which has been

26. Frank, P. Modern Science.

27. *Ibid.*

28. Hilgard, E. R. Psychoanalysis as Science, Edited by E. Pumpian-Mindlin, Stanford University Press, 1952.

29. Sears, R. R. Survey of Objective Studies of Psychoanalytic Concepts, Social Sci. Res. Council Monogr., Vol. 51, 1943.

repressed may become conscious. Misunderstandings of psychoanalytic theory have arisen when statements concerning repression, that originally were intended to refer to unconscious—that is, inferred rather than overt—processes, were erroneously taken as purely descriptive statements of conscious contents. As in physics, a simple identification of statements containing disposition terms with statements about manifest events is not permissible. Still and all, some of the experimental studies have verified even such seemingly farfetched psychoanalytic assumptions as symbolism.

A type of approach other than the experimental, and one that I have tried to develop for a number of years, concentrates on the principle of alternative manifestations of motivational tendencies. This principle describes the basic pattern of interrelationships between the two strata involved in all psychoanalytic theory—the manifest and the latent—and can be shown to underlie most if not all of the specific mechanisms just mentioned. The possibility of analyzing, statistically, the tangled relationships between the two strata after imbuing them with some degree of operational independence may be illustrated by a study dealing with motivation in its relation to overt behavior segments[30] and one dealing with certain mechanisms of self-deception.[31] In the former study, a comparison of over-all motivational ratings with specific behavioral manifestations is used for a rational reconstruction of the cues underlying the so-called intuitive inferences made by the clinician; the same general procedure would apply in case of the more explicit and more scrutinizing inferences concerning motivational dynamics made by the psychologist as a scientist rather than as a synoptic rater. Knowledge of the type of drive-variable involved seems to hold good promise for behavior prediction of an "either-or" type, further specification of which must hinge on other than dynamic factors. Among these further factors determining whether, for example, underlying aggression is worked out in a socially constructive form or in neurotic symptoms, such situational factors as social and economic or occupational conditions must be assigned a major role.

In our study of self-deception, certain formal criteria of distortion, which may take their place alongside the more content-oriented type of diagnostic criteria favored in psychoanalysis proper, were established by means of a linguistic analysis of the individual's responses. For example, favorable self-descriptions that do not correspond to the manifest

30. Frenkel-Brunswik, E. Motivation and Behavior, Genet. Psychol. Monogr., 1942.
31. Frenkel-Brunswik, E. Mechanisms of self-deception, J. Social Psychol., 10:409, 1939.

behavioral realities are frequently formulated in exaggerated terms. The use of such linguistic or semantic devices as superlatives, generalizations, and repetitions was found to be statistically concomitant with a shortcoming rather than a strength in the area concerned.

In the verification of psychoanalytic hypotheses, the systematic evidence furnished by academic psychology constitutes only one of several avenues. Psychoanalysis itself has provided confirmatory, though seldom rigorous, empirical evidence of overwhelming scope, ranging from the wealth of material accumulated from individual patients to a synopsis of dream mechanisms, of lapses of tongue and memory, of pathologic symptoms, and of certain relevant features of folklore, myth, and other cultural phenomena. Regardless of how imperfect psychoanalytic theory may be in its formal structure, it has no rival manog psychological theories as far as the range of both its evidence and its explanatory power is concerned.

Some of the obstacles encountered in the efforts to separate manifest behavior and latent motivation—or surface and depth in general—go beyond the merely methodological difficulties encountered in the process of scientific verification. One of these additional difficulties is a semantic one. The vocabulary of everyday language does not furnish us consistently with two separate sets of terms, one for overt behavior and the other for underlying motivation. Unless we drastically depart from familiar usage, the term "friendliness," for example, stands for the basically friendly outlook on life, or for the techniques of friendliness—genuine or fake—by which this basic outlook may be implemented or pretended, or for both. This dilemma is in a formal sense similar to the one presented by the twofaced meaning of our common perceptual terms.[32] These terms also tend to have double reference, one to the personal and somewhat variable perceptual response and the other to the interpersonal, measured physical stimulus. Most perceptual qualities exhibit highly tangled relationships to a variety of measured stimulus variables. The conceptual separation of perceptual stimulus and perceptual response can thus no longer appear as a case of entities superfluously multiplied; neither can, we may add, the separation of behavior and motivation with their similarly tangled relationships, as outlined in some of the foregoing paragraphs.

Certainly, both the motivations and the behaviors are constituted from overt behavior, as both stimuli and perceptual responses are constituted from different types of observational experiences. But motivations are arrived at through a synopsis of the constant elements in many bits of behavior. The problem of the genuineness of behavior (that

32. Brunswik, E. Wahrenehmung.

I have pointed out as crucial in the context of proving psychoanalytic hypotheses) illustrates the need that the two sets of events be made conceptually and operationally independent of each other so that their far-reaching actual independence under the principle of alternative manifestations can be brought out. An independent nomenclature for the different levels will thus have to be established in the end. This would remove much of the temptation to fall back into an oversimplified, pre-psychoanalytic, single-level or surface treatment of the motivational aspects of behavior.

It has been observed that each time separations of the kind just described had to be substituted for previous identifications in the history of science, there was irrational, emotional resistance against the recognition of the equivocations or ambiguities involved. Besides their applicability to our outlook on psychoanalysis in particular, these resistances have some bearing on another topic, the acceptance or rejection of scientific theories in general. They may also be linked with what I have called "intolerance of ambiguity."[33] Acceptance of the ambiguous relationship between motivation and manifestation, which is the chief discovery of psychoanalysis, requires cognitive tolerance of ambiguity on the part of the scientist. Its opposite, the concretistic, compulsive, and dogmatic patterns of perception and thought that have been so vividly described among scientists, are not conducive to the acceptance of psychoanalysis.

A final word must be added concerning the true or alleged ethical implications of psychoanalysis. Together with the cognitive resistances just outlined, ethical connotations may be the chief determinants of the acceptance and further destiny of any scientific theory. It has been objected against psychoanalysis—perhaps more often in the past than in the present—that its orientation is fundamentally amoral. Arguments of this kind were raised, not only by philosophers in search of a system of absolute values, but also by empirically oriented social scientists and psychologists of major stature, among them Max Weber.[34] Weber saw in psychoanalysis an expression of a tendency to loosen our basic ethical principles. In a letter of 1907, Weber had accused Freud of proposing a psychiatric or "nerves" ethics characterized by the prevalence of the "hygienic" point of view.[35]

Against these strictures it may be said that, with all the reservations

33. Frenkel-Brunswik, E. Intolerance of ambiguity as an emotional and perceptual personality variable, J. Personality, 18:108, 1949.

34. Weber, Max. The Protestant Ethic and the Spirit of Capitalism, New York, Charles Scribner's Sons, 1930.

35. Weber, Marianne. Mex Weber: Ein Lebensbild, Heidelberg, Lambert-Schneider, 1950.

that psychoanalysis has voiced against an overly naive rational interpretation of ethics, it has merely turned against the assumed major executive principle of the traditional forms of ethics rather than against their basic constructive content. This particular executive principle is the mechanism of repression. Most pre-psychoanalytic ethical systems stress such inhibitory devices as the looking away from evil, or its denial, or its mastery through strength of will. From psychoanalysis we have learned about the inefficiency and the dangers of these various forms of repression; from the same source we have learned of the importance of consciousness, integration, and maturity. All that is considered an essential ingredient of maturity in psychoanalysis, such as rationality, the overcoming of aggression, cooperativeness, the ability to love and to work, and the courage to face inside and outside threats that oppose these characteristics, bespeak standards that stand up well among the traditional systems of ethics. In psychoanalysis, every neurosis is in and by itself considered as failure at moral control. The important historical contribution of traditional systems of ethics is the attempt to strengthen consciousness and conscience against the invasion of the instincts; through psychoanalysis we have become aware that such strengthening can be achieved only by facing and working through, rather than merely condemning, the forces threatening our conscious personal and social values. From this latter viewpoint, the mortal sin is self-deception and lack of insight rather than a lack of repression.

It may be that the diversion of attention from the functions of reason in psychoanalysis has contributed to the semblance of ethical relativism. As we have seen, psychoanalysis was so overwhelmed by its epoch-making discovery of the role of irrational forces that the explicit exploration of reasoning processes was temporarily obscured, even though it was reason and not the irrational that held the top spot so far as the evaluative attitude of psychoanalysis is concerned.

There is an illuminating reversal in the role played by reason when we compare the direct verbal formulations made by Freud, on the one hand, and Weber or Durkheim,[36] on the other, with the actual function of reason in the theoretical edifices of these men. Both Durkheim and Weber have repeatedly been described as rationalists, albeit both see the foundations of society in fundamentally nonrational moral qualities. Freud, on the other hand, has been criticized for having given too much prominence to the irrational, while in fact his one hope is the overcoming of the irrational in a society built on reason. Freud neglected to explore reason directly and challenged the potency of reason in

36. Durkheim, E. The Rules of Sociological Method, Glencoe, Ill., Free Press, 1950.

guiding human conduct. But in his evaluations of the goals of human development he has an exalted esteem for reason, and his understanding of the vicissitudes of unreason has sharpened his grasp of the fundamental nature of reason. In this more crucial respect he is a believer in reason in the best sense of the word.

REFERENCES

FRENKEL-BRUNSWIK, E. Psychoanalysis and the Unity of Science, Boston, American Academy of Arts and Sciences, 1954.

HARTMANN, H., KRIS, E., and LOWENSTEIN, R. Function of theory in psychoanalysis, Drives, Affects, and Behavior, Edited by R. Loewenstein, New York, International Universities Press, 1953.

KRIS, E. The nature of psychoanalytic propositions and their validation, Freedom and Experience, Edited by S. Hook and M. R. Konwitz, Ithaca, Cornell University Press, 1947.

9

Theory Construction and Validation in Psychoanalysis*

Leonard Horwitz

Psychoanalysts, in contrast to academic psychologists, have not been particularly concerned with problems of theoretical methodology. This trend is beginning to change as the psychoanalytic movement in the past two decades has made increasing contact with the other behavioral sciences and has begun to see itself through the lenses of other disciplines. Contrary to the view of most psychologists, Freud was actually quite sophisticated about problems of theory construction and kept in mind more carefully than did many of his disciples the distinction between theorizing which was close and that which was distant from empirical data (Frenkel-Brunswik, 1954). Until relatively recently, academic psychologists have been fairly unanimous in viewing psychoanalysis as a kind of demonology, given to all of the sins of metaphysical and anti-scientific speculation (dogmatism, vague concepts, reification, etc.). These views have been considerably tempered in recent years with the result that many psychologists now look upon psychoanalytic theory as a legitimate scientific displine, though perhaps still not quite respectable.

*Reprinted from *Theories in Contemporary Psychology* by Leonard Horwitz with permission of the Macmillan Publishing Co., Inc. Copyright © 1963 by the Macmillan Publishing Co., Inc.

The suggestions and comments of Drs. Gardner Murphy, Robert S. Wallerstein, Richard S. Siegal, and Harold M. Voth are gratefully acknowledged.

Many persons interested in problems of methodology now hold that academic psychology was burdened down by an overly severe scientific "superego" which placed excessive demands for precision both upon itself and upon the findings and theories of psychoanalysis. The academicians have been accused of attempting to strait-jacket prematurely all psychological research in a model of science where methods tend to determine problems rather than vice versa. The procedural tail has tended to wag the substantive dog. The handicap of such approaches, claim the analysts, is suggested in the contrast between the bodies of knowledge about human behavior accumulated by academic psychology on the one hand and psychoanalysis on the other. Clinicians usually cannot conceive of understanding their patients without using the concept of unconscious motivation; experimental psychology has only recently begun to incorporate this concept into its studies, as in the areas of unconscious and preconscious perception. In its long struggle over the admissibility of introspective data, psychology has cut off from its observational base some extremely rich and valuable data concerning the determinants of human behavior and therefore has understandably lagged far behind Freud and his followers, who did not shut their eyes on philosophical grounds to certain simple facts of observation.

The trend toward the relaxation of unrealistically rigid standards of scientific procedure has occurred both in psychology and in the philosophy of science. The shift in philosophy is largely exemplified by the modification of the requirement, originally proposed by the logical positivists, that *all* concepts used in scientific discourse be operationally defined. Most philosophers now recognize that rigid operationism leads to an undue narrowness and sterility in science and that only through the use of "fictitious concepts" (Hempel, 1952) or "hypothetical constructs" which may have but a tenuous tie with the level of observation can the creative scientist construct the theories which will ultimately clarify the unknowns in nature. The requirement that concepts be defined by operations upon observables has been replaced by the more reasonable caution that one be aware of the extent of the connections between observation and theory. This shift away from radical operationism now allows for hypotheses if they are *indirectly* confirmable and for theoretical constructs if they are part of a network which connects them with terms designating data of direct observation (Feigl, 1956). The rationale of this point of view has been expressed by Scriven (1956, p. 113): "A term is fruitful only if it encourages changes in its own meaning; and, to some considerable extent, this is incompatible with operational definition." The challenge posed by psychoanalytic theory to be admitted into the household of the respectable sciences has possibly at least partly contributed to the demise of the strictly operationist approach.

A parallel shift has started to occur during the last decade within academic psychology itself and is best exemplified by the introduction of the conception of "construct validity." Cronbach and Meehl (1955), in one of the most important methodological papers in psychology in recent years, have proposed that psychologists begin to accommodate their tests and measurements to the fact that many of the concepts in psychology are as yet incompletely defined. The so-called independent criterion in the measurement of such significant concepts as anxiety or aggression is an ideal which we can only approach slowly by a system of successive approximations. The rationale for this approach was stated as follows (p. 294):

> Since the meaning of theoretical constructs is set forth by stating the laws in which they occur, our incomplete knowledge of the laws of nature produces a vagueness in our constructs. We will be able to say "what anxiety is" when we know all the laws involving it; meanwhile, since we are in the process of discovering these laws, we do not yet know precisely what anxiety is.

This methodological conception represents a radical departure from the conventional view of validity, which disallowed any test which was not linked to a fully defined criterion measure. The authors have demonstrated, for example, the operation of a "bootstraps effect," by which a test and its independent criterion, after a period of refinement, may ultimately find their positions reversed. This has occurred with regard to intelligence test measures and teachers' ratings, where the tests have now become the criterion measure against which teachers' ratings are "validated." The introduction of the construct-validity idea into academic psychology may have two salutary effects. It may help to bring psychoanalytic studies and research, with their un-operationist concepts, within the purview of its respectable scientific confreres. Second, it emphasizes the importance of doing research upon concepts embedded in a "nomological network" in which the various links between theoretical constructs and observables are spelled out as clearly as possible and the relationship between the construct at hand and related constructs is defined. This suggestion may help to curb the numerous piecemeal studies, unrelated to any kind of comprehensive theory, from flooding the literature—studies which often add little to the advancement of psychological science.

STRUCTURE OF THE THEORY

Rapaport (1960) has suggested that psychoanalysis contains the potential for a systematic, hypothetico-deductive structure, although it has not achieved this form as yet. This kind of systematic treatment was regarded by Freud as an ideal (Frenkel-Brunswik, 1954) and had been started by Rapaport shortly before his untimely death (Rapaport, 1960; Rapaport and Gill, 1959). Largely based upon Freud's theorizing and supplemented by Hartmann's contributions in ego psychology as well as Erikson's psychosocial emphasis, Rapaport and Gill have suggested some of the broad outlines of the kind of theory which may eventually emerge.

They dealt primarily with the "metapsychology," a term which undoubtedly conjures up images of mysticism, armchair theorizing, and an anti-empirical approach. But metapsychology is not intended as transcendent psychology, as is true of metaphysics in relation to the science of physics. Rather, it is the study of the assumptions upon which the system of psychoanalytic theory is based. Like any good theory, it takes speculative leaps, but, its critics to the contrary, it is also reasonably responsive to empirical investigations (Gill, 1959). The beginning systematizing efforts of Rapaport and Gill consisted of designating the five "points of view" in psychoanalysis, referring to those aspects of a mental event which must be described in order to present a complete psychoanalytic explanation of the phenomenon. The five "points of view" consist of the dynamic, economic, structural, genetic, and adaptive.

Under each of these rubrics is a set of assumptions which have been abstracted from a related set of psychoanalytic propositions. The structural point of view, for example, contains the following assumptions "a) There are psychological structures. b) Structures are configurations of a slow rate of change. c) Structures are configurations within which, between which, and by means of which mental processes take place. d) Structures are hierarchically ordered" (Rapaport and Gill, 1959, p. 157-158). These assumptions underlie a series of propositions which move toward an empirical base. Thus, the assumption about the existence of psychological structures would include the propositions from the general psychoanalytic theory concerning ego, id, and superego as well as the more recent propositions concerning "apparatuses" (Hartmann) and "modes" (Erikson). These would then subsume the propositions from the special theory of psychoanalysis (referring to pathological developments). Such statements, in turn, would subsume empirical propositions. Rapaport and Gill (1959, p. 157) illustrate these distinctions as follows:

> *Empirical proposition:* around the fourth year of life boys regard their fathers as rivals; *specific psychoanalytic proposition:* the solution of the oedipal situation is a decisive determinant of character formation and pathology; *general psychoanalytic proposition:* structure formation by means of identification of anti-cathexes explains theoretically the consequences of the "decline of the oedipal complex"; *metapsychological proposition:* the propositions of the general psychoanalytic theory which explain the oedipal situation and the decline of the Oedipus complex involve dynamic, economic, structural, genetic and adaptive assumptions.

Several points need to be made about the hierarchical structure described above. Although the system would appear to be of a hypothetico-deductive form, it is by no means a tightly-knit axiomatic system in which, as in Euclidean geometry, all of the propositions are ultimately derived from the basic givens, or axioms. Axiomatization is an ideal in every science which none, not even physics, has yet achieved. Indeed, the outline presented above is hardly even a system; it is little more than a program, a beginning effort towards systematizing and integrating the assumptions in the metapsychology with the many diverse propositions at different levels of the hierarchy.

The major shortcoming in achieving a more adequate systematization of the theory is the lack of precision of its concepts. This point is acknowledged by Rapaport and Gill (1959, p. 11) when they state: "We are not yet in a position to present formal definitions of the terms used in stating these assumptions. We are, however, aware that without such definitions a set of assumptions is of limited value and that, indeed, some of the assumptions presented here are little more than covert definitions. Thus the formulation of the definitions will probably modify this statement of the assumptions." At the level of the observation language, even such a key clinical concept like ego strength is as yet only vaguely defined. Barron's (1953) definition in terms of selected MMPI items is considered by most clinicians to be incomplete, narrow, and restricting. On the other hand, the recent efforts by Karush et al. (1962) to construct an ego-strength scale seemed to err in the opposite direction by including practically every significant aspect of personality functioning. This latter effort was a distinct contribution toward defining the concept insofar as it pointed up the complexity of the variable; optimal ego strength was viewed as a balance which avoided the extremes of excessive inhibition on the one hand and lack of control on the other. One large-scale psychoanalytic study (Wallerstein, Robbins, et al., 1956) attempts to avoid the pitfalls of excessive narrowness and over-inclusiveness by defining the concept as only one of a score of significant personality variables. But no clinician would contend that an adequate conceptualization of this variable has yet been achieved. This reservation applies to all of the currently used intrapsychic variables, such as self-concept, anxiety tolerance, psychological mindedness, etc. They are viewed by clinicians as highly significant but still not adequately conceptualized. This is not to say, however, that we are unable to achieve reliable judgments about them which can be used to formulate predictions and thus test hypotheses. But these concepts are highly complex and are not in a one-to-one relationship with observable behavior. The judgments, therefore, must be derived from a wide range of observational data which are not always easy to specify in advance.

If we take the notion of construct validity seriously, we should not be too alarmed by the lack of precise operational definitions, even for the more empirical propositions. The definitions of concepts should be regarded as tentative working definitions which must gradually be sharpened and clarified. The only cause for concern should be a sense of complacency about the acceptability of inadequate formulations.

The danger of rigidification of theoretical constructs is also raised by the hypothetico-deductive form into which the system appears to be moving. Marx, (1963)* mentions several objections to the premature formalization of theory that was typified. by the Hullian system. In essence he pointed to the excessive narrowing, both in methodology and in theorizing, which such systematizing may encourage, particularly in the more immature sciences like psychology. Similarly, critics of psychoanalysis have levelled charges of dogmatism, orthodoxy, and inflexibility against analytic theory. While every branch of science has its fanatic adherents to the status quo, evidence exists that the system is responsive to new discoveries and modifications at every level of its structure. Gill (1959) particularly addressed himself to this problem in a recent paper and has cogently documented the shift in the past two to three decades from an id psychology to an ego psychology: a greater concern for overt behavior as opposed to an exclusive preoccupation with depth psychology, a shift in emphasis from primary to secondary process thinking, and an increased attention to environmental factors as opposed to the purely internal psychological processes. These developments have been reflected in the inclusion of the "adaptive point of view" as a major rubric of psychoanalytic assumptions.

*Marx, M. H. (Ed.) *Theories in Contemporary Psychology.* The MacMillan Co., N.Y. 1963.

One of the safeguards against a self-contained and sterile system is its openness to a broad range of psychological phenomena. Insofar as its main observational base had been the psychoanalytic treatment situation, psychoanalytic theory has tended to emphasize the intrapsychic, the irrational, and the pathological. To some extent the danger of excluding from its range of study certain phenomena, particularly conflict-free functioning, remains a hazard. At the same time psychoanalysis, in contrast to many of the other systems of psychology, significantly includes within its sphere a wide array of human behavior ranging from experimental observations of the laboratory to naturalistic, cross-cultural studies.

SPECIAL PROBLEMS OF THEORY CONSTRUCTION IN PSYCHOANALYSIS

Before delving into the particular methods of research in psychoanalysis and the issues associated with them, we would do well to examine some of the special problems with which a theory of human behavior is confronted. The complexity and variability of the human organism, plus the uniqueness found in every individual, presents the behavioral scientist with problems which the physical scientist need never consider.

The problem of exercising adequate controls, particularly with regard to matching subjects, is enormously difficult and may only be solved by some method of approximation. This is particularly true when the researcher is investigating the larger, molar segments of behavior (like a patient's response to psychotherapy), as usually occurs in psychoanalytic studies. In attempting to match pairs of subjects for control purposes, the clinician is immediately struck by the lack of congruence between people. Despite similarities along many dimensions, the subtle uniqueness of every individual when studied as a unitary functioning organism makes it well nigh impossible to conceive of matching individuals over a broad spectrum of personality variables. A solution which is now being tried (Wallerstein, Robbins, et al., 1958) and which appears to be more satisfactory than matching pairs, but is far from being a final answer to this problem, is the use of the subject as his own control. As used in studies of psychotherapy, this method is based upon the assumption that the person, at least the adult patient, is unlikely to manifest substantial personality changes over a period of time and the changes which he shows during treatment will be the result of psychiatric intervention. While the assumption is far from correct and does not, for example, take into consideration the phenomenon of spontaneous remissions, it has enough of a core of validity to warrant application. This is particularly true when, as in certain studies (Wallerstein, Robbins, et al., 1958), an effort is made to assess the patient's life situation as a possible contributing factor to the change or lack of change in the patient.

Another complexity is the problem of the relationship between surface and depth, or between phenotype and genotype. Psychoanalytic constructs are such that there is a considerable distance between the levels of overt, observable behavior and its related intrapsychic variables. Basic clinical concepts like anxiety tolerance or ego strength are still vaguely defined in their own right and are weakly linked to behavioral phenomena. Also, identical-appearing surface behavior may be based upon widely different, or even opposite, motives. Generosity or altruism may be the result of a genuine, tender concern for another human being, or it may be a defense against less benevolent wishes. The necessity to see beyond, or behind, the superficial aspects of behavior impinges upon the whole problem of objectivity of observation. Academic psychologists have often recoiled from the highly speculative and inferential interpretations which the depth psychologist feels he must make. While no one can deny that psychoanalysts have often been guilty of "wild analysis" and an over-readiness to engage in unfettered intuitive guesses, neither can one assert that the solution to the problem is to restrict oneself to a narrow range of observational data for the sake of exactness and objectivity. In a very significant contribution to the methodology of psychoanalytic research, Sargent (1961) has proposed that clinical judgments by well-trained observers be used as the primary data of clinical research. Elaborating a basic postulate of a long-term research project on psychotherapy at The Menninger Foundation, she suggested that objectivity be attained by intersubjective agreement among judges rather than at the level of the behavioral data themselves.

Another complicating feature of behavioral research is found in an underlying principle of psychoanalytic theory, e.g., multiple determination. Based upon the observation that human behavior is complexly determined and emerges as a final common pathway for multiple impulses and defenses, this state of affairs enormously complicates psychoanalytic research methodology as compared with the physical sciences. The classical experimental situation in which everything is held constant except for the single experimental variable is a model which is usually inapplicable to behavioral research. Escalona (1950) has described the futility of studying the effects of breast feeding versus cup feeding, for example, in a research which assumes everything else is equal. The context in which the feeding occurs, particularly the mother-child relationship, is an integral part of the hypotheses regarding oral gratification and frustration and therefore must be studied concomitantly in any investigation of infant feeding. This kind of failure to recognize the complexity of psychoanalytic theory on the part of many experimental psychologists attempting to evaluate the validity of its hypotheses is what has contributed to the jaundiced eye which many clinicians cast upon experimental approaches to psychoanalysis.

Over-determination also leads to major problems in evaluating the relative weights of the multiple factors leading to a given behavior at any given time. The same act may be determined by a combination of A, B, C, and D, and may look superficially the same when A is the dominant factor and when D is the dominant factor. Not only are identical overt behaviors produced by a variety of different motives, but the configuration of motive and defense within the same individual leading to identical behaviors may vary from time to time. This phenomenon is a commonplace observation in the analytic situation. The appearance of a given symptom, although determined by several factors, can best be understood in terms of a shifting hierarchy of causes: now it may be understood in terms of a resurgence of oral conflicts, and later it may result primarily from a struggle with hostile impulses.

We have mentioned some of the major problems with which psychoanalysis must cope in attempting to devise more adequate methods of research. Related problems, like the difficulties inherent in being both a participant and observer in certain kinds of research enterprises, will be discussed at greater length below. Suffice it to say that the complexity of the subject matter of psychoanalysis has made the diagnosis of difficulties easier than the prescription of solutions.

The Psychoanalytic Interview
as a Research Method

Freud believed that the major tool of psychoanalytic research was the interview method and, more particularly, the procedure of free association by a patient upon a couch. His tremendous discoveries, almost exclusively based upon the case study method, have set a model of "research" in psychoanalysis which continues to this day. Only in recent years have any notable attempts been made to broaden the base of psychoanalytic study to include a variety of controlled observational methods as well as laboratory experimentation. Benjamin (1950) has expressed the opinion that the psychoanalytic interview is still "our most powerful weapon of psychological research" but is not capable alone of solving, for example, the problems of the differential etiology of personality development. His own intensive long-range studies of personality development in children is a model of psychoanalytic research which is not confined simply to the analytic interview. As will be shown later, a number of controlled experimental studies have been undertaken in recent years in the attempt to validate and extend psychoanalytic theory.

Before discussing the issues raised by the use of the psychoanalytic interview as a research method, we would do well to consider the importance of accumulating simple facts and observations about human behavior which pertain to psychoanalytic hypotheses. Psychoanalysis has emphasized the importance of the experiences and modes of thinking which occur in childhood. Only since the recent "cultural revolution" induced by psychoanalysis have we become aware of the importance of creating an atmosphere of freedom from shame and embarrassment as a way of eliciting from children the wishes and fears which constitute an important fabric of the human personality. The rich nuggets of information that can be easily elicited from children contain material about personality functioning which can be understood with a minimum of interpretation and which do not seem to the analysts to require elaborate confirmation. The observations of Piaget (1929) and the writings of Werner (1957) are filled with data concerning primary process modes of thinking which need to be extended rather than merely confirmed. Kubie (1952) has argued against the uselessness of making "pallid facsimiles in the laboratory of the data which are already manifest in nature, merely to get around the human reluctance to look human nature in the eye."

Although the psychoanalytic situation alone is not a suitable vehicle with which to test theory, it has no peer in uncovering many important facets of personality functioning. We shall be dealing here, however, with the phase of verification, as well as the phase of discovery in scientific research. The psychoanalytic situation obviously is a locus par excellence for the generation of hypotheses. But less obvious is the extent to which this method can be used in the process of confirming or disconfirming theory.

The psychoanalytic situation has certain unique characteristics in contributing to our understanding of the intrapsychic mental life of the patient. We are enabled to observe, or at least infer, the dominant unconscious motivations and defenses which the person is forced to conceal, under other circumstances, both from himself and from others. If one accepts the existence and the importance of unconscious motivation in shaping human behavior, one is hard put to find a situation which is comparable to this one for the investigation of the relationships between the conscious and unconscious life of the individual. Thus, all of the hypotheses concerning the arousal of anxiety as a function of a breakdown of repression, the heightening of defensive and adaptive efforts in dealing with increments of anxiety, and other phenomena which are dependent upon the understanding of intrapsychic functions are relatively inaccessible to us without this kind of investigation in depth.

One objection frequently raised about the use of this method is the fact that the data with which we are presented are derived from pathological states. But experience with patients suffering from psychic distress has explained the apparent paradox of attempting to understand the human personality through the use of a relatively restricted sample of subjects. Only under the pressure of considerable discomfort and the hope of finding relief is a person willing to undergo the painful process of attempting to uncover thoughts and feelings which ordinarily remain inaccessible. Furthermore, the fact is now accepted fairly widely that the principles of personality functioning are broadly applicable across the whole spectrum of human behavior, normal as well as abnormal. Particularly with the advent of psychoanalytic ego psychology with its emphasis upon conflictfree spheres of functioning and of adaptive processes which are relatively autonomous from drives and instincts, psychoanalysis has increasingly been moving in the direction of becoming a general psychology as opposed merely to being a special theory of psychopathology or of therapy (Hartmann, 1958).

But despite the potential value of findings in the psychoanalytic situation and its broad applicability, a researcher using this method is confronted with serious methodological problems which may be summarized under the heading of the participant-observer. On the one hand, we are unable to gather certain essential information except via psychoanalytic therapy, and on the other hand, inevitable distortions occur by virtue of the fact that the analyst-researcher is combining several functions at once: he is attempting to observe and record the patient's behavior; he is attempting to evaluate his own reaction to the patient; and he must act in order to induce change in the person who has come for help (Kris, 1951). The therapist's observations are affected and distorted by his own involvement in the process of attempting to induce change, and the patient's productions are inevitably biased by the therapist's interventions and suggestions, however minimal.

These are serious obstacles to research efforts using such a tool. Is it necessary to discard the method, despite its uniquely fruitful data, because of its inherent sources of error, contamination, and subjectivity? The reluctance of psychologists to attempt controlled studies within the context of the psychoanalytic situation has resulted in protests by psychoanalysts and others that proofs are demanded of them by persons who refuse to use their instruments.[2] Kubie (1952) has likened this attitude to the objections in Leeuwenhoek's day to his findings while at the same time refusing to look through his microscope. A similar point was made by Ruth Tolman (1953, p. 276), who reported the reaction of a prominent physicist to the demand for independent confirmation of psychoanalytic findings.

> Does anyone not trained in experimental physics ever say to Carl Anderson: "Look, I will not believe there is such a thing as a positron unless I can discover it for myself by some other independent method"? . . . In any other science, no one expects to step in without training in the specific method and verify or refute a finding.

It is generally agreed that the analyst is not able to be both researcher and therapist at the same time without distorting each function. The reconciliation has been suggested by Shakow (1960). The pitfalls of subjectivity and conflict of interest can be avoided by 1) divorcing the therapist from any but the purely therapeutic function, the research duties falling upon others, 2) having data collection depend primarily upon recorded psychoanalytic interviews, preferably motion pictures, and 3) getting additional pertinent data regarding the therapist's reactions to the patient in post-session reactions.

This point of view is obviously a shift from the notion, held by some, that every analyst is performing a "research study" upon each case he treats. The contention is that controls are introduced by means of the minimal participation of the analyst and by the therapeutic method of maintaining the analytic incognito. Furthermore, this view holds that the therapist is able to test his hypothesis via the patient's reactions to the analyst's interpretations. The now famous Cordelia story (Frenkel-Brunswik, 1940) is often quoted to illustrate the manner in which an interpretation leads to a recovery of a buried memory and to the confirmation of an analytic hypothesis concerning a daughter's relationship to her father. Such incidents, however convincing to the practitioner, lack the controls necessary for scientific confirmation or disconfirmation. The systematic investigation of hypotheses requires greater objectivity than can be attained in the consulting room, and repetitions of such testing under comparable circumstances is necessary to raise the level of probability of the proposition. Without the introduction of the kind of controls suggested by Shakow, the analytic situation is of only limited value for hypothesis-testing.

2. It is true, of course, that analysts have been guilty of the converse attitude. On the grounds that research into their methods by a third party would interfere with the therapeutic process, many analysts have objected to the study of their work.

A further difficulty, not confined to the interview method but highlighted in this context, is the dearth of canons of interpretation of clinical observations. No definite rules for the inference process have been established. The analyst must call upon his theoretical understanding, his empathy, his clinical acumen, and his observational skills to interpret the significance of a given piece of behavior, to translate the covert or unconscious meanings. This process is obviously fraught with possibilities for error and subjectivity, part of which the analyst has conceptualized as "countertransference." This problem harks back to the dilemma of the objective molecular observation versus the more adequate molar observation which is also more subjective. Until a more adequate method has been devised, control by means of intersubjective agreement among trained observers must be the solution to the dilemma. Obviously, this method does not solve the problem of smuggling in the confirmation of the theory by means of the interpretation. If the interpretation is based upon a working theory, whether or not used by more than one judge, the danger of circularity is a distinct possibility. This danger is particularly great when validation is attempted by persons who are trained within a given frame of reference and are affectively disposed toward finding confirmation. Ideally, the investigator should have no personal commitment to validate or invalidate the propositions under study.

EXPERIMENTAL APPROACHES

Despite the fact that the psychoanalytic interview provides a unique situation for the study of the relationship between conscious and unconscious phenomena, and despite the controls which may be applied in such a study, this method cannot be relied upon exclusively for either the discovery or testing of propositions. A major set of hypotheses in analytic theory concerns psychosexual development during the first few years of life. These findings were mainly inferred from the productions of adults in treatment and obviously must be investigated more directly in longitudinal and cross-sectional studies of children. While much important information can be gained from the patient's reconstructions in treatment concerning his early experiences, we can only know the patient's psychic reality, not the actual situation. The checking of hypotheses regarding parent-child relationships should ideally be done by direct observations of such situations.

In addition to the incomplete base of observations provided by the psychoanalytic situation is a need for the control and manipulation of experimental variables which is not possible in the analytic setting. Recent studies on dream deprivation (Fisher and Dement, 1961), by means of interruption of sleep when the subject begins to dream or by drugs to inhibit dreaming, have been used to explore the adaptive function of dreaming. The McGill studies of sensory deprivation have contributed to a generalization concerning the need for sensory input as a means of maintaining adequate autonomy of reality testing and other executive functions of the ego (Rapaport, 1958). Hilgard (1952) has suggested that projective instruments enable the experimenter to test psychoanalytic hypotheses more adequately than does the therapeutic situation because of the use of standard stimuli in contrast to the more uncontrolled situation in relationship to the analyst.

The relative lack of interest of psychoanalysts in experimental approaches may be understood in terms of several factors. First, many of the experimental efforts have consisted only of attempts to establish the existence of well-known and widely accepted clinical phenomena. It is of no interest to the clinician to learn that the mechanism of repression exists. But it is very much to the heart of the matter to learn more about its operation, why certain individuals use it more heavily than others, its relationship to other defenses, and a host of other questions. The lack of fertility of most experimental attempts, observed by analyst and experimentalist alike (Kubie, 1952; Hilgard, 1952), has served as a deterrent to extensive experimentation.

Even more discouraging to the analyst have been the studies which have shown a remarkable neglect of the actual content of the theory. Propositions have been ripped out of context and translated into naively over-simplified experimental tests. The series of studies on the recall of pleasant and unpleasant words are an instance of this abuse. Some experimentalists have innocently believed that their finding of the superior recall of words like "sugar" over "quinine" test the psychoanalytic hypothesis concerning the repression of unacceptable impulses. There is no substitute for the thorough understanding of psychoanalytic concepts in any effort to study them experimentally.

But even given a mastery of the theory and a sophistication about the pertinent problems needing investigation, the experimentalist must steer an uneasy course between oversimplification and unwieldy complexity. It is now well accepted that the traditional method of manipulating one independent variable while observing its effect upon another (dependent) variable and keeping all other conditions constant is not suitable to psychoanalytic investigation. Rather, it is usually necessary to observe and manipulate a number of pertinent variables at both ends of the observational base. Any study which arbitrarily focuses upon a single set of independent and dependent variables while arbitrarily neglecting other factors known to be important is fated to be unproductive. The studies on subception which originally related only the factors of traumatic content and perceptual threshold failed to yield consistent results because of their neglect of the factor of individual differences in dealing with stressful material. When the experimenters began to introduce the additional variable of characterological differences and separated the "sensitizers," who tend to become hyper-alert in the presence of danger, from the repressers, who tend to blind themselves to danger, the results began to fit with the predictions (Stein, 1953).

This is not to say, of course, that every study requires the consideration of the total and infinite complexity of all possible factors in order to do justice to the phenomenon. Naturally one must ignore or neglect certain variables in order to focus upon others. There appear to be no definite rules of procedure for the optimal restriction or inclusion of pertinent variables. As Benjamin (1959) has pointed out, the hallmark of the gifted researcher is to know which factors can be excluded, or set aside temporarily, while other factors are being investigated. He suggests that a rule of thumb might be that "formulations which ignore parameters known to be relevant are oversimplified" (p. 72).

One method of avoiding the exclusion of pertinent variables is to engage in naturalistic studies where the phenomenon being investigated is not experimentally manipulated. Controls are imposed by means of the conceptualization and study of the pertinent variables. This is the major method used in such fields as astronomy and geology, where the "laboratory" is generally some part of the natural world. As a result of catastrophe, war, or other crises, situations have arisen which provide excellent bases for the study of variables which could not have been studied otherwise, primarily because humane considerations would have precluded the experimental induction of such changes. The best-known of these are the now-classic investigations by Spitz (1945) on hospitalism in infants raised in orphanages and by A. Freud and Burlingham (1944) on children separated from their families during the bombings in Britain. The "controls" introduced into these studies depended upon the kinds of variables the investigator deemed important: the length of separation from the natural mother, the age at which a stable figure becomes essential, the effect of changes in mother surrogates, as well as the variety of behavioral deviations which result from these situations.

Projective techniques also offer opportunities for controlled observation which at the same time do not excessively narrow the field of study. On the one hand, a standard stimulus is presented to the subject, and his responses are recorded verbatim. On the other hand, a broad spectrum of responses is possible, which enables the subject to reveal behavioral reactions from the points of view both of surface and depth. As in the use of the psychoanalytic interview, the controls over subjectivity of interpretation must be introduced at some point, and the use of independent judges or some other control is necessary. The use of projective testing has been fruitful, for example, in Holt's (1956) studies of the primary process as it relates to individual differences in reacting to altered states of consciousness.

The applicability of animal studies to psychoanalytic propositions appear to be at best somewhat limited. Benjamin (1950) holds that the sole contribution of such experiments has been their confirmatory effect of fairly well-accepted hypotheses, such as the importance of crucial early life experiences or the effect of oral deprivation upon later behavior. Recent studies by Harlow (1958), however, on cloth-and-wire mother surrogates may prove to be valuable in elucidating the major variables leading to normal sexual and maternal behavior. Despite the advantages afforded by the control and manipulation of the environment which is possible among animal subjects, the major shortcoming such studies have in relation to humans is the absence of language and verbal behavior, a crucial determinant in human development.

THE PREDICTION METHOD

One of the most promising methods of analytic research, be it used in psychoanalytic therapy or on other kinds of observational data, is that of predicting future developments on the basis of analytic theory. During the past decade several studies have been reported in which the prediction method is the major approach to validating and extending the theory. This is in contrast to Freud's method, which was essentially post-dictive (Rapaport, 1959). In the course of his investigations in depth on an individual case or a series of cases, Freud reconstructed the genesis of personality development and set forth certain generalizations about crucial life experiences which molded the person. Philosophical support for this position is supplied by the contention that satisfactory explanations of the past are possible even when prediction of the future is not possible. Scriven (1959) points to Darwin's theory of the survival of the fittest, which has very weak predictive value but which is a potent explanatory principle. Rapaport (1959) asserts that post-diction is theoretically as valid as prediction, provided care is taken not to invoke *ex post facto* explanation.

But we should mention that post-dictive explanation does not have the explanatory power of a prediction, which must be based upon a universal law in which both necessary and sufficient conditions are elucidated. Although the theory of evolution is not readily subject to test by prediction, psychoanalytic theory should be. Psychoanalytic phenomena only encompass some portion of an individual's life span, in contrast to hypotheses about eons of time such as occur in evolution. Also, the post-dictive method appears to be useful in the early phases of science and is appropriate to the process of formulating hypotheses, as Freud did. The validation of propositions, however, is more effectively done through efforts to forecast future developments than by explaining past events.

The primary method still being used in psychoanalytic study is that of post-diction. Psychoanalytic literature abounds in detailed case studies in which, following Freud, hypotheses are formulated after a patient has been studied intensively by the analyst. Several reasons may be at the basis of the reluctance of analytic researchers to use the more stringent method of prediction. One of these is the difficulty of formulating predictions about situations in which a variety of unforeseeable events or situations, not within the realm of what is being predicted but capable of affecting the outcome, have to be considered. The vicissitudes of life circumstances which impinge upon the person, including the birth of a sibling, the death of a parent, a divorce—all constitute potential environmental changes which are often unforeseeable and could alter the expected course of events in a person's life. Benjamin (1959) has attempted to deal with these contingencies by formulating his predictions concerning personality development in children to include at least some of these events, although obviously it is impossible to predict for the infinite variety of important life circumstances. They are special contingency predictions, and they have the form of "if this, then that."

The predictive method is also faced with the problem of the relative immaturity and incompleteness of the theory. Psychoanalysis has formulated a number of necessary conditions for the development of certain behaviors but has not begun to approach a delineation of sufficient conditions. Benjamin (1950) suggests that the discovery of sufficient conditions may be a "possibly unattainable ideal." We know, for example, that personality variables like anxiety tolerance, impulse control, capacity for the development of a transference neurosis, and freedom from strong regressive trends contribute to a prediction concerning successful resolution of intrapsychic conflict in a psychoanalytic procedure. But no one claims that these personality factors constitute all of the pertinent variables. Similarly, M. Kris (1957) has pointed out that our knowledge and competence in certain areas are still quite deficient, as demonstrated by the Yale longitudinal studies of child development. Their predictions were fairly accurate in designating areas of difficulty for the developing child, but they were not nearly as successful in designating the particular form or manifestation of the difficulty. Similarly, they were much better at predicting the occurrence of pathology than conflict-free functioning and the use of normal defenses. But these deficiencies in our understanding should not be a deterrent to prediction studies. Predictions not only test theory but have a heuristic value as well. Whether or not psychoanalysis will ever arrive at a formulation of sufficient causes, the prediction method undoubtedly is capable of helping to validate, refine, and extend its present causal explanations. Increasing efforts to use and perfect this method in a variety of contexts, mainly in research upon psychotherapy and upon longitudinal studies of children, is one of the brighter lights in the horizon of research in psychoanalysis.

Perhaps the main source of reluctance to engage in prediction studies has been what Rapaport (1959) refers to as the lack of "critical tests" in psychoanalysis. This is also the major criticism that has been leveled against psychoanalysis in discussions of its scientific status. Proponents of psychoanalysis say that it is not possible to formulate a clear-cut set of alternatives one of which would eventuate from one theoretical formulation and another tending to confirm an alternative and mutually exclusive postulate. This apparent lack of alternative hypotheses to explain the same observations is based upon two different factors. First, no alternative theory, or set of theories, attempts to deal comprehensively with the scope of human behavior in the way that psychoanalysis does. The Neo-Freudian theories do not appear to constitute definite alternatives; rather they constitute changes in emphasis, such as the Sullivanian focusing upon interpersonal relations rather than intrapsychic conflict. These conceptions are gradually being incorporated into the mainstream of analytic theory, particularly through the work of Erikson (Rapaport, 1959). Learning theory has not actually joined the issue with psychoanalytic theory, partly because psychoanalysis itself lacks an explicit theory of learning.[3] One is tempted to add that the dearth of alternative theories is probably the basis for the feeling of clinicians, more implicit than explicit, that psychoanalysis is not the best theory of human behavior; it is the *only* theory.

The second aspect of the problem of no critical tests being available refers more to the nature of the theory itself. The theory contains propositions which embrace a wide range of alternative possibilities, any one of which may emerge and yet be compatible with the theory.

---

3. Rapaport (1959) believes that the scientific struggles will eventually occur in this arena, and not around the psychoanalytic theories of motivation which are its present core.

This point is made, for example, in relation to the use of reaction formation to explain the appearance of one form of behavior or its opposite. Thus, psychoanalysts claim that the presence of marked anal conflicts may lead either to stinginess or to extravagance. The analyst is often unable to predict the form of the behavior, since the final emergence of the instinctual derivatives is extremely complex. Hence the reliance upon post-dictive explanation. Such a state of affairs is naturally the bane of the experimentalist, who not only fails to see operational definitions but is confronted with propositions which appear to be disconfirmable. Although there may be shifting fashions of scientific canons, the one requirement of a scientific proposition which is not likely to be altered is that the generalization be subject, now or in the future, to empirical test (Richfield, 1954).

It is surprising, therefore, that a leading psychoanalytic methodologist like Rapaport (1959, p. 120) should have expressed pessimism about ever being able to confirm the special (clinical) theory of psychoanalysis via prediction and even wondered about confirmation of the general (psychological) theory of psychoanalysis:

> Clinical predictions are always fraught with the fact that all motivations have multiple, equivalent means and goals. Thus, such predictions usually cannot specify which of these alternatives are to be expected and therefore, the results of experimental tests on predictions must first be interpreted before their bearing on the theory can be established.

This pessimism does not appear to be entirely justified. In the first place, even a prediction about areas of difficulty or change, provided the area is specified, is a legitimate prediction, though perhaps not the most satisfactory. Predictions made in the Psychotherapy Research Project of The Menninger Foundation (Wallerstein, Robbins, et al., 1956), for example, range all the way from highly specific behavioral outcomes (the patient will not return to the family business) to very non-specific changes (the patient will show increased impulse control) requiring clinical judgment and interpretation to confirm. The latter prediction is similar in some respects to a prediction stating that the person will evidence difficulties in managing anal conflicts. Such predictions pose methodological problems in confirmation but are not devoid of important content which bears on the theory.

Furthermore, there is no *a priori* reason to assume that simply because psychoanalytic predictions so far have not been able to attain the highest possible level of specificity, they will not be able to do so in the future. Of course, we may have to settle ultimately for a more general, rather than a more specific, prediction, because we never derive the sufficient, as well as necessary, causes of behavior. This point of view has been expressed by those who describe certain parts of psychoanalysis as only capable of formulating "tendency statements" (Farrell, 1961). These are statements which are neither universal nor statistical in character and therefore are incapable of being verified or, at best, are capable of only partial verification. To predict that a person will show a tendency toward stinginess, for example, means that such behavior will occur only under certain conditions which may not be entirely specified. But such statements appear to be a reflection of our *current* inability to specify the circumstances of the appearance of this behavior. Such a prediction is not worthless, although it has a limited value in attempting to prognosticate for specific instances. Similarly, whether stinginess or its opposite or both in alternation will appear may not always be possible to predict. But these approximations toward increased specificity are signs of an immature science and do not necessarily mean that critical tests will never be possible. Frenkel-Brunswik (1954) has demonstrated experimentally that the same genotype may give rise to behaviors that are often in opposition to each other. Thus, irritability and exuberance were correlated negatively with each other, but both were correlated with a drive for aggression. The intervening factors giving rise to one manifestation as opposed to the other still remains as a problem for study in order to increase predictive power.

Despite these barriers to prediction studies, they are gaining in popularity and in refinement. One reason for this development is the relatively simple but cogent observation that all clinical work actually involves prediction, implicit or explicit (Sargent, 1961; Kris, 1957). When we say that a patient is suffering from an anaclitic depression, we are in effect predicting that he should respond favorably to treatment in which his dependency needs find gratification. The decision of the therapist to emphasize supportive rather than expressive techniques is based upon the prediction that the patient will react to such treatment with more effective and adaptive behavior in his environment. The treatment situation, long the subject of post-dictive study, is now becoming the locus of predictive studies. Bellak and Smith (1956) have reported a carefully controlled study of short-term predictions concerning the expected developments in the analytic treatment of patients whose preceding hours had been carefully studied by a group of analyst-predictors who were not themselves treating the patient. Robbins and Wallerstein (1956, 1958, 1960) have initiated a long-range study of both process and outcome in which a major method is the formulation of predictions prior to beginning treatment. A key feature of this investigation is the formulation of the theoretical assumptive base for each prediction in an effort to validate and extend psychoanalytic theory.

SUMMARY AND CONCLUSIONS

1. The trend in both philosophy of science and in academic psychology has been towards a de-emphasis upon strict operationism. Philosophers now regard radical operationism as excessively restricting to creative scientific work and stress the importance of hypothetical constructs in any growing science. Similarly, psychologists are beginning to adopt the point of view that the adequate definition of many psychological concepts can only be approached gradually by a system of successive approximations (construct validity).

2. Recent efforts to systematize psychoanalytic theory suggest that it may be formulated as a hypothetico-deductive system. The "metapsychological" rubrics embrace the higher order assumptions which subsume, in decreasing hierarchical order, the general psychoanalytic propositions, special psychoanalytic propositions, and empirical propositions.

3. The major unsolved problems in theory validation consist of the difficulty in matching subjects over a broad range of personality variables, the distance between the intrapsychic variable and its behavioral manifestations, and the fact that multiply-patterned factors usually underlie a given behavior.

4. The psychoanalytic interview is still the major, but not the only, observational method in psychoanalysis. While invaluable in hypothesis-finding, it can be used for hypothesis-testing only insofar as the therapeutic and research functions are carefully separated from each other.

5. For purposes of broadening the base of psychoanalytic observations and in the interest of increased control and manipulation of variables, controlled experimentation is necessary. The major pitfall in this approach has been the danger of oversimplification of complex theoretical constructs.

6. The traditional methodological approach in psychoanalysis has been that of post-diction, formulating explanations and theoretical constructs after the observations have been collected. An increasing number of psychoanalytic studies based upon a prediction method are now appearing, and these should eventually answer the question whether sufficient, as well as necessary, causes for behavior will ultimately be discovered. The lack of "critical tests" in psychoanalysis is seen as a problem relating both to a dearth of rival theories and to the

lack of specificity in the propositions themselves, perhaps related to the immaturity of the science.

REFERENCES

BARRON, F. An ego-strength scale which predicts response to psychotherapy. *J. Cons. Psychol.*, 1953, *17*, 327-333.

BELLAK, L., and SMITH, M. B. An experimental exploration of the psychoanalytic process. *Psychoanal. Quart.*, 1956, *25*, 385-414.

BENJAMIN, JOHN. Methodological considerations in the validation and elaboration of psychoanalytic personality theory. *Amer. J. Ortho.*, 1950, *20*, 139-156.

———— Prediction and psychopathological theory. In L. Jessner and E. Pavenstedt (eds.), *Dynamic psychopathology in childhood*. New York: Grune and Stratton, 1959.

CRONBACH, L. J., and MEEHL, P. E. Construct validity in psychological tests. *Psychol. Bull.*, 1955, *52*, 281-302.

ESCALONA, S. K. (Roundtable 1949). Approaches to a dynamic theory of development. III. Discussion. *Amer. J. Orthopsychiat.*, 1950, *20*, 157-160.

———— Problems of psychoanalytic research. *Int. J. Psa.*, 1952, *33*, 11-21.

EZRIEL, H. The scientific testing of psychoanalytic findings and theory. *Brit. J. Med. Psychol.*, 1951, *24*, 30-34.

FARRELL, B. A. Symposium of psychoanalysis and validation. II. On the character of psychodynamic discourse. *Brit. J. Med. Psychol.*, 1961, *34*, 7-13.

FISHER, C., and DEMENT, W. C. Dreaming and psychosis. Unpublished paper, 1961.

FEIGL, H. Some major issues and developments in the philosophy of science and logical empiricism. In Feigl, H., and Scriven, M. (eds.), *The foundation of science and the concepts of psychology and psychoanalysis*, Vol. I. Minneapolis: University of Minnesota Press, 1956.

FRENKEL-BRUNSWIK, E. Psychoanalysis and personality research. *J. Abnorm. Soc. Psychol.*, 1940, *35*, 176-197.

———— Motivation and behavior. *Genetic Psychology Monograph*. 1942.

———— Psychoanalysis and the unity of science. *Proceedings, Amer. Acad. of Arts and Sci.*, 1954, *80*, 271-350.

FREUD, A., and BURLINGHAM, D. *Infants without families*. New York: International Universities Press, 1944.

GILL, M. M. The present state of psychoanalytic theory. *J. Abnorm. Soc. Psychol.*, 1959, *58*, 1-8.

HARLOW, H. F. The nature of love. *Amer. Psychologist*, 1958, *13*, 673-685.

HARTMANN, H. *Ego psychology and the problem of adaptation.* New York: International Universities Press, 1958.

HEMPEL, C. G. Fundamentals of concept formation in empirical science. *Intern. Encycl. Unified Sci.*, Vol. II, No. 7. Chicagó: Univ. of Chicago Press, 1952.

HILGARD, E. Experimental approaches to psychoanalysis. In E. Pumpian-Mindlin (ed.), *Psychoanalysis as science.* Stanford, Calif.: Stanford Univ. Press, 1952.

HOLT, R. R. Gauging primary and secondary processes in Rorschach responses. *J. Proj. Tech.*, 1956, *20*, 14-25.

KARUSH, A., et al. The evaluation of ego strength: a scale of adaptive balance. Unpublished paper, 1962.

KRIS, E. Psychoanalytic propositions. In Marx, M. H. (ed.), *Psychological theory.* New York: Macmillan, 1951.

KRIS, M. The use of prediction in a longitudinal study. *Psa. Study of the Child*, 1957, *12*, 175-189.

KUBIE, L. S. Problems and techniques in psychoanalytic validation and progress. In E. Pumpian-Mindlin (ed.), *Psychoanalysis as science.* Stanford, Calif.: Stanford Univ. Press, 1952.

MURPHY, G. The current impact of Freud upon psychology. *Amer. Psychologist*, 1956, *11*, 663-672.

PIAGET, J. *The child's conception of the world.* New York: Harcourt, Brace, 1929.

RAPAPORT, D. The theory of ego autonomy: a generalization. *Bull. Menninger Clin.*, 1958, *22*, 13-35.

——— The structure of psychoanalytic theory: a systematizing attempt. *Psychological Issues*, 1960, No. 6.

RAPAPORT, D., and GILL, M. M. The points of view and assumptions of metapsychology. *Int. J. Psychoanal.*, 1959, *40*, 153-162.

RICHFIELD, J. On the scientific status of psychoanalysis. *Sci. Mon.*, 1954, *79*, 306-309.

SARGENT, H. D. Intrapsychic change: methodological problems in psychotherapy research. *Psychiatry*, 1961, *24*, 93-108.

SCRIVEN, M. A study of radical behaviorism. In H. Feigl and M. Scriven (eds.), *The foundations of science and the concepts of psychology and psychoanalysis*, Vol. I. Minneapolis: Univ. of Minnesota Press, 1956.

——— Explanation and prediction in evolutionary theory. *Science*, 1959, *130*, 577-582.

SEARS, R. R. *Survey of objective studies of psychoanalytic concepts.* New York: Social Science Research Council, Bulletin No. 51, 1943.

SHAKOW, D. The recorded psychoanalytic interview as an objective approach to research in psychoanalysis. *Psa. Quart.,* 1960, *29,* 82–97.

SPITZ, R. A. Hospitalism. *Psa. Study of the Child,* 1945, *1,* 53–74.

STEIN, K. B. Perceptual defense and perceptual sensitization under neutral and involved conditions. *J. Pers.,* 1953, *21,* 467–478.

TOLMAN, RUTH S. Virtue rewarded and vice punished. *Amer. Psychologist,* 1953, *8,* 721–733.

WALLERSTEIN, R. S., ROBBINS, L. L., et al. The psychotherapy research project of the Menninger foundation. *Bull. Menninger Clin.,* 1956, *20,* 221–276.

_____ The psychotherapy research project of the Menninger foundation: 2nd report. *Bull. Menninger Clin.,* 1958, *22,* 115–166.

_____ The psychotherapy research project of the Menninger foundation: 3rd report. *Bull. Menninger Clin.,* 1960, *24,* 157–216.

WERNER, H. *Comparative psychology of mental development* (3rd ed.). New York: International Universities Press, 1957.

WHITE, R. W. Motivation reconsidered: the concept of competence. *Psychol. Rev.,* 1959, 297–333.

10

The Validation of Psychoanalytic Interpretations and Theories*

Robert Waelder

THE NEED FOR VALIDATION

The question of validation of psychoanalytic results has often been raised—more often by critics of psychoanalysis than by psychoanalysts themselves. As usual, there is a great variety of opinions. Some are satisfied with the validity of psychoanalytic interpretations as made by well-trained and experienced analysts and hence with the validity of the theory which is based on them, and do not see any need for further proof. Others wish interpretations to be subject to more controls within the analytic procedure while rejecting extra-analytic means of verification. Others, for the most part not analysts, request nonanalytic forms of verification as prerequisite to their consideration of analytic claims.

There is also a wide spectrum of opinion regarding the degree of exactitude that is requested. Some merely present their results as projects of analytic study, often without clearly distinguishing between the raw material of observation and its interpretation, and without stating the

*Reprinted from *Basic Theory of Psychoanalysis*, by Robert Waelder, by permission of International Universities Press, Inc. Copyright © 1960 by International Universities Press, Inc.

criteria according to which the latter follow from the former. In extreme instances, free rein is given to speculation. On the other end of the spectrum are those, mostly people without passive or active analytic experience of their own, who request for every interpretation or proposition the kind of evidence we expect in the physical or chemical laboratory, i.e., evidence sufficiently conclusive to eliminate every possibility of doubt. With such requirements, of course, nobody could ever claim to be his father's issue, and it would need generations of work and millions of expenditure to establish with this degree of exactitude even the most trivial psychological proposition.

The student of animal behavior, Konrad Z. Lorenz, pointed out that certain features known to the field observers are very difficult to reproduce in the laboratory under controlled conditions:

> "Should these experiments seem incredible to the animal psychologist who works in the laboratory, he must consider the fact that the experimental animal in a confined space has fewer experiences which he can differentiate qualitatively than does the dog which is always free to accompany his master . . . Every dog owner is familiar with a certain behavior in dogs which can never be produced under laboratory conditions . . . Imagine what complicated experimental method and how tiresome a training would be necessary to achieve an analogous result under artificial conditions in the laboratory" (Lorenz, 1954, p. 135 f.).

Somewhere between uncritical speculation and the insistence on an impossible mathematical certainty, we must look for the degree of certitude that we can at best expect to reach in these matters, a degree of certitude where interpretations and propositions can be established beyond reasonable, though not necessarily beyond all possible, doubt.

In the literature which deals with the problem of validation, one can distinguish between attempts to justify the validity of psychoanalytic interpretations, or to formulate rules which have to be observed so that such interpretations will be valid, on the one hand; and attempts to test psychoanalytic results by nonanalytic means, on the other. In the first group, Bleuler (1910) was an early contributor. In his defense of psychoanalysis, he emphasized the inner consistency of psychoanalytic interpretations: innumerable facts seem to fall in their place, and everything fits in, like in the solution of a picture puzzle. Bleuler pointed at the great improbability that all this should be due to mere coincidence, and he even tried to estimate the mathematical probabilities involved.

Bernfeld (1932, 1934) emphasized that psychoanalytic interpretations, as a rule, cannot be fully proved by induction, but he thought that under certain circumstances valid conclusions can be drawn from a single observation, and he looked toward Gestalt theory to provide the logical justification for such inferences. He referred to certain experiments in Gestalt theory in which a person is given a few words and has to find the story in which they occur (e.g.: cooking stove, kitchen cupboard, glass vials, chemicals, drawing board, inks, money bills, arrest). There is often *only one* plausible solution (as e.g., in this example: workshop for counterfeit money); only one has a "strong Gestalt." This reasoning is substantially identical with Bleuler's.

But on the other hand, Bernfeld was quite aware of the fact that the feeling of evidence by itself alone is not complete proof of correctness. He thought that if the whole clinical material were combed to extract all "invariants" from it, i.e., all features that occur as common denominators of a group of "associations," support or correction of individual interpretations could be found.

In my treatment of the subject (1936, Chapter II; 1939) I was guided by the consideration that inner consistency alone is not a sufficient criterion of correctness, because quite erroneous ideas, and indeed even paranoid ideas, can show a high degree of inner consistence; the whole web of interpretations must, at least in one place, be supported by independent evidence. I also tried to discuss the validity of psychoanalytic interpretation in the simple example of a neurotic symptom of a child caught *in statu nascendi* by the analyst-mother (1936, Chapter VI).

The present stage of the question of validation has been comprehensively surveyed by Kubie (1952). See also the report on a panel discussion at the American Psychoanalytic Association (Brosin, 1955) and the paper by Schmidl (1955) enlarging on Bernfeld's ideas.[1]

A Science of the Mind and of Human Destiny and the Exact Sciences

In recent years there have been instances in which representatives of the exact sciences showed themselves clearly aware of the fact that the exactitude of physics and chemistry and related sciences, which the so-called "behavioral sciences" lack, is due to certain favorable circumstances inherent in their subject matter rather than due to their supposedly greater maturity. The prominent mathematician, Warren Weaver, e.g., said in his Presidential Address at the American Association for the Advancement of Science:

> What made possible the great success that the physical sciences have experienced, particularly during the last century and a half? The

1. A Symposium on this subject, chaired by Sidney Hook, was published recently (1959) but appeared too late for discussion in these pages.

explanation appears actually to be rather simple. *Physical* nature, first of all, seems to be on the whole very *loosely coupled*. That is to say, excellently workable approximations result from studying physical nature bit by bit, two or three variables at a time, and treating these bits as isolated. Furthermore, a large number of the broadly applicable laws are, to useful approximation, *linear*, if not directly in the relevant variables, then in nothing worse than their second time derivatives. And finally, a large fraction of physical phenomena (meteorology is sometimes an important exception) exhibits stability; perturbations tend to fade out, and great consequences do not result from very small causes.

These three extremely convenient characteristics of physical nature bring it about that vast ranges of phenomena can be satisfactorily handled by linear algebraic or differential equations, often involving only one or two dependent variables; they also make the handling *safe* in the sense that small errors are unlikely to propagate, go wild and prove disastrous. Animate nature, on the other hand, presents highly complex and highly coupled systems—these are, in fact, dominant characteristics of what we call organisms. It takes a lot of variables to describe a man or, for that matter, a virus; and you cannot often usefully study these variables two at a time. Animate nature also exhibits very confusing instabilities, as students of history, of the stock market, or genetics are well aware [Weaver, 1955, p. 1256].

The phenomena which we study in psychoanalysis are certainly highly coupled. A middle-aged person may suffer from depressions. We may approach this study with ideas gained in prescientific experience, viz., the idea that depressions may hang together with severe frustrations and disappointments, and we may look for them in this person's life. There may be many—in his marriage and family life; disappointments with his children or with their attitude toward him; disappointment in extramarital love relationships; a decrease of sexual prowess or of attractiveness; illnesses or a general feeling of aging; disappointments in work, career, or social recognition; or financial worries. All this may be complicated by organic, perhaps involutionary, processes. Then there are the factors suggested by psychoanalytic theories that would have to be considered, such as, e.g., the loss of an object, abnormal forms of object relationships in terms of introjection and expulsion, loss of love from the superego, aggression turned against oneself, or a feeling of discouragement, fatigue, and defeat (See, among others, Freud, 1917; Abraham, 1924; Klein, 1935, 1940; E. Bibring, 1953). Several of these factors will probably be present in any one case, and many of them can be found in people of the same age group without depressions. In our search for the etiological importance of any one of these factors, or any other factor that may be suggested, we are not able to isolate it, while keeping all others unchanged, and so to study its consequences alone. We will always have many more unknowns than we have equations, so to say, so that no conclusion can be made without the exercise of judgment which may be considered arbitrary.

This factor makes for a very great difference between the physical sciences and such disciplines as psychoanalysis. I do not know whether the other two points which Professor Weaver has advanced as contributing to the privileged condition of the physical sciences—linear, or, in any case, simple laws, and relative stability—are quite as important under the circumstances. Stability is not a universal characteristic of the subject matter of the physical sciences, as Professor Weaver has noted himself. But it is true, in any case, that organic and psychic systems, or social systems, for that matter, show a great instability and that relatively small causes can have radical consequences. A small lesion in certain parts of the brain can completely incapacitate a person. Human behavior is largely the result of inner conflicts, and a small change in the relative strength of the competing forces may lead to an entirely different outcome, just as a shift of a small fraction of the vote can lead to a different outcome of an election—perhaps with great consequences.

Another prominent mathematician, Professor Weiner, also ascribes the enormous success of the natural sciences to peculiar circumstances; his point is different from Professor Weaver's, though not without relation to it.

All the great successes in precise science have been made in fields where there is a certain high degree of isolation of the phenomena from the observer. We have seen in the case of astronomy that this may result from the enormous scale of certain phenomena with respect to man, so that man's mightiest efforts, not to speak of his mere glance, cannot make the slightest visible impression on the celestial world. In modern atomic physics, on the other hand, the science of the unspeakably minute, it is true that anything we do will have an influence on many individual particles which is great *from the point of view of that particle*. However, we do not live on the scale of the particles concerned, either in space or in time, and the events that might be of the greatest significance from the point of view of an observer conforming to their scale of existence, appear to us—with some exceptions, it is true, as in the Wilson cloud chamber experiments—only as average mass effects in which enormous populations of particles cooperate. As far as these effects are concerned, the intervals of time concerned are large from the point of view of the individual particles and its motion, and our statistical theories have an admirably adequate basis. In short, we are too small to influence the stars in their courses, and too large to care about anything but the mass effects of the molecules, atoms and electrons. In both cases, we achieve a sufficiently loose coupling with

the phenomena we are studying to give a massive total account of this
coupling, although the coupling may not be loose enough for us to be
able to ignore it altogether [Wiener, 1948, p. 189 f.].

Professor Wiener emphasizes the change that the observer, by the
very fact of observing, works on his object, and sees science successful
either where this influence is negligible as in astronomy, or where we are
interested only in large aggregates. We are all aware of the many
objections that have been raised against psychoanalysts on this ground.
The crudest version of the argument claims that analytic interpretations
are accepted by the patient through the analyst's suggestions, under the
influence of a positive transference; analysis appears as a kind of brainwashing. In a less crude form the validity of psychoanalytic results can
be questioned on the ground of the subtle but undeniable influence that
a combination of various factors—the analyst's personality, scientific
interests, opinions or prejudices; the needs of the patient's resistance;
and, occasionally, the influence of unrecognized satisfactions in the
analytic situation (due, perhaps, to countertransference or to reality
factors, unavoidable or not avoided)—can have upon the selection of the
material that appears in the analysis and, hence, upon the development
of the analytic treatment and the picture derived from it.

Weaver summed the situation up as follows:

> In the world of living things, the progress of science was not so rapid,
> and we ought to be able to surmise why this was bound to be so. As far
> as its stretching (at a fixed temperature) is concerned, one single
> descriptive number completely describes a spring. A second descriptive
> number tells us how the behavior varies with temperature. One single
> number describes how hard, so to speak, it is for direct current to pass
> through a certain wire. One single and simple equation describes the
> temperature-volume-pressure behavior of all perfect gases. One concise
> law states the gravitational attraction between all particles of matter in
> the entire cosmos. Although there are indeed great complications and
> refinements in modern physical and chemical theories, the amazing
> fact is that enormous and very practical progress could be achieved
> with exceedingly simple and yet exceedingly general laws.
>
> But how many variables does it take to describe a flower, an insect,
> or a man? How many subtly interacting and essentially interlocked
> factors must be taken into account to understand an emotional state?
> How complicated is the set of influences that affect behavior?
>
> In other words, physical science was able to get started several
> centuries ago because the world is so built that physics is relatively easy
> . . . Biology, broadly speaking, is several cuts harder. A living
> organism is essentially more complicated and has many more
> interacting characteristics. It is much more restrictive (and can be
> wholly misleading) to study these characteristics one or two at a time,
> and underneath all this is the massive fact, at once mystical and

practical, that when one takes a live organism apart to study it, an essential aspect of the problem has vanished, in that what is on the experimenter's table is no longer an organism and is no longer alive [Weaver, 1957, p. 1227 f.].

The psychoanalyst has nothing to add to these words; they clearly state the conditions and limitations, which are imposed upon us by the nature of our subject, the living man. The desire, praiseworthy in itself, for the exactitude of the physical sciences, together with a lack of appreciation of the conditions that had made the latter possible, have produced an enormous amount of literature of a pseudo-exact variety in which *highly coupled systems are treated as though they were loosely coupled*. Interpretations are duly avoided, and a vast amount of data is collected with many apparent safeguards and is statistically elaborated; but every individual item of these data is often an interpretation, made without awareness and, hence, without the criticism to which interpretations consciously arrived at can be subjected. In psychoanalysis as well as in other behavioral disciplines, or in the social sciences, I often prefer the report of an experienced and cautious field observer, or clinical observer, to the semblance of exactitude of the Gallup poll variety.

The conviction that only the results of experiments can be taken seriously while the observation, however prolonged, of the natural course of events with a view to discovering its patterns is hopelessly inexact—at least if these events do not favor us with a display of simple and obvious regularities as do the planetary movements—has greatly influenced, or indeed determined, during the last three or four generations, what problems were considered worth studying; the results of this selection have partly been excellent and partly not so excellent. In medicine, e.g., it has led to a concentration of effort on the study of specific etiological agents and to a neglect of the ecological aspects of disease, viz., the unbalance between the organism and its environment, because the former present single-variable problems that can be studied exactly in the laboratory or with reasonable approximation to exactitude in the clinic, while the latter involve innumerable variables that are particularly difficult to isolate. Thus, apart from surgery, a large part of the progress of medicine in the last few generations has taken place where conditions came closest to being the outcome of single factors such as, e.g., the invasion of pathogenic organisms into a human body as yet without previous contact with them. Successes were least, on the other hand, in dealing with the degenerative diseases of middle and old age—unless they were controllable by surgery—which involved an intricate relationship between the organism and its environment, including the frozen residue of past adjustments and maladjustments.

The Validity of Historical
and Psychological Propositions

A discussion about the possibility, or impossibility, to establish psychoanalytic propositions "scientifically" should begin with a consideration of the kind of evidence on which propositions such as those advanced by psychoanalysis, i.e., historical and psychological propositions, are based, and under what conditions we are prepared to admit statements on such subject matter as "scientifically" valid.

Whoever challenges psychoanalysis on the ground of allegedly lacking verification should be asked whether or not, or under what conditions, he believes that the following statements can be verified:

Ia.   John Doe, Jr., is the son of Mrs. John Doe (historical statement based on memories and testimony of witnesses);

Ib.   John Doe, Jr., is the son of Mr. John Doe (historical statement based on circumstantial evidence);

IIa.   John Doe loves his wife; he told me so himself (statement about a person's conscious emotional life);

IIb.   John Doe thinks that he loves his wife, but he deceives himself; he does not recognize (or fights against the recognition of) the fact that he has grown tired of her and is interested in Miss X. (Psychological statement about another person's emotional life on the basis of alleged give-away in his behavior, involving judgments about self-deception and unconscious processes.)

Ad Ia. Mater semper certa is a principle of the Roman law, but on what is this certitude based? There is Mrs. Doe who remembers having Junior delivered in the hospital and having brought him home; and he has always been home thereafter until he was grown up; there is a continuity in her memory. So it is in Mr. John Doe's from the day he saw Junior behind a glass wall in the hospital nursery. And there are the neighbors and the friends of the family who have seen Junior periodically throughout the years. All this is of course enough for all practical purposes, but the question is whether it is adequate for scientific accuracy. It is all based on memories or testimony of witnesses, but memories can fail and witnesses can lie or err. Mrs. John Doe, e.g., may not have delivered a child at all but, with the complicity of a few persons, may have presented an illegitimate child of another woman as her own; or she may have delivered and her child was exchanged in the hospital nursery by inadvertence, etc. All these are extremely unlikely contingencies, but they are not entirely impossible. In fact, our judgment that they are extremely unlikely is itself based on prescientific experience or impressions rather than on scientifically controlled investigations, and may therefore be deemed to carry little weight. In order to make the statement Ia exact, it would probably be necessary to have a complete film of Junior's delivery that would keep Junior uninterruptedly in the picture, at least until the footprint has been taken if footprints are considered to be reliable identification marks. But if the latter proposition would, as I fear, have to be proved first, the film would have to run uninterruptedly until the emergence of distinctive features; from then on, perhaps, occasional shots may suffice. Needless to say, there has been no case so far in which maternity has been so established.

Ad Ib. The proof of paternity is, of course, more difficult. In actual life it is based on psychological estimates such as these: It is most unlikely that Mrs. Doe conceived out of wedlock; perhaps she loved her husband, or there was no opportunity for adultery, or nobody has seen her interested in any other man at the time, or adultery would be inconsistent with her character, etc. All this is convincing enough but does not rule out any possible doubt. A fully scientific study may require controlled conditions, with a running cinematographic record, in which Mrs. Doe is kept isolated for a sufficiently long period preceding her delivery, in addition to the data required in the first example.

Ad IIa. The evidence of self-observation has been recognized by many, but others hold that psychic data are purely subjective and, as a matter of principle, not verifiable for others; and universal verifiability, or demonstrability, is alleged to be a fundamental requirement of science. While in the earlier-mentioned historical statements exact conditions can, even though at great labor and cost, be devised for future work, it would seem impossible, if this objection is upheld, to accept any data of self-observation.

Ad IIb. Against the validity of psychological judgments made about others on the ground of their behavior, it can be held that these judgments have never been established. Even if self-observation were admitted, there has never been a comprehensive study to correlate exactly, e.g., facial expressions, described in terms of exact measurement, with reported feelings such as hatred, fear, hope; such investigations, even at the simplest level, would be immensely difficult and time-consuming. On the whole, it could be argued, estimates of things that are supposed to go on in another person's mind and that are not given to his self-observation are speculative and not demonstrable.

To those who are satisfied that valid historical and psychological statements can be made, however, psychoanalytic propositions can be shown to be either valid or invalid; to others, they can probably not be validated.

Psychological and Historical Judgments
Implicit in the Exact Sciences

At this point one may well stop and wonder whether this is not a semantic question after all. Perhaps, so the argument may run, historical statements based on memories, testimony of witnesses or circumstantial evidence, and psychological statements about an inner life, or about unconscious psychic processes, can be made with a degree of certitude that is adequate *for all practical purposes* but falls short of the standards developed, and lived up to, in the physical sciences. We may then go ahead with our psychoanalytic work, confident about what we are doing as an investigating commission may be confident that it has unraveled the facts of a case; but whether it should be termed science, i.e., whether the representatives of the physical sciences would be willing to recognize that our work. can qualify as scientific, or whether we psychoanalysts should actually ask for this recognition, is another question, important for the vanities involved on all sides but entirely irrelevant for an assessment of the validity of the psychoanalytic work itself. Psychoanalysts could go on claiming, if they wished, that they are students of a science of the mind, and practitioners of a technique based on it, while representatives of the older, physical sciences[2] may, if they wished, go on refusing their credentials. But things are not quite as simple as this, and if historical and psychological judgments are inadmissible in science, it is not only psychiatry, psychoanalysis, sociology, or related disciplines, that are excluded, but the physical sciences themselves would face the necessity of re-establishing most of their propositions because *in the work of all scientists a considerable number of things are taken for granted on the ground of historical and psychological judgments.*

Material for experiments has been purchased from a commercial firm and the specifications are accepted because the firm is known as reliable. It is assumed that authors, or at least authors who have an established reputation or work in a respected institution under the supervision of respected scientists, do not deliberately falsify their data, nor suffer from hysterical conditions that would make them doctor their

---

2. This picture is, in fact not quite correct. The deriding of psychoanalysis does not really come from the representatives of the old, well-established exact sciences, but rather from the representatives of disciplines on the fringe of the republic of science who have themselves to fight continuously for their recognition. The examples, quoted above, of the views of two prominent mathematicians show a full realization of the fact that the success of the exact sciences is largely due to favorable circumstances not duplicated elsewhere, and a full realization of the difficulties which confront those who study man.

data without being aware of it. The laboratory setup has not been under constant surveillance by machines; there is no guarantee that other individuals have not bribed the night watchman or otherwise got around him and tampered with the setup so as to bring about a certain result, or that the experimenter himself has not done so, with dishonest intent or in a state of fugue. Of course, all these are possibilities that, practically, need not be taken seriously; any one of them is enormously unlikely, outside of mystery stories, and if it should ever occur it would soon be found out. But this judgment, though sound enough in itself, is based on a mostly prescientific experience and common-sense psychology rather than on precisely controlled conditions, and if such judgments are not deemed admissible, a vast number of scientific experiments would have to be repeated under conditions in which nothing has been taken for granted. One cannot have it both ways: historical and psychological judgments either can, or cannot, be accepted as valid. If they cannot, many results of physical sciences which had been won with such judgments being implicit during the work would have to be re-established under more exact conditions; or if such judgments are admissible, they surely can be used not only implicitly by the physical scientists but also explicitly by the students of human behavior.

And it must be further added that even if all these precautions were taken, it would still remain true that conclusions drawn from experiments rest on the assumption that the experiments have been carried out as claimed, and that nobody has tampered with the setup; and this assumption *must*, in some point, rest on the testimony of persons, and confidence in the reliability of this testimony rests on psychological judgments. Hence, in the last analysis, the psychological factors can never be entirely eliminated.

It was probably for considerations such as these that the philosopher and historian of science, Arthur David Ritchie, stated recently (1958, p. 7): ". . . The paradigm or model type of fact is not the desiccated, artificial fact of the experimental sciences which cannot exist outside the laboratory but a more robust if less precise kind of fact, the evidence of the lawyer or historian. This is an affirmation by a person or subject to other persons or subjects about reactions between them. . . . All public scientific facts depend on these prior affirmations."

A Compensatory Advantage of Psychology

But it is time to consider the other side of the coin. It is true that we cannot prove any psychological proposition by viewing it from outside as we do in the physical sciences, with any exactitude approaching the exactitude that is rightly expected from research work in those fields; but it is equally true that *we know a great deal about the proposition from the inside already*. The molecules, atoms and subatomic particles, the cells and viruses we can study only from the outside, but in mental life what we study is *ourselves*, or subjects closely similar to ourselves, and about ourselves we know, or are able to know, a great deal immediately. It is true that the physicist has great advantages over us on account of the loose coupling of his variables, as Professor Weaver has pointed out, and on account of the great difference in size between us and the atomic particles and the consequent concentration of our concern on matters involving large aggregates of atomic particles only, as Professor Wiener has pointed out; but it is equally true that we will never know anything about atomic particles, or large aggregates of them, for that matter, except through observation from the outside, while we know much about the mind from the inside. There is a sense in which one can say that the common man knows more about the mind than the scientist will ever know about gases or atoms. We know that we love or hate, are afraid or panicked or hopeful, jubilant or desperate, tempted or repelled or both. And we know the mood and the feelings of others, too, all the better the more we are in "contact" with them. The sources of our knowledge of the psychic life of others have been said to be an interpretation of their expressions, or an act of intuition (in the sense of the Latin *intueri*—to look inside), or so-called empathy, identification, or a "perception" of the mental life of others (Scheler) in the sense in which we might say that we come to a strange place and "perceive" poverty or provincialism or terror or culture. But whatever the source of our knowledge of psychic processes in another person may be, whatever the mechanisms or processes by means of which we perceive or understand or infer them, there is no doubt that such knowledge exists and is constantly at the bottom of human relationships (or, if you want to use the favorite term of the "neo-Freudians": of interpersonal relationships). The lover either knows that he is loved or is in doubt about it and is anxious to find out, but both imply the possibility of knowing; a part of the game between the two sexes is sometimes to leave a carefully dosed amount of doubt on this point in the partner. The diplomat must be able to gauge the intentions of his opposite number through the deliberately controlled exterior; so does the good poker player. Social life is largely the constant mutual reaction of people to each other's feelings, as swift and, as a rule, unverbalized, as is the reaction of drivers to each other on the road.

And we know, too, that infants and children are highly sensitive reactors to the mood of the adults, particularly their mothers. Infants react immediately to a disturbance not so much in the environment in general as in their biological environment, i.e., their mothers and other adults who take care of them; they react to anxiety or hatred even if the adult tries to conceal them. Neuroses of a severity and tenacity not otherwise easily accountable have often been observed in persons whose mothers went through a depression during their first year of life. The close interaction between mother and child, early observed by analysts (G. Bibring, A. Balint, Peto, et al.) is now the subject of systematic studies through simultaneous analyses of mother and child at the Hampstead Child Therapy Clinic (see, e.g., Burlingham et al., 1955), and at the Child Study Center, Yale University.

It is conceded, or it is not conceded, that this sort of understanding has some validity. If this is conceded in principle, it is not too difficult to prove or disprove specific psychoanalytic interpretations or hypotheses; or it is not conceded and the rules of the game are so set that only external, behavioristic, physical data are admissible, and in that case it is probably impossible, or close to impossible, to verify psychoanalytic propositions or any other propositions involving man's inner life.

In his survey of experimental approaches to psychoanalysis, Professor Hilgard states: "Anyone who tries to give an honest appraisal of psychoanalysis as a science must be ready to admit that as it is stated it is mostly very bad science, that the bulk of the articles in its journals cannot be defended as research publications at all" (1952, p. 44). The latter is true; these articles are not "research publications"; they are mostly clinical papers, comparable to clinical case reports in medicine or to field reports in the social sciences. But my thesis is that *clinical, or field, studies can, and must, be admitted* in a science in which, on the one hand, *research*, i.e., on the whole, the study of one or two variables in isolation, is *impossible* because variables are too highly coupled; while, on the other hand, *introspection* and *perception* are *possible*.

It must be added, however, that the validity which we claim for psychological self-observation and the observations of others is *not absolute*. Just as the perception of the inanimate world through our senses may be misleading, so may our psychological self-observation and our reasoning, intuition, empathy or perception, whichever it may be, about others. We hear the thunder later than we see the lightning, but we would not be justified in claiming, on this ground, that the thunder occurred later. We see the moon disappear in its eclipse, but we would not be right in saying that it had actually temporarily vanished. The wanderer in the desert may clearly see an oasis on the horizon which is not there, etc. And there is the so-called personal equation in all investigations. In the same sense, the results of our self-observation are incomplete and distorted—this is, indeed, the fundamental thesis of psychoanalysis—and we are often deceived in our judgment of others, too. The young man may have erred in thinking that the girl loved him, or did not love him, and the diplomat or the poker player may have been outwitted. What we have to do, however, is not to discard this source of knowledge because it may at times mislead us, just as we do not discard the testimony of our senses because they may produce the desert mirage but to *correct it by comparing data from different sources and cross-checking on all of them.* This is, after all, the way the fallacies of sensual perception have been recognized, made the subject of systematic study, and have become corrigible. This is essentially how psychoanalytic interpretations and evaluations of individual situations, or of persons, are actually arrived at: we take the data of a person's self-observation; and the data of our psychological observation of this person, with the material of our observation vastly enriched by the psychoanalytic rule by which a person commits himself to permit anything to enter his mind and to say everything that did enter it; and the data of outside, physical, observation. We accept none of these sets of data by themselves as necessarily reliable, uncritically, and cross-check each against the others.

The pressure, brought to bear on psychoanalysts, to validate the propositions of psychoanalysis through experiment or statistics, is a predominantly American phenomenon. The situation in the German-speaking countries is almost the opposite and psychoanalysis is far more likely to be censured for any such attempt at validation than for the failure to supply it. This is due to the fact that in the German cultural orbit, a philosophy has been widely accepted which distinguishes sharply between "nature" and *Geist*—an untranslatable word of many meanings which, in this context, means approximately "mind" and "culture" rolled into one. History, according to this philosophy, deals not with nature but with *Geist,* and so does any psychology that goes beyond peripheral problems such as, e.g., sense perception. Nature can be described by a finite number of quantifiable variables, while mind, culture or existence consist of structures, or Gestalts, which can only be comprehended in their totality. There was the famous, endlessly quoted dictum of Dilthey's: We explain nature, but we understand psychic life.

From this point of view, experimental or statistical investigations in matters of *"Geist"* betray a fundamental misunderstanding of the subject; they are something like intellectual original sin.

This dichotomy has dominated German thought for a century, widely accepted not only by philosophers but also by psychiatrists and medical men. An article of mine was recently published in translation in a German periodical; in it I had said that a satisfactory validation of psychoanalytic theory may involve a very detailed, longitudinal study of a large number of individuals, from the beginning to the end of their lives; that such a study would be enormously expensive and would probably take a century or two until the results could become conclusive; but that it may well be undertaken eventually. Thereupon, the distinguished chief of a department in the medical school of one of Germany's leading Universities wrote me and expressed his astonishment at this passage. Was that really what I had meant to say? Was it not in the very essence of our psychology to claim that the mind was something different from nature?

The German and the American points of view in this matter are perhaps a modern edition of the ancient controversy between Platonism and Aristotelianism. It seems to me that both viewpoints are stronger in their negative, critical part than in their positive, constructive, one. The German philosophy has a strong point inasmuch as the living organism, and even more the human mind, is more than any number of physical parameters can describe; there is, as Warren Weaver called it in the earlier quoted passage," . . . the massive fact, at once mystical and practical, that when one takes a live organism apart to study it, an essential aspect of the problem has vanished, in that what is on the experimenter's table, is no longer an organism and is no longer alive."

The American view, on the other hand, is strong in its criticism, too, because it is not quite clear what the criteria of that "understanding" of the mind, of which Dilthey speaks, are and how one can distinguish between correct interpretations, on the one hand, and guesswork, speculation or even paranoid ideas, on the other. There do not seem to be any intrinsic criteria *within* the experience of understanding itself to sift the one from the others (see p. 6). In view of the fact that people differ in what they feel they understand in mental life, Dilthey's formula would need the setting up of an authority to decide which understanding is, and which is not, correct.

In the light of these difficulties, it seems to me that a solution can be found only in the integration of both viewpoints; or that it has to be eclectic, if one prefers this more modest expression.

A Pentathlon Theory

The pentathlon was a form of athletic contest in ancient Greece, consisting of competition in five activities; running, jumping, wrestling, throwing the discus, and the javelin. Competitions in five, or in ten (decathlon), athletic disciplines have been revived in modern times. In this kind of contest it is quite possible that the victor is, in any part of the contest, inferior to other athletes who have, or have not, entered the pentathlon competition. The victor's result in running or in jumping, e.g., may fall short of the result of the best Olympic runner or jumper who has not entered into this specific competition, or may fall short of the results of fellow contestants in these branches of the pentathlon itself because it is the average mark that counts. The Greeks have therefore used the term to characterize a type of man whose merits lie more in the width of his pursuits than in his success in a narrow area.

Psychoanalytic interpretations of single events, or a psychoanalytic chart of an individual person, or general psychoanalytic propositions can hardly be proved on the basis of external, physical, measurable data alone. But I submit that the combination of such data with the data of a patient's self-observations (including the self-observations pursuant the tentatively proposed interpretation) and with the data of our observations of his behavior, including his verbal behavior, viewed as expressions of psychic processes, each of these sets of data viewed critically in the light of the other data, form a kind of evidence which is just as convincing[3] as the evidence found in the study of a single variable in such fields where single variables can be meaningfully studied in isolation.

This is actually the way the psychoanalytic practitioner proceeds— or should proceed. The analyst constantly oscillates between an inside and an outside view. There are thoughts and feelings reported by the patient and features in the patient's behavior both inside the analytic situation and in his life, or past memories, which, to the analyst, seem to "click," to tell their story; no sooner is such a hypothetical interpretation won, through the patient's self-observation and/or the analyst's empathy—e.g., in terms of our previous example, about the psychological meaning of the patient's depressions—that the analyst changes his vantage point and looks upon the matter from outside and asks himself: is this hypothetical interpretation in conformity with all the facts; e.g., do conditions with these particular implications always bring about depressions? And he will probably gain further material from the outside view by proposing the interpretation, or part of it, to the patient and watching whether there is any reaction to it. Or, if he has gained any information from the outside, e.g., that depressions always occur at a particular date, or after specific events, he will immediately try to view things from the inside and try to grasp the possible connection of things. In this oscillation the analysis proceeds.

3. Provided, of course, that the analyst has learned to "restrain speculative tendencies" (Freud, 1914a, p. 22) and really practices the cross-checking described above. Carl Becker once spoke of writers of history *sans peur et sans recherche;* it is not astonishing that they can be found among psychoanalysts, too.

According to newspaper reports, the Water Company in a Midwestern city noticed a few years ago that water consumption rose several times every evening for a few minutes to a high level. The matter was investigated and it was found that these maxima in the consumption curves coincided with the commercials on television; they were due to the flushing of many toilets at the same time. I do not know whether this has actually occurred in this way or was just a good story. In any case, it is a good analogy for the reasoning that goes on in psychoanalysis. It may be that the Company officials discovered the external fact, i.e., the coincidence of the peaks in the consumption curves with the television commercials, first, and then understood psychologically what was going on; or they may have started with a guess that consumption peaks were perhaps due to the simultaneous flushing of many toilets, then considered the possible reasons for such simultaneity, and thereafter proceeded to search directly for specific situations which many people may consider as proper moments to interrupt their activities. In a similar way, the psychoanalyst may either observe a coincidence first and then understand its meaning; or he may "understand" the meaning of a symptom or behavior trait first and then investigate whether the observable facts are in accordance with it.

There is the further analogy that once the connection has been grasped, it can be further corroborated by predicting the consumption peaks under various schedules for the commercials, in one case, and the occurrence of symptoms or other phenomena under varying conditions, in the other.

The Question of Universal Demonstrability

The admission of "empathy" or perception of psychic processes in others as admissible evidence will meet with the objection that it is subjective in the sense that not all people can "see" what some claim can be seen. Some people are "intuitive," have "empathy," "are in good contact with people," others are not.[4] Some are, indeed, almost blind to

4. It is among the desiderata that students of psychoanalysis should have this ability of "good contact with the patient" and "intuition," or "empathy." This requirement may seem particularly odious from an epistemological point of view; we can hardly call it evidence that practitioners of psychoanalysis can "see" certain connections if they have first been chosen for their "empathy," i.e., for their ability to see them. It looks like circular reasoning, but it is no more so than the exclusion of the color-blind from a certain type of work which is discussed farther down in this chapter; and it is not essentially different from what happened in the early years of investigation of the splitting of the atomic nucleus; in those days, research was mainly carried out through observation of extremely minute fluorescence phenomena caused by the impact of individual protons on a zinc sulfide screen, and many students had to be dropped from this kind of work because they did not get the right results (see Waelder, 1955, p. 3).

psychological material and the incidence of "psyche-blindness" is perhaps in no group as high as among the devotees of the exact sciences—for reasons about which psychoanalysis could venture some guesses. But, however that may be, the fact appears as a serious barrier against using this kind of "perception" because scientific results must be demonstrable to everybody—they must be *intrasubjectiv verifizierbar*— at least in principle, whatever that may mean. So at least it is stated and propositions in the physical sciences are, it is claimed, universally demonstrable.

Yet are they? For one, there are many things that are not demonstrable to those who are deficient in one of their senses—are blind, or deaf, or, to mention minor deficiencies, are color-blind or lack the ability to differentiate between musical tones. A certain area of scientific propositions about nature cannot be demonstrated to them; nevertheless, we do not on this ground question the validity of these propositions but accept it that they are correct and that it is due to personal shortcomings that some people cannot corroborate them.

Then, there are the mentally sick—hallucinating psychotics, e.g.— or the intellectually underdeveloped—oligophrenics or morons—to whom many scientific propositions cannot be demonstrated. One might try to circumvent this difficulty by stating that general demonstrability merely means demonstrability to the mentally normal. This would be a satisfactory way out if we could define this group through characteristics independent of the matter at issue, e.g., through organic characteristics; in such case, we could say that it must be possible to verify scientific propositions to every person except those suffering from a defined anatomical or physiological abnormality. But as things are, we can characterize the psychotics usually through a lack in their sense of reality and are therefore in a circular reasoning if we state that scientific laws, an important part of reality, can be demonstrated to all but the insane, and the insane are those who cannot appreciate reality.

But let us not belabor the point and assume that a way has been found to settle this matter in a logically satisfactory fashion; there still remains the large issue of mathematics. An understanding of the physical sciences, particuarly of anything beyond the most elementary facts, depends to a large degree upon the use of mathematical tools. I do not know how large a percentage of high-school students actually understands algebra or trigonometry as different from having memorized formulae to the point of being able to pass the tests; but this is still elementary mathematics. How great a percentage of the whole population, excluding psychotics and morons, could actually grasp higher mathematics to the point of being able to understand the reasoning in modern physics? I suspect that there are many more people who could see or feel a great deal of their neighbors' moods, fears, or aspirations than can understand the tensor calculus.

Even in mathematics it may happen that a proposition is at a time not universally demonstrable, not only to all people but not even to all ranking mathematicians. J. Hadamard (1945) speaks of the possibility that the "psychology of different individuals may differ in some essential points" and gives the following examples: ". . . a question which, though a mathematical one, was contiguous to metaphysics raised a lively discussion . . . between myself and . . . the great scientist Lebesgue. We could not avoid the conclusion that evidence—that starting point of certitude in every order of thinking—did not have the same meaning for him and for me . . . we recognized the impossibility of understanding each other.

"The subject in question belonged to the theory of 'sets'. Now, when . . . Georg Cantor communicated his fundamental results on that theory (now one of the bases of contemporary science), one of them looked so paradoxical and upset so radically all our fundamental notions that it unleashed the decided hostility of Kronecker, one of the leading mathematicians in that time. . . . Of course, the proof of that result is as clear and rigorous as any other proof in mathematics, leaving no possibility of not admitting it" (p. 92).

Thus, the results of physics and chemistry cannot really be demonstrated to everybody; nor even to everybody not insane. They can be demonstrated only to a small fraction of the people at the present time. The others can see or hear the visible or audible *results;* every sane individual who is not deaf can hear that the radio messages do get through the air, but only a few can understand how this happens. The notion that the older, physical sciences are universally demonstrable boils down to the fact that they have gained a vast prestige, partly because of the demonstrability and usefulness of their technical *applications,* partly because of the relative unity of their exponents, and that the people are satisfied that the structure of science is sound. In this, and only in this sense can one say that the propositions of the physical sciences are universally demonstrable.

The younger psychological and social sciences have nothing of this prestige. They have not yet delivered many applications which people find useful—though the psychoanalytic contributions to education and to preventive psychiatry may in the not far distant future come close to this specification—and their conspicuous representatives do not show the unity which alone can inspire confidence among outsiders. As far as psychoanalysis is concerned, I see no reason, if our free society survives,

why a similar state of affairs should not be reached in several generations: that the people at large accept the judgment of experts as correct
though they cannot themselves check on it, and that the propositions are
thereafter considered as "universally demonstrable."

REFERENCES

ABRAHAM, K. (1924). A Short Study of the Development of the Libido
Viewed in the Light of Mental Disorders. *Collected Papers of Karl
Abraham.* London: Hogarth Press, 1942.
BERNFELD, S. (1932). Der Begriff der Deutung in der Psychoanalyse. *Z.
angew. Psychol.,* 42.
———, (1934). Die Gestalttheorie. *Imago,* 20.
BIBRING, E. (1953). The Mechanism of Depression. In: *Affective Dis-
orders,* ed. P. Greenacre. New York: International Universities Press.
BLEULER, EUGEN (1910), *Die Psychoanalyse Freuds. Verteidigung und
kritische Bemerkungen.* Wien: F. Deuticke, 1911.
BROSIN, HENRY W. (1955). Report on the panel: Validation of Psycho-
analytic Theory. *J. Amer. Psychoanal. Assn.,* 3.
BURLINGHAM, D. and A. GOLDBERGER, A. LUSSIER (1955). Simultaneous
Analysis of Mother and Child. *The Psychoanalytic Study of the Child,*
10. New York: International Universities Press.
FREUD, S. (1914a). On the History of the Psychoanalytic Movement.
Standard Edition, 14.
———, (1917). Mourning and Melancholia. *Standard Edition,* 14.
HADAMARD, JACQUES (1945). *The Psychology of Invention in the
Mathematical Field.* New York: Dover.
HILGARD, ERNEST R. (1952). Experimental Approaches to Psychoan-
alysis. In: *Psychoanalysis as a Science,* ed. E. Pumpian-Mindlin.
Stanford, California: Stanford University Press.
KLEIN, M. (1935). A Contribution to the Psychogenesis of Manic-
Depressive States. In: *Contributions to Psychoanalysis 1921-1945.*
London: Hogarth Press, 1948.
———, (1940). Mourning and Its Relations to Manic-Depressive States.
In: *Contributions to Psychoanalysis 1921-1945.* London: Hogarth
Press, 1948.
KUBIE, LAWRENCE S. (1952). Problems and Techniques of Psychoanaly-
sis, Validation and Progress. In: *Psychoanalysis as a Science,* ed. E.
Pumpian-Mindlin. Stanford, California: Stanford University Press.
LORENZ, K. (1954). *Man Meets Dog.* London: Metheun.
RITCHIE, ARTHUR DAVID (1958). *Studies in the History and Methods of
the Sciences.* Edinburgh: University Press.

SCHMIDL, FRITZ (1955). The Problem of Scientific Validation of Psychoanalytic Interpretations. *Int. J. Psychoanal.*, 36.

WAELDER, R. (1936). The Problem of the Genesis of Psychical Conflicts in Earliest Infancy. *Int. J. Psychoanal.*, 18, 1937.

———, (1939). Kriterien der Deutung. *Int. Z. Psychoanal.*, 24.

———, (1955). The Functions and the Pitfalls of Psychoanalytic Societies. *Bull. Phila. Assn. Psychoanal.*, 5.

WEAVER, WARREN (1955). Science and People. *Science*, 122 (No. 3183).

———, (1957). Science and the Citizen. *Science*, 126 (No. 3285).

WEISSBERG-CYBULSKI, ALEXANDER (1951). *Hexensabbath*. Frankfurt a. M.: Verlag der Frankfurter Hefte.

WEINER, NORBERT (1948). *Cybernetics*. New York: John Wiley.

11

Comments on the Scientific Aspects of Psychoanalysis*

Heinz Hartmann

In this lecture I will examine the body of facts and theories we call psychoanalysis from a point of view not altogether widely discussed in our literature. We all consider psychoanalysis, among other things, a science. It is, however, not always clearly understood to what degree and in what respects this statement is true, nor is it always easy to say what are the distinctive formal and methodological characteristics of this science. If the analyst is often shy of discussing such questions with representatives of other, more highly systematized and methodologically more firmly established fields of science, this may well be due to the rather forbidding difficulties to explain to these others even comparatively simple aspects of analytic method or content. But it is also true that not many of us give much thought to such matters, and that with even fewer it is in the foreground of their interest and work. This is undoubtedly the result of a characteristic feature of psychoanalysis as a profession which is a union of practical with scientific activities, and of the development of our profession. It easily leads to what E. Kris (1947) has called a lack of "trained clarifiers" of the kind we find in the physical sciences. But I think that progress in the clarification of our hypotheses,

*Reprinted from *Essays on Ego Psychology*, by Heinz Hartmann, by permission of International Universities Press, Inc. Copyright© 1964 by International Universities Press, Inc.

and systematization, and the consideration of methodological principles is no less important in analysis than in other sciences. The
possibility fully to extricate their meaning from our observations
depends on it. Later I shall briefly speak about attempts in this direction,
coming, in part, from outside professional analysis. It is true that
hypotheses used in our work can be tested, for instance, experimentally.
Still, this statement is not generally true. Moreover, the function of these
propositions in the context of analysis as a whole is unquestionably very
hard to evaluate from an extra-analytic viewpoint. Because of these
circumstances, I am convinced that the major part of this work of
clarification and testing will fall to the analysts' lot.

As so much of every aspect of psychoanalysis has originated in the
work of Freud, I may briefly comment here on what he felt about its
scientific character. Freud has been decried because of his narrow
scientism, because of his positivism—and equally often because of
rather opposite tendencies which some writers thought to discover in his
work, for instance, a bent toward metaphysical speculation, or even
mysticism; he has been called a rationalist and an irrationalist, a
humanist and an antihumanist. Such judgments, though often
primarily aimed at his philosophy, or at what some people believed his
philosophy to be, imply as a rule also judgments of analysis. In spite of
this great variety of partly antithetical evaluations, it should be clear to
every student of his works that Freud had early in his life developed a
strict belief in the scientific methods of thinking and that this belief
continued unshattered till his end. The word "belief" here points to his
conviction that reliable and testable knowledge can be ascertained in no
other ways but those of science. It is equally clear that in what we might
call his "cautious optimism" he expected rational thinking to have the
power of slow, gradual expansion. Finally, there is no doubt that for
him psychoanalysis meant the conquest, for scientific study, of human
behavior in the broadest sense; a field that in its essentials had never
before been touched by scientific exploration. He thought, as many
psychoanalysts do, that even the therapeutic aspect of analysis would in
the long run be overshadowed by its importance for a science of man.
This primacy of scientific aims and the responsibilities vis-a-vis the rules
and procedures of scientific thinking that go with it have become
essential in the development of psychoanalysis—in contradistinction to
other psychological schools, though they have grown, in part, in the
same soil. Neither with Jung, nor Adler, nor Rank do we find the same
dedication to scientific method, or the unquestioned readiness to submit
to its demands, nor do we find there the same energetic and consistent

endeavor to wrestle with the untold difficulties our subject matter forces us to face.

Precisely because of his sense of responsibility toward the demands of scientific thinking, Freud never denied, or disowned, or passed over the imperfections of psychoanalysis as a science. After a visit Einstein had paid to him, he wrote to a friend (Jan. 11, 1927): "He has had the support of a long series of predecessors from Newton onward, while I have had to hack every step of my way through a tangled jungle alone. No wonder that my path is not a very broad one and that I have not got far in it" (Jones, 1953–57, 3:131). We have the right to disagree with the last sentence. But this passage clearly shows that Freud was very far indeed from considering psychoanalysis a closed or completed, or, in many respects, even a satisfactory system. Being well aware of the many white spots on the map of analysis, he did not believe "to have all the answers"—a notion about the state of analysis occasionally met with inside and outside of it. Freud was fully aware of the need for reformulation of many aspects of psychoanalysis, and of the tentative character of some of his statements. Also, concerning an important aspect of analysis he stated that one cannot yet deal with it without introducing "uncertain assumptions and unproven guesses." But he did not doubt the superiority of analysis over all other approaches to a psychology of personality in explaining not only the phenomena he had been the first to discover, but in explaining also an ever broader sector of human behavior in general.

We know today (from the letters to W. Fliess) that the field this science was meant to cover was, not only in Freud's later years but from his beginnings, psychology in the most comprehensive sense. It was never meant to be limited to the study of pathological phenomena, though even today psychoanalytic psychology is sometimes presented as "theory of neurosis." I want to emphasize, then, Freud's very broad conception of psychoanalysis as a science, despite the fact that his first decisive insights were gained through the study of neurosis and despite the fact that this study has remained in the center of our therapeutic work. What actually happened was that Freud in learning to understand neurosis uncovered at the same time the essential features of mental functioning in general: conflict, defense, dynamic unconscious processes, etc. His broad approach was foreshadowed in his "Project for a Scientific Psychology" and explicitly stated in *The Interpretation of Dreams.* But he often said that he obviously could not approach all parts of psychology at the same time; moreover, the fact that he had not, or only cursorily, approached a subject, he maintained, should not be misconstrued as meaning that he did not appreciate its importance. Actually, even today not all the implications of this comprehensive conception have been worked out and the process of broadening and reformulation continues. What, then, is the field of analysis?

The question is somewhat obscured by the idea, mentioned before and occasionally found both inside and outside analysis, that it is somewhat like a closed system. This is a very simple, but a very un-Freudian approach. The need for growth and development is already implied in the very outline Freud gave us. Everything we can focus on and explain with its conceptual tools, and its method, is part of it—as long, of course, as it is not contradicted by observation or another more reliable theory. We may also, if we prefer, make a distinction between "actual" and "potential" analysis—the latter, as I said before, probably comprising its application to every chapter of psychology. I may add here that also another attempt at broadening our conception of psychoanalysis as a science has become more or less accepted. We would no longer limit it to what has its immediate origin in the use of the analytic method in the analytic situation. We include work in applied analysis, in various fields of medicine, social science, and so on. Also the use of psychoanalytic concepts and hypotheses in the direct observation of children is today recognized as part of scientific analysis.

Psychoanalysis is richer in theoretical complexities than any other approach to psychology, though the complexities of some physical sciences may be greater. This complex theorizing in analysis is, I think, dictated by the special features of its subject matter. It can stand any comparison with physical sciences as to its originality and ingenuity and particularly as to the unique combination of logical and imaginative power of its creator. Still, some of our terms are ambiguous. The hypotheses are frequently not clearly differentiated as to their closeness to observation, or as to the degree to which they have been confirmed. The level of systematization is, in general, comparatively low, in spite of efforts to remedy this state of affairs. The suggestion, made by many, to achieve a higher degree of clarification and systematization by reformulating psychoanalytic theory according to newer developments in biology or physics might occasionally be helpful—as has been the borrowing of such models by Freud. But such suggestions too often ignore the special conditions in our field and, more generally, the fact that the use of such borrowings has to be checked in every case as to its fruitfulness in the field into which they are transplanted. In addition, simply to translate our experience into the language of a field that appears somehow more tangible (as is the case, e.g., with brain physiology) but about which (as certainly was the case with brain physiology) we know even less, is not always feasible or fruitful. And recently suggestions for a renewed collaboration of psychoanalysis with the study of the brain abound. These are questions not only of a theory of science—as which they are commonly presented—but also of, if I may say so, practical considerations with regard to a given science in a given stage of its development. The methodological demands on science are generally made from the vantage points of its most advanced field. It will not always prove profitable to apply them rigidly or literally to a beginner among sciences, as analysis is. It is not wise to limit, in the beginning, the field to those parts that can easily be approached in a methodologically unobjectionable way (see also Rapaport, 1958). In many instances, methodological considerations had to be postponed. But I may also mention that some hypotheses, rather questionable from the viewpoint of a philosophy of science, have in the case of analysis proved their heuristic value.

It is difficult to describe clearly, in logical terms, what is generally called "clinical research." The fact that the analysts' observations are made in a clinical setting has, in more ways than one, determined also the development of the scientific aspects of analysis. That much is obvious. What is less obvious—it has, as a matter of fact, never been systematically studied—is the comparative scientific potential of the various ways of clinical approach. It would be worth while to examine this question more closely. On the other hand, clinical work seems, in a certain sense, often more "scientific" in analysis than in many other clinical fields. I state this only as an impression, but it is certainly one shared by many. The problem has a variety of aspects. There are, first of all, the great case histories of Freud in which the scientific problems are explicitly stated and which usually combine the presentation of his clinical findings with the discussion of the theoretical (and often also technical) problems involved. They show the constant mutual promotion of observation and theoretical thinking at work. But this style of his case histories has, one could say, remained unique. It has only rarely been imitated, and hardly ever successfully.

There is, then, this second factor. Findings in analysis have been presented in very different ways. There are the reports on "pure" observations (mostly, as we shall see, only comparatively "pure"), more frequent in the earlier years of analysis, though they are not entirely absent today. But the insight into relations of a dynamic, or genetic, or structural nature is more in the foreground than the reporting of isolated data. The placement of the data with respect to mental functioning and its vicissitudes has become the immediate concern not only of the theoretician. That is, the observations are viewed also from the angle of

our theoretical knowledge, as validations or invalidations of a hypothesis and in the most fortunate circumstances as crucial experiments. The
analyst is thus no longer like a naturalist who discovers and describes a
new flower or a new animal. Explanatory concepts enter the picture, and
there are several levels of them. Some are still comparatively close to
observation, while others are far removed from overt behavior and from
immediate experience. This development in analysis has its parallels in
the development of other sciences. Once lawlike propositions on the
structure of neuroses, on the instinctual drives, on typical phases of
development, and so on, had been formulated, our knowledge of mental
processes and their interactions became less tenuous and many hypotheses became less tentative in character. The analyst learned to feel more
secure, more at home with them, and the corresponding concepts
entered more and more the reporting of clinical material. This is indeed
a characteristic feature of clinical discourse in analysis, in contradistinction with many other branches of clinical work. It shows the theoretical
training of the analyst and his scientific interest; it shows above all a
relation of fact finding and theory, imposed by our subject matter and
typical of analysis.

Reviewing a great number of analytic papers or lectures, you find
certain distinct types as to the ways in which the clinical and theoretical
aspects are combined. There is of course the classical type in which
clinical material is presented, compared with earlier findings, and
classified, and then searched for theoretical implications. Other papers,
though clinical in appearance, actually set out to prove or illustrate a
hypothesis which is the main concern of the author; it may be presented
as such, or it may be presented as derived from the clinical data, while in
reality the latter are mere illustrations of the thesis and not its origin.
There are many other types and the subject would no doubt deserve a
special study.

The case of hypothesis preceding observation is, of course, an
entirely legitimate procedure (Hartmann, Kris, Loewenstein, 1953)
which has played a considerable role already in Freud's beginnings (and
plays an analogous role in other fields). Predilections for certain forms of
thinking or presentation appear in a continuum, from the case in which
what looks like a clinical contribution is actually directed by thinking
on a high level of abstraction, to the other extreme at which an essay
formulated in terms of theory is actually closely geared to observation.
Obviously, this is also one result of the impossibility to present in a
paper, or even in a book, all the observational data gathered in analysis.
Thus abbreviations become necessary. What one calls "clinical" and
"theoretical" presentations in analysis are divergent styles of abbrevia-

tion. In this paper, I merely wish to demonstrate that due to specific features of the psychoanalytic approach the demarcation line of clinical and theoretical work is often not easily traceable. These circumstances may also help to explain why it is that in analysis complex and imaginative construction may be presented in data-language, or clinical language, as well as in concept-language or theoretical language. This is indubitably so, and the statement of these facts implies, of course, no criticism. But this state of affairs, characteristic of psychoanalysis, poses a problem in communication. Every reading of psychoanalytic literature asks of the reader a labor of reconstruction if he wants to view it in its aspect as a scientific contribution: what was the background in terms of observables? What are the hypotheses, either presupposed by the author, or deducible from his work?

We cannot expect to find in every analyst the beautiful harmony between theoretical, clinical, and technical insight and skill which was the hallmark of one genius. As we find individual preferences for one aspect, a certain degree of specialization is natural enough. But it is still true in analysis—and this again is different in other fields—that "good theory" cannot be written without broad clinical experience and that every clinical understanding presupposes knowledge in theory. The full meaning of clinical findings can only be developed in the framework of theory. Therefore, as I said, clinical work is generally permeated by hypotheses, as, for instance, not even the simplest statement concerning unconscious processes could be made without them. This example shows that what I am describing here is not an accidental occurrence but directly traceable to a basic feature of analysis.

There is, in this, of course, also an element that can easily become, and not infrequently has become, a handicap to scientific work in analysis, and this is another reason why I mention it in this context. That is, the hypotheses may interpenetrate with fact finding in such a way that their hypothetical character is not always clearly recognized (Hartmann, Kris, Loewenstein, 1953). Highly abstract hypothetical constructs (as libidinal cathexis, etc.) are then reported in a descriptive sense, as data of observation. Such a procedure induces confusion in both clinical practice and theory. If the hypotheses are not, as they should be, spelled out as such, they cannot be tested by further research. Second, that constructs are sometimes described as findings may well be one of the reasons (though certainly not the only possible one) why "findings" cannot be confirmed by other observers. This factor makes it particularly desirable in psychoanalytic research—it is, of course, a principle of every science—that if there is construction, we indicate how it has been arrived at; that is, our hypotheses should be as clearly and as explicitly stated as possible, in order that their relations with others become apparent and that they may be checked by further work. This level of scientific work has not yet been reached in all aspects of analysis, but it has been achieved in some, as a result mainly of a more meticulous study of the theoretical assumptions we bring to bear on our material.

This is the point at which to refer to the problem of interpretation. I do not mean here interpretation as part of our therapeutic technique, but rather as a cognitive tool. Loewenstein has spoken recently about its different aspects (1957). Now, interpretation is tentative explanation, therefore close to hypothesis. Here, too, we find different levels which we could distinguish as "deep" and "superficial"—in analogy to, but not identical with, the meanings these terms have in technique. Interpretation may be just the pointing to common elements in a sequence of associations and thus establishing a connection. On another level of cognitive interpretation, a great number of data, by far transcending the immediate givens of a situation, and a considerable amount of hypothetical thinking have to be introduced, in order to come to a conclusion. Here we meet again the problem of the ratio of observational and hypothetical elements I discussed before. It would be quite wrong, in analysis, to expect a simple correlation between this ratio and the scientific value of an interpretation. Experience decides against this easy answer. Interpretations introducing even a great many variables often prove superior—if they are based on an adequate constructive power of the analyst who integrates his knowledge and theoretical thinking. Fortunately, in analysis "deeper" insight is often truer insight too. This is another aspect which analysis shares with the theoretically highly developed sciences.

Due to the pervasive nature of the genetic aspect in analysis, the reconstruction of early childhood experiences or situations is of essential interest in this connection. We have learned how to gear theoretical expectations to observables in "predicting the past." It works beautifully, as far as we can suppose that the structure of the mental apparatus and the laws governing it are not too different at the stage we are reconstructing from their more familiar later stages—and if enough experiential checks are available. Both these conditions are not fulfilled in dealing with the preverbal stages of development. Hence our extrapolations referring to that stage have mostly a rather tenuous character. What appears as evidence is of necessity often but a reflection of the hypotheses we introduced; such extrapolations are implied in their points of departure. Given the paramount interest of analysis in these preverbal developments, it is imperative that they be studied also by every other method at our disposal. This has been done in direct child observation by psychoanalysts, by investigations that are analytic as to concepts and hypotheses without using the analytic method. The concepts devised for later stages of development not always being sufficient, it has become one of the main endeavors especially of ego psychology today, to find concepts which fit reconstructive data as well as data of direct observation and which facilitate their interrelation. Freud's reformulation of the theory of anxiety, emphasizing the genetic role of external danger, made this broadening of the field of psychoanalysis possible. Later concepts, of the conflict-free sphere, of the ego apparatuses, of primary autonomy, and so on, point in the direction of such a unifying theory, which includes the direct study of both maturation and development in the scope of psychoanalysis.

If there is some discontent, outside of analysis but often also shared by psychoanalysts, as to the relation of facts to theories, this can certainly not be attributed to a lack of data. The amount of the data available to the experienced analyst is rather overwhelming. In this respect, too, analysis leaves every other approach to a psychology of personality far behind. It is sometimes argued that psychoanalysis has actually studied only a comparatively small number of cases. But this argument misses the point. In every individual case we often gather hundreds of data pertinent to a problem in question, contiguities in free associations or other observed regularities. That is, every clinical "case" is actually hundreds of cases, scientifically speaking. Or, rather, we can say that for every "case" there is often a great wealth of instances in which every single hypothesis that comes into play can be tested. And our technique is constantly based on predictions of future responses.

This wealth of data is growing, but it is not always easy to impart this knowledge, to make it intersubjective—though, of course, some ways of communication in teaching or professional contacts of other kinds have been worked out.

On the other hand, our demands on clarification and systematization of theory have remarkably increased. The recent paper by Rapaport and Gill (1959) is an important step in this direction. Still there are, as I said before, broad sectors of our theories in which this clarification and systematization, insight into the relations between various aspects of theory, distinction between confirmed and nonconfirmed parts of it, between hypotheses close to observation and hypothetical constructs have not yet been achieved. This is mainly due to the fact that, compared to other branches of psychology, we work in analysis with a quite unusual number of variables; and in the last instance to the nature of the subject matter that is in the center of psychoanalytic interest.

There are some other general features of analysis which counteract an easy "scientification" (if you will excuse this term) and which it is good to keep in mind. Each one of these would deserve a thorough investigation. But for the purpose of this lecture I have to abbreviate and to simplify a highly complex subject. The data gathered in psychoanalytic observation are primarily behavioral data. And the aim is clearly the explanation of human behavior—though in a broader sense than at least the older schools of behaviorism would have found acceptable. These data, though, are interpreted in analysis in terms of mental processes, of motivation, of meaning. Our concepts of mental processes are usually more than one step removed from behavioral data—and, as I may mention right here, also from immediate experience. The remoteness from the behavioral aspect is one reason why an objective, or maybe we should better say intersubjective, testing of analytic propositions becomes in most instances an arduous task. Hence the conviction of many analysts that these propositions can be tested only in the analytic situation itself. This, again, is often but not always true.

In analysis, as in other fields, investigation obviously proceeds in different layers. There is a chiefly descriptive aspect to it. There is one level, still close to observation, but already going beyond it in one or another respect. Then there is the level of theoretical discourse. The relations between these levels can well be studied in psychoanalytic case histories. Many of the most important concepts are explanatory in nature, e.g., the concept of unconscious mental processes, of libido, of cathexis and many others (Hartmann, 1927; Feigl, 1949; Frenkel-Brunswik, 1954). This element was essential in making a comprehensive psychology of personality possible.

As I said, this characteristic of analytic discourse often removes it rather far from overt behavior and from immediate experience. The frequent remoteness from the subjective experience has been deplored by some; yet, given the kind of conceptual tools analysis uses, it would hardly be otherwise (see also Wisdom, 1953). The problems of "subjectivity" and "objectivity" are posed in analysis in a way somewhat different from the usual one in that we attempt an objective study also of the psychological factors accounting for subjectivity. I may add, though it might not appear to the point in the context of this presentation, that in the course of analysis the new insights the patient gains by way of objectivation can be gradually integrated, in a secondary way, also in his immediate experience.

We find the explanatory character, the comparative remoteness from the descriptive level, in many main aspects of analytic thinking. It means, among other things, that elements of behavior, similar in a descriptive sense, may be considered dynamically or genetically as rather different, and vice versa. We encounter this problem, of course, also in other fields of science, but hardly to the same extent in other branches of psychology. As this level of conceptualization is often met even in clinical work, readers not used to this style of thinking will often experience a feeling of discomfort.

As to individual clinical observations versus the formulation of lawlike propositions, I want to say the following: one works in analysis between the extremes of two attitudes. One attitude would, for the sake of closeness to colorful clinical experience, let the wealth of phenomena stand unformed and insufficiently connected; and another one would force precociously their variety into the procrustean bed of too narrow theorizing (Hartmann, 1929). On the other hand, critics of analysis are often not aware of the wealth of observations on which it rests; but they also frequently misjudge the role of theory in it. Theoretical concepts (as libido, the mental systems, etc.) are then discussed as if they were meant in a descriptive sense.

While the position of psychoanalysis to behaviorism is, in a general way, clear, we become naturally interested in the question: what, then is its position vis-à-vis the introspective schools of scientific psychology? I do not want to stress the obvious, namely that analysis is to a large extent based on introspection, nor the difficulties which arise in an attempt to make an introspective psychology scientific in the usual sense of the term. I rather want to say that this difficulty has in this case partly been overcome by the theories of analysis which lead to generalizations and objectivation beyond immediate experience, and in turn to hypotheses which are accessible to testing. I think our experience bears out the point that it is only by the introduction of hypotheses on different levels, and sometimes on a high level of abstraction, that the full meaning of the observables can be gathered, which means above all that predictions become possible.

Today, nobody would consider science a mere summary of facts; also, the role of imagination in science has come to be clearly recognized in our days (Einstein and others). But it is not too well known how far imagination based on self-observation can contribute to hypothesis formation in the field of psychology. It probably plays a considerable role with what one is wont to call "intuitive" psychologists. According to Freud, such "intuitions" are the result of mostly preconscious observation and induction. While hunches, guesses, unaccountable insights, or intuitions are likely to play a role in the formation of hypotheses in other fields, too, it is possible—though not sufficiently explored—that in psychology those based on self-observation are often an important element, which could mean that some aspects of mental processes can be approached in this way. That this possibility is increased if the objectifying devices of the psychoanalytic method are brought to bear on it, I have said before. Also one should not overrate the degree to which nonchecked self-observation is relevant in psychoanalytic thinking. But it is striking that there are thinkers who seem to have the capacity of developing, without systematic and controlled observation, hypotheses that are later confirmed by way of induction; also of course that among those thinkers who have abundantly written, on the basis of their "intuition," about human behavior, we find only some who have this capacity. It might well be that in psychology this kind of capacity for fruitful hypothesizing plays a different and more important role than in other fields. I certainly do not want to overestimate the merits of uncontrolled guesses. But I point to this because it could become a fascinating object for the study of creative thinking in psychology, and one that only psychoanalysis could dare to approach. Where conclusions, later confirmed, have been arrived at on grounds of scanty observations which one would consider an insufficient basis for induction, it is conceivable that in those cases self-observations of yet unknown breadth and complexity might have been one determining factor. The possibility that self-observation may have this function does not, of course, obviate the necessity to check systematically such apparent "intuitions" with every available method.

It is very likely that in the work of Freud and other analysts such unaccountable insights have occurred. If so, it is clear that, certainly with Freud, his striving for scientific discipline, his patient accumulation of observational data, and his search for conceptual tools to account for them have kept their use under control. Many subjects approached in analysis, had, before Freud, been studied by so-called intuitive psychology only. But he was wont to oppose psychoanalytic psychology to intuitive psychology, and the development psychoanalysis has taken bears out this point. Still the relation between the cues used and theory is no doubt a rather complex one in psychoanalysis. This consideration leads us back to what I said before about this relationship. I do not think that concept formation in analysis differs in principle from concept formation in science in general (see Hartmann, 1927). But the complexity of the theoretical structure and the fact that validation, at least as to some of its aspects, is extraordinarily difficult, pose problems which are not always clearly understood and have not always been solved in a satisfactory way.

Suggestions to translate psychoanalytic theory into the language of operationism have been made repeatedly (Ellis, 1956; and others). But such attempts have not gone very far. Moreover, the nature of the special problems with which analysis has to deal was not always sufficiently realized. On the other hand, I may at least mention here that Flew (1956), facing some of these special problems with which psychoanalysis is confronted, has come to the conclusion that "these peculiarities are such as to ensure that their central and basic place in psychoanalysis must give this discipline a logical status different from, though not of course for that reason either inferior or superior to, that of sciences concerned with things other than human beings, and even from that of sciences concerned with less distinctly human aspects of human beings."

I pointed before to that constant use of predictions and their checking which is an essential part of the technique of psychoanalysis. However, this refers mostly, though not exclusively, to hypotheses still comparatively close to observation. But beyond this level, a great number of constructs figure in analysis for explanatory and predictive purposes and for the direction of further research. The "logical gap" (Einstein) between the level of constructs and observation, very obvious in modern physics, is apparent also in the less highly systematized fields like psychoanalysis. Its constructs originate, in the last instance, in observation, to which we have to add the legitimate role of imagination in theory formation (to which I referred before). It is, of course, difficult to assess their comparative distance from the data of observation in analysis and in other fields, but we will agree that essential aspects of psychoanalytic theory are rather far removed from clinical observation. Freud and some other analysts were not shy of theorizing. It was felt, in analysis, that too puritanic an attitude toward the introduction of hypotheses, or toward the introduction of complex hypotheses, had not proved and could not be expected to be beneficial to the development of scientific psychology. A great number of hypotheses were, then, introduced, in cognizance of their function, and accepted, modified, or rejected according to the usual criteria. They were not to be in contradiction with experience and with each other, and had to prove their explanatory value. For some levels of theorizing the acceptance of "good" and rejection of "bad" hypotheses appeared to be comparatively easy; but this is certainly not true of all levels of theory, neither in analysis, nor in other sciences. I may say here that the complexity of the theoretical structure of psychoanalysis seems to me not just a theorizing for theory's sake. Despite opposite and rather generally shared demands for simplification, this complexity may be a necessary and fruitful response to the demands a more comprehensive conception of personality makes on our thinking today. Historically it is true that in psychology before Freud a definite distrust of theory prevailed; and this attitude is still apparent in various aspects of social science. As to the present stage in analysis there is no doubt that it is a stage of growing complexity. All attempts at simplification, of which there are many, at a concentration on only one aspect at the expense of others, had to be paid for by a severe limitation of the explanatory reach and the predictive value of analysis. It is possible that the optimal relation between complexity of theory and explanatory fitness differs in different stages of the development of a theoretical system. Thus one may hope, possibly even expect, that at some future time we may reach a decidedly more beautiful and satisfactory stage, when simple formulations will become of equal or superior value.

It is partly due to this intricate interdependence of variables that the problem of quantification, difficult enough to approach in some other fields of psychology, seems even more inaccessible in psychoanalysis. Obviously, measurement which has been defined as "the business of pinning numbers on things" (S. S. Stevens) is not equally easy in every field of science. We compare the strength of impulses, the tenacity of resistances, the impact of rational tendencies, etc., we infer from the strength of a resistance the force of repression; but one cannot measure these factors. It may be that "more, less, greater than, fewer of, increase or decrease in, etc., may be used more profitably" than numeration (Brower, 1949). One can measure overt behavior, or physiological processes in the central nervous system, etc., but not mental processes in the sense we use the term in analysis. We assume relationships between the former and the latter, thus an approach to measurement by way of the former is not unthinkable. Often "processes that are difficult to measure may be studied in behavioral as well as in physical sciences by analyzing the frequency, duration, and degree of their interference with a more easily measured process" (Lindsley, 1957). Actually, though, these connections are in our case always highly complex and have mostly not been sufficiently clarified. Quantification is possible and has been widely achieved in nonanalytic branches of psychology as to those psychological processes which are, viewed from the vantage point of a psychology of personality, of a peripheral nature. They may, since analysis moves toward a general psychology, become more important than they have previously been also in psychoanalysis proper. Still, I have to remind you at this point of what I said before of the relative remoteness of the factors predominantly considered in analysis from this aspect of psychology, which means that the translation from the language suitable for this aspect into the one dominant in analysis is no easy matter; it has been tried, though, with respect to certain problems and has proved feasible.

There is no doubt, of course, that systematization in science can, in principle, benefit from measurement. But it is possible that at the present stage of development of psychoanalysis, measurement at all costs, as some want to have it, considering the variables only from the angle of our capacity to measure them, would sacrifice an essential aspect of analytic research.

Despite what I just said about measurement, in regard to psychoanalysis, quantification is implied in many analytic concepts, in the "force" of the drives, in the "strength" of the ego, in the principles of regulation, etc. As a matter of fact, we find this quantifying concept formation even at a level of hypothesis formation comparatively close to clinical observation. We trace the vicissitudes of cathectic charges from one dream element to another, or from an instinctual tendency to a symptom. This introduces an element of coherence into our psychological hypotheses. Of course, such a quantifying concept formation without possibility of measurement poses à problem and this problem has been widely discussed. I will not go into it any further here, beyond saying that I do not consider this procedure logically unacceptable.

It is obvious that the endeavor to validate psychoanalytic hypotheses by all means suitable to the purpose is welcome in analysis as it might help toward a clarification of its theories. Experimental work, outside of the analytic situation, with this purpose in mind has also been done by analysts themselves, of which I shall quote two examples. Certain psychoanalytic ideas concerning the use and meaning of symbols could be confirmed extra-analytically by Roffenstein (1923) and by Betlheim and Hartmann. Recently, Fisher (1954, 1956, 1957) has validated some aspects of Freud's ideas on perception, imagery, and dreams, and has in other respects suggested modifications of analytic theory.

Direct observation of psychotic patients confirmed on a large scale what Freud had inferred about the characteristics and main contents of primary processes. Indirect validations of psychoanalytic propositions have become available as a consequence of their use in psychology, anthropology, etc., since the demarcation line between analysis and neighboring fields has become less strict than it had been before. Such studies are often an incidental profit from studies frequently not primarily aimed at validation. To give you again an example, I remind you of G. Klein's (1954) investigation of the impact of needs (thirst, in his case) on cognition, and on the influence of "cognitive styles" on it. This problem of the interaction of needs (taken as representing drives) and cognition (a function of the ego) is, of course, close to the center of analytic interest. "Cognitive styles" have been described, and their explanation has been attempted, e.g., in Freud's presentation of the problems of obsessive thought. Among the studies of the motivation-cognition problem I may also mention the work of Frenkl-Brunswik (1949).

There exists, as you all know, an extensive literature on experiments in animals and in man that aim at the testing of psychoanalytic hypotheses, or hypotheses derived from analysis. These studies have so far not decisively contributed toward a reformulation of psychoanalytic theory. But it is true that the best of them lead us to a better insight into certain difficulties inherent in our field and may lead us to renewed efforts to strive for better formulations of our hypotheses, sharper definitions, and greater systematic coherence. Early criticisms of analysis often gave the impression that those stumbling blocks could easily be overcome, but for the disinterest or the ineptness of the analysts. If one were to let those critics do the theorizing, everything could be comfortably arranged according to the best available standards. This approach was entirely ignorant of the specific characters of our subject matter and of the complexities encountered by every method that seriously strives for an explanation of personality. It entirely overlooked the essential insight that hypotheses are primarily tools, to be adapted to the demands of a given field. To accept these directions and warnings would have meant, for the analysts, to become "acceptable" in the sense of methodological standing—but also to pay for it by accepting a disastrous curtailment of the reach and the depth of his work. Fortunately, this brand of criticism has somewhat receded today. Still even now it sometimes needs emphasizing that this understanding of hypotheses as tools, a principle widely accepted in every science, leads to the conclusion: that in a considerable part of our field scientific progress can be expected in the first line from those who are not only able to judge the logical nature of such tools, but also to test their fruitfulness in actual psychoanalytic work.

The achievement of greater clarification and systematization, then, still rests primarily on the analysts themselves. But every step in this direction might well, in turn, increase also the potential relevance for this process of contributions coming from outside psychoanalysis.

I will conclude this lecture, which was mainly on method and theory, with a practical suggestion. Speaking of the scientific aspects of analysis, one should really also speak of the analyst as a scientist. If what I said is true, namely, that the methodological development of analysis will mainly rest on the work of the analysts themselves, one would hope them to be prepared for this additional task. It has often been said that his personal analysis endows the student with the degree of objectivity essential for scientific work. But such statements, while not actually false, are incomplete. The personal analysis is certainly a prerequisite for that kind of work, but is not in itself sufficient. Obviously, there are also questions of gifts and of interests involved—but they do not concern us here. My point is rather that as the logic of experimentation or of statistical work is taught in other fields, there is something—as a matter of fact, very much—that is teachable and learnable about the special methodological aspects of psychoanalysis as a science and one would wish that our curricula will find it possible to include opportunities for such studies.

REFERENCES

BROWER, D. (1949), The Problem of Quantification in Psychological Science. *Psychol. Rev.,* 56.

ELLIS, A. (1956), An Operational Reformulation of Some of the Basic Principles of Psychoanalysis. In *The Foundations of Science and the Concepts of Psychology and Psychoanalysis,* ed. H. Feigl & M. Scriven. Minneapolis: University of Minnesota Press.

FEIGL, H. (1949), Some Remarks on the Meaning of Scientific Explanation. In: *Readings in Philosophical Analysis,* ed. H. Feigl & W. Sellars. New York: Appleton-Century.

FISHER, C. (1954), Dreams and Perception. *J. Amer. Psychoanal. Assn.,* 2.

——— (1956), Dreams, Images and Perception. *J. Amer. Psychoanal., Assn.,* 4.

——— (1957), A Study of the Preliminary Stages of the Construction of Dreams and Images. *J. Amer. Psychoanal. Assn.,* 5.

FLEW, A. (1956), Motives and the Unconscious. In: *The Foundations of Science and the Concepts of Psychology and Psychoanalysis,* ed. H. Feigl & M. Scriven. Minneapolis: University of Minnesota Press.

FRENKEL-BRUNSWIK, E. (1949), Intolerance and Ambiguity as an Emotional and Cognitive Personality Variable. *J. Personal.,* 18.

——— (1954), Psychoanalysis and the Unity of Science. *Proc. Amer. Acad. Sci.,* 53.

HARTMANN, H. (1927), *Die Grundlagen der Psychoanalyse.* Leipzig: Thieme.

——— (1929), Uber genetische Charakterologie, insbesondere über psychoanalytische, *Jb. Charakterol.,* 6.

——— ———(1953), The Function of Theory in Psychoanalysis. In: *Drives, Affects, Behavior,* ed. R. M. Loewenstein. New York: International Universities Press.

JONES, E. (1953-57), *The Life and Work of Sigmund Freud*, 3 Vols. New York: Basic Books.

KLEIN, G. (1954), Need and Regulation. In: *Nebraska Symposium on Motivation*, ed. M. R. Jones. Lincoln: University of Nebraska Press.

KRIS, E. (1947), The Nature of Psychoanalytic Propositions and Their Validation. In: *Freedom and Experience*, ed. S. K. Hook & M. R. Konwitz. Ithaca, N.Y.: Cornell University Press.

LINDSLEY, E. O. (1957), Operant Behavior During Sleep: A Measure of Depth of Sleep. *Science*, 126.

LOEWENSTEIN, R. M. (1957), Some Thoughts on Interpretation in the Theory and Practice of Psychoanalysis. *The Psychoanalytic Study of the Child*, 12.

LOTTIG, H. (1931a), *Hamburger Zwillingsstudien*. Leipzig: Barth.

RAPAPORT, D. (1958), *The Structure of Psychoanalytic Theory: A Systematizing Attempt*. *Psychological Issues*, Monogr. 6. New York: International Universities Press, 1960.

———— & GILL, M. M. (1959), The Points of View and Assumptions of Metapsychology. *Int. J. Psycho-Anal.*, 40.

RAFFENSTEIN, G. (1923), Experimentelle Symboltraüme. *Z. ges. Neurol. & Psychiat.*, 87. Translated in part in: *Organization and Pathology of Thought*, ed. D. Rapaport. New York: Columbia University Press, 1951.

WISDOM, J. (1953), *Philosophy and Psycho-Analysis*. New York: Philosophical Library.

12

Psychoanalytic Theory and Evidence *

Wesley C. Salmon

The distinction between considerations which are in a broad sense logical and those which are empirical is a fundamental one for the philosophy of science; indeed, this distinction constitutes the basis for differentiating philosophy from the empirical sciences. It is the business of the philosopher of science to investigate and explicate the logical criteria a scientific theory must satisfy and, in cooperation with the empirical scientist, to determine whether a particular theory does satisfy them. Failure to meet these logical criteria would be an insuperable objection against any scientific theory. If it satisfies the logical criteria it must still passs the test of empirical confirmation. The logical criteria are within the domain of philosophy, but the actual empirical confirmation is not. The collection, evaluation, and interpretation of the evidence is strictly the business of the empirical scientist.

It is not the aim of the present essay to formulate and discuss the general philosophical principles which are applicable to all of the empirical sciences. Rather, the attempt will be made to apply some of the more familar and relatively noncontroversial principles specifically to parts of psychoanalytic theory.[1] The general area of investigation will be

*Reprinted by permission of the New York University Press from *Psychoanalysis, Scientific Method and Philosophy*, edited by Sidney Hook. Copyright © 1959 by New York University.

1. Terminological note: In this essay the term "psychoanalytic theory" will be used to denote the empirical theory in a general way and to distinguish it from psychoanalysis as a therapeutic technique. I make no attempt to state precisely what I take to be the content

the logical relations between observational evidence and hypothesis or theory. No attempt will be made to deal comprehensively with the nature of the evidence which supports psychoanalytic theory as a whole. The discussion will take up some restricted but important issues concerning the confirmability of psychoanalytic theories and hypotheses.

I

Freud and his followers have repeatedly emphasized the fundamental role of a principle of determinism in psychoanalytic theory.[2] Since the concept of determinism has had a long and varied philosophical history, it may be useful to distinguish several of the more important philosophical doctrines of determinism, indicate the roles these doctrines have been intended to fulfill, and show how the psychoanalytic principle differs from them in content and function.[3] I hope to show that the philosophical interpretations of determinism are inappropriate to psychoanalytic theory, and I hope to present a formulation which will be appropriate. In reformulating the psychoanalytic principle I am not attempting to state what Freud or any other psychoanalytic theorist had in mind when he referred to a principle of determinism.[4] I shall be attempting to state with reasonable precision a principle which will have the theoretical import required by psychoanalytic theory. This formulation bears directly upon the problem of evidence, the subject of this essay as a whole.

of psychoanalytic theory—that in itself would be a colossal task. I appeal only to those parts of the theory which are accepted by analytic theorists of a relatively orthodox Freudian kind. "Hypothesis" is used to refer to statements about individual cases; presumably such statements result from the application of the theory to these cases. Hypotheses are not directly verifiable by observation; they are indirectly confirmable on the basis of observational evidence. "Theory" is reserved for the generalizations which are supposed to hold for all cases and which constitute the substance of the scientific discipline. "Logical" is used in a broad enough sense to comprehend both inductive and deductive considerations as well as semantic ones.

2. Statements to this effect abound. For example, see Sigmund Freud, *A General Introduction to Psychoanalysis* (Garden City, N. Y.: Garden City Publishing Co., 1943), pp. 27, 95 n.; Sigmund Freud, *The Psychopathology of Everyday Life* in *The Basic Writings of Sigmund Freud* (New York: Random House, 1938), pp. 150 ff.; and Charles Brenner, *An Elementary Textbook of Psychoanalysis* (Garden City, N. Y.: Doubleday and Co., 1957), chap. I.

3. Two of the most famous classical statements are those of Kant and Laplace: *Immanuel Kant's Critique of Pure Reason*, ed. Norman Kemp Smith (London: Macmillan and Co., 1933), p. 218; P. S. Laplace, *A Philosophical Essay on Probabilities* (New York: Dover Publications, 1949), pp. 2–5.

4. Quite possibly Freud associated the psychoanalytic principle of determinism with a philosophical doctrine; indeed, he seems to regard determinism as a presupposition

(1) Philosophers have often taken determinism as an a priori principle. Some of these philosophers have used the principle to circumvent the Humean problem of the justification of induction. To avoid the circularity of using inductive reasoning to establish a principle which would serve to justify induction, the principle of determinism has been regarded as a priori. In psychoanalytic theory there is no problem of the justification of induction; like any other empirical science, it makes use of inductive methods without involvement in the problem of their justification. The problem of induction is a problem in the philosophy of science, and one that should in my opinion be taken seriously, but it is not a problem in any one of the empirical sciences. Hence, no empirical science need include a special a priori principle to secure for itself a justification of the inductive method.

If the principle of determinism were a priori, either it would be a synthetic a priori metaphysical presupposition of science[5] or it would be an analytic a priori truth of logic. It has been argued effectively by many authors that neither science in general nor any particular science has need of metaphysical presuppositions.[6] On the other hand, if the principle of determinism were a truth of logic it would be tautological and therefore empirically empty. In neither case would it be required as a basic principle within the empirical discipline of psychoanalytic theory; it could be deleted from the theory without affecting the empirical content of the theory in any way.

In psychoanalytic theory the principle of determinism is a posteriori. In Freud's work it is supported by a large body of empirical evidence taken, for example, from the investigation of slips of the tongue or pen, dreams, and neurotic symptoms. Whether or not this evidence can be regarded as conclusive, it is the kind of evidence upon which the principle rests.

(2) The philosophical doctrine of determinism has often been stated in a very general way which may be rendered somewhat inaccurately as "Every event has a cause." Apart from the fact that determinism in the inanimate world is irrelevant to psychoanalytic theory, there are two important reasons why this sort of formulation

---

of empirical science. See Sigmund Freud, *A General Introduction to Psychoanalysis*, pp. 27, 95–96.

5. Kant is probably the most important historical representative of this point of view.

6. Herbert Feigl, "Scientific Method without Metaphysical Presuppositions," *Philosophical Studies*, Vol. 5, No. 2, February 1954; Arthur Pap, *Elements of Analytic Philosophy* (New York: The Macmillan Co., 1949), chap. 16.

misses the psychoanalytic principle. First, it need not be taken as a basic postulate of an empirical science that every event in the range of the subject matter of that science be subject to causal determination and explanation. Even if we adopt the dubious assumption that it is the business of science to discover causal relations, we do not need to postulate beforehand that such relations exist. The most we need is a regulative principle that the discovery of such relations is important to the scientific discipline in question—that it is worth while hunting for such relations. A regulative principle would be a directive for the conduct of science, not part of the content of a particular science. Whether such relations exist need not be decided beforehand; it may be left to the investigators to see whether they can be found. There is nothing logically peculiar in looking for something even though we cannot be given iron-bound assurance that it exists. We merely need to know that it would be worth finding if it did exist. Of course, we would not undertake the search if we knew ahead of time that the object did not exist. But we are certainly justified in the search if we simply do not know whether it exists or not. Furthermore, even if it were not true that every event is subject to complete causal determination, it might still be true that some very interesting causal relations exist. The investigation of these relations would unquestionably form an appropriate part of a scientific discipline.

Second, psychoanalytic theory is not .content merely with the statement that certain events, such as slips of the tongue, have some cause or other. For psychoanalysis it is important that these causes be psychic causes. If such events were completely determined by physiological causes, this would not be sufficient for psychoanalytic theory. Psychoanalytic theory holds that such events as slips, dreams, and neurotic symptoms have as their causes such occurrences as conscious or unconscious impulses, wishes, desires, etc.[7] This point will be discussed more thoroughly below; here it is sufficient to point out that the psychoanalytic principle specifies the *kinds* of causes involved whereas a philosophical principle would not.

(3) The philosophical doctrine of determinism has often been related to ethical issues, and often in conflicting ways. It has sometimes been argued that determinism excludes freedom and moral responsibility; at other times it has been held that determinism is a necessary condition of freedom and moral responsibility. Philosophical disputes

7. Antony Flew, "Motives and the Unconscious" in *Minnesota Studies in the Philosophy of Science*, Vol. I, *The Foundations of Science and the Concepts of Psychology and Psychoanalysis*, ed. Herbert Feigl and Michael Scriven (Minneapolis: University of Minnesota Press, 1956).

of this sort are perennial; there is no need to enter upon them here.[8] We need only remark that such ethical issues are irrelevant to the methodology and empirical content of psychoanalytic theory. We cannot countenance the acceptance or rejection of a fundamental principle of an empirical theory on grounds of alleged desirable or undesirable ethical consequences.

(4) In philosophy of science the controversy over determinism has often been a controversy over the kinds of laws that are fundamental in science. Those who reject determinism hold that statistical laws are fundamental and that events are determined probabilistically. At least, the opponent of determinism holds we have no good ground for asserting that deterministic laws must be fundamental and that all probabilistic relations must be explainable in terms of deterministic ones. The determinist, on the other hand, maintains that all events are governed by unexceptionable and nonstatistical laws. We may use statistical laws because it would be impractical to trace out all the causal determinants of some events or because of our ignorance of some of the causal laws, but the determinist maintains that complete causal determination obtains in the real world nevertheless.

The issue of determinism is widely discussed in the philosophy of quantum mechanics, but it is doubtful that psychoanalytic theory needs to make a commitment on this sort of issue. It is one thing to deny that certain events are completely haphazard and unrelated to previous events. It is quite another to claim that events of a certain kind are related to their predecessors by deterministic laws. It is a distinct possibility that there are stable probability relations between events and their predecessors in which the degree of probability is sometimes high. There would hardly be grounds for complaint if psychoanalytic theories could be shown to be well-confirmed statements of probabilistic relations which would enable us to explain any event as following from certain predecessors with a high degree of probability. In such a case we would have every right to deny that events such as slips, dreams, and neurotic symptoms are haphazard and meaningless, and this is what the psychoanalytic principle of determinism is concerned to deny.

The foregoing discussion has not been intended as an exhaustive survey of philosophical principles, doctrines, or controversies; it has been intended to show that these are quite irrelevant to the psychoanalytic principle of determinism. We might characterize the psychoanalytic principle provisionally in the following way: it is an empirical postulate subject to confirmation or disconfirmation by empirical

8. For discussions of this topic see *Determinism and Freedom in the Age of Modern Science*, ed. Sidney Hook (New York: New York University Press, 1958).

evidence; it asserts the existence of definite relations among events; but the relation may be either deterministic or probabilistic; and it specifies that the "causes" involved are of a rather specific sort. Perhaps it is misleading even to call a principle that fits this description a "Principle of determinism"; however, the usage is so well established it would be futile to recommend a change at this point. It is better to emphasize the difference between philosophical determinism and psychoanalytic determinism and hope that confusion will be minimized. It is probably advisable always to speak of psychic determinism when the latter principle is involved.

There is a good deal to be done before we can state the principle of psychic determinism in a satisfactory form. It is not sufficient to say that all psychic events have psychic causes, even if we understand the statement probabilistically. In many cases, at least, when we apply the principle of psychic determinism, only the determinants are psychic while the event which is probabilistically determined is an event of behavior—a movement of the body, for example. On the other hand, we do not wish to say that every event of human behavior has psychic determinants; blushing has, but flushing often has not. Nor will it do to say merely that voluntary behavior has psychic determinants. In the ordinary sense of "voluntary," such behavior as a nervous tic is not considered voluntary, yet we would hold that it has psychic determinants. Rather, what we want to say is that the organism's responses to stimuli fall into two classes; first, responses which are mediated only by constitutional mechanisms, i.e., mechanisms which cannot be modified by stimuli (except perhaps of a physically traumatic sort), and second, responses which are not thus mediated by constitutional mechanisms. Psychoanalytic theory says that there are psychic mechanisms in such cases, whether or not there are neurophysiological mechanisms. Roughly, if there are neurophysiological mechanisms, they can be modified by experience.

Stimuli and responses are publicly observable phenomena.[9] In addition, there may be certain privately observable psychic phenomena such as conscious wishes, feelings, and emotions; this is a matter of controversy with which we need not become involved here. However, on any theory whatsoever, unconscious psychic phenomena are not directly observable by anyone, subject or other observer. They are inferred entities or events.

9. This seems to be the point of departure adopted by Ellis, who, incidentally, emphasized the probabilistic character of his reformulations. Albert Ellis, "An Operational Reformulation of some of the Basic Principles of Psychoanalysis" in Feigl and Scriven, editors,

If we begin by thinking of the organism as a container whose surface and environment we can observe but whose interior cannot be directly observed, then our problem can be regarded as that of understanding the output of the organism.[10] It becomes obvious that the output is conditioned by the input; there is a relationship between stimulus and response. In some cases the relationship is constant—a certain type of stimulus is followed by a certain type of response with a high degree of probability, unless a definite physical pathology can be discovered. In such cases we have simple reflexes and the like—stimulus and response are mediated by a constitutional mechanism. Perhaps it is possible to give a completely physiological explanation of this mechanism; whether it is or not is beside the point here. In other cases a psychic mechanism can readily be found; at least, the organism can report the existence of such a mechanism which he claims is an object of his immediate awareness. "He called me a fool, and this made me angry so I left the room." Conscious anger is the mechanism according to this report. It may be desirable to investigate this mechanism further, since being called a fool does not always lead to conscious anger, and conscious anger under these circumstances does not always lead to leaving the room, but at least we have a good start toward an understanding of the behavior when we realize that conscious anger occurred. When behavior occurs which is not the result of a stimulus setting off a constitutional mechanism which the subject can report, then, according to the principle of psychic determinism, there is an unconscious psychic mechanism which causes the behavior in question. The existence of this unconscious psychic mechanism cannot be established by direct observation (including introspection); it can only be inferred on the basis of indirect evidence. In order for the principle of psychic determinism to be empirically meaningful, then, it is necessary that there be independent evidence for the existence of this psychic mechanism, apart from the specific item of behavior it is supposed to explain. If no such independent evidence were possible, then the assertion of the existence of the mechanism would add nothing to the statement of the behavior to be explained. Other parts of psychoanalytic theory indicate what the independent evidence is. The theory gives a limited list of inferred entities such as unconscious feelings, desires, impulses, conflicts, and defense mechanisms. In some cases, at least, the theory states that such entities are created (with a high degree of probability) under certain

10. For a discussion of such models see Egon Brunswik, *The Conceptual Framework of Psychology, International Encyclopedia of Unified Science* (Chicago: University of Chicago Press, 1955), Vol. I, No. 10, Part IV. See also Otto Fenichel, *The Psychoanalytic Theory of Neurosis* (New York: W. W. Norton and Co., 1945), Part I-A.

specifiable conditions. The occurrence of such conditions constitutes independent inductive evidence for the existence of the entity. Furthermore, according to the theory, if one of these unconscious psychic entities exists, it is possible under specifiable conditions to elicit a certain kind of conscious entity (which may go under the same name without the qualification "unconscious"). Free association, hypnosis, and narcosynthesis are ways of eliciting the conscious entity. It is not that the subject becomes aware of an unconscious entity—there is a sense in which this is impossible by definition. Rather, according to the theory, the occurrence of the conscious entity (or the report of it if one insists upon excluding introspective evidence) under the specified conditions constitutes inductive evidence for the existence of the inferred entity at an earlier time. Other items of behavior such as slips, dreams, and neurotic symptoms constitute further inductive evidence for the existence of the inferred entity. It may be, and often is, the case that none of these items of evidence is by itself very conclusive, but we must keep in mind that inductive inferences often involve a concatenation of evidence each item of which is quite inconclusive. Nevertheless, the whole body of such evidence may well be conclusive.

In view of the preceding discussion, then, we may attempt a formulation of the principle of psychic determinism. It will be quite different from any formulation of a philosophical doctrine of determinism.

Every item of human behavior constitutes indirect inductive evidence concerning the inferred mechanisms by which the organism mediates between stimulus and response. Particularly, behavior which cannot be explained on the basis of constitutional mechanisms alone constitutes indirect inductive evidence for the existence of conscious or unconscious psychic mechanisms for which other indirect inductive evidence is also theoretically available. In short, no item of behavior is inductively irrelevant as evidence concerning the mechanisms by which the organism mediates between stimulus and response.

I offer the foregoing formulation, tentatively, as an adequate statement of the principle of psychic determinism. Whether this is what psychoanalytic theorists have always meant is beside the point. It is offered as an empirically verifiable statement which will fulfill the required function in psychoanalytic theory. It is empirically verifiable in the sense that it asserts the existence of certain objective probability relations. These relations are fundamental to psychoanalytic theory.

II

In the preceding section I have spoken of psychoanalytic theory as a theory of the mechanisms which mediate between stimulus and response. It is a theory which postulates the existence of certain unobservable events, entities, and mechanisms. In that section I spoke of indirect inductive evidence for the existence and nature of these unobservables. The charge has sometimes been made that all of this is vacuous because the relationship between observables and unobservables is stated in such a way that *any* evidence supports *any* hypothesis about the unobservables. In this section I wish to examine such criticism.

The kind of situation I shall take up is this. A subject X is observed by a psychoanalyst. On the basis of his observation of X and on the basis of psychoanalytic theory the psychoanalyst hypothesizes that X has a certain unconscious feeling. For example, from his knowledge of X's childhood he may hypothesize that X has an unresolved oedipal conflict. On the basis of this hypothesis he may derive the conclusion that X has unconscious hostility toward his father. This latter statement is another hypothesis, for unconscious hostility cannot be observed directly. When it comes to confirming this hypothesis, trouble may arise. Suppose X is observed to treat his father with a great deal of affection and solicitude. Rather than withdrawing the hypothesis that X has unconscious hostility toward his father, the psychoanalyst may say that X also has unconscious fear of hostility and exhibits behavior of the opposite extreme in defense against his own feelings of hostility. At this point the critic will very likely rise in objection and say that the psychoanalyst is making his hypothesis about unobservables immune to any negative observational evidence; hence the hypothesis is empty. If affectionate behavior is not evidence against hostility, the critic might say, then nothing could be.

If it were true that the hypothesis is compatible with any conceivable evidence, then it would be empirically empty and thus useless from the point of view of empirical science. In order to be nontautological a hypothesis must be falsifiable in principle. If it is impossible consistently to describe observable conditions which would, if they occurred, falsify or render improbable a psychoanalytic hypothesis, then the hypothesis could not be considered an empirical one.

There are at least two ways to answer the objection in the specific instance cited above. First, we might point out that overt hostility and extreme affection and solicitude do not exhaust the possible modes of behavior of X toward his father. The modes of response cover a continuum ranging from the one extreme to the other and including more moderate forms of behavior such as appropriate filial affection, indifference, and covertly hostile neglect. One way to answer the above objection is to maintain that behavior at either extreme of the continuum is evidence for the existence of hostility, while the more moderate forms would constitute evidence against the hypothesis. This answer can be made rather plausible by citing a great deal of clinical and everyday evidence for the fact that behavior at one extreme of a continuum often replaces that of the other extreme.

A second and better answer can be given. Rather than maintaining that a few restricted items of behavior can constitute conclusive evidence for or against the hypothesis, we can point out that a large range of facts is relevant to the hypothesis and the hypothesis must be judged on the weight of total evidence. Any single item of behavior or any small sample may be compatible with the hypothesis that X has unconscious hostility. We know that conscious hostility can be expressed and handled in a wide variety of ways. According to psychoanalytic theory, unconscious hostility can be dealt with in an even wider variety of ways. The unobserved mechanisms are extremely complex, and this means that the variety of modes of response is large. But it does not mean that every total behavior pattern is compatible with the hypothesis of unconscious hostility. It does mean that a good deal of evidence is required to determine whether the unconscious hostility exists, and this evidence must be taken in conjunction with a complex set of theories and hypotheses. A dialectically clever psychoanalyst might be able to argue rather convincingly that any given behavior pattern is compatible with any hypothesis concerning unconscious entities, but such forensics are no part of psychoanalytic theory and are not sanctioned by it.

What then, is the character of the total evidence bearing upon the hypothesis that X has unconscious hostility? What counts as evidence for the hypothesis, and, more important, what would count as evidence against? It is, of course, impossible to give a complete and detailed answer to these questions, but it is not too difficult to give a fairly clear indication of what the answer must be. Here are some kinds of relevant considerations. How does X generally deal with anger and hostility? Does he express conscious anger or does he suppress it? Do situations which would arouse conscious anger in most people arouse conscious anger in X? If X generally avoids the expression of conscious anger and tends not to feel conscious anger in situations which would ordinarily arouse conscious anger, then this would tend to confirm the hypothesis that X's hostility will be unconscious if he has any. On the other hand, if X does not show tendencies to suppress and repress anger, that would tend to count against the hypothesis. Does X have dreams in which violence occurs, and in which the object of the violence is associated by X with his father? Does X make slips of the tongue which are associated with anger toward or abuse of his father? Does X "unwittingly" hurt his father's feelings? Does X "accidentally" break things belonging to his father? In the process of psychoanalysis does X develop conscious hostility toward his father? If the answers to all the foregoing sorts of questions are negative, then the hypothesis of unconscious hostility toward his father is disconfirmed; if there are a fairly large number of affirmative answers, then the hypothesis tends to be highly confirmed.

If criteria like those roughly indicated above are applied to a large number of subjects and it is found that with a high degree of probability a subject with a certain type of background turns out to have unconscious hostility toward his father, this tends to confirm the larger theory which would yield the prediction of hostility in such cases. When the larger theory has been confirmed, then the very fact that the subject X has a certain background lends weight to the hypothesis of his unconscious hostility. Indeed, if the larger theory is well enough confirmed, this may be the greatest evidence there is for the hypothesis of unconscious hostility. Then, the fact that a subject Y whose background is similar to that of X developed conscious hostility toward his father in the course of psychoanalytic treatment will lend weight to the hypothesis that X has unconscious hostility.

The ideal that the theory attempts to approach is, of course, to be able to predict with a high degree of reliability which individuals will have unconscious hostility toward their fathers and which will not, and then to predict, with respect to those who do have such hostility, the exact mode in which they will deal with it. Some progress has been made in this direction, but a good deal is left to be done.

The whole point of this section of this essay is well illustrated by an example taken from Freud's work. In Chapter IV of *The Interpretation of Dreams* Freud attempts to defend his thesis that all dreams are wish fulfillments. He explains how many dreams which appear not to be wish fulfillments can be shown to be wish fulfillments upon analysis. But there is one type of dream that he calls "counterwish dreams." These can be explained as wish fulfillments only by interpreting them as fulfilling the wish to produce a dream which does not fulfill any wish, that is, as fulfilling the wish to refute the theory that all dreams are wish fulfillments. The critic of psychoanalytic theory may look upon this as almost a paradigm of the interpretation of any evidence, however adverse, as compatible with or even supportive to psychoanalytic theory. Surely, the critic might say, the hypothesis that every dream is a wish fulfillment is a tautology if we are allowed to count as wish fulfillment dreams any dream which cannot be the fulfillment of any other wish than the wish to have a dream which is not a wish fulfillment. Any possible evidence contrary to the theory is thus automatically made compatible; negative instances are automatically transformed into positive instances.

Such a criticism would be superficial and unjustified. First, we must note that the wish to refute a scientific theory is a genuine wish in every sense of the word. It would be an unexplained peculiarity in the theory if it held that this particular type of wish is somehow incapable of being expressed in a dream. When we consider the emotional fervor that rose in opposition to Freud's theories during his lifetime, and when we consider, in terms of psychoanalytic theory, how important it must be to patients in psychoanalysis to deny the existence of certain wishes, such an exception would seem even stranger. The wish to deny the thesis that all dreams are wish fulfillments is no casual wish. However, this does not answer the critic's charge. In order to answer his criticism we must state what would constitute evidence against the theory: First, if one of these dreams which cannot be explained as any other kind of wish fulfillment were to occur to someone who had never heard of Freud's theory, this would be most damaging. Second, if a counterwish dream were to occur to someone who had not been negatively inclined toward Freud's theory, that would count as negative evidence. Freud points out carefully that every such counterwish dream occurred to someone who gave ample independent evidence of being negatively disposed toward the theory. In particular, these dreams were had by persons hearing Freud's lectures for the first time and reacting negatively to them, and by patients in analytic treatment who were experiencing strong resistance. Freud said he could almost predict when a patient would have such a dream. Third, if such a dream occurred to someone who was negatively disposed towards Freud's theory, but at a time when the issue was not under consideration, that also would count as negative evidence. Freud explicitly states that events of the previous day constitute the occasion for a dream. Furthermore, he points out that oftentimes the counterwish dreams occur the very night after the individual first heard Freud's theory. In other cases, perhaps, this happens when the issue has arisen during the day. But, according to the theory, these dreams can occur only to those who vehemently reject the theory and only when the day preceding the dream has occasioned resistance to the theory. Such a dream, occurring under any other circumstances, must count as negative evidence.

Psychoanalytic theory has been discussed as a theory of the unobservable mechanisms which mediate between stimulus and response in the human organism. According to the theory the mechanisms are complex, and they undergo changes which constitute a complex history. The main point of this essay has been to indicate the wide range of evidence which is relevant to the inference concerning these mechanisms, and to show that it is in principle possible to state the kind of evidence which should count as positive and that which should count as negative. In so far as this kind of case can be made for the various parts of psychoanalytic theory, to that extent the theory is shown to be empirically meaningful. Whether it is empirically *confirmed* is an entirely different question, and one which can be answered only by empirical investigation.

13

Psychoanalysis: Protoscience and Metapsychology*

Gail Kennedy

In these comments I shall limit myself to Freud's own version of psychoanalytic theory. During the opening session on Psychoanalysis as a Scientific Theory it was asserted that this theory could not be considered "scientific" for at least three sets of reasons: (1) It has the stigmata of a theory that is so formulated as to be by its very nature irrefutable; (2) no adequate methods for establishing the data on which the theory is based, or the predictions from the hypotheses formulated, are provided; and (3) Freud's metapsychology depends on speculative conceptions which are, in crucial instances, inconsistent with well-established results of other sciences, or are beyond the range of scientific confirmation.

I

Is psychoanalysis an "irrefutable" theory and therefore pseudo-scientific? Irrefutability may take several forms: (1) Such a statement as "All events are due to Divine Providence" cannot be disproved. It precludes inquiry by begging the question. (2) A theory may be irrefutable because its proponents always admit what is favorable to the

*Reprinted by permission of the New York University Press from *Psychoanalysis, Scientific Method and Philosophy*, edited by Sidney Hook. Copyright © 1959 by New York University.

theory, and deny whatever is adverse. (3) A theory may be irrefutable because its proponents resort to *ad hominem* arguments when it is attacked. (4) It may be irrefutable because its concepts are so vague that they can always be extended in a way that will yield an *ad hoc* explanation of any apparent exception.

None of this first group of objections is, I think, of much importance. Of course, psychoanalytic theory might be so formulated as to preclude the logical possibility of negative cases. That it need be so formulated, or that the theory as it is actually used corresponds to such a formulation, is questionable enough to throw the burden of proof upon the critic. A proponent of psychoanalysis might use the theory in a way that presupposes conclusions which *should* be open to question. This is something that with a certain amount of logical ingenuity can be done in defense of any theory. No doubt in the heat of the controversy over psychoanalysis it has occurred. Freud himself may have lapsed on occasion into question-begging arguments. But is there something in the psychoanalysis theory which especially lends itself to this sort of reasoning, or which logically requires it? I do not think so. Is it a *typical* mode of reasoning in this field? I do not think that it is. Again, a proponent of psychoanalysis might be the sort of person (as Huxley said of Herbert Spencer) whose "conception of tragedy is the murder of a beautiful theory by an ugly fact." Also he might "have you going and coming" by explaining your objections away as due to your "resistances." Karl R. Popper charges that both these kinds of argument are characteristic of Marxism, psychoanalysis and Adler's "individual psychology." Speaking of his student days, he says:

> These theories appeared to be able to explain practically everything that happened, within the fields to which they referred. Their study had the effect of an intellectual conversion or revelation—of opening your eyes to the truth hidden from those not yet initiated. Once your eyes were thus opened, you saw confirming instances everywhere: the world was full of *verifications* of the theory. Whatever happened always confirmed it. Thus its truth appeared obvious; and unbelievers were, clearly, people who did not want to see the truth—either because it was against their class interest, or because of their repressions which were still 'unanalysed,' and crying aloud for treatment.[1]

What this amounts to, however, is saying that the individuals Popper has in mind subscribed to these theories as articles of faith. It is not the theories themselves but their uncritical adherents who are here condemned as pseudo-scientific.

---

1. "Philosophy of Science: A Personal Report," *British Philosophy in the Mid-Century*, ed. C. A. Mace (London: 1957).

Finally, do proponents of psychoanalysis habitually resort to the device of explaining away apparent difficulties? Often it is difficult to draw the line between an *ad hoc* explanation and the legitimate extension of a concept. No doubt, proponents of psychoanalysis have sometimes failed to hew to the line. But in a young science *many* concepts are bound to be vague; and in any science concepts must be either abandoned or amended to take account of novel data. An idea, as Peirce remarked, is "a little person," and any live theory is a growing body of ideas. Freud himself understood this well. In one of his rare comments on scientific method he said:

> The view is often defended that sciences should be built up on clear and sharply defined basal concepts. In actual fact no science, not even the most exact, begins with such definitions. The true beginning of scientific activity consists rather in describing phenomena and then in proceeding to group, classify and correlate them. Even at the stage of description it is not possible to avoid applying certain abstract ideas to the material in hand, ideas derived from various sources and certainly not the fruit of the new experience only. Still more indispensable are such ideas—which will later become the basal concepts of the science—as the material is further elaborated. They must at first necessarily possess some measure of uncertainty; there can be no question of any clear delimitation of their content. So long as they remain in this condition, we come to an understanding about their meaning by repeated references to the material of observation, from which we seem to have deduced our abstract ideas, but which is in point of fact subject to them. Thus, strictly speaking, they are in the nature of conventions; although everything depends on their being chosen in no arbitrary manner, but determined by the important relations they have to the empirical material—relations that we seem to divine before we can clearly recognize and demonstrate them. It is only after more searching investigation of the field in question that we are able to formulate with increased clarity the scientific concepts underlying it, and progressively so to modify these concepts that they become widely applicable and at the same time consistent logically. Then, indeed, it may be time to immure them in definitions. The progress of science, however, demands a certain elasticity even in these definitions. The science of physics furnishes an excellent illustration of the way in which even those 'basal concepts' that are firmly established in the form of definitions are constantly being altered in their content.[2]

All this first group of alleged faults are different ways of begging the question. They are fallacies to which impassioned believers are peculiarly prone. The real issue raised by those who criticize psychoanalytic theory on this ground is not one of the validity of the theory as a set of statements which might eventually be confirmed or

---

2. "Instincts and Their Vicissitudes," *Collected Papers* (London: 1925), IV, 60-61.

disproven as a whole, or in part, but about the attitude of its proponents.
Have they been partisans, or inquirers, or a mixture of both? Earlier
controversies in the history of science, where powerful emotions are
aroused,—for example the one over evolution in the sixties and seventies
of the last century—show that highly competent individuals, such men
as Agassiz and Owen, Huxley and Gray, may be both, and yet, on the
whole, act as scientists, not propagandists, in carrying on the argument.
Is this true of Freud and of many of those who have extended and
developed the theory? I do not see how anyone who has tried to read
without bias iñ the extensive literature of this field can fail to arrive at
the conclusion that psychoanalysis is an attempt by responsible
inquirers to establish a new branch of science.

II

The second charge is that psychoanalysis is an elaborate theory
depending on wholly inadequate methods of confirmation. Neither the
data on which the theory is based nor predictions derived from the theory
are subjected to public and repeatable tests which meet the canons of
scientific method. This assertion is made on two major counts:
(1) psychoanalysis developed as the consequence of experiments in the
therapy of mental illness, yet there is little correlation between claims
made for the theory and actual therapeutic results; (2) the psychoanalytic method has to be employed in an atmosphere of privacy,
even secrecy, which precludes an objective judgment of the results.

It is true, of course, that many analyses are unsuccessful or but
partly successful, and it is also true that there are many alternate ways
of being "cured." Some persons recover from a mental illness
"spontaneously"—that is, we do not know why nor how they got well.
Religious conversion, and other kinds of experience with sufficient
emotional impact to produce a secular conversion, may mobilize latent
resources within the individual powerful enough to effect a "change of
heart."[3] Other reputable methods of psychiatric treatment produce their
cures. And many a patent quack can claim his quota of successes
through the use of auto-suggestion, electrotherapy, hydrotherapy, a
sugar-free diet combined with breathing exercises, or whatnot.

Psychiatry is not the only branch of medicine where statistics of
"cures" and "failures" are unreliable. In tabulations of cases treated by

---

3. There is an example of this in *As You Like It*. The cruel Oliver, who had tried to
kill his younger brother Orlando, has been rescued by Orlando from a savage lioness.
When he tells Celia of this, she says, "Was't you that did so oft contrive to kill him?" And
Oliver replies: " 'Twas I; but 'tis not I. I do not shame / To tell you what I was, since my
conversion / So sweetly tastes being the thing I am."

psychoanalytic methods the number cited is small, and there are so many variant factors entering into the treatment of each one that the crude statistics have little probative force. At most, they may suggest problems for more detailed and circumstantial investigation. There is, then, a gap between the theory and the therapeutic results of its application to the treatment of mental illness. Yet, its status as a scientific theory is not necessarily invalidated by this discrepancy. To Freud himself the practice of psychoanalysis was largely a means; he was not inclined to be unduly optimistic about the future of psychoanalysis as a mode of treatment and was primarily interested in it as a method of investigation. His real goal was a better knowledge of the structure and mechanisms of the human mind. And it is psychoanalysis as a method of research with which we are here concerned.

A more serious objection than the gap between theory and therapeutic results is that the method is inherently unscientific because of the way in which it must be used. How in the private, even secret, relation between analyst and patient can the subjective element possibly be eliminated? Statements of the patients themselves cannot always be taken at face value—Freud early discovered that many of the "memories" disclosed were false, that in some crucial instances patients were unable to distinguish their fantasies from what had actually occurred. Worse than that are the effects of the transference which develops in the analytic situation. When the analyst makes interpretations, the patient's unconscious may all too willingly comply by furnishing associations in the form of fantasies, dreams, and selected memories which serve either submissively to corroborate the interpretation (though it may be wrong) or defiantly to corroborate the interpretation *because* it is wrong. And under the influence of the countertransference the analyst himself may be seduced into accepting the patient's own subtly and indirectly proffered interpretations, or he may project his own unconscious conflicts on to the patient and end up by treating the wrong person. How is it possible to get out of this quagmire?

When we consider the multitude of theories that can always be "thought up" to explain supposed "facts" and the variety of dissident theories both psychoanalytic and nonanalytic in the field, why not regard the Freudian version of psychoanalysis as just one set of conjectures among many? Why take its pretensions seriously? Yet there are, I believe, good reasons for regarding psychoanalysis as a protoscience—the beginnings of a science that is still in the *clinical* stage of development (as described by Freud in the passage quoted), the stage in which there is constant interaction between a rapidly growing body of observations and theories that are continually being altered in order to accommodate new discoveries.

First, the evidence is not *all* private. There are mitigations. Predictions made in the course of an analysis, such as those that the patient must have had an early traumatic experience of a given sort, can often be checked.[4] Case histories are reported. Recordings of whole analyses (a Gargantuan task) have been made. Psychoanalysis has infiltrated the field of psychiatry. Medical schools, hospitals, clinics and established institutes for the training of analysts provide opportunities for systematic observation and discussion of neurotic and psychotic patients from the psychoanalytic point of view. An increasing consensus has thus grown up within the medical profession. The belief in psychoanalysis may be a group illusion of these practitioners—phrenology and mesmerism once had large numbers of reputable and experienced adherents—but none the less this substantial consensus is relevant, and the systematic observations may well be important indirect evidence for the essential validity of the theory.

Moreover, as is the case with any comprehensive theory, psychoanalysis can be broken down into a large number of subsidiary hypotheses. There is available a large body of circumstantial evidence, drawn from a wide variety of fields, which is relevant to the testing of these hypotheses. Among the sources from which this evidence may be drawn are: detailed studies of the overt behavior of neurotics and psychotics; the use of drugs, in narcosynthesis, and of hypnotism to investigate repressed emotions and memories; the controlled use of drugs which produce a temporary simulation in normal persons of neurotic and psychotic states; the experimental production of neuroses in animals; experiments on animals and with human subjects dealing with such basic mechanisms as repression, displacement, fixation and regression, dream symbolism, etc.;[5] studies of children raised as orphans or in other abnormal situations;[6] the comparative study of child-rearing practices in different cultures;[7] the comparative study of institutions, of rituals and myths, of art works and literature, etc. From all these diverse sources, and others as well, converging evidence may be drawn that is

4. An example of this sort of verification is given by Marie Bonaparte in "Notes on the Analytic Discovery of a Primal Scene," *The Psychoanalytic Study of the Child* (New York: 1945), I, 119–25.

5. For a brief recent survey and discussion of this particular type of experimental work see Ernest R. Hilgard, "Experimental Approaches to Psychoanalysis," *Psychoanalysis as Science*, ed. E. Pumpian-Mindlin (New York: 1952, 2d ed., 1956), pp. 3–45.

6. Cf. Anna Freud and Dorothy Burlingham, *Infants Without Families* (New York: 1944).

7. Cf. *Childhood in Contemporary Cultures*, ed. Margaret Mead and Martha Wolfenstein (Chicago: 1955).

relevant to the accuracy of the data upon which psychoanalytic theory is based and the confirmation of specific hypotheses which may be derived from that theory.

If then, psychoanalysis is susceptible to piecemeal confirmation or disconfirmation through circumstantial evidence drawn from many diverse fields, it should be an embryonic science, a system of hypotheses as yet not fully unified but testable by ordinary scientific methods. That, I think, it now is—a protoscience.

III

The third set of criticisms is that Freud's metapsychology depends on speculative theses which are, in crucial instances, inconsistent with well-established results in other sciences, or are beyond the range of scientific confirmation.[8] Three of these, in particular, are open to this charge. They are (1) that certain basic inhibitions, which Freud thinks of as now being generic human traits, the prohibition of parricide, cannibalism and incest, are the result of early racial experiences, traumatic in character, which have been inherited through the id; (2) that the Oedipus complex is a recapitulation by each individual, under the stimulus of emotional attachments to the parents (or parent surrogates), of this traumatic experience undergone by his remote ancestors; (3) that there are two basic sets of complementary and opposed instincts, the erotic or life instincts and the aggressive or death instincts, and that this basic dualism pervades all of organic nature.

Freud willingly admits that he cannot prove these assertions. His account of the initial organization of society and of the revolt of the brothers in *Totem and Taboo* he calls a "scientific myth," and in *Beyond the Pleasure Principle,* where he first advanced his conception of the universal polarity of erotic and death instincts, he says that it is so highly speculative "I am neither convinced myself, nor am I seeking to arouse conviction in others." None the less, Freud did come increasingly to "believe" in these three propositions as basic to his metapsychology.

Two separate contentions are involved in the first of these statements. One is the inheritability not only of instinctual dispositions, "the ability and tendency to follow a certain direction of development and to react in a particular way to certain excitations, impressions and stimuli," but also of archaic memory traces. The inheritance of

---

8. There is an oddity here. If the metapsychology is refuted by facts, then surely *it* is not untestable. And if the metapsychology is testable, then how is it related to its allegedly untested, perhaps untestable, psychology? Can one have a testable metapsychology for an untested, even perhaps untestable, psychology? I owe this point to my colleague, Professor Joseph Epstein.

"dispositions," however they may have originated, is not in doubt. What seems implausible is the inheritance of memory traces and Freud's explanation of the way in which it came about. A memory, he says, enters into the archaic inheritance "when the experience is important enough, or is repeated often enough, or in both cases. With the father-murder both conditions are fulfilled."[9] This seems contrary to established findings of present-day genetics. Freud makes no attempt to answer this objection, nor to supply any alternative explanation. His attitude, as indicated in other contexts, seems to be that psychology and ethology are *prior* to the biological sciences in the sense that they describe behavior for which the biological sciences must ultimately give an explanation. Similarly, he believes that the anthropologists (who as a body have rejected his theory of the primal group) must eventually explain somehow what he regards as psychologically well grounded facts.[10] There are, I think, alternative ways, perhaps more plausible, of attempting to explain the archaic memory trait: (1) If the primal murder occurred often enough it might be explicable through the operation of natural selection.[11] (2) By social inheritance the archaic memory might be directly transmitted from the unconscious of parents to the unconscious of children. Freud believed that there could be communication at the subconscious level without any conscious awareness, but he did not consider this possibility.

On the universality of the Oedipus complex, whether or not it be a recapitulation of ancestral experiences, Freud gets more support. Ethnologists believe that some form of "nuclear family" exists in every human culture, and many would agree that an Oedipus complex, or some complex which would be an equivalent for that type of social organization, occurs as a result of the prolonged dependence of the human child upon the care of parents or parent surrogates.

9. *Moses and Monotheism* (New York: 1955), p. 129.

10. Cf. *Moses and Monotheism*, p. 169. Recently F. D. Klingender has published an article, "Palaeolithic Religion and the Principle of Social Evolution," *The British Journal of Sociology* V (1954), in which he says (p. 150): "Human society did not therefore, on this hypothesis, begin with the act of revolt to which our children still secretly aspire, while they are in the grip of the Oedipus conflict, but with its far more difficult sequel: the renunciation and redirection of natural impulses which put an end to what was virtually a state of perpetual revolt in the primate group. This way of looking at the matter may imply a shift in the emphasis generally placed on Freud's theory, but the main burden of my argument was published forty years ago in *Totem and Taboo* (1913)."

11. An interesting hypothesis which might explain how instinctive patterns of behavior have gradually evolved from what were originally learned responses is suggested by W. H. Thorpe in chapter 8 of his *Learning and Instinct in Animals* (Cambridge, Mass.: 1956).

Freud's dualistic theory of instincts when stated at the level of Empedocles' principles of Love and Strife is clearly beyond the bourne of science. What is important for psychoanalytic theory is the question: Are there two basic sets of instincts, the erotic and the aggressive? Freud thought it easier and more plausible to explain such phenomena as the repetition compulsion, ambivalence, sadism and masochism, and melancholia as manifestations of a partial defusion of these two normally fused sets of original instincts. To say that aggression is a product of frustration ignores the question: Where does the aggression come from? To argue that an aggressive act is the deflection of an initial positively toned (possessive) drive toward the barrier still leaves the problem of how a drive is changed into its qualitative opposite. A simpler and more plausible hypothesis is to suppose that the original drive is a fusion of erotic and destructive impulses. To possess is originally to incorporate, it is both a having and a destroying of the object. And all "creative" exercise of energies involves an element of destructiveness. Something must be done away with or else forcibly remolded (incorporated) in whatever we make.

There is some evidence from physiology for this dualism. Certainly the erotic drives depend upon mechanisms of the body, and the now classic research of Walter B. Cannon did a good deal to disclose the physiological basis of aggression. More recently it has been found that the adrenal medullae of "constitutionally" aggressive animals such as the lion contain a relatively high amount of noradrenalin, while in animals such as the rabbit whose safety lies in flight adrenalin predominates. The drug meprobamate (Miltown) apparently blocks the secretion of adrenalin. Tweak the whiskers of an ordinary mouse and he rushes off in panic, but the "tranquilized" mouse when tweaked maintains his equanimity. Men are not mice, but there is evidence that outwardly directed anger accompanied by aggressive behavior is associated with the production of noradrenalin, whereas aggression directed inward accompanied by fearfulness, anxiety, and depression is associated with the production of adrenalin.[12]

These highly controversial theses are not the whole of Freud's metapsychology. Other parts of it, such as his topological division of the psyche into an id, ego and superego, are more immediately derived from clinical data, and less doubtful. And by far the greater part of psychoanalytic theory consists of what I have called protoscience. One *can* get along without these far-reaching contentions in the form Freud stated

12. Daniel H. Funkenstein, "The Physiology of Fear and Anger," *Scientific American*, May, 1955, pp. 74–80.

them. They are not essential, many practicing analysts would say, to therapy, nor even to the formulation of a logically coherent theory of the etiology of neurotic and psychotic disturbances. Yet Freud found them indispensable. When even the faithful Ernest Jones expressed scepticism concerning his ideas on the erotic and death instincts, Freud replied in a letter that "he could no longer see his way without them, they had become indispensable to him."[13] This is a revealing statement. The parts of Freud's metapsychology which are most speculative and implausible were not just the divagations of a genius who could also be a cautious and uncannily sensitive observer; they do not indicate, as some critics have thought, that Freud was rather inept when it came to the construction of theories. What Freud meant—quite literally, I am sure—was that he could not see his way in a hitherto uncharted field without them. Without imagination the perceiver is blind. Without an increment of excitement there are no fresh perceptions. As Carl Hempel has pointed out, it is "the fictitious concepts rather than those fully definable by observables" that stimulate predictions and thus afford *new* observations, of something that was not previously discerned. Hence, Freud was tentative, yet also tenacious, about these hypotheses. They were essential to him in the way a set of working plans is to the creator of any novel construction. Throughout his life Freud altered the plans as he went along. Subsequent inquirers may and should modify them in accordance with their needs. Eventually they may present a more fully developed, more precise, even more plausible metapsychology as the framework of psychoanalysis. It is easy, then, to conclude that Freud's metapsychology is "unscientific"; but could he have founded psychoanalysis without it?

13. *The Life and Work of Sigmund Freud* (New York: 1957), III, 276.

FREUD
and the Science
of Psychology

And this time again it has been my guiding purpose to make no sacrifice in favor of apparent simplicity, completeness and finality, not to hide any problems and not to deny the existence of gaps and uncertainties. In no other field of scientific work would it be necessary to insist upon the modesty of one's claims. In every other subject this is taken for granted; the public expect nothing else. No reader of a work of astronomy would feel disappointed and contemptuous of that science if he were shown the point at which our knowledge melts into obscurity. Only in psychology is it otherwise; here the constitutional incapacity of men for scientific research comes into full view. It looks as though people did not expect from psychology progress in knowledge, but some other kind of satisfaction, every unsolved problem, every acknowledged uncertainty is turned into a ground of complaint against it.*

*(S. Freud, *New Introductory Lectures on Psychoanalysis*, New York: Norton Press, 1933, p. 6)

14

The Position of Psychoanalysis in the Science of Psychology[*]

Junius F. Brown

Introduction

As an academic psychologist who has recently completed a training analysis I meet people everywhere who want to "pump" me about my experiences in and my opinions of psychoanalysis. Not only in social intercourse but in the discussion periods following occasional addresses or technical papers, the same series of questions almost invariably comes up. A few of these queries are pertinent and sophisticated, but the vast majority are confused and naive. I regret to say that those asked by my colleagues who are professional psychologists are as often in the second as in the first category. There are psychological reasons for this state of affairs, some of which will be given in a later section of this paper. My chief purpose in writing it, however, is not to tread on toes but to make the discussion of psychoanalysis by psychologists more intelligent.

In a controversial field the questions of both the bias and

*Reprinted from the *Journal of Abnormal and Social Psychology*, 35, 1940, 29-44. Copyright © 1940 by the American Psychological Association and reproduced by permission.

competence of the author are bound to arise. I had studied the psychoanalytic literature and had had a considerable bias in favor of psychoanalysis for some years previous to my own analysis. I have expressed this bias in some previous papers (5; 6; 7). A brief quotation from one of these (7) will indicate my theoretical position before analysis.

> The academic psychologist who has really studied psychoanalytic theory (and he is a very rare individual), is apt to be overwhelmed by the systematic complexity of the theory and by the importance of the problems with which psychoanalysts are concerned. Be he Titchenerian Structuralist, Behaviorist, or Gestalt theorist, he must in honesty admit that his own particular school neither answers nor even poses questions of such wide systematic implication nor of such vital interest. If he is a teacher he must be further impressed with the fact that psychoanalysis is concerned with just those problems which his students expect him to answer and for which he has no answer, at least from the standpoint of his own theoretical persuasion. Psychoanalytic theory deals with *psychological problems*, it deals with *nearly all* psychological problems, and the problems basic to it are *vital*.
>
> The academic psychologist, however, has some advantages which many psychoanalysts lack. He has been trained in the logic of science and in the experimental method. As a logician and an experimentalist, he feels, and rightly so, that many aspects of psychoanalytic theory are in need of conceptual clarification and of a somewhat more rigorous type of proof. He has been trained to accept as scientific those statements concerning experience to which competent observers give universal assent. And although he does not consider himself competent to gather the data which psychoanalysts use in making their theories, he does consider himself competent to criticize the manner in which these theories are built. He further considers himself right in demanding from psychoanalysis that type of experimental criticism which is essential to the healthy growth of any science. To put the present status of both psychoanalysis and academic psychology briefly, the psychoanalyst is equipped with an extensive knowledge of the most vital psychological facts, but he is not equipped to deal with these in critical experiments. Most academic psychologists continue to use the experimental method on facts which are all too often banal or simply *curiosae*.
>
> The outcome of this state of affairs is most unfortunate. The psychoanalysts are inclined to consider the academic psychologists curious fellows in no way concerned with those real problems which they as psychotherapists have to meet. The psychologists, on the other hand, are inclined to look on the psychoanalysts as "mystics" or "cultists." Nothing is gained by either side and the resulting disdain and suspicion are mutual.

Since my analysis, although I now accept some of the contentions I previously criticized and reject some I previously accepted, by and large the judgment remains unchanged. The process of being analyzed, however, has given me insight into why I hold such opinions. And this fact may give my present paper more authority. I by no means hold to the often-expressed dictum that only the analyzed have any right even to entertain an opinion about psychoanalysis. I do, however, feel my own opinions are much better founded since going through analysis than before.

By psychoanalysis, I mean that portion of psychology which deals with the sources and distribution of the psychic energy underlying the integrated behaviors of the whole organism. As such it embraces three different fields of endeavor which although interrelated, must be evaluated separately. These three different fields are:

(a) A method of *psychological observation* in which free association and dream analysis and study of the transference of early acquired libidinal and aggressive attitudes towards the analyst are used to uncover the unconscious.

(b) A systematized *set of theoretical constructs* which are used to order the psychological data found by this method.

(c) A method of *psychotherapy* in which these techniques are used in a special sense to change the structure of the human personality.

A great deal of confusion arises in that critics, failing to consider these fields separately, draw implications from one field to another when such conclusions do not follow. Thus one often hears that since the *therapy* is long and expensive, the *method is worthless and the constructs* methodologically inadequate. Or it is alleged that the *therapy* is very successful but owes its success to suggestion, so that both the *method* and the *constructs* are not worthy of consideration.

Such statements are of course illogical, but I hear them *ad nauseam*. In this paper, consequently, I shall try to evaluate method, system of constructs, and therapy separately with regard to the adequacy of each in its own field. I shall also have something to say about the methodological shortcomings of each and inquire how far these may be avoided. Psychoanalysis represents a vast amount of research, and its literature is tremendous.[1] I shall make no pretense, therefore, of elucidating the details of the theory, nor will I give scholarly documentation. The few appended references provide easily available sources where the topics in questions are treated more or less extensively.

A METHOD OF PSYCHOLOGICAL OBSERVATION

No matter what one thinks of psychoanalysis as a systematic set of concepts or as a psychotherapy, one is "forced" to admit that it is a

---

1. Cf. the imposing *Index Psychoanalyticus* compiled by Rickman (19).

method of psychological observation of great importance. Some time before the word *psychoanalysis* was invented, the fact of unconscious motivation of both psychological and physiological processes had been established. William James called this discovery the most important made by psychology during his lifetime. It is well known how the combined efforts of Bernheim's school and Charcot's (plus the at times acrid debates between them) established the fact that hypnosis is created by suggestion (8; 17). They then showed that hypnotic suggestion could influence both psychic and physiological processes, so that the symptoms of conversion hysteria could be artificially created in hypnosis. From here it was easy to prove that hysteria itself is a sort of "self-hypnosis" in which both physical and psychological symptoms are produced without the conscious cognizance of the patient. There is no point at this time in quibbling about the methodological status of the concept "unconscious." We must accept the fact that *some behavior originates from motives of which the subject is not aware in his normal waking state, but which may be discovered by hypnosis by a specially trained observer.*

If the science of psychology is to cover all the phenomena of human behavior, methods must be devised for the observation of these unconscious mechanisms. What is needed is a sort of "psychological microscope" by which the psychologist can observe in the subject those processes that he cannot observe with the unaided eye and ear. Now it may be that sometime we shall have a "physiological microscope" so that bio-chemistry and bio-physics of the nervous system may be observed directly. That time, apparently far away at the end of the nineteenth century, seems just as far away today. The "apparatus" for such a psychological microscope cannot even now be a "brass instrument" but must be a condition of observation.

As we have already seen, the discovery of the laws of hypnosis leads to the possibility of using hypnosis as such an instrument.[2] Freud began to play with this new instrument with certain neurotics. When, after a period of five years' experimentation (1890–1895), he discovered that the method of free association was superior to that of hypnosis for the purpose of observing unconscious motivation, he began to use the former exclusively. It would take us too far afield to go into Freud's reasons for replacing hypnosis and suggestion by free association (9; 10).

2. The discovery of law and instrument is always closely interrelated. The viewpoint that empirical observation aided by instruments leads inductively to law is seriously to be questioned. Knowledge of laws more often creates the possibility of making new instruments than do existing instruments create the possibility of discovering new laws. Cf. Brown (4).

The chief of these, however, is that in free association not only the observer but also the observed becomes gradually cognizant of the unconscious factors involved and so the study of total life histories is greatly facilitated.[3] There have been now some forty years of extensive experimentation with free association by Freud and his followers. I think we must accept the fact that *most human behavior originates from motives of which the subject is not aware in his normal waking state.* These motives, however may sometimes be discovered by psychoanalysis. Psychologists, furthermore, are themselves human beings and similarly influenced by unconscious motives, a fact which led Freud to the belief that psychologists themselves should be analyzed.

Dr. Franz Alexander (1) has given us a very keen analysis of the sources of error in unaided psychological observation and has pointed out how psychoanalysis as a method overcomes or at least minimizes these. According to him there are four sources of error in every communication regarding motives between two individuals, such as the psychologist and his subject.

The first of these is the danger that the subject will limit his communication to what he wants to tell the experimenter. He may wish for reasons which are quite conscious (pride, prestige, guilt) to place himself in a different light. He may, in other words, lie to the experimenter. Academic teachers know how frequent such behavior is in students suspected of cheating in examinations. Psychoanalysis as a method minimizes this source of error, practiced as it is chiefly either on ill individuals who desire to get well, or on candidates who themselves wish to become psychoanalysts. Both categories of individuals will tend to be honest, particularly as confidence in the analyst is established. Resistance (i.e., the persistence of the wish not to face the unconscious basis of our motives) and transference (i.e., the personal emotional relationship which arises between analyst and analysand) enhance this source of error, however, and help make psychoanalysis a long and laborious process. It is often urged that psychology has more objective methods ("lie-detectors") to determine whether individuals are telling the truth. Although it is true that such devices may detect deception, in themselves they cannot create honesty. The use of methods of measuring the physiological concomitants of emotional states during analysis is not impossible and perhaps in the future will be regularly undertaken.

The second source of error (which we have already dealt with in some detail) lies in the fact that the subject does not himself know all his

---

3. That free association has greater therapeutic value than hypnosis and that not all individuals may be hypnotized are other important reasons.

motives. In the process of psychoanalysis (the free association method and dream analysis) he gradually becomes cognizant of them. The extent to which this awareness occurs depends, of course, largely on the length and adequacy of the analysis and on the structure of the subject's personality. Physical microscopy itself depends on the power of the lenses and the nature of the specimen under observation. That analysis is a long process and probably never completed cannot be held against it as a scientific method. It is the best we have.

The third source of error lies in both the experimenter and the subject. They ·may not know each other or not "speak the same language." This source of error is largely overcome by the daily interviews between the experimenter and the subject, taking place over a considerable period of time. Since basic similarities and differences in the personalities of both parties do play a role, however, the choice of the best suited analyst is a matter of extreme importance.

The fourth source of error resides in the experimenter. The psychologist like any mortal is subject to unconscious motivation. If his own unconscious has been explored, however, he may compensate for this effect. He may learn his own "personality difficulties" and psychological "blind spots." Communication is a bipolar relationship. The subject may not know or want to tell; the experimenter may not know himself, or wish to hear. The demand that psychoanalysis be practised only by thoroughly analyzed individuals minimizes this source of error.

Seen from this viewpoint, then, psychoanalysis has no parallel in the science of psychology as a method of studying human motivation. Psychology has other methods which are better suited to other problems, such as perception and learning. For the study of the dynamic sources of total human behaviors, however, analysis is unique and indispensable. It would be an exaggeration to state that the sources of error of unaided communication are eliminated in psychoanalysis. They are only so far minimized as our present state of knowledge permits. Further technical refinements may be expected in the field of "psychological microscopy" just as they have occurred in the field of physical microscopy.

We may summarize by stating: *granting the role of unconscious motivational processes in determining human behavior, psychoanalysis is a uniquely "successful" way of studying them.* This conclusion stands independent of the methodological value of psychoanalysis as a set of constructs or its value as a psychotherapy.

A SYSTEMATIC SET OF THEORETICAL CONSTRUCTS

A vast array of psychological facts has been gathered through observing humans by the method of psychoanalysis. I think it is no exaggeration to say that more scientific information concerning the springs of human action has been accumulated through forty years of psychoanalysis than through the centuries of unrefined psychological observation. These facts have become ordered and systematized through the aid of certain theoretical constructs.

Psychology has come to methodological maturity. The naive belief that science is solely a product of empirical observation unaided by either theory or guiding principles has been given up even by the modern behaviorists. Science consists of a set of propositions about nature to which competent observers assent. That the propositions are observable under certain controlled situations is the reason why such assent is obtained. No sensible person thinks of debating with physicists unless he knows physics. The same state of affairs should be, but is unfortunately not, true in psychology. Everyone claims a "right to an opinion," even without knowledge of the facts. I must state dogmatically that certain facts have been established by the psychoanalytic method which are as undebatable as the facts of thermodynamics or gravitation, albeit of course not so mathematically deducible or easily demonstrable. It is not my purpose in this paper to touch on these facts except incidentally as they are integrated with the theory.

The facts of a science, once established, become systematized through theoretical constructs. The history of psychoanalysis has been methodologically sound in that fact and theory have been organized hand-in-glove fashion from the time of Freud's earliest writings. We accept the necessity for some sort of coordinating definitions and theoretical constructs. My purpose in this section is to inquire into the adequacy of those adopted by the psychoanalysts. In a single paper the whole theoretical structure of psychoanalysis may not be examined. Elsewhere (6) I have tried to show how the theory is related to the various theoretical positions in academic psychology. Consequently here we shall examine methodologically only certain of the outstanding theoretical propositions.

The theory of the basic urges (1; 12; 13; 15). The theory that the basic sources of human psychic energy are to be found in the libidinal and aggressive instincts is the *starting-point* but by no means the *cornerstone* of psychoanalytic theory. Inasmuch as Freud was forced to accept something to start with, as a late nineteenth century biologist he accepted what all nineteenth century biologists believed in, namely the instincts for racial and self-preservation. These he called the libidinal and the ego instincts. The realization that hate was as great a force as love came much later (1920). In the world as we know it today this statement needs no particular proof. Hate and aggressiveness are not rare and pathological but frequent and "normal." The question of *where* both the libidinal and the aggressive urges originate is, however, a different one. Freud accepted them as instinctual (i.e., innate, teleological, and occurring without foresight into the end), but of course subject to environmental modification.

Modern methodological research led by Dunlap in psychology and Bernard in sociology has raised severe doubts as to the adequacy of the concept of instinct. Some of their criticisms are undoubtedly applicable to certain writings by psychoanalysts. But psychoanalysis as a systematic psychology stands quite independent of the theory of instincts. Although Freud himself retained his faith in the instinct theory, some of his followers no longer accept it. Whether the libidinal and aggressive urges are instinctual or early acquired is of vast importance for the implications of psychoanalysis for sociology (it is claimed, for instance, that "war is inevitable" or that "socialism is impossible" because of the death instinct), but of practically none for the development of a systematic psychology. No matter where they come from, the facts of love and hate are ever with us. I wish but can scarcely believe that these lines will prevent sociologists and psychologists from dismissing psychoanalysis with a sneer because it is "based" on a theory of "instincts."

The theory of the structure of the personality (12; 14; 1). The naive belief that human beings are controlled by unitary conscious souls or egos is today held only by fundamentalist theologians and by the completely uneducated laity. We have already seen that much of the energy for human behavior lies in the unconscious. Besides the unconscious, psychoanalysts posit the conscious and the foreconscious. These represent the topological divisions of the human psyche, i.e., the locations in which the changes in dynamic energy take place. The earlier Freudian theory supposed that behavior was the resultant of conflicts between the conscious and unconscious elements of the psyche. After 1902 Freud (14), realizing the necessity for positing directive forces within the psyche, developed the theory of the ego, super-ego, and id. Thus beside the topographical problem (i.e., the problem of the location of the conflict) there arises the dynamic problem (i.e., the problem of the nature of the conflicting forces).

In addition to the topographic and dynamic problems every behavior also presents an economic problem. Freud states that every conflict is resolved by the dynamic redistribution of psychic energy in the most economical fashion possible considering the total situation. Thus a psychosis is economical when it is the only alternative to suicide, or a conversion hysteria economical when it is the only alternative to continual psychic conflict. The Freudian theory thus supposes that all behavior results from the disequilibration of the existing distribution of *psychic energy.* This disturbance gives rise to conflict. A new equilibrium is established through the *dynamic forces* (id, ego, super-ego) working out the conflict in the *topographical segments* (conscious, foreconscious, unconscious) of the mind in an *economic* fashion.

There is today little doubt that any theory of the mind must allow for its structuredness. The only question which arises is whether the Freudian theory is the "best" which can be made. Of all the various theoretical constructs of psychoanalysis those concerned with the structure of the person seem to me to be the least adequate methodologically. In general, psychoanalysis has done more than any psychological school to overcome the theory of animistic souls characteristic of pre-scientific psychology, but in the concepts of the ego, super-ego and id much animism still remains.

Although these concepts are realized to be of an auxiliary nature by most analysts, occasionally one comes across statements by psychoanalysts which describe a given behavior as the result of a personal quarrel between a nasty little homunculus called the id, a moral little one called the super-ego, and a selfish little one called the ego. These creatures seem to live in not very definitely circumscribed areas of an ill-defined place called the psyche. The conceptions of many analysts of conscious and unconscious are also much too rigid. The idea of the economy of psychic processes is not at the present time subject to logical or experimental proof. I believe that the conceptions of the topological psychologists are methodologically more adequate to describe the now well-established fact of the multiple-structured person and its relations to the environment (6). In fairness it must be admitted that the research of the psychoanalysts much more than that of the topologists has established the fact in question.

The theory of psychosexual genesis (13; 15; 20). All modern theories of personality agree that personality has its genesis in the way in which organisms of specific biological constitution overcome or fail to overcome environmental barriers. The chief arguments are concerned with the nature of the basic urges and with the nature of environmental frustrations. The psychoanalysts suppose that the personality has its genesis through the frustration of the basic libidinal and aggressive urges. To develop this theory requires the demonstration of infantile sexuality and hostility. That Freud conceived of sexuality in a very broad sense is finally being realized. In this sense I think we can say that infantile sexuality is an established datum of psychology. That very young babies (certainly under one year of age) show marked libidinal and aggressive attachments (to parents and siblings) is now scientifically established. That the vast majority of neonates live for a period of time in a family is not debatable. That sexual "perversion" is normal in children and is a frequent phenomenon in adults is known to all psychiatrists. With these facts in hand the Freudian postulate of infantile sexuality becomes an indispensable one for genetic psychology.

The status of the theory of psychosexual development (as opposed to the postulate of infantile sexuality) is but little more open to question. We have already seen how personality development is a dialectical process in which established personality organizations become disequilibrated through the frustration of emerging urges, so that a new organization ensues. In choosing the frustrations concomitant with weaning, toilet training, and infantile masturbation on which to build the theory, Freud has certainly chosen most if not all the major frustrations of childhood in our culture. Undoubtedly other frustrations concomitant with other new adjustments such as walking and talking are of importance in child development. Freud has touched on these only incidentally. Undoubtedly also, as the anthropologists have shown, if one changes the nature of the culture (i.e., of the frustrations), personality differences ensue. But the fact remains that as long as human beings are conceived through copulation, are born of the womb, are nursed as mammals, are forced to eliminate urine and faeces under socially controlled conditions, and are sexually differentiated, Freud's "Three Contributions to the Theory of Sex" remains a basic text in psychology.[4]

We may summarize this section by stating: *granted the necessity for theoretical conceptions in systematic science, those of psychoanalysis are the most adequate we have in accounting for the sources and distribution of energy in the integrated behavior of the organism as a whole.* They need methodological and logical refinement and demonstration by a more direct experimental approach. As concepts they do not have the same degree of scientific adequacy as does psychoanalysis as a method of psychological observation. Again, it must be borne in mind that their validity is equally independent of the efficacy of psychoanalysis as a method of psychotherapy.

Psychoanalysis as Psychotherapy

Academic psychologists are medical laymen and, like all medical laymen, inclined naively to accept the "myth" of the infallibility of the physician. They are, however, students of the mind and inclined not to

4. For the thought of this sentence I am grateful to the anthropologist, Dr. Weston LaBarre.

accept the "myth" of the infallibility of the psychotherapist. They are hence more inclined to emphasize the failures than the success of psychoanalysis as a therapy.

Psychoanalysis as a psychotherapy is based on Freud's finding that the unconscious motives made conscious by psychoanalysis as a method of observation were then subject to conscious intelligent control. Its efficacy as a therapy depends, then, on the skillful use of the method and on the use of the conscious intelligence of the subject. Since even in the longest psychoanalysis the whole unconsciousness is not brought to light and since no intelligence is perfect, immediate limitations are placed on psychoanalysis as a therapy.

Psychoanalysis as a therapy is not, as it has often been called, a "mental surgery." Certain pathologic organs—an inflamed appendix, tonsils, and the like—may be excised without seriously upsetting the integration of an organism in surgery. Surgery is chiefly concerned with structural pathologies. The development of certain other pathologic processes may be prevented by immunization in the blood stream or sterilization of the environment. Through the field of medicine, however, there are functional pathologies which are not subject to excision, on the one hand, and have already developed, on the other— such as diabetes, hypertension, tuberculosis. For these medicine has no cure in the sense of single specific treatments such as operations or immunizations. They must be treated by arresting the pathologic process and then controlling its future course. The success of the treatment depends on the stage of development of the pathogenic process and its severity.

Most mental diseases are functional pathologies. The idea that a phobia or a mania which has its etiology in a long psychic development may be excised by "mental surgery" is absurd. What may be done is to arrest the particular psychological development which makes it inevitable. There are various psychotherapies which specifically attempt such a check. Of these psychoanalysis is probably the most ambitious because it aims at a fairly complete examination of the unconscious. It attempts, in other words, a causal rather than a mere symptomatic cure. But even if psychoanalysis is the most ambitious of the psychotherapies it does not pretend to remove "complexes" in the way that surgery does tumors, and it cannot assure complete immunity from further "complexes" in the way that vaccination assures immunity from smallpox. What it usually does is to teach the patient the sources of his complexes so that he can understand them and live with them. Occasionally, however, the complexes themselves disappear in the process of becoming conscious.

Although psychoanalysts are more and more accepting research cases, in general only those with pecuniary reserves can afford to do so. The psychoanalyst is a highly trained medical specialist whose practice is limited to around seven patients at any period. The psychoanalysis of the individual (for reasons we gave in the first section) is a long process. Consequently, except for research cases, only the well-to-do may be psychoanalyzed. In general, youth, if not a prerequisite, is at least an advantage in the prospective analysand. Since psychoanalysis requires a more or less complete reliving of the past and since the older the individual the longer such a review requires, psychoanalysis has had greater success with young than with old people. We have already seen that intelligent conscious control of previously unconscious impulses is the aim of psychoanalysis. Thus intelligence becomes a prerequisite for a successful psychoanalysis. The overcoming of resistance and the establishment of transference is necessary if psychoanalysis is to work. Since this cooperation is almost impossible in deeply psychotic individuals, psychoanalysis has had its greatest success with psychoneurotics.

When one considers all the foregoing, psychoanalysis compares very favorably with the functional therapies of internal medicine.[5] Recent studies (2; 3; 18; 20), furthermore, indicate its great importance in the understanding of many of the functional pathologies usually treated solely by internal medicine. Despite the growing importance of psychoanalysis as a specific medical discipline, its value as a psychotherapy remains decidedly limited. There are reasons for believing that all medicine of the future will be more concerned with preventive than with therapeutic problems. I believe the mental hygiene of the future will be concerned more with psychoanalysis than with any of the other schools of medical psychology. Lack of space prevents me from giving my precise reasons for this statement.

We may summarize by stating: *when one keeps in mind the difficulties which confront all psychotherapy and also the ambitiousness of psychoanalytic therapy, psychoanalysis has been unquestionably successful with certain types of mental disorder.* Its efficacy is, however, limited by economic, medical, and psychological considerations.

Relation to Psychology

The past three sections have summarized the methodological adequacy of psychoanalysis and related it to psychology as the science of

---

5. I base this statement on the printed reports of the Berlin, London, and Chicago Psychoanalytic Institutes.

human behavior. We have seen that it is the "best" method for observing the sources of human action and the most systematic set of concepts concerning the nature of these sources. In this section, as an academic psychologist I wish to outline very briefly how I think psychoanalysis should be related to the training of the academic psychologist.

It would be useless to deny that there is at present a schism between academic psychology and psychoanalysis. Although psychoanalysis is increasingly taught in the neuropsychiatric departments of the medical schools, so far as I know there is no academic department of psychology where a basic training in psychoanalysis is part of the routine curriculum for undergraduate majors and graduate students. Psychoanalysis has fared and continues to fare badly in the universities. Thus the psychoanalysts have been driven to develop their own training centers outside the universities.[6]

This state of affairs works to the disadvantage of both psychoanalysis and the universities. Although psychoanalysis is of the greatest importance to medicine, it is, as I have tried to show in this paper, of even greater importance for the science of psychology. The present psychoanalytic training centers, primarily for psychiatrists, only occasionally have the opportunity to train research psychologists. The teaching staffs are made up almost exclusively of practising physicians, often with little teaching experience. Library and laboratory facilities are usually inadequate; the atmosphere of leisure necessary for scholarly research scarcely prevails in them.[7] And the training centers have hardly any opportunities to develop research programs into problems other than those of psychiatry. Thus psychoanalysis suffers as a branch of psychology by its lack of the research facilities which characterize the first-rate universities. Academic psychology, on the other hand, is not being fertilized by the vital and pertinent questions which psychoanalysis is throwing up on every side. Psychoanalysis has more legitimate implications for the field of social psychology—which for our times is of such importance—than have introspectionism, behaviorism, gestaltism (which are now part of every curriculum) combined. Thus contemporary psychology suffers from a rigidity of academic tradition with regard to psychoanalysis, just as philosophical psychology suffered from the same rigidity of tradition regarding experimental physiological methods seventy-five years ago. The result is

6. Such institutes or training centers are located in the United States in Boston, New York, Chicago, Washington, Baltimore, Topeka, and Los Angeles.

7. In some of the institutes, particularly that of Chicago, persistent efforts are being made to overcome these difficulties and actually to establish the true university atmosphere.

an academic psychology which is precise but sterile, and a psychoanalysis which is badly in need of scientific criticism but vital and fruitful.

Both sides are to blame for such a state of affairs. The psychologists object particularly to psychoanalysis as a "cult" or "sect." Probably all great scientific discoveries or schools have had to behave in a "cultish" fashion at first. The psychoanalyst has been forced by the defection of nonanalytic individuals whom the public confuses with psychoanalysts, to insist on a strict adherence to psychoanalytic doctrine. The refusal of the universities to give psychoanalysts a proper hearing has forced them to develop their own institutes and societies. The academic psychologists claim it is impossible for them to get training in psychoanalysis and without training they cannot practise it for research purposes. That psychoanalysts are "right" in requiring a didactic psychoanalysis for practitioners follows from reasons set forth in the opening section of this paper. On the other hand, I think training in psychoanalysis has been unduly expensive. To this the psychoanalyst, of course, can reply that in the early days the universities could well have adopted psychoanalysis in their curricula and made it less so.

The psychoanalysts regret that they do not get a fair hearing. That their complaint is well founded may be readily attested by a survey of the most frequently used texts in academic psychology. If psychoanalysis is presented at all, it is presented incorrectly and in an inadequate fashion, naively criticized on impertinent grounds. The psychoanalysts on their side incline to look on psychologists as men of self-limited vision whose compensations take the form of running rats through mazes and investigating hearing with brass instruments, rather than concerning themselves with vital problems. And so it goes.

If I am right in my opinion that psychoanalysis is the major contribution to psychology made in our times and that it should be part of the basic training of all psychologists, sooner or later its inclusion in the university curriculum will be accomplished. When this occurs, the necessity for the separate psychoanalytic institutes will be overcome. The only question which remains is how the change may best be brought about. To so difficult a problem this paper will attempt no answer. Through it I hope, however, to convince some psychologists of the importance of psychoanalysis as a science and of the consequent importance of cooperation with psychoanalysts.

REFERENCES

1. ALEXANDER, F. *The medical value of psychoanalysis.* New York: Norton, 1932.

2. ALEXANDER, F. Psychological aspects of medicine. *Psychosom. Med.*, 1939, *1*, 7-18.

3. BENEDIK, T., and RUBENSTEIN, B. B. Correlations between ovarian activity and psychodynamic processes. *Psychosom. Med.*, 1939, *1*, 243-270.

4. BROWN, J. F. A methodological consideration of the problem of psychometrics. *Erkenntnis*, 1934, *4*, 46-61.

5. BROWN, J. F. Freud and the scientific method. *Phil. Sci.*, 1934, *1*, 323-337.

6. BROWN, J. F. Psychoanalysis, topological psychology and experimental psychopathology. *Psychoanal. Quart.*, 1937, *6*, 227-237.

7. BROWN, J. F. Freud vs. Marx: Real and pseudo problems distinguished. *Psychiatry*, 1938, *1*, 249-255.

8. CHARCOT, S. M. *Oeuvres completes*. Paris: Louis Battaille, 1892.

9. FERENCZI, S., and RANK, O. *The development of psychoanalysis*. New York: Nervous and Mental Disease Publishing Co., 1925.

10. FREUD, S. *The history of the psychoanalytic movement*. New York: Nervous and Mental Disease Publishing Co., 1917.

11. FREUD, S. *General Introduction to psychoanalysis*. New York: Liveright, 1920.

12. FREUD, S. *New introductory lectures on psychoanalysis*. New York: Norton, 1933.

13. FREUD, S. *Three contributions to the theory of sex*. New York: Nervous and Mental Disease Publishing Co., 1930.

14. FREUD, S. *The ego and the id*. London: The Hogarth Press, 1927.

15. FREUD, S. *Beyond the pleasure principle*. London and Vienna: International Psychoanalytic Press, 1922.

16. FREUD, S. *Collected works*. London: The Hogarth Press, 1933. Vol. II.

17. JANET, P. *Psychological healing*. New York: Macmillan, 1925.

18. MENNINGER, K. A. *Man against himself*. New York: Harcourt, Brace, 1938.

19. RICKMAN, J. *Index psychoanalyticus*, 1893-1926. London: Hogarth Press, 1928.

20. STEPHEN, K. *Psychoanalysis and medicine*. New York: Macmillan, 1933.

21. Various. Symposium on hypertension. *Psychosom. Med.*, 1939, I, 93-198.

15

The Scientific
Status of
Psychoanalysis*

Ernest R. Hilgard

Psychoanalysis is, first of all, a medical psychology concerned with the treatment of human suffering, and as such represents the procedures used by those trained in it as they treat the patients who come to them for help. It is also a general psychology, with its interpretations of human development, memory, thought processes, creativity, social behaviour— fitting all of the subject matter of psychology into its categories. Finally, it presents a general view of man's place in nature, of how man may live with his heritage of unconscious processes if he is to be at peace with himself, and if he is to be as rational as he can be in planning for the future of human society. The influence of psychoanalysis upon literature and drama rests upon this implied *Weltanschauung*.

Every young science goes through a number of stages in its development from naturalistic observation, through the detection of areas of lawfulness and construction of more limited theories, to more comprehensive, parsimonious, and elegant theories. While these states can be assigned some sort of historical order, observations are guided by theories, theories are modified by observations, and some theories of very wide scope may be proposed early, to be supplemented later by less

*Reprinted from *Logic, Methodology, and Philosophy of Science*, edited by Ernest Nagel, Patrick Suppes, and Alfred Tarski, with the permission of the publishers, Stanford University Press. © 1962 by the Board of Trustees of the Leland Stanford Junior University.

ambitious models. Hence any particular body of scientific material can be assessed only according to its history, its achievements along the way, the course of revision, and its promise for the future.

Psychoanalysis has a special history because it was dominated so long by Sigmund Freud, a man of great genius, who made most of the observations upon which psychoanalysis is built, who began theory construction at the very start of his career, and fought the social battles for recognition against a hostile clientele. He thus defined the field of inquiry, invented the techniques of investigation, proposed the theories, and set the stage for the fervent social interactions that have characterized psychoanalysis as a profession. He continued to think, to change his mind, to propose new ways of looking at things, throughout a long life. Despite the changes in detail, there is a remarkable unity to his thinking, if one looks for the guiding ideas rather than for the changing metaphors that expressed them. One guiding idea is ·the *continuity of development* from earliest infancy; new ways of behaving are built on earlier ways through subtle transformations and shifts, in which the old and outgrown ways are somehow carried along, also, on occasion becoming manifest. This idea has had a profound influence upon general psychology. The notion that these residues from earlier experience affect behavior *unconsciously* is a second guiding idea. The nature of the active unconscious, the number of fundamental drives, the nature of repression, may be matters of some dispute, but some equivalent of unconscious motivation, of the regulation of what man does by thought-like processes that are out of awareness, is now part of general psychological thinking. A third guiding idea, that present behaviour is often a resultant of *conflict* and exhibits ways of meeting, resolving, or compromising issues, brings the results of the past into the present. This feature of Freud's teaching has also become a commonplace of academic psychology. There are many other guiding ideas, such as the distinction between impulse-driven thinking, called primary process thinking, and more rational or conceptual thinking, called secondary process thinking. This distinction has not yet been fully domesticated in academic psychology, but it is influential in current research. The special processes assigned to the dreamwork (condensation, displacement, symbolization) are significant original formulations. Thus far I have not discussed the contributions of the psychoanalytic method. Again, to Freud we owe free association, the role of interpretation, and the very important problems of transference and countertransference.

Most of these ideas were spelled out in the seventh chapter of *The Interpretation of Dreams* (1900) (5), Freud's major announcement of his theory, but they had already been worked out in 1895 in his "Project for a scientific psychology" that came to light only recently with the Fliess papers (6). It is significant that Freud was searching for a theoretical framework for his ideas before the turn of the century, and had four more decades in which to develop them before his death in 1939.

For philosophers of science, the history of psychoanalysis provides a unique opportunity to study the evolution of a science. It of course had many roots and was influenced by the *Zeitgeist*, but it would not have been the same without Freud. We know now the kinds of germinal ideas he had as early as 1895. Many of these were imaginative, novel, inventive, but they were not weird or fantastic, and they foreshadowed developments in neurophysiology as well as in psychoanalysis. Freud built upon the available methods and scientific ideas that were current, molding them honestly and courageously on the basis of his careful observations of himself and of his parents. Frenkel-Brunswik (4) assessed his inferred variables from the point of view of the logic of science, and she found that in *principle*, he was doing what any conceptualizer of science does. He was aware of the problems of scientific logic; while he often used metaphor when events were too difficult to systematize more precisely, he would have preferred to abandon metaphor for better anchored concepts. The interaction between creative imagination, on the one hand, and careful observations, on the other, as exemplified in Freud, bears dispassionate study. His speculations doubtless outran his data at some points, but this is perhaps essential if a young science is to grow.

We are now considering where psychoanalysis stands today, twenty years after Freud's death. As students of the history of science, we need to recognize the personal and social problems that faced psychoanalytic practitioners and theorists following his death. There had been defections from the ranks during his lifetime by such early favorites as Adler, Jung, and Rank, so that the central core of psychoanalysis was both defined and dominated by Freud. During his lifetime a unity within a developing theory could be maintained by accepting his leadership; after his death those who wished to remain within the tradition then had to retain a kind of unity that would be social as well as intellectual. That is, those who now remained within the mainstream of psychoanalysis had to be free to modify their views (as Freud would have done were he still alive), but they felt some obligation to show that they followed Freud's main teachings both as to method and theory, enough at least to preserve unity among themselves. This has inevitably resulted in a certain amount of in-group rigidity and out-group antagonism, understandable in view of the social history of psychoanalysis during Freud's lifetime. Seldom has a man with a new scientific message been greeted with as much antagonism and hostility as Freud met, from both medical and non-medical groups. This is part of the social history that we have to understand if we are to study the evolution of psychoanalysis as a science. Post-Freudian psychoanalysis has its own social history, too, with in-group and out-group relations internal to psychoanalysis. The nature of these relationships, in the light of their history, will some day contribute an interesting chapter to the sociology of knowledge. There is no point at present in passing judgment on these matters, except to note that there is flux. For example, in several large cities psychoanalytic institutes have fissioned into separate groups differing on some matters of doctrine, yet leaders at the national level have managed to keep these factions united within the American Psychoanalytic Association, with graduates of the separate institutes validated as psychoanalysts. Thus the groundwork exists for the eventual reduction of the barriers between the groups that now find themselves somewhat in conflict.

In order to proceed with an assessment of the status of psychoanalysis as a science today, some choices have to be made. I have chosen to discuss what the analysts call their *metapsychology* rather than their theory and technique of psychoanalytic treatment of patients. There fortunately exist two papers providing information about contemporary psychoanalytic thinking within the social tradition of classical psychoanalysis. One is a long chapter by David Rapaport in Koch's *Psychology: A Study of a Science.* (12). The chapter is entitled "The structure of psychoanalytic theory: a systematizing attempt" (17). Prepared after this chapter, but appearing in print at about the same time, is a paper also by Rapaport, in collaboration with Merton Gill, entitled "The points of view and assumptions of metapsychology" (18). These papers are serious efforts to state the structure of psychoanalysis "from the inside," and can be taken as a fair specimen of the best of current thinking among those who feel themselves at home within the classical Freudian tradition, while yet ready for new developments ahead. My initial task becomes a review and commentary upon these statements. I shall lean primarily upon the paper by Rapaport and Gill (18).

PSYCHOANALYTIC METAPSYCHOLOGY

In undertaking their formal statement of the propositions of metapsychology, Rapaport and Gill begin by distinguishing four kinds of propositions within psychoanalysis: empirical propositions, specific psychoanalytic propositions, propositions of the general psychoanalytic theory, and propositions stating the metapsychological assumptions. Their own examples follow.

Empirical Propositions. "Around the fourth year of life boys regard their fathers as rivals."

This is empirical in the sense that it could be investigated directly by available methods, and is thus either demonstrably true or false on the basis of directly relevant evidence.

Specific Psychoanalytic Propositions. "The solution of the Oedipal situation is a decisive determinant of character formation and pathology."

This is a step removed from direct empirical study because it implies some substantiated theory regarding the Oedipus complex, character formation, and pathology. It is specific in that its reference is to a set of events taking place at one time in the life cycle. Even though the proposition were confirmed, its explanatory value would be limited to this set of events.

General Psychoanalytic Proposition. "Structure formation by means of identifications and anticathexes explains theoretically the consequence of the 'decline of the Oedipus complex.'"

Note that this proposition says something more about the preceding one, placing it in the larger context of identification and cathexes, that will be used to explain other events as well. Hence this proposition is of more general scope.

Metapsychological Proposition. "The propositions of the general psychoanalytic theory which explain the Oedipal situation and the decline of the Oedipus complex involve dynamic, economic, structural, genetic, and adaptive assumptions."

This is, of course, the most general statement of all.

In their paper, Rapaport and Gill attempt to limit themselves to the metapsychological propositions in relation to general psychoanalytic propositions, avoiding the two levels of specific psychoanalytic propositions and the empirical propositions. The metapsychological theory that they present, already hinted at in the illustration, can be restated as follows: *The psychoanalytic explanation of any psychological phenomenon must include propositions reflecting the dynamic, economic, structural, genetic, and adaptive points of view.*

Those familiar with psychoanalytic theory will recall that Freud formulated three metapsychological points of view, which he called dynamic, topographic, and economic. Rapaport and Gill, in order to make explicit what was implicit in Freud, and to include current developments within psychoanalytic ego psychology, accepted the three points of view of Freud (modifying topographic to structural, in view of changes during Freud's lifetime), and added two points of view (genetic and adaptive). These five points of view are in some respects five separate models. Let us see how each of them is characterized.

1. *The Dynamic Point of View.* This is perhaps the most widely understood aspect of psychoanalysis, and gives psychoanalysis its designation as a dynamic psychology. The general psychoanalytic propositions of the dynamic point of view employ the concepts of *unconscious forces and conflicts,* and the concept of *drive or instinct.* Contemporary psychoanalysts commonly refer only to the two specific innate drives of sex and aggression; other drives (if any) are thought to be derivatives of these.

The metapsychological assumptions within this point of view are thus summarized by Rapaport and Gill:

The *dynamic* point of view demands that the psychoanalytic explanation of any psychological phenomenon includes propositions concerning the psychological forces involved in the phenomenon.

The major assumptions are:

a.   There are psychological forces.

b.   The effect of simultaneously acting psychological forces may be the simple resultant of the work of each of these forces.

c.   The effect of simultaneously acting psychological forces may not be the simple resultant of the work of each of these forces.

It is evident that these assumptions are a mere scaffolding upon which a more precise theory has to be built. For example, the third assumption as stated negates the second, so that the two can be combined into this statement: "The effect of simultaneously acting psychological forces may *or may not* be the simple resultant of the work of each of these forces." In this form the statement is a mere truism, but of course there is more intended. The third assumption actually implies something like this: under some circumstances the effect of simultaneously acting forces is modified by drive fusion and overdetermination; under these circumstances the effect is not a simple resultant of the work of each of these forces. This statement draws in, however, some notions from general psychoanalytic theory (e.g., drive fusion and overdetermination), and hence belongs with a next elaboration of the theory rather than with the metapsychological assumptions at the level of generality that Rapaport and Gill seek to hold.

2. *The Economic Point of View.* This is the point of view that all behavior is regulated by psychological energy, and concerns the principles by which psychological energy is disposed of. The term "economic" means "economical," that is, that psychological energies

operate along paths of least effort, leading toward tension reduction and homeostasis.

Psychoanalytic theory when approached from this point of view has to do with the processes by which tension is reduced by energy discharge either directly or through devious means, or by suspending energy discharge until conditions are more favourable. The basic concepts here are primary and secondary process, wish fulfillment, cathexis and countercathexis. There are additional related concepts of binding and neutralization of psychological energy. The level of concepts represented by primary and secondary processes and cathexes belongs, however, to the general psychoanalytic theory, rather than to the metapsychological assumptions.

The metapsychological assumptions are that there are psychological energies, that they follow laws of conservation and entropy, and that these energies are subject to transformations that increase or decrease their entropic tendency.

The use of physical analogies in the assumptions of both the dynamic and economic points of view requires discussion, to which we shall return.

3. *The Structural Point of View.* The structural point of view replaced the earlier topographic one when Freud introduced the tripartite division of id, ego, and superego to displace (or supplement) the emphasis upon unconscious, preconscious, and conscious topography. More recently there has developed within classical psychoanalysis an emphasis known as ego-psychology in which various kinds of structure are proposed: e.g., defense-, control-, and means-structures. The control- and means-structures are considered to be relatively autonomous structures within the ego, and thus part of the conflict-free sphere (8).

I shall not repeat the formal language of the assumptions with respect to structure. The main points are that structures are configurations with a slow rate of change, that these structures have a hierarchical order, and that mental processes take place within, between, and by means of these structures.

4. *The Genetic Point of View.* The course of individual development is very important within psychoanalytic theory, and emphasis upon early childhood is one of the most influential contributions of psychoanalysis to general psychology. The developmental point of view was so taken for granted within psychoanalysis that it has not traditionally been separately formulated as parallel to the dynamic, economic, and structural viewpoints. The general theory of psychosexual development is well known, in which the child passes through the anal, oral, phallic, latency, and genital stages on the way to maturity.

This aspect of the theory is the source of some controversy between those who insist that the crises related to these stages are primarily rooted in the nature of the organism (the more classical position), and those who attribute a major influence to the impact of the culture in which the child is reared (the more dissident position). The terminology is somewhat unfortunate, because "genetic" means ontogenetic or epigenetic, and not gene-controlled as in the more familiar current use of the term. However, we may continue here to use the term as synonomous with developmental.

The metapsychological assumptions of the genetic point of view are that all psychological phenomena have an origin and development, originating in innate givens that mature according to an epigenetic ground plan. The earlier forms of psychological phenomena, though superseded by later forms, remain potentially active; at any point in psychological history the totality of potentially active forms codetermines all psychological phenomena.

It may be noted, in passing, that the level of generality of these assumptions is such that the content of general psychoanalytic theory could be greatly changed without violating them. For example, psychosexual development could be replaced by some other content without violating any of these assumptions.

5. *The Adaptive Point of View.* This relative newcomer to psychoanalytic theory permits statements that cover most of the ground familiar to functional psychology, and frees the psychoanalyst from the need to find a libidinal explanation for all behaviour. Among the conceptions are the organism's preparedness (through evolution) for an average expectable environment, "apparatuses" that are essentially abilities by which to cope with the environment, dependence upon external stimulation, achieved relative autonomy from the environment.

The adaptive assumptions include statements concerning adaptation to internal states, to the physical and social environment, and the mutual adaptations between man and environment.

This completes the listing of the five points of view and their assumptions, according to Rapaport and Gill. This summarization cannot do justice to their treatment, which at many points includes reservations, nor to the sources they have used in arriving at the assumptions. They illustrate each of the assumptions by reference to the psychoanalytic theory of affects; for the sake of brevity, these references have been ignored in my summary. Only a reading of their original paper can fill in these gaps.

Rapaport and Gill concluded their paper by a statement of confidence that the five points of view are likely to prove necessary and sufficient "to a degree which recommends that they should be accepted—for the time being—as the framework of psychoanalytic metapsychology." They felt less sure about their assumptions: "It is not yet possible to assess whether all these assumptions are necessary, and whether this set of assumptions is sufficient—when coupled with observational data—to yield the existing body of psychoanalytic propositions."

FIVE MODELS OR ONE?

What is implied in the assertion that a psychoanalytic explanation requires a minimum of one proposition from each of the five points of view? It could mean that this is a five-dimensional system, with the coordinates of any event being the five yielded by the dimensions. The dimensions are not of this kind, however, and this interpretation can be rejected. A second possibility is that there are five independent models. An event can be explained according to *any one* of the models, but the explanation has not become exhaustive until it has been explained according to *every* model. That this is possibly the intent of Rapaport and Gill appears to be demonstrated in the empirical use of the five-model scheme in the interpretation of hypnotic phenomena by Gill and Brenman (7). Each point of view in turn serves for the characterization of what happens within hypnosis; the story is completed when the last of the five points of view has been discussed. The models of course overlap, and references to other points of view are not excluded when a given view provides the background for discussion. The manner of the interaction is not specified, however, and this is one of the weaknesses of the Rapaport and Gill presentation. It is not clear, for example, whether non-interchangeable kinds of information emerge from each model, or whether, by appropriate transformations, the yield of one of the models could be made more powerful by using information from the others.[1]

We have Rapaport saying of the points of view:

"The 'points of view' seem to be the equivalents of 'principles' in psychoanalytic theory. Yet their form shows that the time to examine them one by one, for their long-range significance, has not yet arrived. Instead of formal principles, we will present here a few general conceptions, which compound the various points of view, and which

---

1. A statement that "*all* psychoanalytic propositions involve *all* metapsychological points of view" does not clarify the status of the separate points of view.

seem likely to survive whatever the fate of the more specific ingredients of the psychoanalytic theory should prove to be" (17, p. 152). His discussion then proceeds at a level quite different from that of the Rapaport-Gill paper.

The vacillation between the points of view as models, as principles, as components to be compounded, is understandable in view of the complexity and looseness of contemporary psychoanalytic formulations.

It is in accordance with good scientific practice to seek for principles of unification, and I have therefore examined the five viewpoints to see if some sub-grouping might be plausible. One principle that appears to be a possible guide for combining the five models into a smaller number is the *time-span* of the processes to which the models refer. The reference of the dynamic and economic models is to events which have primarily a *short* time-span: the resolution of forces, and the transformation of energy into work. The reference of the other models is to events with a *long* time-span: genetic, structural, and adaptive models refer to processes developing over the life-span, changing slowly, and leading in the end to the contemporary situation which the dynamic-economic model is called upon to explain. A first step in simplification would be to unite the dynamic-economic models into one and the genetic-structural-adaptive models into a second one.[2]

If there are just two models, one historical covering a long time-span, one a historical covering a short time-span in the present, then both the independence and the interrelationship of the models are easier to comprehend. Let me give an analogy from problem-solving. The *historical* understanding of problem-solving requires that we know what the problem-solver brings to the situation from his past learning, what relevant information he has, what techniques he knows, what attitudes he has toward himself as a problem-solver. We can make certain assertions or predictions on the basis of this knowledge. The *ahistorical* understanding of problem-solving requires that we know the manner in which our problem-solver makes use of his past experience in relation to the present, how he analyzes the problem, selects the relevant information and techniques, how the present display of the problem influences what he is able to do. There are many relationships here that cannot be discussed in purely historical terms. One way of putting this is that sufficient past experience to solve a problem does not guarantee that the subject will solve the problem, unless the present demands upon him

2. Hartmann and Kris (9) have also recognized that the explanatory propositions of psychoanalysis classify chiefly into two groups: genetic and dynamic.

are made in an appropriate manner, and unless he has his past experiences available in a form suitable for use.

Translating this example into the language of the clinic, we might say that an individual's relations to his parents in childhood were such as to produce an abiding structure of anxiety-dependency. Now he takes a job in which the boss reminds him (unconsciously) of his father, the anxiety (based on the dynamics of transference) overwhelms him, and he develops neurotic symptoms. The abiding structure is a historical fact, to be explained by the genetic-structural-adaptive model; the breakdown with the present boss is to be explained by the dynamic-economic model. Obviously the two interact in that we understand the individual's present behaviour in relation both to his life history and to the provocative circumstances of the present.

The separation of the two models is a practical convenience because data come both from the life-history.and from the present, though as a scientific enterprise the two models should be combined. If a single equation is written to describe what is happening in the present, it can have terms in it that represent the present. Thus Hull's equations for reaction potential (11) include the simultaneous interactions of habits (including generalized habits) built up in the past, along with the drive state, stimulus dynamisms, and so on, in the present. There is no formal obstacle to including historical and *ahistorical* data in the same equation.

For convenience, we may discuss the five Rapaport-Gill models as though they were two, turning aside from the problem of their eventual integration into one.

THE DYNAMIC-ECONOMIC MODEL

Some contemporary model of this kind is needed to deal with the problem of conflict and its resolution, and the energetics of behaviour, including facilitation, inhibition, distortion, symbolization.

The physical metaphors as used at present are unsatisfactory, but perhaps they can be built upon to do what the models are intended to do. The physics is not literal: there is no mass for force to accelerate, there is no distance by which to determine how much work a force has done, there is no dissipation of energy into unavailable heat by which to make precise the meaning of entropy; when energy is transformed it is not changed from potential to kinetic (19). Non-psychoanalytic psychologists have also used physical metaphors, such as threshold and drive, not out of the vocabulary of systematic physical science, or force, distance, direction, as by Kurt Lewin, with more of the flavour of systematic physics. When the vocabulary remains too close to that of strictly. physical science, the metaphors are strained and the result has usually been unsatisfactory (14, 16).

Uneasiness with the quantitative concepts of the dynamic-economic model has been expressed by psychoanalysts. Thus Kubie (13) states:

> Assumptions as to changes in quantities of energy are admissible only if alterations in the pattern of intrapsychic forces are ruled out. A failure to recognize this has made all so-called economic formulations a species of ad hoc speculative allegory in quantitative terms.

Note that this statement of Kubie's not only is critical of the economic theory, but indicates clearly that the dynamic-economic models must be thought of at one and the same time.

Colby (1) has given thoughtful consideration to these problems. He finds the hydraulic analogy used to describe psychological energy (i.e., a reservoir with pipes to regulate the flow) entirely unsatisfactory, and builds his own cyclic-circular model. He recognizes that his energy concept is actually far removed from the physicist's concept: "Our psychic energy provides a synoptic way of talking about activity and change" (1, p. 27 f.). While energy within his system has some descriptive characteristics (pulsation, period, synchrony, etc.), it is transported through the system essentially as a modifiable message, and its "energetic" aspects are minimal. He is struggling with genuine problems within the psychoanalytic description of events and processes, and finds some sort of "feedback" model essential. Without going into his solution of the problems, we can here merely indicate that this is a serious effort to find an alternative to the classical model. It supports the position that the status of the dynamic-economic metapsychology of contemporary psychoanalysis is very provisional.

THE STRUCTURAL-GENETIC-ADAPTIVE MODEL

Freud's tripartite structure—id, ego, superego—is a heuristic convenience in the discussion of typical intrapsychic conflicts. The impulsivity of the id, the intellectual realism of the ego, and the moral flavour of the superego epitomize ways of talking about stresses within the person that are familiar in the Hebraic-Christian tradition. Thus the spirit may be willing while the flesh is weak, one may start out on a course of action but be troubled by a nagging conscience. Anyone raised in Western culture can easily understand the id-ego-superego conflicts, at least in their broad outlines.

This simplicity, while an initial advantage, rises up as an obstacle when the parts of the personality become reified as almost three persons, the id telling the ego what to do, the ego actively fighting the id, the superego being a party, too, to the internal battles. Actually, as Colby says, "its simplicity (i.e., that of the tripartite scheme) makes it insufficient to conceptualize specifically enough the manifold functions of psychic activity" (1, p. 77).

The id, ego, superego structural divisions have been supplemented more recently chiefly by differentiations within the ego. The ego-psychology of Hartmann has multiplied the structures within the ego, calling them "ego-apparatuses." Some of these apparatuses are said to rest on constitutional givens (e.g., perception, motility, intelligence) (8). Other secondary apparatuses develop through interaction with the environment; both kinds may be relatively autonomous, that is, free of control through the instinctual drives. These ego-apparatuses and structures are very numerous and I have not found a systematic list of them, if indeed, such a list is possible. Apparently some primary process defense mechanisms such as displacement, content, and projection, can be included among ego-apparatuses or structures (17, p. 154). Other structures include control- and means-structures, which are not defenses.

The acceptance of conflict-free ego structures has been viewed as a great advance within classical psychoanalysis, permitting not only the greater differentiation of the structural viewpoint, but the addition of the adaptive viewpoint. The psychoanalyst no longer faces the burden of explaining everything in terms of one or two primordial drives; he can now accept the drive theory as he has always done, but can supplement it with the structures of the conflict-free ego sphere, and thus comprehend the problems of perception, problem-solving, esthetics, play, that were forced into a somewhat artificial perspective when everything had to be derived from drive. The concept of sublimation no longer has to be stretched to cover everything that appears on the surface to be non-sexual. While the multiplication of apparatuses and structures within the ego gives this new freedom, some of the unifying value of the older structural theory has been sacrificed. This is probably inevitable when a theory is in transition, and seeks to encompass new facts under new assumptions.

Because the structural conceptions relate to enduring aspects of the personality, aspects with slow rates of change, these conceptions are intimately bound to the developmental ones represented by the genetic and adaptive viewpoints. Erikson (3) has combined the psychosexual states of classical psychoanalysis with adaptive crises associated with each of these stages, thus integrating the genetic and the adaptive viewpoints as these are characterized by Rapaport and Gill.

While Erikson takes off from Freud, accepting the psychosexual stages associated with the prominence of certain body orifices as the individual matures, he attempts to go beyond Freud and to meet the problem of interaction with the environment, showing how the resolution of each developmental crisis affects the manner in which later crises are met. He introduces some stages beyond the Freudian genital stage, or perhaps as differentiations within it, with the three successive polarities in adolescence and adult life of ego identity versus role diffusion, generativity versus self-absorption, and integrity versus despair and disgust.

Erikson's proposals are insightful, sensitive to the human situation, and provide important supplements to the encapsulated and intrapsychic flavor of the more traditional psychosexual theory of psychogenesis. Yet from the point of view of a logical or systematic plan of human development, intended to hold across cultures, it lacks criteria by which its stages are distinguished and according to which the major problems associated with each stage have been identified.

In general, examination of the structural-genetic-adaptive model indicates that, like the dynamic-economic model, it is a very provisional one, although useful in giving direction to the kind of tighter theory eventually to be achieved.

THE VALIDATION OF PSYCHOANALYTIC PROPOSITIONS

There have been many attempts to submit theoretical propositions from psychoanalysis to experimental tests, either of a quasi-clinical sort (as in projective tests and hypnosis) or in non-clinical tests (as in studies of memory, animal behaviour, child development in other cultures, etc.). While indeed many of these have come out rather favourably to psychoanalytic conceptions, the general attitude of the classical psychoanalyst has often been one of skepticism, if not of hostility, to these attempts. Why should this be?

1. The first reason for a negative attitude by the psychoanalyst toward these attempts is his confidence that the psychoanalytic method is the only appropriate method for revealing some of the relationships. A depth psychology, it is said, requires a depth method for its study. The only person qualified to interpret evidence is the one who has himself been through a psychoanalysis, and is thus familiar first-hand with the phenomena. Thus psychoanalysis is needed to produce the phenomena and a psychoanalyst is needed to interpret them.

We may accept this objection to studies by non-psychoanalysts, but with two qualifications. First, it applies to *some* aspects of the psychoanalytic theory only. We need to become clearer about which aspects require the analyst and the analytic method, and which do not. Second, when a psychoanalyst obtains the data and assists in its interpretation, then third persons (including non-psychoanalysts as well as other psychoanalysts) may be helpful in arranging for critical hypothesis testing.

2. The second reason for a negative attitude by some psychoanalysts toward empirical attempts at testing psychoanalytic propositions is the complexity of psychoanalytic theory, and hence the fear that tests of separate propositions will be either trivial or irrelevant. According to Rapaport, most of those who try to test the theory either do not understand it, or they ignore what they know. "The overwhelming majority of experiments designed to test psychoanalytic propositions display a blatant lack of interest in the meaning, within the theory of psychoanalysis, of the propositions tested" (17, p. 142).

This second argument has some force, but it can be overstated. To be sure there have been those who interpreted the Freudian theory of forgetting to mean that unpleasant things are forgotten and pleasant things remembered; then they went about constructing lists of words including quinine (unpleasant) and sugar (pleasant) to test the Freudian theory. This sort of thing has not happened much in the last few years, as the knowledge of psychoanalytic theory has become more sophisticated.

The reason that the argument may be overstated is that psychoanalytic propositions at all levels lack the tightness of conceptual integration that makes the very general test possible. Hence more low-level propositional testing is in order before the larger system can be tightened up for testing within the larger network of theory.

The empirical propositions to be tested are not necessarily trivial, and they usually imply some of the special or general psychoanalytic propositions as these are outlined by Rapaport and Gill. For example, it is not easy to get good evidence as to the age ranges within which boys are especially rivalrous with their fathers. This information (and other of the same general sort) is important to test some of the inferences from the more general theory.

We are led into a paradox when we insist that the superstructure of psychoanalytic theory (including metapsychology) ought to be accepted before we attempt to test theory. Sophistication demands that we do test theory. The idea that a single hypothesis can be disconfirmed by evidence, but not confirmed, is logically sound, but scientifically trivial. A single hypothesis, embedded in a theory, can be neither confirmed nor disconfirmed in any important sense without knowing more about the theory. That is, one needs to know the interactions: for example, under one circumstance praise will improve learned performance, under another it will handicap performance. The proposition "praise improves performance" is thus not established by a score-card, in which it more often improves than handicaps, but rather by additional propositions which specify when it does one and when it does the other. Thus we test what Cronbach and Meehl (2) call the *nomothetic network;* we do not test one proposition at a time, or, if we do, we do not draw our conclusions from these tests in isolation from each other. The paradox arises because the psychoanalytic theory is not quite good enough for systematic testing. Hence the best we can do is some theory construction, integrating a few of the propositions that appear consonant with the general theory. Then it is *these* propositions that we test. These smaller models, or miniature systems, as Hull called them, will not reconcile the devotee to the whole system, but is the best that can be done at this stage.

Who is to do the testing: For some purposes the psychoanalytic interview is the best source. It may yield inferences that can be checked in other ways, however, and if experimental and clinical evidence agrees, so much the better all around. For example, the adult consequences of loss of a parent in childhood (10) can be studied through interviews with the adult, but these will raise conjectures about what went on at the time of parent loss. These conjectures can be studied by doing some investigations of children who have recently lost a parent. Thus the nature of the hypotheses being tested will often rule on the best method of studying them. There need be no *a priori* decision that the best method will be the psychoanalytic interview, or observational studies of children, or experimental studies. The nature of the hypotheses, and availability of methods and of facilities, will guide investigations within psychoanalysis as they do in any other field of science.

There are some inhibiting factors within professional psychoanalysis that tend to reduce the research productivity of the analysts themselves. One is the long course of training, so that training is typically completed at about age 40, when families are established, obligations are great, and research initiative is on the decline. Another is the nature of a practice involving long and expensive commitments to aid the suffering, so that the analyst must have faith in what he is doing. This leads to a conservative tendency with respect to change of doctrine or method, which, while not to be condemned, is less favourable to research than a situation lacking such commitments. The training institutes have tended to neglect research in their training programs; in the recent report on training in psychoanalysis (15) covering 460 pages, but four pages were devoted to research. Only three of the 14 institutes bring research at all prominently into the training pattern. The job of consolidating psychoanalysis as a science will continue to call for the collaboration of others if it is to move ahead with any rapidity.

The reconstruction of psychoanalytic theory can be expected to take time. It would be undesirable to throw present formulations aside, and to start all over again, for too much would be lost, even though some communication today is by way of rather loose metaphor. The gradual reconstruction may in time produce drastic revisions, but that possibility does not mean that these revisions have to be made all at once. The theory has enough body that investigators can choose segments of the theory within which to work out smaller models to be coordinated with others as the work advances. There are a number of avenues available to them besides those that open up only within the psychoanalytic interview. Among these are the study of child development and child rearing (including studies by anthropologists), studies of perception, learning, and memory (especially where there is ambiguity and perhaps conflict), projective tests, hypnosis, and the study of sleep and dreams. A great many pertinent investigations are now under way in these fields, and we have every reason to expect a reconstruction of psychoanalysis to emerge from them. It will be a reconstruction rather than a validation, for the very act of validation requires reconstruction. In the process a better science will emerge, with firmer data encompassed within a more elegant system.

REFERENCES

1. COLBY, K. M. *Energy and Structure in Psychoanalysis*. New York: Ronald Press, 1955.

2. CRONBACH, L. J., and P. E. MEEHL. Construct validity in psychological tests. *Psychological Bulletin*, Vol. 52 (1955), pp. 281–302.

3. ERIKSON, E. H. Identity and the life cycle. *Psychological Issues*, 1, No. 1, New York: International University Press, 1959.

4. FRENKEL-BRUNSWIK, ELSE. Psychoanalysis and the unity of science. *Proceedings of the American Academy of Arts and Sciences*, Vol. 80. (1954), pp. 271–350.

5. FREUD, S. *The Interpretation of Dreams*, 1900. New York: Basic Books, 1955.

6. FREUD, S. *The Origins of Psychoanalysis: Letters to Wilhelm Fliess, Drafts, and Notes:* 1887–1902. New York: Basic Books, 1954.

7. GILL, M. M., and MARGARET BRENMAN. *Hypnosis and Related States: Psychoanalytic Studies in Regression*. New York: International University Press, 1959.

8. HARTMANN, H. *Ego Psychology and the Problem of Adaptation*, 1939. New York: International University Press, 1958.

9. HARTMANN, H., and E. KRIS. The genetic approach in psychoanalysis. In *The Psychoanalytic Study of the Child*, Vol. 1. New York: International University Press, 1945, pp. 11–29.

10. HILGARD, JOSEPHINE R., MARTHA F. NEWMAN, and FERN FISK. Strength of adult ego following childhood bereavement. *American Journal of Orthopsychiatry*, Vol. 30 (1960), pp. 788–798.

11. HULL, C. L. *A Behavior System*. New Haven: Yale University Press, 1952.

12. KOCH, S. *Psychology: A Study of a Science*. Vol. 3. *Formulations of the Person and the Social Context*. New York: McGraw-Hill, 1959.

13. KUBIE, L. S. The fallacious use of quantitative concepts in dynamic psychology. *Psychoanalytic Quarterly*. Vol. 16 (1947), pp. 507–518.

14. LEEPER, R. *Lewin's Topological and Vector Psychology: A Digest and a Critique*. Eugene, Oregon: University of Oregon Press, 1943.

15. LEWIN, B. D., and HELEN ROSS. *Psychoanalytic Education in the United States*. New York: Norton, 1960.

16. LONDON, I. D. Psychologists' misuse of the auxiliary concepts of physics and mathematics. *Psychological Review*, Vol. 51 (1944), pp. ·266–291.

17. RAPAPORT, D. The structure of psychoanalytic theory: a systematizing attempt. In Koch, S. (Ed.), 1959, pp. 55–183. (Also in *Psychological Issues*, 2, No. 6, 1960).

18. RAPAPORT, D., and M. M. GILL. The points of view and assumptions of metapsychology. *The International Journal of Psychoanalysis*, Vol. 40 (1959), pp. 153–162.

19. SKINNER, B. F. Critique of psychoanalytic concepts and theories. In Feigl, H., and M. Scriven (Eds.) *The Foundations of Science and the Concepts of Psychology and Psychoanalysis*. Minneapolis: University of Minnesota Press, 1956, pp. 77–87.

16

Pavlov, Freud and Soviet Psychiatry[*]

Lawrence S. Kubie

FOREWORD

It is not easy to make an accurate appraisal of the attitude of Soviet psychiatrists to current trends in psychiatry. The behavioral scientist in America and England is constantly seeking an harmonious integration of organic and psychological approaches to the causes of psychopathological processes, and to their resolution (21). The more-or-less official attitude of Soviet psychiatrists to these same problems seems to contrast sharply with this. The attitude to psychoanalysis is one indicator of their position, but not its sole manifestation. In seeking to explore these attitudes we have had to depend chiefly on accounts by the few informed psychiatrists who have travelled in Russia and talked to Russian psychiatrists there, plus our own opportunities to talk to Russian psychiatrists in Western Europe towards the end of the war, and more recently in this country, many of these interchanges requiring the intermediation of a translator. The author of this paper is depending on notes made during the course of several such encounters, and upon a recent article written by Fedotov (2), the reply by Reider (31), and the book on psychology in the Soviet Union (32) which has recently been published. The latter confirms an impression that the Russians still think of the physiological and psychological approaches as irreconcilable, instead of as bands on a continuous spectrum.

*Reprinted from *Behavioral Science*, Vol. 4, No. 1, 1959, pp. 29–34, by permission of James G. Miller, M.D., Ph.D., editor.

Thus the bibliographical references in that volume contain no reference to psychoanalytic articles or writers: neither those which have been translated and which are listed at the foot of each page, nor those which are available only in Russian and which are listed in the bibliography at the end of the volume. Almost the only non-Russians listed in either bibliography are those who translated the work of Russian writers into other languages. The exceptions are J. B. Watson, Clark L. Hull, Marx, Engels, and one reference in a footnote to Kazanin's book on *Language and Thought in Schizophrenia*, which is characterized as a popularization of the experimental work of Vigotsky. There are, however, references to and quotations from Lenin's pronouncements on the nature of matter and of sensation. In a chapter summarizing the 14th International Congress of Psychology which was held in Montreal, the works of some non-Russian contributors are listed briefly.

In the text of the volume there is one direct reference to psychoanalysis and its concepts. On page 5, psychoanalysis is characterized as a psychological system which "tends to reduce all human behavior to dark, inexplicable, biological urges expressed through the unconscious." Each word in this statement is inaccurate. It would have been accurate to say that analysis finds unconscious components among the determinants of most behavior. Yet to call these "inexplicable" would still be inaccurate. Furthermore, it seems strangely inconsistent that a Russian, with his presumptive biological emphasis, should criticize psychoanalysis on the grounds that its emphasis on the biological determinants of behavior "reduces behavior to dark biological urges."

The chapter on the formation of associative connections contains no reference to free associations. The chapter on the theory of memory does not refer to its selectivity, to duration, to the distinction between recording and ease or difficulty of recall, to the inseparable problem of forgetting, or to the play of emotional determinants in all of the multiple phenomena of memory.

Repeatedly throughout the book consciousness is identified with the process of verbalization, precisely as Watson tried unsuccessfully to do many years ago. The use of the concept of automatic *(viz.,* unconscious) behavior corresponds roughly to that which analysts would call preconscious. There is much confused debate over whether such behavior is under any directional control, or whether by "automatic" one must imply free-of-any controls. There is no recognition of the difference between preconscious and unconscious, although the problem of accessibility to consciousness is referred to on one or two occasions. In short one comes reluctantly to the conclusion that many of the most important and difficult issues in human psychology are evaded by the simple device of not even mentioning them.

Thus insofar as Soviet Psychiatry takes any attitude towards psychoanalysis, one can say that it is one of hostile depreciation. Their position purports to derive from the data and work of Pavlov; yet the arguments which are advanced betray many elementary misconceptions not only about analysis and analysts, but surprisingly enough about Pavlovian psychophysiology and psychology as well. Moreover, the Soviet writers make no reference to the series of careful studies of the areas of agreement and of disagreement between Pavlov and Freud which have appeared since 1930: (1, 3, 4, 5, 6, 7, 9, 10, 11, 12, 16, 21, 22, 23, 24, 25, 26, 27). In these studies certain basic facts emerge.

Areas of Agreement
Between Pavlov and Freud

(1) As is true of all creative minds Pavlov's own point of view evolved and changed with the years to such an extent that were he alive today he would not be in accord with the present attitude of Soviet psychiatrists towards psychoanalytic theory and technique. It is true that at the start Pavlov had exacted fines from any student in his laboratory who used such words as "conscious" or "voluntary." Only a few years later, however, he found not only that he had to use these terms himself, but that he had also to make a differentiation between conscious and unconscious psychological processes. He discussed how the one can influence the other; and he wrote of those "favorable conditions under which the unconscious synthesis may enter the conscious field." Anyone who deals with the problems of behavior in such terms as these is thinking psychoanalytically, by whatever name he chooses to call it. To this evolution of Pavlov's thinking there is an illuminating parallel in the development of Watsonian Behaviorism. In his early days Watson would not use the words "Conscious" and "Unconscious." In a later period he found himself forced to use "Verbalized" and "Unverbalized" as equivalent terms (10, 12, 28, 29, 30).

(2) Furthermore, Pavlov explored the occurrence of mutual interference among concurrent mechanisms. He wrote of the mode and role of conflict among various conditioned and unconditioned reflexes, and of the corresponding conflicts among derivative psychological states. Here again he was thinking and writing in terms which parallel psychoanalytic data.

(3) Pavlov and Freud approached all problems of behavior and of psychology from a biogenetic basis. This is an important bridge between the two. Yet Soviet psychiatrists seem to be unaware of it; misled perhaps by the fact that the investigator of conditioned reflexes and the psychoanalyst work at different levels of the continuum called "Behavior." At these different levels the method of study and the criteria of validity and of prediction must differ (15, 17); but the study of no level of integration can replace or make unnecessary the study of other levels. In all integrative hierarchies, science must investigate every level, confident that in the course of time they will converge to illuminate one another (16). Therefore, there is nothing inconsistent in the study of such neurophysiological mechanisms as the conditioned reflex, and the study of those psychological phenomena to which the conditioned reflex makes a vital contribution.

(4) Both Freud and Pavlov made use of techniques of sampling under conditions the constancy of which is maintained carefully, so as to control all variables except those whose changes are to be studied. In Pavlov's work the sampling device is the conditioned reflex under the constant conditions of the laboratory. In psychoanalysis the sampling device is the technique of free association under the constant conditions of the analytic procedure. How constancy of extrinsic variables is achieved in psychoanalysis has been fully described in certain technical studies (15, 17, 18).

(5) Finally, it has been shown that the psychoanalytic technique of free association is actually the mirror image of the conditioned reflex itself (9).

Each of these five points involves complex technical issues which are developed in detail in the appended references. They indicate that although there are are differences, there are no irreconcilable conflicts between these two systems for the exploration of behavior. Concurrently they are making fruitful contributions to our understanding of human psychology and its aberrations. Therefore it is regrettable that Soviet psychiatrists seem still to be unaware of the studies which have built a bridge between them. It is further regrettable that their misinformation about and misconceptions of analysis are so elementary, as Reider has shown (31, v.i. Epilogue).

A consideration of the philosophy and methodology of scientific development gives further support to my argument that these two disciplines are mutually supplementary and not opposed. Thus it is an obvious fallacy to maintain that to study the properties of hydrogen and oxygen is irreconcilable with a study of the properties of water; merely because we cannot as yet predict all of the properties of water from the properties of its components. What one can say is that in the meantime it is essential for the investigator at each level to understand the work of others, to search out their implications for his own, and above all never to misrepresent the work of others for the empty satisfaction of attacking his own misconceptions. Yet this is what many Soviet psychiatrists are doing today in their criticisms of what they mistakenly believe psychoanalysis to be.

If he wanted to engage in this kind of useless interdisciplinary warfare, the psychoanalyst could point out many limitations to the relevance of the conditioned reflex to human psychology. Thus the conditioned reflex is operative only when conditioned and unconditioned stimuli are separated by relatively brief intervals of time, intervals measurable in seconds and minutes. Human mental processes on the other hand can bind gaps in time and space that span both oceans and years. Similarly the conditioned reflex plays only a minor role in the development and function of symbolic processes, which are man's most unique trait. To the analyst, however, it is of less value to emphasize the limitations of the conditioned reflex than its contributions. He wishes that a similar attitude towards psychoanalysis would prevail in Russia.

REASON FOR BIAS

There may be reasons for this bias, the origins of which are not scientific. In fact, underlying this needless controversy is an array of sociological, ideological and economic issues, which should play no role in arguments about scientific problems. Indeed, their intrusion always weights the scales with irrelevant considerations. Not long ago extraneous ideological considerations threatened to distort the work of Soviet geneticists. In psychiatry similar extraneous considerations based on a series of erroneous assumptions are injected into this discussion.

(a) One such assumption is that psychoanalysis attempts to make people accept without protest or concern the existing inequities of any given social, cultural, or economic system. The invalidity of this charge has been demonstrated in detail on other occasions (13, 14). Actually it is wholly unfounded. The goal of analysis is to emancipate a man from his enslavement to those unconscious mechanisms over which he has no voluntary control, precisely because they are unconscious. This frees him from the dominion of automatic repetitive mechanisms, whether compulsive or phobic. The man who is psychologically free in this specific sense is not afraid to fight and sacrifice for human betterment. nor is he on the other hand an automaton under the dominion of his own unconscious. Therefore he is not blindly conformist, blindly enslaved, nor blindly rebellious. He is not readily subjugated by any form of party-line thinking, whether economic, political, religious or scientific (19, 20). A psychologically healthy man accepts dictation from no one. Can it be an accident therefore that the two human institutions whose opposition to psychoanalysis has been most bitter have been the most authoritarian of all churches[1] and the most authoritarian of all politico-economic systems? And is it not likely that the misinformation and ignorance which is manifested in such statements as those of Fedotov (2) have their origins in bias?

(b)   The psychoanalyst can study and treat only a few people at a time. Therefore his use of his technique constitutes at best a pilot demonstration of methods which can lead gradually to prevention, but which can never hope to be used as a mass cure-all. Those who want rapid mass cures will be impatient of the slow and humble methods by which analysis has acquired microscopic data on the neurotic process. In the early years of psychoanalytic history, because it could gain no official acceptance in teaching hospitals or medical schools (and for other reasons as well which are not relevant here), most psychoanalytic patients were relatively wealthy, or at least comfortably off. Consequently it is easy to jump to the conclusion that the analyst protects the special interests of the wealthy and is blind to human suffering and poverty. This fallacy has also been fully exposed elsewhere (14, 20).

(c)   The data on human life which confronts the analyst makes it impossible for him to make a scapegoat of either poverty or wealth, of excessive leisure or fatigue, of indolence or overwork. He knows that the neurotic process arises out of roots which are more universal than any such circumstances. It is clear to him that unhappy life situations have many serious secondary consequences for the neurotic process; but he also knows that they are never its primary source (20).

(d)   The analyst has learned to distrust the consequence of naked competition for power, even more than the consequences of competition for wealth. He has come to realize that although many of the by-products of the struggle for wealth and display denigrate human values, these are rarely as brutal or as destructive to life and liberty as is the direct struggle for power. The bread-line is not a pretty spectacle; but it is neither as savage nor as irreversible as is the mass liquidation of those who stand in the way of ambitious men who conspire for power. Consequently in the

---

1. Lest this be misunderstood and misquoted I would point out that the Roman Catholic attitude to psychoanalysis while wary is not officially hostile. Some Catholic dignitaries talk, preach and even write as though they expressed an official condemnation. They do this without official reproof, but also without official sanction. There are Freudian analysts who are devout Catholics.

present stage of human culture, the analyst views the struggle for money, in spite of its many sordid and neurotic features, as a socially protective device. Money, like the policeman, is for the time being a necessary if imperfect protection against the frailties of man. Although the psychoanalyst deplores these frailties and the inequities of distribution in which they result, he looks upon them as a symptom of human maladjustment rather than its cause. Consequently he feels that the Utopian expectations of those who believe that the elimination of competition for wealth and display will solve the problem of human neuroses are merely an expression of good-hearted naivete. This skepticism about an assumption which is basic to orthodox communist philosophy is naturally a challenge which the dedicated communist finds disturbing and unwelcome (14, 19).

Lest this argument be taken as an expression of blind ideological partisanship, I would point out that recently, in a still unpublished lecture, I discussed before the American Academy of Arts and Sciences in Boston on December 11, 1957, the difficulties and possibilities of a truly preventive psychiatry (Daedalus in press). In considering this I pointed out that human ingenuity has not yet succeeded in devising a political, economic, educational, cultural or religious system which does not mask, exploit, reward and thus intensify the workings of the neurotic process. I indicated that authoritarian forms and democratic forms interact with the neurotic process in different ways; but that neither is free of guile or responsibility with respect to it. Similarly, I stressed the fact that despite the differences in the neurotogenic effects of the Russian and American systems, both must devote themselves to searching self-examination and self-criticism if either is to rid itself of those features which are destructive to human values and human life. Therefore, there is no self-righteous chauvinistic bias in my pointing out that the Soviet view of psychoanalysis is warped by ideological refractive errors. We have our own refractive errors, too; but they happen not to be relevant to this particular issue.

EPILOGUE

In 1935, Dr. Ralph W. Gerard (now Director of Laboratories in the Mental Health Research Institute of the Department of Psychiatry of the University of Michigan) was on a trip for the Rockefeller Foundation to various European laboratories and centers for the study of neurology, neurophysiology and psychiatry. He visited Pavlov in his laboratories in Leningrad. They were discussing his work on conditioning and especially the production of experimental "neuroses" in dogs by presenting them with a task of discrimination which was too difficult.

To Dr. Gerard's surprise, Pavlov said with a twinkle, "Do you know that I was led to try these experiments by reading some of Freud's work?" He then proceeded to speak of his indebtedness to Freud for stimulating his thoughts and his experiments into this productive channel, and added that he anticipated that deeper understanding of behavior would come from a fusion of the concepts of the conditioned reflex and of psychoanalysis. Subsequently Dr. Gerard related this conversation to Freud during the course of a visit to him in Vienna. Freud was impressed, and then said ruefully, "It would have helped if Pavlov had stated that publicly a few decades ago."

My own hope is that this short review of the problem may help towards that synthesis of studies of psychoanalysis and of the conditioned reflex, the value of which was felt both by Pavlov and Freud.

REFERENCES

1. ·ANDERSON, O. D. and PARMENTER, RICHARD. A Long-Term Study of the Experimental Neurosis in the Sheep and Dog (With Nine Case Histories). *Psychosomatic Medicine Monographs*, Vol. II, III, IV. Published with the sponsorship of the Committee on Problems of Neurotic Behavior, Division of Anthrop. and Psychol., National Research Council, Wash., D. C., 1941, p. 150.

2. FEDOTOV, F. The Soviet View of Psychoanalysis. *The Monthly Review* (in press, 1958).

3. FRENCH, T. N. Interrelations Between Psychoanalysis and the Experimental Work of Pavlov. *Am. J. Psychiatry*, Vol. XII (No. 2), May 1933, pp. 1165–1203.

4. FROLOV, Y. P. *Pavlov and His School—The Theory of Conditioned Reflexes.* Oxford University Press, New York, 1937, p. 291.

5. GANTT, W. HORSLEY. *Experimental Basis for Neurotic Behavior— Origin and Development of Artificially Produced Disturbances of Behavior in Dogs.* Hoeber-Harper, New York, 1944, p. 211.

6. HILGARD, ERNEST R. and MARQUIS, DONALD G. *Conditioning and Learning.* D. Appleton Century Co., Inc., New York, 1940, p. 429.

7. ISCHLONDSKY, N. E. Neuropsyche und Hirnrinde: Band 2, Physiologische Grundlage der Tiefenpsychologie under besonderer Beruksichtigen der Psychoanalyse. Berlin, Urban and Schwarzenberg, 1930; Der Bedingte Reflex und seine Bedeutung in der *Biologie, Medizin, Psychologie und Padogogik, Ibid.*, Vol. I.

8. KUBIE, LAWRENCE S. Review: *The Nature of Human Conflicts: An Objective Study of Disorganization and Control of Human Behavior;* Luria, A. R., Liveright, N. Y., 1932, p. 431; *Psychoanal. Quart.*, 1933, Vol. 2, pp. 330, 336.

9. KUBIE, LAWRENCE S. Relation of the Conditioned Reflex to Psycho-analytic Technique. *Arch Neurol. and Psych.*, Dec. 1934, Vol. 32, pp. 1137–1142.

10. KUBIE, LAWRENCE S. Review: *Pavlov and His School*, by Frolov, Y. P.; Oxford Univ. Press, N. Y., 1936, p. 286; *Psychoanal. Quart.*, 1941, Vol. 10, pp. 329–339.

11. KUBIE, LAWRENCE S. A Physiological Approach to the Concept of Anxiety. *Psychosom. Med.*, July 1941, Vol. 3 (No. 3), pp. 263–270.

12. KUBIE, LAWRENCE S. Review: *Lectures on Conditioned Reflexes*, Vol. 2. *Conditioned Reflexes and Psychiatry: by Pavlov, I. P.:* Inter-nat. Pub. Co., N. Y., 1941, p. 199; *Psychoanal. Quart.*, Oct. 1942, Vol. XI (No. 4), pp. 565–570.

13. KUBIE, LAWRENCE S. Psychoanalysis and Moral Responsibility, Chap. 18, pp. 155–166 from *Practical and Theoretical Aspects of Psychoanalysis.* Int'l. Univ. Press, N..Y., 1950, p. 252.

14. KUBIE, LAWRENCE S. Psychoanalysis in Relation to Social, Eco-nomic and Political Changes, Chap. 20, pp. 174–186 from *Practical and Theoretical Aspects of Psychoanalysis*, Int'l. Univ. Press, N. Y., 1950, p. 252.

15. KUBIE, LAWRENCE S. Problems and Techniques of Psychoanalytic Validation and Progress, pp. 46–124, from Hixon Fund Lectures of the Calif. Inst. of Tech., on *Psychoanalysis As Science*, Pumpian-Mindlin, E. (ed.), Stanford Univ. Press, Calif., 1952, p. 158.

16. KUBIE, LAWRENCE S. Some Implications for Psychoanalysis of Modern Concepts of the Organization of the Brain, *Psychoanal. Quart.*, Jan. 1953, Vol. 22 (No. 1), pp. 21–68.

17. KUBIE, LAWRENCE S. Psychoanalysis as a Basic Science, pp. 120–145, from *Twenty Years of Psychoanalysis*, Alexander, F. and Ross, H. (eds.); W. W. Norton, N. Y., 1953, p. 309.

18. KUBIE, LAWRENCE S. The Use of Psychoanalysis as a Research Tool: *Psychiatric Research Reports 6*, Amer. Psych. Assoc., Oct. 1956, pp. 112–136.

19. KUBIE, LAWRENCE S. Freud's Legacy to Human Freedom (Read in part before the Rudolf Virchow Med. Soc. of N.Y.C. on May 7, 1956); printed in the *Proceedings of the Rudolf Virchow Med. Soc.*, Vol. 15, 1956, pp. 34–48. Reprinted in *Perspectives in Biology and Medicine*, Autumn, 1957, Vol. 1 (No. 1), pp. 105–118.

20. KUBIE, LAWRENCE S. Social Forces and the Neurotic Process; Chap. 3, pp. 77–99, from *Explorations in Social Psychiatry;* Leighton, Alex. H. (ed.). Basic Books, Inc., N. Y., 1957, p. 452.

21. KUBIE, LAWRENCE S. The Neurotic Process as the Focus of Physio-logical and Psychoanalytic Research. Read before the Roy. Soc. of

Med., in London in Sept., 1957, *J. Mental Science*, London, Apr. 1958, Vol. 104 (No. 435), pp. 518-536.

22. LIDDELL, H. S. Conditioned Reflex Method and Experimental Neurosis, Part III, Chap. 12, pp. 389-412, from *Personality and the Behavior Disorders*, Vol. 1; Hunt, J. McV. (ed.). The Ronald Press Co., New York, 1944, p. 618.

23. LIDDELL, HOWARD S. Conditioning and Emotions, *Scientific American*, Jan. 1954, Vol. 190, pp. 48-57.

24. LIDDELL, HOWARD S. Stress, Emotion, and Mental Health. *Annual Lectures, Nat'l Inst. of Health*, 1954. Public Health Ser. Publ. No. 467. U. S. Govt. Printing Office, 1956, pp. 67-85.

25. LIDDELL, HOWARD S. A Biological Basis for Psychopathology. Pres. Address, Amer. Psychopath. Assoc., 1957, Hoch, P. and Zubin, J.: *Problems of Addiction and Habituation*, Grune and Stratton (in press).

26. MASSERMAN, JULES H. *Behavior and Neurosis—An Experimental Psychoanalytic Approach to Psychobiologic Principles*. University of Chicago Press, Chicago, 1943, p. 269.

27. MASSERMAN, Jules H. *Principles of Dynamic Psychiatry: Including an Integrative Approach to Abnormal and Clinical Psychology: with a Glossary of Psychiatric Terms*. W. B. Saunders, Philadelphia, 1955, p. 790.

28. PAVLOV, I. P. *Conditioned Reflexes—An Investigation of the Physiological Activity of the Cerebral Cortex*. (Transl. and ed. by G. V. Andrep); Oxford Univ. Press, England, 1927, p. 430.

29. PAVLOV, I. P. *Conditioned Reflexes and Psychiatry*, Vol. 2, Lectures on Conditioned Reflexes. (Transl. and ed. by W. Horsley Gantt); Int'l Publishers, New York, 1941, p. 199.

30. PAVLOV, I. P. *Experimental Psychology and Other Essays*. Philosophical Library, New York, 1957, p. 653.

31. REIDER, N. A Psychoanalyst Replies. *The Monthly Review:* (in press, 1958).

32. SIMON, BRIAN (ed.). *Psychology in the Soviet Union* (collected papers of various Russian psych.). Stanford Univ. Press, Calif., 1957, p. 305.

17

Freud and Hull: Pioneers in Scientific Psychology*

David C. McClelland

To a group of psychologists at least, an attempt to discuss these two men at the same time would be somewhat surprising—Sigmund Freud, the cultured European, expert on dream-life, founder of psychoanalysis; Clark L. Hull, backwoods American, expert on learning, founder of a kind of latter-day Newtonian system of behavioral psychology. Yet both claimed to be scientists, both contributed in a major way to psychological theory, and both are key figures in contemporary psychology. Certainly no Ph.D. candidate in psychology today can safely ignore either of them and even most undergraduate students of psychology must study rather carefully both psychoanalysis and Hull's system of behavior theory.

So we have an apparent paradox: here are two men who differed radically in personality, in cultural background, in scientific approach, in the kind of behavior they cared about, yet both are major figures in contemporary psychology. Why is this? To try and find an answer, let us look at some of these differences a little more closely. Fortunately we have at last an eminently sane and thorough biography of Freud by Ernest Jones (3) which gives a great many details about Freud's early scientific career which have subsequently been lost sight of in the furious controversies over psychoanalysis. As for Hull, he is too recently dead for anyone to have attempted a systematic evaluation of his career;

*Reprinted by permission from *American Scientist,* Journal of the Society of the Sigma Xi, Vol. 45, No. 2, March 1957.

but we do have his own autobiographic statement and in his case I can draw on my own personal knowledge since I studied under him at Yale University in the late 30's. Freud (1856–1939) lived most of his life in Vienna, and was in many ways a vintage product of a rich center of European culture. His family was not very well off and he was always short of money in his student days, but he was nevertheless encouraged in his early intellectual and cultural interests by the traditional Jewish respect for knowledge and learning. He grew up to be a true scholar in the old sense, knowing some eight different languages, and being well-versed in the classics of all cultures. He is one psychological scientist who has sometimes been more accepted in literary circles than in scientific ones. He started his professional career as a physiologist and neuro-anatomist but was forced, in the end, to go into the practice of medicine to earn a living.

Hull (1884–1952) by way of contrast, was almost the stereotype of an American pioneer. He was brought up in a log cabin in Michigan and spent his early years attending a one-room school and clearing stumps from the land to prepare it for farming. His formal education was as poor as Freud's was rich, although he seems to have read a good deal on his own, and mentions in particular Spinoza's *Ethics*. His father was practically illiterate and did not finish learning to read until his wife taught him after they were married. The family had been strongly Protestant, but his parents were "free thinkers," just as Freud's parents were with respect to their strong Jewish tradition. Hull originally planned to enter some practical profession like mining engineering but on a summer job he contracted poliomyelitis (at the age of 24) which permanently crippled one leg and forced him to change his occupation to that of school teaching—fortunately for science. What could be a more extreme difference in background than this—Freud, the cultured, well-educated European; Hull, the practical pioneer American! How they both ended up in psychology is a fascinating problem in itself, but we cannot take time to dwell on it here. It will have to do to say that Hull apparently decided quite on his own during his prolonged con-valescence from poliomyelitis that psychology was the field for him and got his mother to read him James' *Principles of Psychology* since his own eyes were too weak at the time. Freud on the other hand, seems to have been drawn into psychology gradually from the experience he had in his clinical practice with "nervous " cases.

As psychologists they differed greatly. Freud began his professional life by studies in neuro-anatomy and then moved on to the aphasias as being somewhere between physical and mental disease and finally ended up in functional neuroses with studies of dream-life, hypnosis, sexual instincts, and the like. In his work we run across concepts like libido, repression, defense mechanisms, the censor, the unconscious, the Superego, etc. In Hull we find a totally different line of development. He began working with serial verbal learning, then turned to aptitude testing, and finally spent the major portion of his career dealing with data derived from studies of learning functions in the white rat at Yale University. At only one point did their empirical interest overlap. They both studied hypnosis—neither, it may be noted in passing, with much success. Freud gave it up because it was an undependable therapeutic instrument, and Hull gave it up partly because he thought that he had demonstrated that it was merely a form of suggestibility similar in kind, if not in extent, to waking suggestibility, and partly because of the opposition of medical authorities in New Haven. Hull dealt in concepts like habit strength, excitatory potential, reactive inhibition, drive and the like. His mature and most developed work is represented by a page of definitions, axioms, deductions, and equations, whereas Freud's is represented by a page of closely reasoned analysis of inner mental life. It is small wonder that people have doubted whether they were in the same field.

In fact, throughout the last twenty or thirty years there hasn't been much tendency to treat them as part of the same discipline. Psychoanalysis grew up quite independently of academic psychology and American behaviorists were not slow in following their European colleagues in branding Freud both unscientific and absurd. Unfortunately we do not have recorded what these two men thought of each other. In fact, we could not really expect that Freud would have taken time out in his late seventies to read Hull's aggressively behavioristic papers which began to appear around 1930, fully 35 years after Freud's major work had begun. The best that we could expect from psychoanalysts on Hull is a terse "no comment," meaning perhaps that most of Hull's system is irrelevant to human psychology. On the other hand, Hull certainly knew about Freud's work through the influence of men like Professor John Dollard whom he knew at Yale, but it does not seem to have influenced his thinking much. Perhaps his comment on one of his early teachers at Wisconsin, the clinical psychologist Jastrow, will serve to represent somewhat his attitude toward men like Freud; "His mind could scintillate in a brilliant fashion, but his approach to psychology was largely qualitative and literary . . . He would sometimes lecture for five minutes at a time in perfectly good sentences, yet hardly say a thing" (2, p. 147).

Yet this is clearly not the whole story. Two facts stand out as contributing strongly to the impression that Freud and Hull basically had something very important in common. First, some of the most extreme systematic behaviorists of the Hull school have had a great personal interest and respect for psychoanalysis. Perhaps it was because Hull's system had little to say about their inner experiences and their own personal problems. So they turned to psychoanalysis as a personal, non-professional interest, perhaps, one might almost say, as providing a philosophy of life. A number of these behaviorists were psychoanalyzed. Secondly, Professors Dollard, Miller, and others at Yale attempted formally to state some of the psychoanalytic concepts in terms of the Hullian principles of behavior. Oddly enough, this did not prove a very difficult task, at least in its initial stage, a fact which strongly suggests that there must have been some basic similarities in approach between the two men. Some of their values at least should have been similar.

Let us look for a moment for these similarities. On the personal level, despite their enormous difference in background, they were alike in several important respects. Both were prodigiously hard workers. Freud, when he was writing "The Interpretation of Dreams" often saw patients eight to ten hours a day and then worked past midnight writing his books. Hull's working habits were the opposite although they were equally intense. He used to wake early in the morning around 5:00 A.M. and think in bed several hours before rising and going to his office at Yale. He kept "a permanent notebook of original ideas, concerning all sorts of psychological subjects as they came to me" (2, p. 147). At his death he had some twenty-eight such volumes in which his ideas had been persistently and continually worked through to their ultimate implications. Freud published more, partly because his active psychoanalytic period lasted for fully 40 years while Hull's mature work was all done in about 18 years between 1930 and 1948. But behind every page of Hull's work there was a vast amount of intricate reasoning and calculation, much of which could be condensed to a single equation taking up one line.

Both men were also tremendously courageous and honest. They both believed that the truth must be pursued at all personal cost. The attacks that Freud had to suffer because he was a Jew and because he persisted in attributing sexuality to infants are too well known to need review here. Hull never was as violently and personally attacked, but it is certain that he came in for his share of ridicule over the tedious and elaborate proofs of his theorems and propositions. Such challenges seem to have led both of them to redouble their efforts to do what they thought the science of psychology needed most.

Thirdly, they were both what might be called "close thinkers." Although Freud's thinking did not result in carefully worked out geometrical or algebraic proofs, no one who has read his works can deny that he wrestled with a problem as closely and thoroughly as did Hull, particularly in his early years when he was still formulating some of his basic ideas. Finally, both men had a grand vision of the great new science of psychology which spurred them on to tremendous efforts. Someone has said that to make a great contribution to any field of knowledge, one must have an image of one's own greatness. Both were modest about it, but the idea that a real science of psychology was possible gripped both of them and they both felt that it was their sacred duty to show how this could be done. And both had confidence in their ultimate success: "We shall win through in the end" (Freud). "It would be nice to know how these and similar scientific problems turn out" (Hull). Neither of them had the slightest doubt that ultimately the problems of understanding human behavior scientifically would be solved.

What was this science of psychology to be like? Again we find they had much in common. Both were extremely anti-religious and deterministic. Both openly disbelieved in God and Freud nearly caused a family crisis by refusing at first to go through the "superstitious nonsense" of a Jewish wedding ceremony. Hull reacted violently against his narrow sectarian upbringing and felt that "religious considerations interfere with the evolution of science" (2, p. 162). Their determinism was thoroughgoing and can perhaps best be illustrated by the way both of them treated the problem of "free will" or "spontaneity." Freud recognized characteristically that the subjective feeling of free will was an important psychological fact to be explained. His explanation consisted of demonstrating that so-called chance acts or trivial "choices" really have an unconscious motive behind them which a skillful analyst can always discover. Thus, no act is uncaused and the *illusion* of free will simply comes from the fact that some of our motives are unconscious (3, p. 365). Hull, on the other hand, in his presidential address before the American Psychological Association in 1936 spends a good deal of time getting rid of such notions as "consciousness" or "spontaneity" as being thoroughly unnecessary in a scientific system. His explanation is, in principle, the same as Freud's. Two acts, A and B, may have different strengths, so that A appears rather than B. But if A is unsuccessful in satisfying a need (motive) its strength will gradually diminish according to known laws of the extinction process, and finally B will "spontaneously" appear because its strength is now relatively greater than A's. No "free choice" is involved. In his own words, "This theorem is noteworthy because it represents the classical case of a form of spontaneity widely assumed, as far back as the Middle Ages, to be inconceivable without presupposing consciousness" (1, p. 12). Both men believed firmly in natural law and took much delight in explaining traditional moral and religious concepts as perfectly natural phenomena.

Their psychologies were also to be quantitative. This comes as no surprise in the case of Hull who spent the last years of his life trying to set up scales and units for measuring his basic concepts like habit strength, but it is perhaps unusual to claim that Freud, who appeared so qualitative in his writing, was also really quantitatively oriented. Yet Ernest Jones, who has analyzed Freud's earliest "general theory" which was never published, leaves no doubt about Freud's ultimate way of thinking about mental phenomena. Jones describes the work thus: "The aim of the 'project' is to furnish a psychology which shall be a natural science. This Freud defines as one representing psychical processes as quantitatively determinate states of material elements which can be specified. It contains two main ideas: (1) to conceive in terms of Quantity which is subject to the general laws of motion, whatever distinguishes activity from rest; (2) to regard the neurones as the material elements in question" (3, p. 385). In another place Freud speaks of a goal which plagues him, "To see how the theory of mental functions would shape itself if one introduced quantitative considerations, a sort of economics of nervous energy" (3, p. 347). It is quite clear from his subsequent work which deals with the libido, or drive concept, and its various ways of being checked and diverted that he had fundamentally in mind a quantitative concept of neural or electrical energy which was seeking to be discharged.

Both men also felt that psychology ultimately rests first on physiology and ultimately on physics. This is clear from the statement quoted above about Freud's first "general theory" and it is well known that Hull always hoped to find some confirmation of his theory at the physiological level. Both men ultimately were disappointed in not being helped more by nerve physiology and had to go on without it, but they believed that ultimately the laws of physiology and psychology would be found to be similar or at least consistent with one another.

Finally, in both of their systems the organism is conceived as being guided in its functioning by the satisfaction of needs or the "discharge of tension." It is difficult here to use words that will apply equally well to both systems of thinking, but clearly they both have very much the same idea in mind. It runs something like this: The organism seeks to preserve a state of equilibrium; anything which disturbs it will call out adjustive responses which will continue until the equilibrium is restored. Freud had in mind apparently a simple reflex model in which a stimulus sets up an excitation which "sets out" through the nervous system until it can discharge itself in a response. Generalizing this idea, he spoke of states of "unpleasure," or, as it has been more recently translated, tension, which keep the organism upset and active until they are discharged either directly or indirectly. The direct discharge, or primary process, as it was called, may simply involve the hallucination of the desired state of affairs as in a dream. The indirect, or secondary process involves an instrumental adaptive response in real life which produces the desired event in fact rather than in fancy. Hull did not concern himself at all with the primary process since, as a behaviorist, he did not concern himself with dreams and the like, but the secondary process describes almost exactly the way he thought the organism functioned. Certain biological needs like hunger, thirst, and sex (here a bow to the Freudians, although he never worked with sex as a drive) made the organism active until it successfully discovered a response which reduced the need. Then in the proposition which is basic to his whole system, Hull postulated that the reduction in need automatically strengthens the connection between the stimulus and response preceding it, a statement of the well-known "law of effect," which is usually thought to have been formulated first by Thorndike in this country. It is interesting to observe, however, that Freud, thinking along very similar lines, had come to an identical conclusion in the 1890's: "When this (the process of satisfying a desire) occurs, associations are forged . . . with the perceptual image of the satisfying object on the one hand, and on the other hand, the information derived from the motor activity that brought that object within reach" (3, p. 392). In Hull's terms, he is saying that need reduction forges a connection between the "stimulus" and the response-produced stimulus, a conception quite similar to Hull's in most respects. It is probably because the basic "model" of how the organism functioned is so similar for the two men that it was so easy to incorporate certain Freudian notions into Hull's system. Both men were essentially natural scientists, who had been strongly influenced by the theory of evolution, and who tended, therefore, to think of the organism as responding and adapting to changes in the environment so that it could survive or maintain its equilibrium.

Having covered some of the superficial differences between the two men and some of their basic similarities, we are in a better position to summarize how they differed in their approach to the scientific study of psychology. In the first place, they differed markedly in their attitude toward experimentation. Freud was no experimenter, as Jones makes very clear. His early success in the laboratory was with the microscope where he spent hours and hours dissecting, inventing new methods of staining, and analyzing different kinds of nervous tissue. He tried experimentation three times, all unsuccessfully according to Jones. His last attempt was to measure the effects of cocaine on muscular strength as measured by a dynamometer, a problem which, except for the nature of the drug used, was quite similar to many similar studies performed by academic psychologists like Hull and others. Freud had a marked preference for "seeing" over "doing." He spoke of experimentation in terms of "mutilating animals or tormenting human beings" (3, p. 53). One of his objections to hypnosis was that it was a "coarsely interfering method." Instead, he preferred to listen carefully and analyze. Hull was much more the practical American "doer." He thought that much valuable time was wasted in controversy that could better be settled by the resort to experiment. In his autobiography he quotes with favor Thorndike's comment "that the time spent in replying an attack could better be employed in doing a relevant experiment" (3, p. 154). It is true, however, that most of his own experiments particularly in his later years, were done not with human beings, but with rats. So one might argue that the logical superiority which experimentation should have given him over Freud was dissipated to a considerable extent because he did not employ it in the areas where it might have revealed the most useful facts for understanding human nature.

Another really basic difference between the two men was in the kind of behavior in which they were interested. Hull, true to the American tradition, was concerned almost wholly with the psychology of learning, with discovering how the organism adapts to new situations. He wanted to know what shape the learning curve took, what its major determinants were, what happened when practice ceased, etc. In all of this he was satisfied to use white rats because they seem to learn pretty much the same way as human beings do, at least so far as the simple kinds of associative learning are concerned in which Hull was interested. Freud, on the other hand, was interested in dreaming rather than in learning. Dreaming provides of necessity a kind of psychological data which belongs exclusively to the human sphere and which leads readily into studies not only of abnormal psychology, but of art and literature. It involved Freud in problems of memory for content and of perception, problems which Hull failed to deal with satisfactorily in his system. To the extent that Hull neglected dream life, Freud neglected the psychology of learning. If one may presume to stand in judgment, we might conclude that to the extent that both of them tried hard to build general systems of psychology, each began from too narrow a base. But this has always been true in the history of science. If each man pushes his insights to the limit, perhaps some future genius can see how they fit together, as Einstein could for certain physical phenomena.

Finally and most important of all, they differed enormously in the relative emphasis they placed on induction and deduction. Hull was fascinated by deductive systems from his earliest youth. While in his teens he "tried to use the geometrical method to deduce some negative propositions regarding theology" (2, p. 144). Later in college he constructed a "logic machine" which would satisfactorily "deduce" all the implications of a set of propositions plugged into it. But let him put it in his own words. "The study of geometry proved to be the most important event of my intellectual life; it opened to me an entirely new world—the fact that thought itself could generate and really prove new relationships from previously possessed elements" (3, p. 144). It is probably fair to say that all of his serious intellectual work was patterned after the geometrical model. He worked out a number of miniature systems complete with axioms, definitions, and derivations of theorems which he would then put to the "observational check." He believed that all secondary laws of human behavior could be derived from certain primary laws and so he dedicated his life to discovering the primary laws "together with the scientifically true and unmistakable definitions of all critical terms involved. These laws should take the form of quantitative equations readily yielding unambiguous deductions of major behavioral phenomena, both individual and social" (3, p. 162). It was his particular *bête noire* to read theorists whose propositions and principles were so unclear, confusing and ambiguous that it was impossible to test any of them experimentally.

Freud, on the other hand, took quite a different tack. He feared the deductive method and consciously set himself against using it for fear that it would lead him into empty philosophical speculation. Here we must invoke the difference in the historical period in which the two men grew up. In Freud's time it was revolutionary to be empirical, to turn one's attention to actual observation of human behavior. To be excessively theoretical was to be identified with philosophers whom one was revolting against. By Hull's time, however, there had already been a considerable mass of data collected by experimentation and observation, and Hull felt that the real problem was now to bring some order into it. He had nothing but contempt for the man who came into his office on Monday morning and looked around the laboratory asking, "Now what shall I do next?" He felt that this "dry as dust" empiricism was getting nowhere, that it did not lead to an accumulation of knowledge in systematic form.

Even though the difference between the two men can readily be explained in historical terms such as these, it remains a fact that Freud, as a person, was always much more impressed by the singular observed fact than Hull was. Freud stayed much closer to his data. After all, his theories had their basis in the consulting room and he had to check them constantly against the symptoms of his patients. In the early days when he was attempting to check his hypothesis that hysteria, as a neurosis, always had a sexual etiology, he had to test it against case after case as they came to him for consultation. He felt that he had to explain every little fact, no matter how small and how apparently insignificant. (See, for example, his "Psychopathology of Everyday Life.") Hull, on the other hand, was much more willing to attribute things to "chance" and in this sense was not so thorough-going a determinist, at least in practice. When a particular rat did not behave the way he was supposed to according to Hull's theory, it did not concern him unduly because, by this time, statistical considerations could be invoked and it was possible to attribute the deviation to some chance factor and still argue that the general results of the experiment were in agreement with the hypothesis. Freud retained throughout his long life the basic conviction that "theory is all very well, but it does not prevent (the facts) from existing" (3, p. 208). The same could not be said of Hull in practice, though I am sure that he would have subscribed to this sentiment in theory. When facts turned up which seemed actually to be inconsistent with his theory his common reaction was: "Give me time. It is not possible to make all deductions at once, the system must be built up gradually." This is certainly a justifiable attitude, but in the end his loyalty was primarily to the system (as indeed it might well be, considering the amount of energy and time he had put into it) rather than to curious, apparently inexplicable, facts in themselves.

As a result of this last difference in particular, both men had their characteristic weaknesses as scientists. In Freud's case, he kept so close to his observations over the years as an inductive scientist that his theoretical system was constantly in a state of flux. The concepts used did not relate to each other in any clear systematic way because they were constantly growing, changing and developing as new observations were made. One may argue that a scientist must keep his theorizing flexible, but one also has a right to expect that it is not so flexible as to make it impossible to test systematically. Freud, himself, was temperamentally disinclined to follow up on the detailed checking of his insights, as Jones points out, and this shows in the end in his system. He could have used some of Hull's rigor.

As for Hull, his weakness ultimately lay in the fact that he whittled away at the inductive process until observation became merely a means of checking his previous theoretical assumptions. This has the disadvantage which has characterized all such elaborate deductive systems in the past. It leads its exponents to look at only those phenomena which are covered by the system. Other phenomena tend to be neglected, though they may be equally important, simply because they do not "fit" in the system anywhere and to make them fit may cause a radical, not to say painful, revision in the enormous superstructure of propositions and derivations which the system involves. Hull speaks rather fondly in his autobiography of a machine which he built over a number of years which would calculate coefficients of correlation automatically. He relates that many of his friends joked with him about it, claiming that it would never work. "But," he concludes, somewhat proudly, "it really worked exactly according to plan" (2, p. 151). What he failed to add was that although it did work, no one ever used it, partly because there are important facts which will have to be accounted for by other theoretical models.

But what is our final evaluation of the contribution of these two men to the scientific study of psychology? To begin with, we must not underestimate the fact that they both inspired in a number of younger men the firm conviction that a science of psychology was possible. Such a belief has not been widely held, and, as we have seen, they both fought valiantly against doubts on this score wherever they arose, but particularly in religious circles. Then if we were to summarize Freud's lasting contribution in one word, it would have to be "ideas." He left behind him probably more important ideas about the nature of human psychology than any other man since Aristotle. Many of these ideas have not been checked by what most of us would regard today as adequate scientific methods, but they are a rich legacy which psychologists will draw on for years to come.

To summarize Hull's lasting contribution in one word, we would have to choose "system." By this we need not refer to his own elaborately worked out mathematico-deductive models. It is more the attitude which his models imply than the particular models themselves. No one, and here I speak from personal experience, could be long associated with Hull without catching some of his enthusiasm for exactitude, clarity, and system in stating propositions and ideas. The following comment is typical: "Too often what pass as systems in psychology are merely informal points of view containing occasional propositions . . . Some authors are prone to the illusion that such propositions could be deduced with rigor in a few moments if they cared to take the trouble. Others assert that the logic has all been worked by them 'in their heads,' but that they did not bother to write it out; the reader is expected to accept this on faith. Fortunately, in science, it is not customary to base conclusions on faith" (1, p. 30).

It would be difficult to make much of a case for Hull as an original thinker or for Freud as a systematic one, but certainly we may agree that the "system" of the one and the creativity of the other are both absolutely essential for a successful scientific approach to psychology.

REFERENCES

1. HULL, C. L. Mind, mechanism and adaptive behavior, *Psychol. Rev.*, *44*, 1-32, 1937.
2. HULL, C. L. Autobiography, in *A History of Psychology in Autobiography*, Vol. IV. Worcester, Mass.: Clark Univ. Press, 1952.
3. JONES, E. *The Life and Work of Sigmund Freud*, Vol. I. New York: Basic Books, 1953.

18

Psychoanalysis and American Psychology *

David Shakow

"Psycho-analysis is not a specialized branch of medicine. I cannot see how it is possible to dispute this. Psycho-analysis is a part of psychology; not of medical psychology in the old sense, not of the psychology of morbid processes, but simply of psychology."

Thus spoke Freud in 1927 (p. 252). And yet, despite his belief, psychoanalysis and psychology can hardly be said to be united. While other schools of psychology have tended, with time, to become absorbed into the mainstream, the relationship between psychoanalysis and psychology has run a different course. This is due mainly to two factors. Whereas the other schools have grown up in the tradition of academic psychology and within its fold, psychoanalysis has developed almost entirely outside this environment, both spiritually and physically. Psychoanalysis also differs because it is not only a school of psychology offering a theoretical system; it is several other things besides. Thus, psychoanalysis may be thought of as (1) a therapeutic method, (2) a method of investigation, (3) a body of observations, (4) a body of theory about human behavior, and (5) a movement going far beyond its scholarly aspects.

This chapter will concentrate on the theoretical system growing out of the body of observations of psychoanalysis and on the influence of this set of ideas on American psychology. I shall, however, have to consider

*Reprinted by permission of the author and Prentice-Hall, Inc., from *Clinical-Cognitive Psychology: Models and Integrations*, edited by Louis Breger. © 1969, pp. 56–79.

several other aspects of psychoanalysis as well. The study of the complicated relationship between psychoanalysis and American psychology
will necessitate an exploration of the various processes which compose
the totality called the *Zeitgeist*. In assessing the impact that Freud has
had on American psychology, I shall begin by drawing the distinction
between the pervasiveness of Freudian conceptions and the misunderstanding of Freud's concepts. This will be followed by an examination
of the nineteenth century milieu in which both Freud and psychology
developed. Next, I shall attempt to trace both the direct and indirect
influences of Freud in the first half of the present century. To complement the general survey, two specific areas—the unconscious and
motivation—will be examined in greater detail because of their particular importance.

The history of psychology (and philosophy) shows many ideas
which bear a resemblance to Freud's theories. Some of them, for instance
the earlier theories of the unconscious of Herbart, von Hartmann, and
Carpenter, appear to have had little direct effect on the development of
Freudian concepts. Freud was probably familiar with a few of them from
his youth and was very likely influenced by them, as he was by Nietzsche
and Schopenhauer, but only in a general way. What seems certain,
however, is that they helped to shape that vague complex of forces called
the *Zeitgeist*, and their influence made the *Zeitgeist* ultimately receptive
to Freud's influence.

The ideas of Freud's immediate forebears, including Meynert,
Brücke, Charcot, Breuer, Bernheim, Brentano, Fechner, Hering, and
Lipps, seem to have had considerable influence on Freud, although they
were not predecessors of his central ideas. They contributed to the
intellectual development of the period, a development which came to a
culmination with the impact of Freud's theories.

The ideas of Freud's early American contemporaries, such as the
functionalists (James, Dewey, Angell), while they do not seem to have
influenced Freud directly, were precursors of some of his central ideas,
and they helped to pave the way for the acceptance of Freud's conceptions. James played an especially important role by his anticipation of
some of Freud's particular insights and by his influence on the thinking
of his students (Holt, Woodworth, Thorndike, and others).

The various concepts of the subconscious held by Freud's later
contemporaries (Janet, Prince, and Sidis, for example) affected Freud's
thinking little, if at all, yet contributed a great deal to the receptivity in
psychological circles to Freud's conception of the unconscious.

I have used the two terms 'conception' and 'concept' and shall be
making the distinction between them repeatedly. By conception I mean

the broad matrix from which theories and concepts crystallize. Concepts have definitions; conceptions make ready use of any term and apply concepts in a common sense way in disregard, or even in ignorance, of their definitions. Theories, by and large, use only terms which have a conceptual status. When terms (for instance, relativity, libido, survival of the fittest) are used outside of the theory, they become conceptions, as they may have been before the theory gave them definition as concepts.

Thus, these predecessors and early contemporaries are not truly genetic antecedents of Freud. They are, instead, representatives of numerous parallel developments.

Those who followed Freud present no less complex a situation. On the one hand, many trends in psychology appeared after Freud's publications which seem to represent direct effects of his influence but are said to derive from independent sources. On the other hand, many theorists who claim that their views are derived directly from Freud seem to have utilized only certain of Freud's ideas in combination with other theories.

In the course of my presentation, I may appear to be suggesting a steady growth of Freudian influence. That such a semblance of continuity is illusory, however, should not surprise anyone who is accustomed to genetic observations and who has learned to think in terms of 'epigenesis' rather than 'preformation,' in terms of saltatory rather than uninterrupted development, in terms of advance by developmental crises rather than along smooth growth curves.

Forewarned against the simplistic assumption, we notice not only the obvious, increasing respect which finally reaches a crescendo of homage to Freud, the man, and his conception of man, but also some of the other attitudes which color whatever acceptance his work has gained:

(1) What is accepted is Freud's new view of man and his pioneering in new areas for psychological study. There has been a slow realization that Freud awakened interest in human nature, in infancy and childhood, in the irrational in man; that he is the fountainhead of dynamic psychology in general, and of psychology's present-day conceptions of motivation and of the unconscious in particular.

(2) Although there are many striking exceptions, it is for the most part his *conceptions* of these fields of study and his *observations* in them, not his *concepts* and *theories* about them, which have been accepted.[1]

---

1. To these considerations may be added the state of psychoanalytic theory itself. The exact meaning of key concepts such as cathexis (see Holt, 1962) and libido (Holt, 1965) is not always clear. Thus, in psychoanalytic writings, and particularly in post-Freud

(3)   When the theory itself is referred to, it is usually transformed into some 'common sense' version or is taken at the level of its clinical referents. In either case, it is likely to be criticized. It can even be said that until relatively recently no serious efforts were made to study thoroughly or to define Freud's concepts before either testing them experimentally or rejecting them.

(4)   The methods by which Freud arrived at his theories have not been used. Only recently has there been some effort made to examine the psychoanalytic method as a tool for research.

Thus, along with the non-linear growth of influence, we find that at almost every step the increase of Freud's influence is accompanied by opposing or confounding trends. What has occurred has been increasing verbal acceptance without proportionate growth of true conversance, acceptance of Freud's conception of man but not of the means by which he derived it. In fact, it has been an influence that was not accompanied by true understanding.

In the case of psychoanalytic theory, barriers in the way of ideal understanding were numerous and weighty among psychologists. Generally speaking, the scientist, because of the limited working time available to him, tries to learn more and more about his area of specialization and inevitably attends less and less to everything outside it. In his specialty, he may try to be completely rational and objective. But outside of it—and for a long while psychoanalysis was outside to most psychologists—where he lacks knowledge, he will act, not like a scientist, but like any other person. Common experience indicates that when tested knowledge is not available, implicit regulations of various sorts, whether ideologies, commitments, biases, predilections, or aversions, will select and shape the understandings he gains and mold the influences which impinge upon him. It is easy to see why many psychologists, involved in their specialized concerns and protected by their ideologies were immune to the influence of this new theory.

The historical influence of a theory cannot be measured by the degree of familiarity with and acceptance of it or its precise parts. Rather, Freud's influence on psychology must be gauged by the reactions of psychologists to any idea which demonstrably originated in Freud's observations and theories, regardless of whether the idea came

---

writings, there is frequently the same blurring of concepts and conceptions found in the popular literature. Klein (see Klein, G. S. *Freud's Two Theories of Sexuality*, 1969) analyzes Freud's concept of sexuality with reference to just this sort of problem. Similarly, Loevinger (see Loevinger, J. *Theories of Ego Development*, 1969) deals with the related problems of the psychoanalytic theory of ego development, and I (see Breger, L. *Dream Function: An Informative Processing Model*, 1969) attempt to do the same for theory of dreams (in Louis Breger (ed.) *Clinical-Cognitive Psychology Models and Integrations*, 1969).

from original sources, secondary sources, popularizations, or hearsay. (Compare Hoffmann, 1957.)

Our task is to trace the details of this influence and to establish how closely the accepted ideas resemble the original theory. This calls for an examination of the ideological commitment of Freud and the channels through which his theory was presented, and the specific ideological commitments of psychology which determined its reaction to the impingements of Freud's theory, as well as some aspects of the broader ideological situation in the United States at the time of the first impact of Freud's theory. For, while such factors are irrelevant to the appraisal of the theory itself, they nevertheless helped determine the character of Freud's influence.

NINETEENTH AND EARLY
TWENTIETH-CENTURY BACKGROUND

The nineteenth century appears to have been a period in which mechanism, naturalism, and positivism were dominant, although represented in a narrower and more materialistic way than they had been during the eighteenth century Enlightenment. An appreciation of the factors which imposed limitations on Freud's influence, including the differing commitments of academic psychology and psychoanalysis, requires reaching back into the nineteenth century philosophical matrix out of which psychology grew.

A partial explanation of the separation between psychoanalysis and psychology is probably to be found in the bifurcation of philosophy into natural philosophy and moral philosophy. Out of natural philosophy grew present-day epistemology and science. In this context, arose the key topics of early psychology—perceiving and knowing. Out of moral philosophy grew present-day ethics, with its relevant psychological problems of willing, wishing, feeling—topics central to psychoanalysis.

Of more immediate relevance for an appreciation of the influence of psychoanalysis on psychology, however, is the nature of their respective commitments to an important scientific outgrowth of nineteenth century philosophy, to what has come to be known as 'the Helmholtz program.' In part, it was psychology's commitment to the Helmholtz program which separated it, and even now keeps it somewhat apart, from those roots which gave rise to moral philosophy.

The Helmholtz program was a reflection of the philosophy embodied in a statement made in an 1842 letter to Eduard Hallman by du Bois-Reymond:

> Brücke and I pledged a solemn oath to put into power this truth, no other forces than the common physical-chemical ones are active within the organism; that, in those cases which cannot at the time be explained

by these forces one has either to find the specific way or form of their action by means of the physical-mathematical method, or to assume new forces equal in dignity to the chemical-physical forces inherent in matter, reducible to the force of attraction and repulsion [du Bois-Reymond, 1918, p. 108].

This statement was accepted in principle by the group which shortly came to include Helmholtz and Ludwig, known later as the Helmholtz school of medicine.

Cranefield (1957, 1959) points out that the '1847 program,' as he calls the program of the Helmholtz school, had three goals: (1) to establish an anti-vitalist position with the accompanying idea of intelligible causality, (2) to provide argument for the use of observation and experiment, and (3) to attempt to reduce physiology to physics and chemistry. Following a searching review of this topic, Cranefield concludes that the program had more or less success in achieving the first two goals. However, with the molar methods then available, the achievement of a truly physicalistic physiology was impossible. Not until present-day molecular biophysics and chemistry was this reduction possible. Thus, even the Helmholtz group turned to the assumption of the "new forces equal in dignity" part of the oath and to an attack upon the multiple problems of physiology by experimental methods using as tools physics and chemistry.

With this clearer understanding of what was actually represented by the Helmholtz program, we are ready to examine the different ways in which psychology and psychoanalysis reacted to and interpreted the philosophy of the program, and how these respective interpretations affected both the course of Freud's thinking and psychology's receptiveness to Freudian theory. If psychology or psychoanalysis were to try to carry out the Helmholtz program, they could not reasonably be expected to do more than physiology itself was then able to achieve. At most, they could adopt a mechanistic-deterministic point of view, apply experimental and observational methods to their phenomena, use physical and chemical techniques, and deal with their phenomena in terms of forces which were of "equal dignity."

Psychology was at first committed by Helmholtz, a physicist, to becoming an exact science in the same sense that physics was an exact science. But, like physiology, psychology had to compromise and settle for an experimental rather than a physicalist approach. Psychology, in the attempt to be exact, restricted itself to the use of the experimental method and consequently to the study of phenomena about which it *could* be exact. What came to be known as sensory psychology and psychophysics appeared to be the general areas to which these methods were applicable.

As we shall see below, it was not the theoretical commitment alone, but rather this commitment in combination with the choice of the experimental method and of the subject matter for the application of the method, which was fateful for psychology. Psychology, in aiming to establish itself experimentally, came increasingly to focus upon introspective reports. This led to an intense preoccupation with the mental elements constituting subjective experience. Finally, in the hands of such structuralists as Titchener, the description of these mental structures seemed to become the very goal. When introspective data proved to be unreliable, the shortcomings of the subjects were held to be at fault. The resultant use of trained 'introspectors' led to still another problem: increasing dependence of experimental results upon the research center in which the subjects were trained with the likelihood of nonreplicable results. A crisis in experimental psychology developed.

The resolution of this crisis split psychology into two camps, one of them rather accessible and the other much less accessible, to Freud's oncoming influence. The first group to rebel against the sterility of the structuralist program were the functionalists (James, and Dewey, J. R. Angell, and the Chicago school). They believed the experimental program had miscarried because of the quest for fixed mental elements (structures).

We can call on William James to illustrate the more general roots of the functionalists' dissatisfaction. James (1890, Vol. 1, pp. 548-549) characterized the exactitude of Fechner's law (and of psychophysics) as pseudo-exactitude, and asserted that whatever validity it had was in physiology, rather than in psychology. He commented as follows: ". . . it would be terrible if even a dear old man as this could saddle our Science forever with his patient whimsies, and, in a world so full of more nutritious objects of attention, compel all future students to plough through . . . his . . . works. . . ."[2]

By raising the question of the use and purpose of psychological structures and processes, the functionalists became involved in issues of adaptation, development, and the relationship between organism and

---

2. James' rebellion against the Helmholtz program and his criticism of Fechner's psychophysics reflects his personality, showing his freedom as a psychologist to look at and think about an amazingly broad range of human phenomena. Through his opposition to the limiting requirements of the 'exact science' commitment he was able to face 'life in the raw' and to consider all facts of life proper subject matter for psychology. Evidence for the similarities between the functionalist and Freudian trends are especially clear in James, who in many respects appears to have anticipated Freud's ideas. Examples of James' anticipation are so abundant that their neglect by both psychologists and psychoanalysts is not only puzzling but embarrassing. Note particularly his discussion of the vague and the fleeting (1890, Vol. 1, pp. 254-225).

environment. Accordingly, they contributed to the growth of naturalistic observation and developmental theorizing. The functionalists' program thus shared with Freud's program allegiances to both the Helmholtz school and to Darwinism and initiated a trend which augured favorably for Freud's influence.

Somewhat later than the functionalists, the behaviorists (Watson and others), the representatives of the second trend, rebelled against the structuralist's miscarriage of the experimental program. This group turned against the introspectionist aspect of the structuralist program, restating and reinforcing the exact science program in a form even more rigorous (or should we say more rigid?) than the original. They saw the fruitless, deceptive shadowboxing of the structuralists' introspections as the cause of the sterility of their experimental program and concluded that consciousness was an epiphenomenon. It was as if they had deliberately agreed that consciousness was not reducible to the forces of "attraction and repulsion" and therefore not of the character demanded by even a modified form of the original Helmholtz program. The behaviorists declared observable behavior to be the only proper subject matter of an exact science of psychology, thus ruling out both consciousness as a subject matter, and the use of introspection as a method. In this way, they reaffirmed the constriction of the field imposed by the exact science interpretation of the original program and exacerbated this constriction by an accompanying blindness to the possibility of "new forces equal in dignigy." Once consciousness and introspection were declared illegitimate, the source of the data on which psychoanalysis was built was, of course, excluded from the behaviorist's scientific psychology.

The general result seems to have been that the functionalists, who were directing their attention to more meaningful areas, made only little progress toward exactitude and unified theory, whereas those who remained faithful to the earlier program made equally little progress in extending their exactitude beyond the confines of limited laboratory problems. While functionalism, through its emphasis on use and adaptation, gave rise to applied psychology and the psychology of individual differences, the mainstream of American psychology came to adhere to the new and extreme form of what was essentially the original exact science program as interpreted by the behaviorists.

Thus, Darwinian influence and functionalism, especially Jamesian open-mindedness and genius, led to psychological thinking akin in many respects to Freud's. It seems reasonable to assume that these account for part of whatever subsequent receptiveness there was to Freud. But functionalism was itself isolated from the mainstream of

American psychology, a circumstance which partially explains the reluctant acceptance of Freud in most Western psychological circles.

It is important to recognize that although psychology's particular interpretation of and commitment to the Helmholtz program was an obstacle to Freud's influence, it nevertheless also served as a link between psychology and psychoanalysis. Freud, too, was committed to the Helmholtz program, and a consideration of this commitment will help to explain this paradoxical situation.

During his years at the University of Vienna, Freud was strongly influenced by Brücke, the "Far Eastern" representative of the Helmholtz group. He worked on neurophysiological problems in Brücke's laboratory and described Brücke as the person who "carried more weight with me than anyone else in my whole life . . ." (Freud, 1927, p. 253). Freud's early speculations concerning the neuroses bear the stamp of this influence, an influence clearly revealed in the "Project for a Scientific Psychology" (1895). In the "Project," Freud made a valiant attempt to develop a neurological theory of psychopathology and psychology, but when he failed in this, he turned to what amounted to a search for forces "equal in dignity" in the psychological sphere. This was not, however, the sphere of academic psychology, for the problems Freud settled on— those of affectivity—were more consonant with the subject matter of moral philosophy.

From about 1900 on, Freud's theories essentially emphasize the psychological—the *motivational* psychological—though there are occasional backward glances at physiology (as in *Three Essays on the Theory of Sexuality*, 1905). Freud's early commitment and the difficulty in giving up this physicalist background led to certain theoretical difficulties that are only recently being clarified (Holt, 1965, 1967, Klein, 1967 . . .). Despite these problems, it seems clear, as Loevinger points up (1969)* that Freud's theories are primarily *psychological,* that they deal with meanings and ideas (conscious and unconscious), symbolic transformations, feelings, human relationships, and the like.

If we re-examine the Helmholtz program in the context of the oath taken by duBois-Reymond and Brücke, we see that the spirit of the program could be fulfilled wholly or in part in three ways: (1) by a true physicalist physiology (which was not attained during the whole Helmholtz period), (2) by an objective experimental physiology (Ludwig, Helmholtz, Brücke, duBois-Reymond, *et al.)* or an objective experimental psychology (Wundt, G. E. Muller, Ebbinghaus, *et al.)*

*Loevinger, J. *Theories of Ego Development in Clinical-Cognitive Psychology.* L. Breger (Ed.). Prentice-Hall, Inc., Englewood Cliffs, N.J. 1969.

which used physics and chemistry as *tools,* or (3) by a consulting-room psychology which used objective observational methods (Freud). The inclusion of the last naturally raises a question, for a consulting room psychology utilizes neither instrumental controls nor the controls usually associated with experiment, coming closer to the naturalistic situation with which biology proper was occupying itself at the time.[3]

In point of fact, the area of psychology Freud chose did not lend itself readily to experiment or to the application of physical and chemical techniques, whereas the area of the experimental psychologists in part did, and that was the part which was most impressive to the scientific public. For the period in which Freud worked, the nature of the material, and the stage of development of the field appeared to call for an acceptance of the kind of observational technique and the kind of theory that he developed. To Freud and others, his endeavor was an indirect but essential step toward the realization of a program which was to include obviously significant and even apparently trivial facets of ordered and disordered human behavior.

The experimental psychologists were so imbued with the narrower interpretation of the Helmholtz philosophy and their interpretation of its methodological restrictions that they limited themselves to areas of psychology in which the method was applicable, that is, to sensation and perception, the fields closest to physiology. This meant that they worked in the laboratory where they could choose their problems and consequently could apply the method without much difficulty. Freud, on the other hand, working in the consulting room, had to deal with the problems which came to him. Careful analysis convinced him that these were affective ones. To these he tried to apply the Helmholtz philosophy as far as possible, but obviously he could not do so as rigorously as could the experimental psychologists with their more limited segmental problems. Nevertheless, he held strongly to the anti-vitalist position of the Helmholtz school and to the use of observation, if not experiment. The essence of the program, common to all its parts, was an exceptionless determinism. For Freud, the "equal in dignity" part of the program took the form of the postulate of thoroughgoing *psychic* determinism. It is true that in a number of places (for example, 1913, p. 182; 1925, pp. 25–26) Freud indicated the hope for an eventual physicalist explanation. It is nevertheless clear from other statements (for example, 1913, p. 166)

3. Scriven, in "Psychology without a paradigm" (L. Breger, ed., *Clinical-Cognitive Psychology,* New Jersey: Prentice-Hall, 1969), argues that it was probably a mistake all along for psychology to have attempted to model itself after physics. He outlines some interesting alternatives that are more consistent with recent thinking in the philosophy of science (Louis Breger, 1969).

that he was not willing to accept superficial and easy biological hypotheses—for instance, Jung's simplistic theory of a toxic cause for dementia praecox—when he felt that psychological ones were much more relevant and meaningful.

The "new forces" which Freud postulated were not "reducible to the forces of attraction and repulsion" by the means he had at his disposal. His methods did serve, however, to encompass in the scope of the scientific program a broad range of phenomena which exact academic psychology could not at that time, nor even now, deal with adequately. It was, then, the equivalent of a psychological extension of the "equal in dignity" part of the Helmholtz program that Freud pursued for the rest of his life. In the present context, it suffices to say that by assuming the existence of such forces, he made *psychological reality* a subject matter of psychological study having for many psychologists the same dignity as did the *impingements of external reality* for psychophysicists and behaviorists.

FREUD AND DYNAMIC PSYCHOLOGY

The course Freud followed was in some respects similar to that of the functionalists who rebelled against the narrower interpretation of the Helmholtz program and concentrated on areas foreign to the dominant behavioristic group, areas such as instinctual drives and emotions. As we have seen, functionalism helped to prepare the ground for Freud's influence on psychology and became the area of psychology most open to his influence. Together, Freudianism and functionalism came to serve as the main sources of nourishment for dynamic psychology. In the long run, however, Freud, not functionalism, was decisive for the survival and growth of dynamic psychology, so much so that, at present, dynamic psychology and Freud are often considered synonymous.

It is true that one trend in clinical psychology, that represented by Witmer, can be said to derive from Wundt and the structuralist point of view. However, this was not the trend which prevailed. Rather, it was the trend initiated by Healy, largely influenced by Freudian psychology, which became the dominant one (Shakow, 1948).

All in all, it is understandable that Boring should conclude: "The principal source of dynamic psychology is, of course, Freud" (1950, p. 693).

The dynamic trend was alien to and combatted by the mainstream of development in psychology. For a very long while, the commitment of the mainstream to "exact science" and the skipping by academic psychology of the naturalistic phase which had been so well represented in biology did not encourage interest in naturalistic observation, let alone in the rough and ready observations and theorizing characteristic of psychoanalysis.

Woodworth clearly saw the intrinsic contrast between Freudism and the main trend in psychology: "As a movement within psychiatry, psychoanalysis was a revolt against the dominant 'somatic' tendency of the nineteenth century, and a springing into new life of the 'psychic' tendency. Just when psychology was becoming more somatic, psychiatry started in earnest to be psychic" (1931, p. 126).

It is obvious that the choice of subject matter and explanatory level, which Woodworth stresses, was important. But there is perhaps something even more crucial in the contrasting methods used in psychology and psychoanalysis. Freud resorted to methods which we still do not know how to describe precisely. The "exact science" of psychology, on the other hand, adhered to exact methods which were not easily, if at all, applied to the subject matter on which Freud developed his theories. Psychology did not have the means to prove or disprove Freud's theories.

While James' commitment was to face unflinchingly life in the raw and Freud's was to carry out, implicitly if not explicitly, the Helmholtz program as well as clinical reality permitted, the mainstream of psychology uncompromisingly stuck to the narrower aspects of the Helmholtz program, which the originators of the program had not been able to carry out even in physiology (Cranefield, 1957). I once speculated how much further developed and more widely applicable our exact scientific methods might now be if all of psychology had initially committed itself to carry out the Helmholtz program on the subject matter of and within the limitations of clinical reality (Shakow, 1953). If nothing else, the question does identify this problem as the age-old one of the difference between working inductively from the material of naturalistic observation and working inductively from narrow premises. It would seem that major scientific advances arise from the interplay of these two quite separate approaches, and it was precisely this interplay that was prevented for a long time by the differing commitments of the mainstream of psychology and psychoanalysis. In such interplay, methods develop which increasingly fulfill both the demands of the material and the demands of the criteria for relevant levels of rigorous proof. It seems that the different commitments of academic psychology and psychoanalysis not only interfered with their taking note of each other's methods, but also resulted in their focusing on different subject matters. Because of these events, the development of rigorous methods applicable to the data of psychoanalysis was prevented.

I have surveyed the differing commitments of psychology and psychoanalysis and some causes of psychology's reluctance to recognize Freud. Later, we shall consider some of psychology's ambivalent feelings further, but at the moment we are faced with another problem. Assuming the accuracy of this description of the relationship between academic psychology and psychoanalysis, it would not be surprising if a stalemate prohibiting any interaction had resulted, with little or no Freudian influence on psychology. The fact that there *has* been a profound Freudian influence calls for an explanation.

GENERAL ASPECTS OF TWENTIETH-CENTURY DEVELOPMENTS—INFLUENCE AND OBSTACLES TO INFLUENCE

In analyzing the way in which psychoanalysis came to affect psychology, two mutually supporting lines of influence, one indirect and one direct, seem to emerge. Although they cannot be completely separated, the indirect influence seems to be that which came predominantly from the surrounding culture, from that part of the *Zeitgeist* which was itself greatly shaped by Freudism. The direct influence appears to be that which came along natural professional lines, from sources more immediately related to psychology and psychoanalysis. Let us first examine the various streams of *indirect* influence.

The American atmosphere of the first decades of the 1900's was a peculiarly favorable one for Freudian ideas. The muckrakers (Tarbell, Norris, Sinclair, Steffens) and early realists (Crane, Dreiser, London) of the last decades of the nineteenth century had already laid the foundations for breaking down the genteel traditions of a primarily Puritan and Victorian culture. This trend was markedly accelerated by the social protesters (Eastman, Goldman, Dell, Debs), the feminists (Schreiner), and the Bohemians (Dodge), all of whom were influential in the period immediately before and after World War I. Freudian ideas were welcomed with open arms by these rebellious forces, and relationships developed among them in which the Freudian influence became paramount. In fact, Freudian ideas became so integral a part of the *Zeitgeist* that this *Zeitgeist* became an indirect but major channel for Freud's influence on professional psychology. The impact of the new ideology led to the development of a simplified and distorting popular and semi-popular literature dealing with Freud which continues even to the present. This, in turn, contributed to the public consciousness of psychoanalysis which led students and members of other disciplines to expect psychologists to deal with dynamic aspects of human behavior. By the nature of the ideas it dealt with, Freudism re-aroused dormant guilts among psychologists for not having met a reasonable obligation—the greater understanding and control of the forces of human nature.

Concurrent with these indirect factors which played varying roles in Freud's influence, more *direct* professional influences were at work. But in spite of the combined pressures of public consciousness, impatient colleagues (such as Tansley, 1920, and Wheeler, 1921), students, and professional influences, psychoanalysis did not immediately become a part of American psychology. It had first to overcome many difficulties, some of which were actually created by the very vehicles that carried it.

There were, of course, many general professional factors which no doubt worked against psychology's receptiveness to psychoanalysis. Freud was a stranger and an outsider, one whose unconventional methods were suspect, whose air of condescension to academic psychology was repugnant, and whose use of the doubtfully defensible resistance argument was particularly antagonizing.[4] A further obstacle was probably the professional medical orientation of psychoanalysis, whose students were trained in independent and non-academic settings, in contrast to the conventional academic setting of the psychologist.

But such factors were, in the end, probably only accessory to the major obstacles. Most of the difficulties grew out of particular qualities of the material provided by psychoanalysis, material which is the usual means of transmitting new theories and ideas. The language barrier, confounded by the circuitous course of psychoanalytic development, made it difficult for the psychologist to be sure what psychoanalysis really was. The subtlety of Freud's writing made understanding of the

---

4. This is the argument that opposition to psychoanalysis is motivated by unconscious resistance on the part of the opponent, that, for example, one cannot accept the idea of the Oedipus complex because it arouses anxiety to think of one's own. In a related argument, it is asserted that only he who has engaged in psychoanalytic therapy can fully understand psychoanalytic theory. There are insidious aspects to these positions and, when carried to their extremes as they sometimes are, they place the theory in the position of a religious dogma that is impervious to all questioning. At the higher levels of theoretical abstraction, the connection between theory and therapy is frequently not clear, making the resistance argument of little relevance.

Nevertheless, the insidiousness with which the argument is sometimes used should not blind us to certain elements of truth in it. For one thing, certain phenomena can best be understood from first-hand experience which is, after all, what distinguishes science from arm-chair speculation. Hence, it is quite reasonable to demand such a first-hand acquaintance with psychoanalytic therapy, either as patient or therapist, as a necessary prerequisite for an informed discussion of it.

The resistance argument itself touches on a somewhat more complicated issue stemming from the peculiar problems that arise from introspective methods. Bakan (1967) points out how Külpe and the others of the Würzburg school around the turn of the

original German difficult, even for those who knew German fairly well, and it was a rare psychologist who could do better than this. Those who went to whatever translations were available were hindered by their general inadequacy. Further, psychologists seemed preponderantly to prefer secondary sources. But it was difficult to find a reliable secondary source which covered even a portion of psychoanalytic theory. Until fairly recently, the secondary sources made no pretense of providing any systematic presentation of psychoanalysis. At the very best, they presented only parts of the theory, frequently emphasizing the clinical rather than the general theory; at the worst, they were misleading. To the general lack of familiarity with psychoanalysis was added the misinformation provided by the oversimplifications and distortions of the more popular sources.

The opinions of outstanding psychologists from James and Hall through Dewey, Watson, Woodworth, McDougall, Thurstone, and Terman, and historians such as Boring and Murphy provide a glimpse of the academic reaction to Freud. Whether the responses were made as a man in the street or as a psychologist, whether they were the result of dormant professional guilt or of the particular quality of the written sources, they ranged from the violently negative, through the indifferent, to the generally positive. At all these levels, however, reactions were characterized by conflict and hesitancy.

Thus, while Freud's influence was being inescapably forced upon psychology by various public and professional pressures in a period of great social and moral upheaval in the United States, particularly during the years just before and after World War I, concrete and practical factors joined cultural and social trends to complicate and obstruct the course of this influence. Clashing philosophical and professional

---

century, in using the method of introspection on the problem of "imageless thought," began using free associative methods very much like Freud's. Their work led them ever closer to psychoanalytic data and methods. For example, Messer posits unconscious processes. Ach stresses the role of motivation in guiding thought and uses hypnosis, and Bühler stresses the importance of empathy with the subjects in such research (Bakan, 1967, pp. 96–97). Suddenly, the work is dropped and Külpe's subsequent publications contain no mention of it, nor of the entire topic of thought! It seems reasonable to assume with hindsight that their methods led the Würzburg group to the same place that they led Freud, that their probing of each others' minds produced unconscious material, generated anxiety or other forms of discomfort and defensiveness or resistance, which in turn led to an abandonment of the whole enterprise.

Resistance, as the above historical example illustrates, is an important psychological phenomenon; it does occur in relation to the data generated by introspective methods, a fact that is extremely important in understanding the historical development of psychology as well as certain reactions to Freud and psychoanalytic theory. (Louis Breger, 1969)

commitments, language and methodological barriers, and mutual defensiveness and misunderstanding prevented any semblance of continuous integration of psychoanalysis into American psychology, leading instead to complex interactions that resulted nevertheless in a fitful, though steadily increasing, growth.

THE UNCONSCIOUS AND MOTIVATION

Of the many major contributions of Freud to psychological theory, we might deal briefly with two of especial importance—the unconscious and motivation. These are selected because they are areas central to the interests of psychologists and lend themselves more readily to examination than do other areas to which Freud contributed, such as dynamic psychology and the understanding of human nature.

The long history of the conception of the unconscious, represented by both Freud's precursors and contemporaries mentioned earlier, laid the foundations for receptiveness to the idea of an unconscious when this was proposed by Freud. On the other hand, it made true appreciation of his concept of the unconscious, which included two different kinds of unconscious, one unrepressed and the other repressed (Gill, 1963), much more difficult.[5] In fact, psychologists often acted as if they were not aware of this distinction.

In the case of motivation, Freud's theory was caught up in the controversies related to various polarities—determinism-teleology, mechanism-vitalism, pro- and anti-hedonism, and nature-nurture. These controversies served as obstacles to the penetration of Freud's concepts but nevertheless helped to spread his general conception of motivation. The very involvement of his theory on both sides of the controversies clearly demonstrates the misunderstandings of it which were prevalent.

When we examine the specific course of Freud's theory of motivation, we see its relationships with certain aspects of the association and act psychology of his predecessors Herbart and Brentano (active ideas and intentionalism) and its similarities to such sibling theories as those of Thorndike, Claparède, and Ach. Definite likenesses can also be seen between Freud and the theories which derived from these latter three psychologists—those of Piaget, Lewin, and the adopters of Thorndike's law of effect, most particularly of Hull and the Yale group.

---

5. See the discussion by Klein (in press) and Loevinger (1966) of the two principles of the dynamic unconscious (or repression) and the "reversal of voice" principle. What Klein and Loevinger present are essentially cognitive formulations of the two forms of the unconscious referred to here. (Louis Breger, 1969)

Piaget's theories show parallels to Freud's theories in their union of nature and nurture, in the pervasive role they give to motivation, and in their hierarchic conception of motivation. Lewin's theories of tension systems and his concern with emotions are also parallels to Freud. The attempt made by Hull and the Yale group to reconcile psychoanalysis with conditioned reflex theory generally resulted in an invasion of the literature by Freudian terms but at the price of turning Freud's concepts into conceptions only barely related and sometimes contradictory to the original concepts. There can be no doubt, however, that Hull's drive concept and the concepts of Dollard, Miller, and Mowrer, all of which differed from the psychoanalytic one, did a great deal to make Freudian ideas familiar and of great interest to psychologists.

If we follow Freud's concepts along another line of development, along the line of instinct, we see a somewhat similar result. The comparison of the instinct conception with Freud's concept of instinctual drive reveals developments which were both an aid in a general way to keeping the instinct idea alive and a hindrance in a specific way to Freudian influence. We see this both in those who rebelled against the instinct idea (Bernard, Watson, and Kuo) and in those who, like Tolman and Woodworth, needed some kind of nativist conception for the completion of their psychological systems. In the case of McDougall, who was particularly concerned with a nativist basis for his psychology, Freud's emphasis on the drive concept appears to have reinforced his persistence in his own hormic psychology.

It is difficult to summarize the meandering course of Freud's influence on the birth and development of motivation theories in psychology. One can only be amazed by the intricate intertwining of influence and by the unpredictable channels through which influences are effected. What appears highly probable, however, is that the passage through a stage of acceptance, which amounts mainly to taking the specificity out of concepts and turning them into vague conceptions, is unavoidable in the historical process.

PROBLEMS AND PROSPECTS
FOR THE FUTURE

Having looked at some aspects of the historical background of the present position of psychoanalysis, it remains for us to examine briefly some of the problems and prospects for the future, as psychoanalysis takes its place as part of psychology. Rapaport, in attempting a systematization of psychoanalytic theory, has presented the main lines of the problems that lie ahead (Rapaport, 1959, pp. 155–167).

The obstacles to the integration of psychoanalysis with psychology are of two types: practical obstacles that lie in both psychology and psychoanalysis, and certain theoretical obstacles that arise from the nature of their common field of study.

The practical obstacles lying within psychology are various. We have already noted some of the problems arising from psychology's self-consciousness, a self-consciousness which is reflected in a preoccupation with *the* scientific method and with experimental design at the cost of substantive concern. There has been, too, a tendency in psychology toward addiction to a single theory or to a single method, a trend closely associated to the prevalence of schools. Another obstacle is the extension to problems in psychology of what Adelson (1956) has called the notion of "perfectibility," the natural American propensity to be optimistic (Shakow, 1960). Although this attitude of optimism has become most obviously involved in problems of therapy, it can also be seen in theories about the basic nature of man (Maslow, 1962). These theories have developed largely in reaction to an exaggerated concern with the pathological but tend to neglect the negative forces with which individuals must contend. Psychoanalytic ego psychology, especially Erikson, appears to have dealt with this area in a much more realistic fashion.

Psychoanalysis, too, has its practical obstacles. The first of these is a problem which was considered earlier: the lack of systematic theoretical literature, especially on the general psychoanalytic theory. Although this situation is to some extent being alleviated by the work of persons like Rapaport (1959) and Gill (1963), it still remains an obstacle to theoretical progress. Another handicap is the training offered by psychoanalytic institutes. Its almost exclusive limitation to physicians, its essentially night school character, and its emphasis on private practice which does not foster theoretical interest and development and results in a limited number and kind of patient are all handicaps to theoretical progress. It is not surprising, therefore, that some demand has grown up in recent years for relatively independent institutes to be associated with both medical schools and with graduate departments of psychology (Shakow, 1962).

In addition to the two kinds of practical problems just considered, there are a number of theoretical obstacles arising from the very nature of the subject matter and the field which psychoanalysis and psychology have in common. Regard for the individual's legal and moral rights is a major empirical barrier to the observation and manipulation of behavior inside and outside the laboratory. This problem also has important theoretical aspects: the effects of such trespass upon the subject, the observer, and the observation. There is, too, the hierarchy problem. Much experimentation lies ahead before laws of hierarchic transformation are developed which will permit adequate handling of field problems taken into the laboratory. Still another problem grows out of the fact that a large proportion of psychological phenomena occur only in the contact of one person with one or more others. The method of participant observation has been developed to deal with this problem, but the implications of the method have not yet been theoretically formulated, and the lack of such systematization has in turn retarded the theory's development. A final obstacle is that of mathematization, including quantification.

Some progress has been made in the attempt to deal with these various problems. First efforts are being made toward handling the difficulties created by participant observation through the development of alternative techniques. Knowledge of dyadic and other social situations is being advanced by the use of techniques for studying organized complexity and modern computational devices (Weaver, 1948). The hierarchy problem has offered more difficulties because the theoretical aspects of heirarchic transformation have not been developed. This difficulty is, of course, somewhat alleviated by the fact that not all problems need to be taken to the laboratory. Although as many problems as possible need to be brought under laboratory control, efforts to deal rigorously with field situations should be continued and increased.

Over a decade ago, I was afforded an opportunity to take stock of mid-century trends in what was broadly defined as the area of experimental psychology (Shakow, 1953). At that time, a number of trends appeared conspicuous. One of these was the growing awareness by psychology of its own overconcern with its formal disciplinary aspects and the resultant ego orientation rather than task orientation. Together with this awareness were early signs of revolt against this preoccupation with our neighbors' presumed interest in our affairs. Another important trend was the growing interest in Jamesian "more nutritious objects of attention," reflected in increasing attention to molar studies, accompanied by a diligent search for methods to handle the organized complexity involved.

Rapaport (1959) has made some important complementary points. More recently, Koch (1959, pp. 729-788) has presented a more systematic statement of a similar point of view. In his concluding perspective, based on his review of the formulations made by the thirty-four contributors to the first three volumes of his work, Koch (1959, pp. 783-785) says:

> *"It can in summary be said that the results of Study I set up a vast attrition against virtually all elements of the Age of Theory* [approximately the 1930-1955 period] *code.* . . . [None of the contributors] is prepared to retreat one jot from the objectives and

disciplines of scientific inquiry, but most are inclined to reexamine reigning stereotypes about the *character* of such objectives and disciplines. There is a longing, bred on perception of the limits of recent history and nourished by boredom, for psychology to embrace . . . problems over which it is possible to feel intellectual passion. . . .

"*For the first time in its history, psychology seems ready—or almost ready—to assess its goals and instrumentalities with primary reference to its own indigenous problems. . . .*

"This preparedness to face the indigenous must be seen as no trivial deflection in the line of history. . . .

". . . at the time of *its* inception, *psychology was unique in the extent to which its institutionalization preceded its content and its methods preceded its problems.* If there are keys to history, this statement is surely a key to the brief history of our science. . . . Never had inquiring men been so harried by social need, cultural optimism, extrinsic prescription, the advance scheduling of ways and means, the shining success story of the older sciences."

·Why do I make so much of these developments? Because they have direct reference to a central aspect of Freud's influence—the long delay in integration of his ideas and the many vicissitudes hindering the achievement of their appropriate place in psychology. But in making these points about the past, am I not, as Koch says, "decrying the inevitable"? Am I not trying to hurry history, questioning the relentless march of historical forces, the forces of the dominant aspects of the *Zeitgeist,* which nothing could have changed? Those of us who have wished that the integration of Freud into psychology had been more rapid recognize that it would have required psychologists who were objective and task oriented, who saw their central concern as the understanding of human nature, who reacted to Freud as a colleague (rather than as an outsider) equally interested in achieving this understanding, who accepted Freud as bringing to the field an insight into areas of crucial importance for psychology, who did their utmost to understand the theories and the methods which were being proposed, who marshalled the forces necessary for developing topics in these areas further, expanding the methods to make them more searching. In fact, earlier integration of psychoanalysis into psychology would have demanded that the psychologists of the period disregard both internal and social pressures, would have demanded that they disregard both their own values and prejudices and those facets of the scientific *Zeitgeist* that impinged on them most ·closely.

It may be, of course, that just as the attainment of hybrid vigor requires different combinations of periods of inbreeding and outbreeding, so the optimal development of a science requires different concentrations of attitudes at different periods in its development. If this is so, then psychology has certainly gone through its period of inbreeding. We have been through a period which has been weighted heavily with the strongly held narrownesses and limited commitments previously described, as well as with the negatives which Boring discusses with such tolerance (Boring, 1942, p. 613). Perhaps these were inevitable for the period.

Can it be, however, that an atmosphere favorable for the outbreeding which some wished for in this earlier period, but which the mainstream of the *Zeitgeist* was not ready to support, is now in the process of developing? Can it be that our judgment is correct in holding that now the main force of the scientific *Zeitgeist* is changing and asserting itself in an emphasis on meaningfulness, even though the new atmosphere is still permeated with the smog of tradition, the heritage of an irreversible history?

As the effects of its early negative characteristics—which I, however, cannot help believing any science needs, in at least some degree, during all phases of its growth—subside, psychology seems to be developing more positive qualities. These include a readiness to face substantive aspects of problems, with insistence on only the degree of rigor necessary to protect the substance; an appreciation of the psychologist's personal motivations for entering the field (Roe, 1953); an appreciation of the stage of psychology's scientific development (Adrian, 1946; Tolman, 1947); a readiness to participate in a group commitment to a field where tolerance for tentativeness needs to be great; above all, an ability to recognize the value of a variety of approaches to psychology, even if one's personal commitment is to one particular approach. These are the qualities of mature psychologists who have to work with an inevitably adolescent psychology.

Freud has at times been compared with various great idea men— Jesus, Leonardo, Newton, Kant, Darwin, Pasteur, Einstein; with great conquistadors—Moses, Columbus, Magellan; and with great methods men such as Socrates. It is actually not surprising to find this number and range, and even exaltedness, of the comparisons. Besides the difficulty of categorizing great men simply by finding their counterparts, there is the difficulty of keeping individual emotions out of the situation. From one point of view, Freud *was*, despite his own denials, a great man, whose ideas revolutionized not only psychology but a large part of twentieth century thought. From another point of view, Freud *was* a conquistador, a great discoverer who opened up and explored hitherto unprobed areas in man. And again, Freud *was* a great methods man (Bernfeld, 1949, pp. 183–184), as the free association method attests.

But one thing characterized Freud above all—the constantly

changing, developing nature of his theoretical system. He continually checked his hypotheses and theories against his observations, always ready to adjust them in reply to demands of new facts. (There was, of course, an element of natural reluctance about revising his views, particularly in cases where new data originated outside of his own experience.) In all his correcting and revising, he was constantly building, basing new ideas on new or old theories and hypotheses, even going back to long abandoned ideas if the new data warranted.

Should we not try to emulate him by avoiding the extremes of either accepting his theories as dogma merely because they are his, or rejecting these same theories merely to indicate our independence from him? Can we not follow his own essential concern for congruence between fact and theory, building in part on what he has already given us, examining his views and testing them to the fullest, and developing new theories as needed?

Freud, after a period of intensive work in various fields of medicine and physiology, turned his attention to problems more directly related to the understanding of human nature. He saw psychological phenomena differently from both his predecessors and contemporaries. When he reported what he saw, he was generally greeted with skepticism. Thereafter, through his long, active and markedly productive life, he developed his ideas in isolation, assisted only by a group who identified strongly with him. In such circumstances, how did his vast influence on the psychology of which he had never been a part come about?

Using a broad definition of influence as a guide in my attempt to answer this question, I found that ideas which demonstrably originated in the Freudian body of theory and observation have indeed permeated virtually the whole range of psychology. In fact, with the cumulative growth of this influence, Freud has become the most prominent name in the history of psychology. Nevertheless, this growth in influence has not, at least as far as psychology is concerned, been continuous; it has had its ebbs and flows, its enhancements and abatements, its leaps and halts.

A separation existed between psychoanalysis and psychology in spite of their common heritage from the Helmholtz tradition, a tradition which permeated the biological and physiological sciences when Freud started his work. It would seem that this gulf actually arose out of the different way in which each viewed its commitment to the Helmholtz program. Psychology did not recognize Freud's serious commitment to the "forces equal in dignity" part of the tradition as parallel to their own concern with the first part of this oath, the part which called for a "reduction to physical-chemical forces." Its own early focus on the "rigor" demanded by the latter led psychology to skip almost entirely the naturalistic stage usual in the development of a science and to identify itself with the "exact" of a hypothetical science, rather than with the "meaningful" that psychoanalysis had chosen. Since psychology had not come to terms with defining the proper place and time for exact measurement and quantification, there arose confusion in the use and meaning of the terms good and bad science—bad science being taken to be that which characterized psychoanalysis. The naturalistic method which fitted psychoanalysis so well was derogated as being unscientific.

What are *psychologists*—all those professionally involved with human nature—to make of Freudian thinking? The answer lies essentially in the recognition that Freudian thinking is part of man's conquest of nature, the understanding of human nature. Psychoanalysis, like psychology of which it is a part, is not the possession of any group, not the property of the members of any organized association; it belongs to man. Being an early Freudian or a trained Freudian (or even a convinced anti-Freudian!) may carry certain rewards and certain claims in other settings but has no relevance here, for psychoanalysis is part of the heritage which great men provide. As the discipline most directly involved, it is up to psychology to understand, develop, and build on this heritage, making the changes that imagination, coupled with careful observation and experiment, indicates.

REFERENCES

ADELSON, J. Freud in America: some observations. *American Psychologist*, 1956, *11*, 467-70.

ADRIAN, E. D. The mental and the physical origins of behavior. *International Journal of Psycho-Analysis*, 1946, 27, 1-6.

BAKAN, D. *On method.* San Francisco: Jossey-Bass, Inc., Publishers, 1967.

BERNFELD, S. Freud's scientific beginnings. *American Imago*, 1949, *6*, 163-96.

BORING, E. G. *Sensation and perception in the history of experimental psychology.* New York: Appleton-Century-Crofts, 1942.

BORING, E. G. *History of experimental psychology*, 2nd ed. New York: Appleton-Century-Crofts, 1950.

CRANEFIELD, P. F. The organic physics of 1847 and the biophysics of today. *Journal of the History of Medicine and Allied Sciences*, 1957, *12*, 407-23.

CRANEFIELD, P. F. The nineteenth century prelude to modern biophysics. *Proceedings, First National Biophysics Conference*, 1959, New Haven.

DUBOIS-REYMOND, E. H. *Jugendbriefe von Emil duBois-Reymond an Eduard Hallmann*. Berlin: Reimer, 1918.

FREUD, S. The project for a scientific psychology. In M. Bonaparte, A. Freud, and E. Kris (eds.), *The origins of psychoanalysis: letters to Wilhelm Fliess, drafts and notes, 1887–1902*. New York: Basic Books Inc., Publishers, 1954, 352–445.

FREUD, S. The claims of psycho-analysis to scientific interest. *Standard Edition, 13*, 163–90. London: The Hogarth Press, Ltd., 1955. (First printed in 1913.)

FREUD, S. An autobiographical study. *Standard Edition, 20*, 1–74. London: The Hogarth Press, Ltd., 1959. (First printed in 1924.)

FREUD, S. Postscript to the question of lay analysis. *Standard Edition, 20*, 251–58. London: The Hogarth Press, Ltd., 1959. (First printed in 1927.)

GILL, M. M. Topography and systems in psychoanalytic theory. *Psychological Issues*, 1963, *3* (2, Whole No. 10).

HOFFMAN, F. J. *Freudianism and the literary mind*, 2nd ed. New York: Grove Press (Evergreen Books), 1959.

HOLT, R. R. A critical examination of Freud's concept of bound vs. free cathexis. *Journal of the American Psychoanalytic Association*, 1962, *10*, 475–525.

HOLT, R. R. A review of some of Freud's biological assumptions and their influence on his theories. In N. S. Greenfield and W. C. Lewis (eds.), *Psychoanalysis and current biological thought*. Madison: University of Wisconsin Press, 1965, 93–124.

HOLT, R. R. The development of primary process: a structural view. In R. R. Holt (ed.), Motives and thought, psychoanalytic essays in memory of David Rapaport. *Psychological Issues*, 1967, *5*, No. 2–3 (Monograph No. 18–19), 345–83.

JAMES, W. *The principles of psychology*, 2 vols. New York: Henry Holt & Co., 1890.

KLEIN, G. S. Peremptory ideation: structure and force in motivated ideas. In R. R. Holt (ed.), Motives and thought, psychoanalytic essays in memory of David Rapaport. *Psychological Issues*, 1967, *5*, No. 2–3 (Monograph No. 18–19), 80–130.

KOCH, S. Epilogue. In S. Koch (ed.), *Psychology: a study of a science*. Vol. III. New York: McGraw-Hill Book Co., 1959, 729–88.

LOEVINGER, J. Three principles for a psychoanalytic psychology. *Journal of Abnormal Psychology*, 1966, *71*, 423–43.

MASLOW, A. H. *Toward a psychology of being*. Princeton: D. Van Nostrand Co., Inc., 1962.

RAPAPORT, D. The structure of psychoanalytic theory: a systematizing attempt. In S. Koch (ed.), *Psychology: a study of a science*. Vol. III. New York: McGraw-Hill Book Co., 1959, 55-183. Also in *Psychological Issues*, 1960, 2, No. 2.

ROE, A. A psychological study of eminent psychologists and anthropologists, and a comparison with biological and physical scientists. *Psychological Monographs*, 1953 (67 (2)), Whole No. 352.

SHAKOW, D. Clinical psychology: an evaluation. In L. G. Lowry and V. Sloane (eds.), *Orthopsychiatry, 1923-1948: retrospect and prospect*. New York: American Orthopsychiatric Association, 1948, 231-47.

SHAKOW, D. Some aspects of mid-century psychiatry: experimental psychology. In R. R. Grinker (ed.), *Mid-century psychiatry*. Springfield, Ill.: Chas. C. Thomas, Publisher, 1953, 76-103.

SHAKOW, D. Psicopatologia y psicologia: nota sobre tendencias. *Revista de Psicologia General Aplicado* (Madrid) 1960, 15, 835-37.

SHAKOW, D. Psychoanalytic education of behavioral and social scientists for research. In J. H. Masserman (ed.), *Science and Psychoanalysis*. Vol. V. New York: Grune and Stratton, Inc., 1962, 146-61.

SHAKOW, D., and RAPAPORT, D. The influence of Freud on American psychology. *Psychological Issues*, 1964, 4, No. 1, 243. Also published as Meridan Book (paperback), Cleveland: The World Publishing Co., 1968.

TANSLEY, A. G. *The new psychology and its relation to life*. London: George Allen and Unwin Ltd., 1920.

TOLMAN, R. C. A survey of the sciences. *Sciences*, 1947, 106, 135-40.

WEAVER, W. Science and complexity. *American Scientist*, 1948, 36, 536-44.

WHEELER, W. M. On instincts. *Journal of Abnormal Psychology*, 1921, 15, 295-315.

WOODOWRTH, R. S. *Contemporary schools of psychology*. New York: The Ronald Press Co., 1931.

19

Orientations from Psychoanalysis*

George S. Klein

A growing self-consciousness about the conventions and objectives
of theorizing and about ways of systematizing evidence for psychoanalytic concepts is discernible within the psychoanalytic community.
Major parts of the psychoanalytic framework are coming under
skeptical scrutiny, not with the objective of showing how Freud was
"wrong," but with the constructive aim of assessing their fruitfulness for
clinical work. In particular the utility of "metapsychology"—that
inelegant label for such speculative attempts as the "structural point of
view" and the energy model to stake out a general theory that would
account for clinical observations through hypothetical structures and
processes—is being questioned (for example, Home, 1966; Rycroft,
1966). In view of this restrictiveness about the theory among
psychoanalysts themselves, it seems paradoxical to say that psychoanalysis continues to provide vital nutriment for research in nontherapy
settings. In this period of stocktaking, of concern with both indispensable and expendable concepts in the psychoanalytic enterprise, it is
appropriate to examine some of the guidelines afforded by the
psychoanalytic theory to researchers in such *nontherapeutic* investigative contexts as the university laboratory.

I hesitated over the word "theory" and was tempted to say
"framework" instead. The hesitation was partly occasioned by my own

*Reprinted from *Perception, Motives and Personality*, by George S. Kline, by
permission of the publisher. Copyright© 1970 by Alfred A. Knopf Inc.

uncertainty about what a theory is, an uncertainty that reading various philosophers of science has intensified rather than diminished. It is probably correct to say that psychoanalysis is not really a theory by any standard put forth by the philosophers of science. Certainly it is not a theory in the sense of being a clear organization of diverse facts according to a few basic principles. It is probably more accurate to describe psychoanalysis as an assemblage of propositions within two classes of theory. On the one hand are what Rapaport (1959a) called the "clinical" principles, those for classifying the meanings of, or "reasons" for, behavior viewed as expressing conflict and defense, sexual and aggressive wishes, conscious and unconscious events, substitutions of aims, and so on. On the other hand is metapsychology, which consists of Freud's attempts to account for clinical meanings or principles in the impersonal causal terms of an energic system. The situation is further complicated by the fact that Freud's own thinking underwent radical shifts and variations; later revisions stand awkwardly beside earlier conceptions. To give but one example, Freud's conception (1900, Chapter 7) of two modes of thinking—primary- and secondary-process—was formulated long before he evolved his conceptions of ego, id, and superego. Yet he never revised his ideas of these different cognitive processes in the light of the later, so-called "structural," theory. It could be demonstrated that a consistent theory demands such a reconciliation. (Even without it, however, I believe that the conceptions of primary and secondary process have investigative utility.) Altogether—and to summarize—psychoanalysis is by no means the monolithic orthodoxy that inspires so much awe and contempt, no tightly developed and unshakable structure deviations from which can be easily recognized and denounced as heresy. Its concepts span an extraordinary range of human complexity, linked by a language that only loosely coordinates one part with another, a situation that moved Rapaport to say, "The general theory, far from being well-ingrained dogma, is a waif unknown to many, noticed by some, and closely familiar to few" (1959a, p. 140).

In examining the body of psychoanalytic thought it is important to appreciate that many of its fundamental concepts are anchored in a distinctive data-gathering, clinical situation. It is distinguished by certain relatively invariant physical and temporal conditions, by a code of responsibility between observer and observed, by a method of eliciting verbalizations, and perhaps most important by a distinctive, deliberately fostered type of relationship between two people—a therapeutic alliance, as Karl Menninger aptly called it (1958)—that is surely one of the most extraordinary forms of long-term interpersonal commitment ever concocted by man. Freud envisioned the psychoanalytic situation as a relatively stable setting for therapeutic effort and—I emphasize—for systematic study of the lawfulness of behavior. Never did he waver in his belief that the therapeutic situation was primarily an *investigative* opportunity and the method of free association its instrument. I think this investigative orientation may be one reason why Freud steadfastly insisted on keeping the psychoanalytic method free from domination by the medical-therapist community, a matter in which he was overruled— to the melancholy detriment of both psychology and psychoanalysis.[1]

In contrast to the observational conditions to which psychologists are accustomed, the psychoanalytic situation is most certainly unique in that the *therapeutic pact* and the *interpersonal relationship* are the indispensable—or at least the most likely—bases for observing many of the dramatic phenomena that constitute its legacy of discovery for psychological science. As a method and setting for observation the psychoanalytic session undoubtedly elicits and highlights a broad range of conflict-determined phenomena—transference, regression, eruption of unconscious fantasies and the like—that are still unmatched by and largely unrepresented even in those bold and imaginative experiments of recent years that involve observations of behavior in stressful environments. How many laboratory scientists can (or would dare) set up a situation in which a subject dissolves into tearful helplessness and permits us to watch him in the tyrannical grip of a peremptory unconscious fantasy—even assuming that it were possible to circumvent the ethical issues?

But the very conditions that contribute to the uniqueness of psychoanalytic observations are at the heart of the difficulties in bringing psychoanalysis into the "mainstream of psychology." For the kinds of data and the observational situation of the psychoanalytic hour present challenges to the systematizing of observations and the inferring of lawfulness that are different from those encountered in the more common experimental models to which twentieth-century psychology has so far anchored its fate.

This consideration throws light on existing dissatisfactions with psychoanalytic theory among nonpsychoanalytic psychologists. I doubt that the distaste among university and laboratory psychologists for psychoanalysis is altogether attributable to the fact of its being "poor" theory. Psychology has always had "poor" theories, and we can even make a case that it had had *only* "poor" theories, which nonetheless

1. He wrote in a letter to Paul Federn (March 27, 1926), "As long as I live I shall resist that psychoanalysis be swallowed up by medicine" (E. Federn, 1967, p. 270).

have been recognized as useful, even welcome, soil for exploration. Undoubtedly the gamey taste of psychoanalysis is partly the result of its unpalatable conceptual novelties, partly of crudities in the manner of theorizing. To my mind, however, the single most important basis of the experimentally minded psychologist's discontent with the theory is the circumstances of data gathering from which psychoanalytic concepts have emerged and the rules of inference by which the analyst arrives at statements of lawfulness. Even were there none of the complications that arise from the fact that therapeutic rather than investigative interest must prevail in the gathering of data, the therapeutic nature of the situation makes direct access to the data impossible for nonpsychoanalysts. The fact that the data depend upon a therapeutic context makes them a pretty exclusive sort of data, accessible to only a few. It is easy to see why this inaccessibility would alienate laboratory and university psychology from psychoanalysis. Moreover, the phenomena are not easily replicable in the university laboratory, and, worst of all, the published glimpses of data show that the application of rigorous criteria for stable evidence and rules of inference is long overdue.

From its beginnings, psychoanalytic investigation has been faced with the dilemma of how to coordinate investigative intentions with therapeutic considerations. Working with a therapeutic context as a source of data presents a persistent and unresolved difficulty: Although the "classical," long-term treatment situation is uniquely valuable from an investigative standpoint for eliciting unusual phenomena, we do not really know if it is uniquely valuable therapeutically. Psychoanalysis has always had faith that the two orientations are harmoniously served; we still do not know whether this faith is justified. If the classical context and procedure are an incomparable source of researchable phenomena but of uncertain therapeutic effectiveness compared with competing strategies, then a dilemma confronts us: how far to modify, or to resist modifying, the clinical situation in the interest of one or the other. Shall we retain the classical therapeutic context and its procedural conventions for their investigative utility, or shall we change therapeutic strategy, even though this change may narrow the range of potentially observable phenomena? Freud chose the former course, possibly because of the investigative richness he observed in the "classical" analytic procedure; he regarded with distrust all attempts to manipulate the psychoanalytic situation for purposes of therapeutic advantage alone. For example, he wrote: "It would be desirable to obtain practical results in a shorter period and with less trouble. But at the present time theoretical knowledge is still far more important to all of us than therapeutic success . . ." (1919b, p. 183).

Another source of difficulty deserves mention. Freud worked in the manner we have come to call "clinical," meaning that a concept is developed through repeated observations under relatively standard conditions in which the determining conditions of a phenomenon are not under tight manipulation or control. This is the time-honored method of clinical medicine. It has been a productive source of physiological discoveries, but it is not an adequate basis for a science of controlled manipulation of variables—experimental science. A vital accompaniment to clinical *medicine* was therefore the physiological laboratory. A hypothesis based on clinical observation can hope for testing, sometimes quickly, in the controlled conditions of the laboratory. But this opportunity is precisely what psychoanalysis does not have, despite repeated valiant efforts to provide it. For, in the attempted translation from consulting room to laboratory, something happens that happens less readily in physiology: either the phenomenon itself changes, or the new interactions created by the altered conditions of observation and method present complications in extracting the phenomenon.

I emphasize the clinical psychoanalytic context of observation not only because it is the key to psychologists' dissatisfaction with the theory but also because it calls into question the view that psychoanalytic concepts can become more useful only if first the logic of the metapsychological theory is cleaned up and tightened and its concepts tested in experimental contexts. The intimate links between psychoanalytic clinical theory and the clinical situation, the difficulties of testing the concepts of the clinical theory outside this situation, suggest that any attempt at propositional rigor and validations begin with *the data of the psychoanalytic situation, not* with those of the experimental laboratory, that such attempts concentrate upon the concepts of the *clinical* theory of psychoanalysis, *not* its metapsychology. The clinical concepts derived from the psychoanalytic data-gathering situation have not yet been cast in a form that is easily translatable to other contexts. The phase of accommodating psychoanalytic *clinical* theory more systematically to the data of the psychoanalytic situation is still ahead of us; it is a phase that would greatly ease the way of translations to nontherapeutic contexts. Those who are primarily interested in achieving formal elegance in the theory must first apply to the original context improved strategies of systematizing observations and inferences (see, for example, Luborsky, 1967). A number of investigators are in fact currently occupied in this fashion (Luborsky, 1967; B. B. Rubenstein, 1965, 1967; Sandler *et al.*, 1962; Sandler & Rosenblatt, 1962; Shakow, 1960; Knapp, 1963, Gill *et al.*, 1968).

But for the *non*psychoanalyst to get observational mileage out of psychoanalytic concepts does not require a formally pure theory. Rigor of this kind is necessary mainly when the central objective is to assess the *predictive power* of concepts and their generality; it is *not* a requirement for other productive, if less systematic, uses of the theory, which I shall summarize. These uses are strictly empirical; they are not geared to improving or "purifying" the theory as a whole. In view of the fact that many of the concepts are still inextricably linked with the data of the psychoanalytic situation and because it is doubtful that experiments can successfully simulate many of the phenomena of the clinical situation, the psychologist who works with psychoanalytic concepts is well advised to take an informal, flexible approach to exploring their surplus meanings and implications. He can hold a concept lightly, ready to modify it radically or discard it entirely according to the vicissitudes of experimental necessity and measurement conditions. Of course, it is incumbent upon him to state as rigorously as possible the distinction between his use of a concept and its application in the clinical situation. And, to be sure, he cannot feel free to claim either proof or disproof of a psychoanalytic proposition; the new context, new methods, new situations may have produced new phenomena and interactions as well.

So then, if he acknowledges difficulties with psychoanalytic theory qua theory and concedes that he can hope to contribute little to the formal elegance of the theory, what nutriment does the body of psychoanalytic concepts hold for the investigator who relies upon experimentation, who is not a psychoanalyst, and whose main concern is not with preserving psychoanalytic theory as such or with the aesthetic appeal of its structure? Those who use psychoanalysis in experimental work can still obtain vital nourishment even though they have only a spectator's interest in the quest for theoretical clarification. I shall try to specify how.

Ultimately, whatever attractions psychoanalysis holds for the nonpsychoanalytic investigator are traceable to Freud's seminal ideas about the dynamics of purposeful behavior, ideas that have implications for virtually every major segment of man's behavior, emotional life, and development—from love to grief, normality to psychosis, infancy to old age. These core ideas have withstood the many vicissitudes of theorizing and controversies among psychoanalysts. They are perhaps the sole bases for accusations of orthodoxy in psychoanalysis. Recalcitrance will be most visible in an analyst's countenance if the three following precepts are challenged.

1. The central, most pervasive condition for the development of motives and of psychopathology is conflict. The usage of many psychoanalytic concepts hinges upon this pivotal interest in conflict. For example, for many analysts the main use even of the concept of ego lies in its relation to conflict rather than in its more popular contemporary meaning as an "adaptive system." Waelder comments, for instance, that to look for ego, superego, and id in the fact that John Doe wants to eat breakfast and enjoys it would not be regarded by psychoanalysts generally as a very valuable enterprise, but that the "situation changes if, e.g., John Doe has been put on a diet by his doctor; in this case, his hunger and his oral desire may be opposed by concern for his health and by conscience reminding him of his responsibilities" (1960, p. 84). In this situation of conflict we see the ego and superego represented, each with its own claims, in his behavior.

Conceptions of the component forces of conflict (for example, sexual and aggressive wishes) and of the forms of their resolution make up a large and incomplete theme in psychoanalytic theory and are at the heart of many changes that have been occurring in the theory. A large body of concepts is ultimately traceable to this emphasis on conflict and its varieties and levels. The concepts of drive and defense are, of course, rooted in it, having evolved from early notions simply of conflict among ideas, to a conception of the stages and crises in psychosexual development that contribute to conflict, to various conceptions of drives, restraints, and controls—all proposals to deal with issues of genesis, forms, intensity and resolution of conflicts.

In recent years this concern with conflict has been revised and expanded, but it is still central. It is from this anchorage in the importance of conflict that ego theory has come to include the conflict-*free* functions and to ponder the distinction between the conflicted and the conflict-free functions. The conditions under which conflict-free functions become involved in conflict and the manner in which conflict stimulates regressive tendencies in certain functions while others are unaffected—such contemporary concerns arise from traditional psychoanalytic concern with conflict.

2. A second seminal idea, stated in its most general form, is that *a person may respond knowledgefully to internal and external stimulation, but be unaware of the meaning that informs his response and even of the response itself.* Here we have the principle of motivated thought, which includes forceful ideation unaccompanied by conscious experience, the critical principle of *repressed* yet *active* ideation. This precept differs from pre-Freudian psychology and even from many theories that followed it; they simply assumed that most memories are silent and uninfluential until activated and that if one motive is active other potential motives are meanwhile inactive. Freud brought to light a kind

of "dynamic knowledge" beyond awareness, showing that it is powerful and capable of exercising a decisive influence on our behavior. The revolutionary principle in this discovery was that an ideational system can exercise motivational force without being introspectively accessible, that such ideas in a state of imbalance can affect action.

. Rather than being simply a basis for redefining mental concepts, the discovery of unconscious motivating and symbol-inducing processes was the discovery of a new range of facts. With it came the implication that we are less free because we are less fully self-conscious than we had previously believed. The discovery of unconscious purposes implied "that the occasions on which we have, to a greater or lesser degree, misrepresented to ourselves what we are trying to do is much more common than we had previously believed" (Hampshire, 1959, p. 180). To this core idea are linked the great distinctions among conscious, preconscious, and unconscious modes of thought, repression, and repression-instigated unconscious fantasies, which underlie a good many psychoanalytic conceptions.

Testimony to the fertility of this assumption comes from none other than B. F. Skinner, not the gentlest critic of psychoanalysis, who credits Freud with having assisted the behaviorist movement through his idea. In Skinner's view the principle of unconscious activity had much to do with moving psychology away from a nonbehavioristic emphasis upon conscious mental events, which had been expressed in the approach of the introspectionists.

> Curiously enough, part of the answer was supplied by the psychoanalysts, who insisted that although a man might be able to see some of his mental life, he could not see all of it. The kind of thoughts Freud called unconscious took place without the knowledge of the thinker. From an association, verbal slip, or dream it could be shown that a person must have responded to a passing stimulus although he could not tell you that he had done so. More complex thought processes, including problem solving and verbal play, could also go on without the thinker's knowledge. Freud had devised, and he never abandoned faith in, one of the most elaborate mental apparatuses of all time. He nevertheless contributed to the behavioristic argument by showing that mental activity did not, at least, *require* consciousness. His proofs that thinking had occurred without introspective recognition were, indeed, clearly in the spirit of Lloyd Morgan. They were operational analyses of mental life—even though, for Freud, only the unconscious part of it. Experimental evidence pointing in the same direction soon began to accumulate. (Skinner, 1963, p. 952)

3. A third basic idea, related to the other two but independent, is Freud's emphasis *upon the preemptive power of ideation, especially the repetitive hold of unconscious fantasy upon thought and behavior.* It is

an interesting historical fact that psychoanalysis did not at first begin with a drive theory but with the notion that *ideas* themselves have a force component that affects behavior (Rapaport, 1958). The first and central elements of the theory in accounting for neuroses were the facts of psychic trauma and conflict among ideas, and the consequences of repetitively insistent, conflicting ideas for behavior. In Freud's early statements of the theory (Breuer & Freud, 1893; Freud, 1894; see also Strachey *et al.*, 1962) the critical force in conflict involved a repressed meaning—the meaning of a real event that was incompatible with the main body of a patient's socially and consciously acceptable ideas. That unacceptable, repressed ideas owed their unique power to sexual involvement contributed, of course, to Freud's eventual emphasis upon drives as the motive power of conflict and unconscious ideation. The core idea that dissociated or unconscious fantasies exert a preemptive hold upon behavior led to tremendous advances in observation, culminating in the theory of dreams; in the conception of two classes of ideation, primary- and secondary-process; in the theory of drive itself; and, of course, in the special theory of the restraining forces of defense.

The theoretical and empirical exploration of these three seminal ideas has been the main objective of the enormous proliferation of concepts and shifts of emphases among psychoanalytic workers ever since. No psychoanalyst would claim that the conceptual links within and among these central themes exist in any acceptable final form or that the parts of the total conception are commensurate either in theoretical origin, observational specificity, or validity. But one need not swallow the theory whole in order to digest some of its parts, nor is there any formal barrier in the theory itself to reflection on different parts with varying degrees of skepticism and acceptance. On the other hand, awareness of the many ramifications of these ideas in all sectors of the theory can very possibly add to the generative implications of a particular part of a theory. For this reason, study of the theory should attempt to embrace as much of it as possible, even if one's central interest is in one of its parts.

I pause at this point to remark on the accusation of orthodoxy that is often thrown at those who refuse to be drawn into the game of showing how Freud was "wrong." I believe that it is not worshipful respect for Freud's genius that keeps one within the so-called "orthodoxy" of working within the framework of these seminal themes of psychoanalysis but rather the still unexplored implications that lead from them. More often than not, attempts to redress imbalances in psychoanalytic theory have only produced new, often worse, ones. On close inspection, such corrective efforts require retreat from Freud's basic respect for the complexities of man's personality. As far as developing a theoretically sounder personology is concerned, Freud's perspectives are still an important safeguard against superficiality.

If this area is ultimately the lifeline from which nonpsychoanalyst students of the theory are to derive nutriment, there is still the matter of how to go about using it. I shall ignore the crucial nonexperimental alternative that would confine investigation to data of the psychoanalytic situation per se. I shall also by-pass efforts directed primarily at the theory's structure. I am concerned here with research objectives whose method is primarily experimental, but even here I am not concerned with research that aims specifically to validate or invalidate psychoanalytic propositions. My view is that the *usefulness* of the theory in expanding discovery and in illuminating phenomena deserves precedence *over considerations of improving the formal rigor of the theory itself.*

I am expressing here a bias about the objectives of science and what is useful in theory for attaining them. I may as well own up to a certain skepticism about whether a full-scale effort to achieve "formal elegance" in the theory as a whole will significantly increase its investigative potential. Emphasis on theoretical rigor can distract attention from a fundamental aim of science, the discovery of *phenomena*—progress in *perception*, if you will—and expansion of the range of the observable in order to help determine the contingent and sufficient conditions of phenomena. Theory helps, but only if *conception* aids *perception,* as when, after the conceptualization of the chromosome, it became possible to *see* chromosomes under the microscope. A good concept or proposition, then, is in the category of an observational instrument. But the perceptual process can be advanced in other ways too; for instance, the development of observational hardware like the microscope may also help—a process of "deanthropomorphizing" observation, as Bertalanffy (1955) calls the development of artificial aids to man's sensory equipment. A beautiful instance of the confluence of concept and instrumental advance is seen in the current research on dreams. Here, Freud's conception of the functions and contingencies of dreams has obvious utility, but it took the almost accidental discovery of the relation of eye movements to dreaming to produce a significant breakthrough in this area.

In the process of uncovering the heretofore unperceived and unperceivable, a theory that is formally inelegant in the lexicons of philosophers of science may serve all the same. Not logic alone but improvements of observation as well unmask a theory as poor, or help to reveal its mettle; formally elegant as well as inelegant theories may suffer either fate. I do not know a psychologist who would not happily exchange all of Hull's rigorously developed propositions for the discovery of the relation between eye movements and dreaming, or the Olds-Milner discovery of positive and negative reinforcement centers, which was, by the way, wholly accidental. *The heart of Freud's success was in refocusing the observational intentions of twentiety-century psychologists* on, for example, the vicissitudes of sexuality and aggression in behavior and development, unconscious determinants of behavior, varieties of conflict, and motivational complexity generally. For an allegedly "inferior" theoretician he did not do badly.

It may seem that I am downgrading theory, but I am not; I am merely putting it in the proper perspective of the aims of science as I see them. We cannot *avoid* theory if only because words always have surplus meanings that must be controlled and accounted for when we plan to *use* our descriptions for purposes of experimental control. But words, concepts, propositions are in the service of observation. They are mediations of the perceptual process, not the perception itself or the regularity observed. People who do not distinguish concept from perceivable regularity are making an error that is well known in the perceptual laboratory: confusing mediation with that which is mediated, the ruler with the object it is measuring. I take issue with the view that reality is itself only a conceptual matter, a view that equates the perceptual regularities observed with the words used to describe them, thus elevating theory to being the objective of research itself.

So—the various strategies for working with psychoanalytic concepts that I am about to mention all have a frankly empirical and rather informal theoretical focus. Two are perhaps even *a*theoretical; the other two start from the theory only with a view to what it can do in generating new observations.

There are four such strategies: *exploring the theory for descriptive concepts that may have utility in specifying and classifying observed regularities; scanning the theory for propositions that may direct a search for new phenomena; conceptual gap filling;* and *searching for small-scale explanatory models within the body of the theory.* I shall take them up in order.

A first important source of investigative usefulness of psychoanalytic theory is its wealth of descriptive concepts that are relatively independent of the psychoanalytic situation and can be used to specify behavioral units observed under conditions of experimentation. Although many psychoanalytic concepts are too much contingent upon the psychoanalytic situation to be of much descriptive value in other contexts, many *are* capable of such use. For example, the conception of

defenses such as "isolation," "denial," and so forth, does have a
descriptive utility in bringing order to behavior observed in contexts
other than the clinical situation.

I draw attention to one such conception that is virtually untapped
for its promise in sensitizing descriptions of thought processes—that of
primary- and *secondary-process* modes of thinking. Freud's idea of two
modes of thought organization was most fully developed in his attempts
to understand dreams (1900, Chapter 7). In Ernest Jones' view, Freud's
description of the altogether different logic of the dream and its similarities to psychotic thinking was at least as monumental a contribution as
his demonstration of unconscious wish-fulfilling contents (1953, p. 397).
Though basically linked to the data of dreams, the concepts have
descriptive utility for classifying behavior in a variety of environments
that tend to undermine the kinds of realistic thinking more familiar to
psychologists. It ought to be mentioned that Freud's account of primary-
and secondary-process modes of thought also implies controversial
assumptions of mechanism as well. Nevertheless, I do not think that
their descriptive value is vitiated by the questionable notions of mechanism in which they are encased.

Experiments at the New York University Research Center for
Mental Health and elsewhere furnish examples of how cognitive
products induced under stress exemplify primary-process thinking.
Behaviors that psychology has previously been able to designate only as
"disorganized" acquire, through this concept, significance as uncommon forms of organization. The concept is proving useful in distinguishing the complex behavioral effects of such drugs as LSD-25
according to how much the drug diminishes secondary-process thinking
(Linton & Langs, 1962, 1964). The concept of primary process has given
a fresh slant on the effects of perceptual isolation (Goldberger, 1961;
Goldberger & Holt, 1961a). It has also been helpful in describing the
kind of thinking that develops when informational feedback from
action and perception is disrupted, as, for instance, when a person is
deprived of the feedback from his own voice while talking (Holmes &
Holzman, 1966; Holzman & Rousey, 1966; Klein & Wolitzky, 1970).

A second way of working with psychoanalytic concepts is to search
the theory for concepts and propositions that promise novel behavioral
observations. (I distinguish propositions generating predictions of
behavior from weaker ones that, though not lending themselves to
rigorous predictive inference, nonetheless suggest new regions of observation.) I think it is fair to say that at the present time not much should
be expected from psychoanalytic concepts in respect to generating
genuinely predictive statements *outside* the psychoanalytic situation.

The main exception may be in developmental studies, but as far as *laboratory* simulation of psychoanalytically observed phenomena is concerned, few, if any, significant discoveries have thus far originated as deductions from a psychoanalytic proposition. Perhaps existing psychoanalytic propositions will in time acquire this power after their predictive capability has been more systematically explored *within* the psychoanalytic situation itself. I do not think that we shall know until such an effort is seriously made. For the present, the difficulty of transferring the concepts to other contexts and across differences in observational technique, situation, and behavioral indicators should make us less sanguine about expecting them in their present form to generate specific predictions in experimental contexts. I take comfort, however, in the fact that prediction is *not* the only goal of the scientist nor the only productive use of theory. A proposition that only *raises a question* is no less useful than one that can generate a specific prediction. Psychoanalytic theory *does* contain many assumptions capable of generating questions about possible mining sites for observational ore.

In this strategy the aim is to find leads to possible conditions determining a phenomenon. Interest in the phenomenon may have developed from outside of the theory, not from the psychoanalytic proposition itself, and may even have been an accidental yield of observations produced by a new laboratory technique. The investigator looks to psychoanalysis for propositions that seem to imply, directly or by analogy, phenomena within his range of observational possibility. He does not, or should not, delude himself that he is thus validating psychoanalytic theory; he is simply exploring a perceived similarity between his data and those *implied* by a psychoanalytic proposition.

I would like to give a recent example of such a use of psychoanalytic concepts, one designed not to validate theory but to flesh out discovery with understanding. Dement and Kleitman (1957a, 1957b) and others have found that dreaming is associated with bursts of rapid eye movements (REMs) and that they occur only during periods of emergent stage 1 sleep, which, in terms of EEGs, are periods of low voltage, relatively rapid brain-wave activity, absence of spindles, low or absent muscular tonus, and respiratory irregularity. An entire night's sleep may yield three to six such dream periods. There is ample reason to think that dreaming sleep differs from other stages of sleep and is triggered and regulated by a different physiological mechanism. Discoveries have, of course, a way of generating further questions, regardless of whether or not theory is present to help the process along, and this area of work has been no exception. The dazzling questions that have been opened up by the discovery of this basic phenomenon are infinitely more varied than could have been provided by deductions from any theory alone, which at best would be only a gap-filling substitute in advance of actual opportunity for observation.

Still, there are points at which psychoanalytic propositions about dreaming *can* raise fruitful questions. For example, Freud's theory holds that the main function of dreaming is to provide an opportunity for the "discharge" of instinctual drives, drives that are endogenously generated from birth on through unknown neurohumoral mechanisms. Second, by virtue of the distorting and disguising effects of the "dream work" (for example, condensation, displacement, and so on), dreams have the function of preserving sleep. Third, although there is a relative deactivation of mental functions during sleep, repressed ideas and ordinarily preconscious ones, called "day residues," remain active. There is plenty to criticize and to clarify in the terms—"discharge," "drive," and so on—of these propositions. But the propositions are nonetheless useful in the laboratory context. In light of the drive conception, the stage 1 REM phase of sleep may be viewed as the periodically insistent physiological concomitant of drive arousal and the accompanying dreams as the cognitive activity motored by the drive process. The main elements of dream cognition would be infantile as well as later concepts and memories that are especially active when the neurohumoral drive structure is in a high state of arousal.

One question that this presumed relationship between dream cognition and drive brings into focus is, How necessary is it to dream? Here psychoanalytic theory, in my opinion, does not offer clear guidelines but does provide launching points for fresh questions. If dreaming is *discharge*, then clearly no good can come from the *suppression* of dreaming, from closing the safety valve. If we accept these assumptions, we would expect *inhibition* of drive discharge to be synchronously associated with intensified pressure *toward* such a discharge. If the dream actually has a discharge function, a highly active need state that persists into the dreaming phase of sleep should receive some relief through hallucinated gratification in the dream. For instance, in our laboratory Bokert (1967) found encouragement for the proposition that dream content may actually have a "discharge" effect. Intensity of thirst following a night's sleep seemed to be significantly reduced if gratification themes were preeminent in the dream content. There is a second alternative, however. The importance of the dream may lie less in "discharge" than in an effort to synthesize or integrate an unassimilated emotional experience; perhaps, to use Erikson's term (1954), a "restitutive" effort (see also Breger, 1967). Possibly dream suppression is harmful from this point of view, too, although I believe that different observational leads proceed from it than from the discharge theory. (The notion of "discharge" is critically assessed in G. S. Kline, *Perception, motives and personality, New York: Knopf,* 1970, chapter 14.)

Be that as it may, the discharge conception has raised interesting possibilities. Experiments by Dement (1960) have shown that increased compensatory dreaming occurs after a period of dream deficit produced by the constant interruption of dreams. On each succeeding night, subjects increasingly attempt to dream. Dement favors the conclusion that dreaming is a necessary psychobiological function and that "more or less complete suppression of it might have serious psychic consequences" in waking day thought and behavior. It is, of course, too early to say what modifications will be required in this generalization.

It is possible, too, that the drive-dream connection proposed by psychoanalytic theory may prove useful in assessing the psychological importance of recent findings about physiological concomitants of dreaming. Jouvet (1961) has discovered that discharges in the caudal pontine nucleus of the reticular formation are closely coordinated with the occurrence of stage 1 REM sleep. This discovery points to a mechanism of dream sleep that is consistent, at least superficially, with the kind of drive activation that psychoanalytic theory says is connected with dreaming. In the end, of course, this hypothesis may turn out to be as mistaken as Columbus' belief that he had found India when he encountered our primitive shores, but the theory of drives will at least have served as a useful starting point for selective empirical inquiry.

The uses of psychoanalytic concepts so far described really proceed less from an interest in psychoanalytic theory as such than from efforts to understand *particular* phenomena. The next two uses I shall describe are also linked with empirical intent, but theory itself is a more explicit objective.

The first approaches the theory with a kind of hypersensitivity to its *gaps*—asking what segments of behavior seem not to be provided for in the theory. Then, by developing conceptual terms coordinate with other terms of the theory, it attempts to enlarge the scope of the theory. Some useful additions to psychoanalytic theory and, I might add, observational incentives have come from this bone-graft type of theoretical surgery. In one example, proceeding from the theory's central emphasis upon *conflict,* Hartmann (1950), Kris (1950), and later Rapaport (1951c, 1957b) and others (Gill & Brenman, 1959, Chapter 4; Holt, 1965a; S. C. Miller, 1962; White, 1963) have raised questions about the conditions and forms in which behavior may be conflict-*free,* questions that have produced far-reaching changes of orientation in psychoanalytic therapy and theorizing. In another example, proceeding from the assumption that drives are pervasively involved in the development of thought functions, Hartmann (1952), Erikson (1951), and recently White (1963) have tried to bring into the theory provision for nondrive determinants of motivation. In still a third example, the dynamic consideration of forces and conflicts, which so long held the center of the psychoanalytic stage, logically demands a concern with the structures that determine the vectors of force. This demand has led to a broadened conception of control and restraint beyond the theory's earlier preoccupation with defense alone (see Rapaport, 1959a).

Attempts to map dimensions of cognitive style, with which I have been associated, are anchored in this interest in ego controls as a way of tackling the age-old enigma of personality constancy (Kline, 1970, Chapters 5, 6, and 7; Klein, Barr & Wolitzky, 1967; Gardner et al., 1959; Gardner & Moriarty, 1968). But the notion of cognitive style also aims at bringing psychoanalytic theory into more direct confrontation with the problem of generalized personality dispositions, which it has long handled in a desultory way as "character defenses." We have viewed personality constants as stable strategies of control that channel drives into adaptively attuned activities, organizing cognitive and affective processes in ways that have little to do with conflict but that give personality much of its individual flavor. This effort at defining general forms of integrative control seeks their manifestations in the various sectors of a person's cognitive behavior. Because this empirical effort to describe cognitive styles requires a detailed regard for cognitive processes, it always has one foot, and sometimes seven others as well, outside psychoanalytic theory, for psychoanalysis has had little to say about the details of cognitive processes. Although psychoanalysis is the most ambitious attempt yet made to describe the pushes and pulls of organismic functioning, it is virtually silent on the details of perception, learning, concept formation, and the like. At the same time, work on cognitive controls and dimensions of cognitive style tries to link them to the larger family of psychoanalytic concepts through terms that are at least commensurate with it. The notion of control implied in the concept of cognitive style seems related to but not synonymous with the notion of defense that has been virtually the only means by which psychoanalysis has dealt with the issue of regulatory constants in personality. The concept of defense, even of "autonomous character defenses," does not seem wholly adequate to describe the behaviors that we have called "leveling" and "sharpening," "focusing" and "scanning," "tolerance for unrealistic experiences," and so on.

The underlying theme of this work has been that those aspects of perception and cognition that analysts currently regard as autonomous secondary-process functions are themselves idiosyncratically organized within individuals. Of course, a personality theory that attempts to define personality dimensions within the psychoanalytic framework but at the same time bases itself on cognitive and perceptual theory must inevitably force revision of, or at least more detailed specification of, segments of psychoanalytic theory.

Another approach to developing psychoanalytic theory for purposes of generating investigation outside the treatment situation—and the final one that I shall mention here—concentrates on extracting from the theory, or applying to portions of its concepts, *models of behavior process*. The term "models" has no single meaning for all psychologists. What I have in mind is a conception of a phenomenon stated in such a way as to offer clues to the variables to be investigated in seeking to understand contingencies of the phenomenon. Models from one area in psychology may be applied to another, as, for example, when a model of the perceptual process is applied to an understanding of personality. Or they may be derived from another discipline, as when the phenomena of thinking are conceptualized in terms of information theory. Ideally, a properly developed explanatory model is not simply a metaphor or an analogy; its power is demonstrated by showing that the terms of relationship holding true within it also hold true of relationships in the sector of behavior under investigation.

Parts of the body of psychoanalytic thought suggest models in this sense; others lend themselves to the application of outside models in an effort to systematize the clinical theory. In bringing the matter of models to the foreground my intention is only to underscore the possibility that parts of psychoanalytic clinical theory may be carried beyond the functional statements in which most of the theory's concepts are cast. Frankly, I am not sure that such attempts will be a fruitful source of new *clinical principles* of meaning that will enlarge the scope of a therapist's interpretive insights. But those who favor this direction have a point in insisting that psychoanalysis will not have maximal usefulness for *experimental* application unless and until it can proceed from models that are able simultaneously to account for both the adaptational or *functional* aspects and the *process* or mechanismlike aspects of a phenomenon. That is a tall order, and, as I say, its feasibility is open to doubt, but it is perhaps achievable for modest segments of the theory in which the model starts with a clearly specified phenomenon to explain.

One such attempt involves a conception of attention cathexis and its deployment developed by Rapaport (1959b) and his colleagues,

Schwartz and Rouse, at the Austen Riggs Center, which in recent years has generated interesting experiments in learning and attention (Schwarz & Rouse,1961; Schwartz & Schiller, 1967, in press). Another example is Engel's attempt (1962) to explicate the psychoanalytic conception of affect in terms of specific discharge and signal aspects of affect.

A third example is a neuropsychological conception developed by Freud (1895) himself almost seventy-five years ago, posthumously published some sixty years later and until recently completely neglected. This early model has intrigued neuropsychologists because it is an attempt to embrace in neurostructural terms basic *functional* trends of psychic behavior that made up the main body of his later work. There are many aspects that have a contemporary flavor: First, it specifies a neurophysiological structure with power and signal capacities; second, the basic systemic principle is not tension reduction but homeostasis, in which neurological structures tend toward the maintenance of optimal rather than zero levels of excitation—in keeping with contemporary notions of open systems; third, it contains a neurone conception capable of accommodating excitation in electrical terms; and, fourth, it involves a system of ascending and descending corticosensorimotor feedback loops. Karl Pribram (1965) points out that an especially interesting feature of Freud's model was his conception of the neurone as a capacitor, capable of graded changes of potential; the nervous system is not simply a conductor but also a means of retaining and building up potential, and neurone activity is interpretable as changes in capacitance of conduction units. It would be fascinating and possibly profitable to study in detail the respects in which Freud's neurological assumptions, freshened by the dramatic changes currently taking place in neurophysiological theory, can convert the functional statements of psychoanalytic theory into process terms. The virtue of such an attempt, again, is not simply worshipful obeisance to Freud but that this model encompasses so much of the scope of his later formulations about the dialectics of conflict and unconscious events.

If, through such investigative application of its terms, psychoanalytic theory as we know it in its therapeutic context takes on a different look, we can draw solace from the thought that, after all, in psychological science the main objective is not theory as an end in itself but theory as a tool for the best accounting of *observed phenomena* and for the discovery of hitherto *unobserved* ones. If the terms of the theory change beyond recognition from their original form, we have lost only a theory—only words and symbols—but we may have gained thereby a means to greater understanding of nature's regularities.

REFERENCES

BERTALANFFY, 1955. An Essay on the Relativity of Categories. *Phil. Sci.*, 22:243–263.

BETTELHEIM, B. 1967. *The Empty Fortress*. New York: Free Press.

BEXTON, W. H., W. HERON & T.H. SCOTT. 1954. Effects of Decreased Variation in the Sensory Environment. *Canad. J. Psychol.*, 8: 70–76.

BOKERT, E. 1967. The Effects of Thirst and a Related Verbal Stimulus on Dream Reports. Unpublished doctoral dissertation, New York University.

BREGER, L. 1967. The Function of Dreams. *J. Abnorm. Psychol. Monogr.*, 72 (5, Whole No. 641).

BREUER, J. & S. FREUD. 1893. On the Psychical Mechanism of Hysterical Phenomena: Preliminary Communication. In *Standard Edition*, 2: 1–18. London: Hogarth, 1955.

DEMENT, W. 1960. The Effect of Dream Deprivation. *Science*, 131: 1705–1707.

DEMENT, W. & N. KLEITMAN. 1957a. The Relation of Eye Movements During Sleep to Dream Activity: An Objective Method for the Study of Dreaming. *J. Exp. Psychol.*, 53: 339–346.

———. 1957b. Cyclic Variations in EEG During Sleep and Their Relation to Eye Movements, Body Motility, and Dreaming. *EEG Clin. Neurophysiol.*, 9: 673–690.

ENGEL, G. L. 1962. Anxiety and Depression-Withdrawal: The Primary Affects of Unpleasure. *Int. J. Psycho-Anal.*, 43: 89–97.

ERIKSON, E. 1951. *Childhood and Society*. New York: Norton.

———. 1954. The Dream Specimen of Psychoanalysis. *J. Amer. Psycholanal. Assn.*, 2: 5–56.

FEDERN, E. 1967. How Freudian Are the Freudians? Some Remarks on an Unpublished Letter. *J. Hist. Behav. Sci.*, 3: 269–281.

FREUD, S. 1894. The Neuro-Psychoses of Defence. In *Standard Edition*, 3: 43–68. London: Hogarth, 1962.

———. 1895. Project for a Scientific Psychology. In Freud, *The Origins of Psychoanalysis: Letters to Wilhelm Fliess, Drafts and Notes, 1887–1902*. New York: Basic Books, 1954, pp. 347–445.

———. 1900. The Interpretation of Dreams. In *Standard Edition*, 4, 5. London: Hogarth, 1953.

GARDNER, R. W. & A. MORIARTY 1968. *Personality Development at Preadolescence: Explorations of Structure Formation*. Seattle: University of Washington Press.

GILL, M. M. & M. BRENMAN. 1959. *Hypnosis and Related States.* New York: International Universities Press.

GILL. M. M., J. SIMON, G. FINK, N. A. ENDICOTT & I. H. PAUL. 1968. Studies in Audio-Recorded Psychoanalysis. I. General Considerations. *J. Amer. Psychoanal. Assn.,* 16: 230–244.

GOLDBERGER, L. 1961. Reactions to Perceptual Isolation and Rorschach Manifestations of the Primary Process. *J. Proj. Tech.,* 25: 287–303.

———— 1961a. Experimental Interference with Reality Contact: Individual Differences. In P. Solomon *et al.,* eds. *Sensory Deprivation.* Cambridge, Mass.: Harvard University Press, pp. 130–142.

HAMPSHIRE, S. 1959. *Thought and Action.* London: Chatto & Windus.

HARTMANN, H. 1950. Comments on the Psychoanalytic Theory of the Ego. In *Essays on Ego Psychology.* New York: International Universities Press, 1964, pp. 113–141.

———— 1952. The Mutual Influences in the Development of the Ego and Id. In *Essays on Ego Psychology.* New York: International Universities Press, 1964, pp. 155–181.

HOLMES, C. & P. S. HOLZMAN. 1966. Effect of White Noise on Disinhibition of Verbal Expression. *Percept. Motor Skills,* 23: 1039–1042.

HOLT, R. R. 1965a. Ego Autonomy Re-evaluated. *Int. J. Psycho-Anal.,* 46: 151–167.

HOLZMAN, P. S. & C. ROUSEY. 1966. The Voice as a Precept. *J. Pers. Soc. Psychol.,* 4: 79–86.

JONES, E. 1953. *The Life and Work of Sigmund Freud,* Vol. 1. New York: Basic Books.

JOUVET, M. 1961. Telencephalic and Rhombencephalic Sleep in the Cat. In G. E. W. Wolstenholme & M. O'Connor, eds., *The Nature of Sleep.* Boston: Little Brown, pp. 188–206.

KLEIN, G. S., H. L. BARR & D. L. WOLITZKY. 1967. Personality. *Ann. Rev. Psychol.,* 18: 467–560.

KLEIN, G.S. & D.L. WOLITZKY. 1970. Vocal Isolation: The Effects of Occluding Auditory Feedback from One's Own Voice. *J. Abnorm. Psychol.,* 75: 50–56.

KNAPP, P. H., ed. 1963. *Expression of the Emotions in Man.* New York: International Universities Press.

KRIS, E. 1950. On Preconscious Mental Processes. *Psychoanalytic Explorations in Art.* New York: International Universities Press, 1952, pp. 303–318.

LINTON, H. B. & R. J. LANGS. 1962. Subjective Reactions to Lysergic Acid Diethelamide (LSD-25): Measured by a Questionnaire. *Arch. Gen. Psychiat.,* 6: 352–368.

———— 1964. Empirical Dimensions of the LSD-25 Reaction. *Arch. Gen. Psychiat.,* 10: 469–485.

MENNINGER, K. A. 1958. *The Theory of Psychoanalytic Technique*. New York: Basic Books.

MILLER, S. C. 1962. Ego-Autonomy in Sensory Deprivation, Isolation, and Stress. *Int. J. Psycho-Anal.*, 43: 1-20.

PRIBRAM, K. 1965. Freud's Project: An Open, Biologically Based Model.

RAPAPORT, D. 1951c. The Autonomy of the Ego. In *Collected Papers*. New York: Basic Books, 1967, pp. 357-367.

———— 1957b. The Theory of Ego Autonomy: A Generalization. *Collected Papers*. New York: Basic Books, 1967, pp. 722-744.

———— 1958. A Historical Survey of Psychoanalytic Ego Psychology. In *Collected Papers*. New York: Basic Books, 1967, pp. 745-757.

———— 1959a. The Structure of Psychoanalytic Theory: A Systematizing Attempt. *Psychol. Issues*, Monogr. 6. New York: International Universities Press, 1960.

———— 1959b. The Theory of Attention Cathexis: An Economic and Structural Attempt at the Explanation of Dognitive Processes. In *Collected Papers*. New York: Basic Books, 1967, pp. 778-794.

RUBENSTEIN, B. B. 1965. Psychoanalytic Theory and the Mind-Body Problem. In N. S. Greenfield & W. C. Lewis, eds., *Psychoanalysis and Current Biological Thought*. Madison: University of Wisconsin Press, pp. 35-36.

———— 1967. Explanation and Mere Description. A Metascientific Examination of Certain Aspects of the Psychoanalytic Theory of Motivation. In R. R. Holt, ed., *Motives and Thought: Psychoanalytic Essays in Honor of David Rapaport*. *Psychol. Issues*, Monogr. 18/19: 20-77. New York: International Universities Press.

SANDLER, J. et al. 1962. The Classification of Superego Material in the Hampstead Index. *Psychoanal. Study Child*, 17: 107-127. New York: International Universities Press.

SANDLER, J. & B. ROSENBLATT. 1962. The Concept of the Representational World. *Psychoanal. Study Child*, 17: 128-145. New York: International Universities Press.

SCHWARTZ, F. & R. O. ROUSE. 1961. The Activation and Recovery of Associations. *Psychol. Issues*, Monogr. 9. New York: International Universities Press.

SCHWARTZ, F. & P. H. SCHILLER. 1967. Rapaport's Theory of Attention Cathexis. *Bull. Menninger Clin.*, 31: 3-17.

SHAKOW, D. 1960. The Recorded Psycnoanalytic Interview as an Objective Approach to Research in Psychoanalysis. *Psychoanal. Quart.*, 29: 82-97.

SKINNER, B. F. 1957. *Verbal Behavior*. New York: Appleton.

STRACHEY, J., et al. 1962. The Emergence of Freud's Fundamental Hypotheses [Appendix to "The Neuro-Psychoses of Defence"]. In

Standard Edition, 3: 62–68. London: Hogarth.

WAELDER, R. 1960. *Basic Theory of Psychoanalysis.* New York: International Universities Press.

WHITE, R. W. 1963. Ego and Reality in Psychoanalytic Theory: A Proposal Regarding Independent Ego Energies. *Psychol. Issues,* Monogr. 11. New York: International Universities Press.

20

Psychoanalysis as a Scientific Theory *

Heinz Hartmann

When some forty-five years ago Freud (1913) wrote for the first time about the philosophical interest in analysis, his main point was that philosophy could not avoid taking fully into account what he then called "the hypothesis of unconscious mental activities." He also mentioned that philosophers may be interested in the interpretation of philosophical thought in terms of psychoanalysis—adding, though, here as elsewhere, that the fact that a theory or doctrine is determined by psychological processes of many kinds does not necessarily invalidate its scientific truth. Since then, the knowledge of human behavior and motivation we owe to analysis has greatly increased, has become much more comprehensive but also more specific; and this development has certainly influenced not only social science, anthropology, and medicine, but also philosophy in a broad sense. Yet this does not mean that analysis can "answer" what one usually calls philosophical problems, though it leads to looking at them from a new angle. Some of its potentialities in this respect have been made use of only rather scantily so far. I am thinking, for example, of its possible contribution toward a better understanding of ethical problems. The interest psychoanalysis may have for philosophers has clearly two aspects: it resides partly in the new psychological findings and theories of analysis, but also in certain questions of methodology raised by Freud's and other psychoanalysts' approach to the study of man.

*Reprinted from *Essays on Ego Psychology*, by Heinz Hartmann, with permission of International Universities Press, Inc. Copyright © 1964 by International Universities Press, Inc.

In speaking of psychoanalysis one often refers to a therapeutic technique. One may also refer to a method of psychological investigation whose main aspects are free association and interpretation; or, finally, to a body of facts and theories (Freud, 1923b). In this last sense, we would certainly consider as psychoanalytic any knowledge gained directly by Freud's method of investigation; but many of us would today consider analysis to include related procedures such as the application of psychoanalytic insights to data of direct child observation, a field which has grown in importance in the last two decades. Of the three aspects just mentioned, it is the method of exploration that has undergone the least change; it is commonly used in a situation defined by a certain set of rules and referred to as the psychoanalytic situation or the psychoanalytic interview. The therapeutic technique has been repeatedly modified, and psychoanalytic theory has gone through a series of more or less radical modifications, by Freud and by others. I want to emphasize that the interrelations among these three aspects are, in analysis, a central topic—though in the context of this presentation I can refer to them only occasionally.

The theories of psychoanalysis follow principles of systematization, as do theories in other fields. Freud, however, did not speak of analysis as a "system," but rather accentuated its unfinished character, its flexibility, and the tentative nature of a considerable part of it. Actually, adjustments and reformulations of various aspects of theory have repeatedly become necessary. There are chapters such as the psychology of the dream, of libidinal development, of anxiety, and of symptom formation, that have been more systematically worked out than others. Psychoanalysis is obviously far from being a closed system of doctrines, though it has sometimes been represented as such. Also, though some fundamental tenets of psychoanalysis are accepted by all (Freudian) analysts, agreement on all of them is obviously lacking.

There is in analysis a hierarchy of hypotheses as to their closeness to observation, their generality, and the degree to which they have been confirmed. It appears that a neater classification as to these points and a higher degree of systematization (considering the different levels of theorizing) than exist today would not only facilitate my task in discussing psychoanalysis as a scientific theory but also clarify the standing of analysis as a scientific discipline. Promising efforts in this direction have been made and are being made by analysts and also by nonanalysts, but as yet no complete and systematical outline drawn from this angle is available; a recent work by David Rapaport (1958) comes close to performing this task. This is probably the reason, or one of the reasons, that in more or less general presentations of psychoanalysis references to its history abound, and the reader will forgive me if they do in this paper too, at least in its first part. I shall mostly refer to the work of Freud, because most of the more general theories of analysis have their origin in it, and because he is in many ways more representative of psychoanalytic thinking than anybody else.

Historical explanations are often substituted for a system; an attempt is made to clarify the function of propositions in their relation to others by tracing their place in the development of analysis. Also, without such historical reference it happens over and over again that analytic hypotheses are dealt with on one level, so to say, which belong to different phases of theory formation, and some of which have actually been discarded and replaced by others. Again, because of the comparatively low level of systematization, I think it is true that even today a thorough knowledge of at least some chapters of analytic theory cannot be acquired without knowledge of its history.

From the beginning, explanations of human behavior in terms of propositions about unconscious mental processes have been an essential part and one characteristic feature of psychoanalysis. I may, then, start by introducing Freud's concepts of unconscious processes. He makes a distinction between two forms of unconscious mental activity. The one, called preconscious, functions more or less as conscious activities do. It is not conscious, in a descriptive sense, but can become conscious without having to overcome powerful counterforces. Where such overcoming of resistances is necessary, as is the case with repressed material, we speak of unconscious processes in the stricter, the dynamic, sense of the word. The dynamic impact of these unconscious processes on human behavior—and not only in the case of mental disease—is one main tenet of Freud's theory of unconscious mental activities.

There is rather wide agreement that conscious data are insufficient for the explanation of a considerable part of behavior, and particularly of those aspects that were first studied in analysis. However, its critics have repeatedly claimed that the introduction of unconscious processes is superfluous. The explanation could be stated, or should be sought for, in terms of the more reliable data of brain physiology. The question here is not just whether, and why, explanations based on such data would be per se more reliable, nor why psychological hypotheses about mental processes ought not to be introduced in explaining human behavior. We have also to consider the fact that, given the actual state of brain physiology, many and even comparatively simple aspects of behavior of the kind we are dealing with in analysis cannot be explained. To rely on brain physiology alone would mean to renounce explanation of the greatest part of the field that psychoanalysis has set out to explain. Or, if one should insist on attempting an explanation on physiological grounds, the resultant hypotheses would of necessity be considerably more tenuous and more speculative even than psychoanalytic hypotheses are suspected to be by its critics today.

Freud, well trained in the anatomy and physiology of the brain, actually started out by attempting to devise a physiological psychology that could provide him with concepts and hypotheses to account for his clinical insights (1895). But beyond a certain point this approach proved of no use. He was thus led to replace it by a set of psychological hypotheses and constructs; and this step represents probably the most important turning point in the history of psychoanalysis. It was the beginning in analysis of psychological theory, the heuristic value of which he found to be greatly superior—a point that, I think, has been corroborated by its subsequent development.

But it is true that even after this radical turn in his approach Freud held on to the expectation, shared by many analysts, that one day the development of brain physiology would make it possible to base psychoanalysis on its findings and theories. He did not think this would happen during his lifetime, in which he proved to be right. In the meantime certain, though limited, parallels between analytic propositions and discoveries in the physiology of the brain have become apparent. Also, the usefulness of some psychoanalytic hypotheses for their field has been recognized by at least some representatives of brain research (Adrian, 1946). As to the psychology of unconscious processes, I think it can be said that Freud in developing that part of analysis was much less interested in the ultimate "nature" or "essence" of such processes—whatever this may mean—than in finding a suitable conceptual framework for the phenomena he had discovered.

While Freud, after the first years of his scientific work, relinquished the attempt to account for his findings in terms of physiology, it is nevertheless characteristic of some of his psychoanalytic theorizing that he used physiological models. He was guided by the trend in German physiology which has been designated as the physicalist school (Bernfeld, 1944), whose representatives were, among others, Helmholtz and Bruecke, the latter being one of Freud's teachers. Certain aspects of the psychology of neurosis, for example, led him to introduce into psychoanalysis the concept of regression (to earlier stages of development), which had been used in the physiology of his day; this concept, though, acquired new meaning in the context in which he used it. Also, in making "function" the criterion for defining what he called the mental systems (ego, id, superego), Freud used physiology as a model. But this no longer implies any correlation to any specific physiological organization (Hartmann, Kris, Loewenstein, 1946). The value of such borrowings or analogies has, of course, to be determined in every single instance by confronting their application with tested knowledge (data and hypotheses). Physiological models (also occasionally physical models, as is obvious, for instance, in Freud's concept of a "mental apparatus") have been used also by other psychoanalysts (see, for example, Kubie, 1953) in order to illustrate certain characteristics of mental phenomena or to suggest a new hypothesis. The use even of metaphors need not of necessity lead into muddled thinking once their place in theory has been clearly delineated. The danger that earlier implications of those model concepts might impair their fruitful use in the new context of psychoanalysis has on the whole been successfully avoided (Hartmann, Kris, Loewenstein, 1946).

The broadening of the scope of psychology that came about as the consequence of the inclusion of propositions about unconscious mental processes meant, first of all, that many aspects of a person's life history that had never been explained before—and that, as a matter of fact, one had not even tried to explain—could be accounted for in terms of the individual's experience and dispositions. Causation in the field of personality is traceable only at its fringes without this broadening of theory. Freud was a strict determinist and often stated that to fill that gap in earlier psychological approaches, partly because of which the study of personality had been unsatisfactory, was one of his primary aims in developing analytic theory. More recently it has been said, by the mathematician von Mises (1939), that the observations correspond rather to statistical than to causal relations. I may mention at this point that this interest in the causation of mental phenomena included, quite naturally, also the interest in what we call the genetic viewpoint, since Freud's attention had been drawn to many facts of early childhood which had been unknown, and regularities in the relationships between early childhood situations and the behavior of the adult had become apparent. For Freud, the investigation of highly complex series of experience and behavior, extending over long periods of time, soon moved into the center of interest. Developmental research was to become equally important for psychoanalytic theory and practice. It is significant that the reconstructive approach in analysis led not only to the discovery of a great wealth of childhood material in every individual case, but also to the ascertainment of typical sequences of developmental phases. The genetic approach has become so pervasive, not only in psychopathology but also in psychoanalytic psychology in general, that in analysis phenomena are often grouped together, not according to their descriptive similarities but if they have a common genetic root (oral character, anal character). It was only much later that this predominance of a genetic conceptualization was counterbalanced by a sharper distinction between genesis and function, to which I shall shortly return in speaking of the structural point of view.

Here I want to add that while I just spoke of the study of the individual's "life history," it would be misleading (though it actually has been done) to classify this aspect of analysis as a historical discipline. This misinterpretation may be traceable to its comparison with archaeology, which Freud occasionally uses. It is true that most analytic knowledge has been gained in the psychoanalytic interview and that the concern with developmental problems refers primarily to the history of individuals. But this should not obfuscate the fact that the aim of these studies is (besides its therapeutic purpose) to develop lawlike propositions which then, of course, transcend individual observations.

At this point I should like briefly to summarize the role of psychoanalysis as a psychology of motivation, still bearing in mind that psychoanalysis takes into consideration the interaction of the individual with his environment, as well as his so-called "inner-psychic" processes. And I have to present to you, at least briefly, a discussion of what, in analysis, we call "metapsychology," a term that signifies not (as it might seem) that which is beyond psychology altogether, but simply those psychological investigations that are not limited to conscious phenomena, and that formulate the most general assumptions of analysis on the most abstract level of theory. Metapsychology is concerned also with the substructures of personality, the ego, the id, and the superego which are defined as units of functions. The id refers to the instinctual aspect, the ego to the reality principle and to the "centralization of functional control" (to borrow a term from brain physiology). The superego has its biological roots in the long dependency on the parents and in the helplessness of the human child; it develops out of identifications with the parents; and it accounts for the fact that moral conflict and guilt feelings become a natural and fundamental aspect of human behavior. The structural formulations, referring to the distinction of ego, id, superego, have several theoretical and clinical advantages. The most important is probably that the demarcation lines of the three systems, ego, id, superego, are geared to the typical conflicts of man: conflicts with the instinctual drives, with moral conscience, and with the outside world. The paramount importance for neurotic *and* normal development of these conflicts, and of the ways to solve them, was one of the earliest discoveries of Freud and has remained central in psychoanalytic practice and theory ever since.

Critics of analysis often tend to underrate the wealth of individual data on which it is built. On the other hand, it also happens that the theoretical nature of concepts like libido is not fully realized; for example, libido is often identified with sexual experience, or as a mere generalization of some observable connections.

In the beginnings of psychoanalysis (even after the importance of unconscious processes had been realized), Freud still adhered more or less strictly to associationism. But when he found conflict to be a primary motivating force of behavior, and specifically an important etiological agent in neurosis, he gradually developed the concept of mental tendencies and purposive ideas. Psychoanalysis became a psychology of motivation, the motives being partly, but not generally, considered in analogy with those consciously experienced. There originated the idea of wishes, in certain circumstances warded off by defensive techniques. He discovered the role of repression and later of other defense mechanisms, like projection, isolation, undoing, and so on. The consideration of mental processes from this angle of synergistic or antagonistic motivating forces is what has been known since as the dynamic aspect of psychoanalysis. The systematic and objective study of conflict has remained one of its essential aspects and has proved a necessary and fruitful avenue to the explanation of human behavior. This was a second bold step in the development of psychoanalysis. The importance of "conflict" had, of course, been known in religious and philosophical doctrines and in literature, but scientific psychology before Freud had no means to approach the subject.

The dynamic factors involved in both sides of a conflict were, for some time, rather poorly defined. It was, then, again primarily data of analytic observation that led to the realization of the importance of the instinctual drives among the motivating forces. I am referring here to Freud's discovery of infantile sexuality. This discovery was, at the time, considered by many as the product of revolting imagination; today, it can easily be confirmed in every nursery.

Even at the period when instinctual motivation seemed to be pretty much ubiquitous, the basic fact of conflict was not overlooked. Self-preservative instinctual drives were, at the time, thought of as the opponents of sexuality. Besides this, the concept of overdetermination, referring to the multiple motivation of all human behavior, continued also through the phase in which motivation was, on the level of general theory, nearly always considered instinctual.

Again, to fit it to his field of observation Freud had to modify the concept of "instinct" commonly used in other fields. His term, in German, *Trieb*, in English, "instinctual drive," or "drive," is certainly not identical with what one refers to as the instincts of lower animals.

His concept of drives had to prove its usefulness with respect to human psychology. Here, the sources of the drives are of much less importance than their aims and objects. The lesser rigidity of the human drives, the comparatively easy shift of the aims, the freeing of many activities from a rigid connection with one definite instinctual tendency, the comparative independence from and variety of possible response to outer and inner stimuli have to be taken into account in considering the role of the drives in human psychology. Still, the psychoanalytic theory of instinctual drives is broad enough to show also many impressive parallels with the findings of a modern school of zoologists (ethologists).

The concept of a continuity of this driving force allows the consideration of a great variety of mental acts from the angle of their investment with drive energy. Furthermore, in this way it is possible to understand the close relationship of many mental processes which, looked at from the surface, would appear to be entirely heterogeneous. The capacity for displacement or transformation into various kinds of human activities; the motivational role traceable through, and specific on, all levels of man's growth from birth to maturity; their central role in typical conflicts; and the fact that they involve relations to human objects—these are some of the psychologically essential aspects of the psychoanalytic concept of human drives. According to Freud, sexuality and aggression are, among all the drives one could describe, those that come closest to fulfilling the demands psychoanalysis makes on a concept of drives.

The concept of mental energy was then elaborated in the sense that it is the drives that are the main sources of energy in what Freud calls the "mental apparatus." However, a strictly quantifying approach to these energic problems has so far not been developed. Or rather: while it is possible to speak of a greater or lesser degree of, let's say, a resistance (against the uncovering of some hidden material), we have no way of measuring it. To account for the difference in the unconscious and the conscious (and preconscious) processes Freud postulated two forms of energy distribution, conceptualized as, respectively, primary and secondary processes. The primary processes represent a tendency to immediate discharge, while the secondary processes are guided by the consideration of reality. This distinction is again both theoretically significant and clinically quite helpful. The thesis that behavior is to be explained also in terms of its energic cathexis is what we call, in analysis, the economic viewpoint.

The regulation of energies in the mental apparatus is assumed to follow the pleasure principle, the reality principle (derived from the pleasure principle under the influence of ego development), and a tendency to keep the level of excitation constant or at a minimum. There are parallels to this in hypotheses formulated by others, and again the use of physical and physiological models played a role in the Freudian concepts.

The three aspects of psychoanalytic theory I have mentioned so far—the topographical (conscious–preconscious–unconscious), the dynamic, and the economic (energic)—represent Freud's first approach to what he called "metapsychology." It is postulated that a satisfactory explanation of human behavior includes its consideration in relation to all aspects of metapsychology. The "meta" in this term points to a theory going "beyond" the investigation of conscious phenomena. The word, generally accepted in psychoanalysis, has proved misleading for many outside analysis. Actually, as I mentioned before, "metapsychology" is nothing but a term for the highest level of abstraction used in analytic psychology.

A fourth aspect of metapsychology, called structural, was explicitly stated considerably later, though it was implicit in earlier theoretical thinking on mental conflicts. The forces opposing the drives in typical conflict situations, warding them off and forcing them to compromise formations (of which the neurotic symptom may serve as an example), are today conceptualized as an essential aspect of what we call the ego. At the core of this concept formation is the recognition of the relevant differences between instinctual tendencies which strive for discharge, and other tendencies that enforce postponement of discharge and are modifiable by the influence of the environment. This means, of course, that the dynamic and economic viewpoints can no longer be limited to the vicissitudes of instinctual drives. Also the original concept of a defensive ego had to be broadened to include in the ego those nondefensive functions of the mental apparatus that are noninstinctual in character. Many of these are not, or not necessarily, part of the conflictual set-up; we call them today "the nonconflictual sphere of the ego" (Hartmann, 1939a). Here belong (though they too may be involved in conflict, without, however, originating in it) perception, thinking, memory, action, and so on. It is likely that in man not only instinctual factors are in part determined by heredity, but also the apparatus of the ego underlying the functions just mentioned. We speak of the primary autonomous functions of the ego. It is true that analysis is, due to its method, directly dealing with environmental factors and with reactions to them, but this has never implied a denial, in principle, of heredity. It is in this sense that we speak of a drive constitution, and today also of constitutional elements in the ego, and of the role of maturational factors in the typical sequence of developmental phases.

To those functions that we attribute to the ego belongs also what one can call the centralized functional control which integrates the different parts of personality with each other and with outer reality. This function (synthetic function or organizing function) is in a way similar to what, since Cannon, we call homeostasis, and may represent one level of it.

The ego is, then, a substructure of personality and is defined by its functions. The instinctual aspect of personality is today conceptualized as the id. Through the development of the ego it becomes possible that the pleasure principle, dominant in the realm of the instinctual drives, can be modified to that consideration of reality, in thinking and action, that makes adaptation possible and is termed, as I said before, the reality principle. Through recent work, the relation between adaptation to outer reality and the state of integration of inner reality has become more accessible. This development in psychoanalytic theory has thus led to an improved understanding of man's relations to his environment, and to the most significant part of it, his fellow men—which is, however, not to say that the sociocultural aspects of mental functions and development had been overlooked in earlier analysis. Psychoanalysis, in contra-distinction to some other schools of psychology, has never been confined exclusively to the consideration of "inner-psychic" processes; it has always, and by no means accidentally, included the consideration of the individual's interactions with the environment. At any rate, the study of object relations in human development has more recently become one of the most fruitful centers of analytic interest ("new environmentalism," Kris, 1950b). Ego psychology represents a more balanced view of the biological and the social and cultural aspects of human behavior. We may say that in analysis cultural phenomena are often studied in their biological context and significance, and biological phenomena in relation to the sociocultural environment (see chapter 14 of *Psychoanalysis: A general psychology*, R. M. Loewenstein et al., eds., New York: International Universities Press, 1966). But this aspect will be discussed more fully later.

Some of the functions of the ego have, in the course of development, to be wrested from the influence of the drives. Gradually, they then reach, through a change of function, a certain degree of independence from instinctual origins and of resistance against reinvolvement with the drives (secondary autonomy—see Hartmann, 1939a; and chapter 7 of *Psychoanalysis: A general psychology*). A similar concept, though less specific in relation to psychoanalytic propositions, has been introduced by G. Allport (1937). This relative independence of the ego is also energically conceptualized, with respect to the sources of energy at the disposal of ego functions. The necessity more clearly to distinguish function from genesis is one of the main implications of the structural viewpoint.

The third unit of functions, considered a substructure of personality, is called the superego. To it we attribute the functions of self-criticism, conscience, and the formation of ideals. The acceptance of moral standards is considered a natural step in ontogenesis. Moral conflict and the guilt feelings that are an expression of it are, from the time when the superego has been instituted, one fundamental aspect of human behavior. The superego has a biological root in the comparatively long dependency and helplessness of the child of the human species, which also means increased importance of the parents for its development. The superego develops out of identification with them, to which, in subsequent layers of development, identifications with others are added. Also obvious in its genesis is a sociocultural factor, which accounts for an important segment of tradition formation. The acceptance of certain moral demands, the rejection of others, the degree of severity of the superego, and its capacity to enforce its demands can very frequently be traced in clinical investigation.

Structural hypotheses are in many ways more comprehensive than earlier formulations of partly the same problems. They have also a considerable value in clinical thinking, because they are particularly fit to account for what has remained dominant in clinical work, that is, the various forms of typical conflict situations. Actually, as I said before, the demarcation lines of those units of functions, or systems, or substructures of personality are so drawn that they correspond to the main conflicts of man, which we now describe as conflicts between ego and id, superego and ego, and ego and reality. It was in this respect that Freud found the older topographical model, the layer model (conscious–preconscious–unconscious), rather disappointing, though in other respects it still retains a certain degree of significance. Defenses as well as drives can be unconscious; thus differences between conscious and unconscious processes cannot be used to account for these conflicts.

I thought it advisable to begin by giving a picture of certain fundamentals of psychoanalytic theory, and of the degree of its comprehensiveness, by indicating at least some of its dimensions, and also the relations between different parts of these theories. Its comprehensiveness means also its actual or potential importance in many neighboring fields. My survey shows also at least some of the points at which questions can be raised from the viewpoint of a philosophy of science. There would have been an alternative to the way of presentation I chose. I could have shown how, in the analysis of a symptom or a dream, our observations lead to anticipations, and how the various levels of our conceptual tools are brought to bear on them; also, how in this process theoretical thinking is constantly brought back to the observables. But this alternative would inevitably demand the introduction of a great number of variables and a discussion of the analytic method and the analytic situation much broader than I am able to give here. Of course, a sector of psychoanalytic propositions can be tested outside analysis, and some have been tested in this way; but it is still true that it is, in the field of analysis, extremely difficult to assay the suitability of the hypotheses for the purposes for which they have been primarily devised without the use, in the analytic situation, of the analytic method.

Since its beginnings analysis has struggled for a system of concepts fit to account for the peculiarities of the subject matter it had to deal with. Freud spoke of his endeavor to "introduce the right abstract ideas" and said, "We are constantly altering and improving them." This work has continued; nevertheless, not all concepts used are equally well defined. The distinction between independent, intervening, and dependent variables is often not clearly drawn. Also the different degrees of confirmation of the various parts of the complex network of psychoanalytic hypotheses are frequently not made apparent in analytic writings. Actually, there are many reasons for the lack of methodological strictness we often find in analysis. Some of them are encountered in every theoretical approach to the central aspects of personality. In addition, there is the fact that for psychoanalytic research there were no traditional methodological models available that could be used in its service; the differences in content as well as in method prevented a borrowing in this respect.

Freud had a firsthand knowledge of experimental method and was thoroughly steeped in the philosophy of science of the great *Naturforscher* of his day. He was fascinated by the theories of evolution, which left their imprint on his thinking, and, of course, there must have been other factors in the intellectual climate of his "formative years" that influenced his development as a scientist. The heuristic character and value of hypotheses were well known to him, as well as the role of basic concepts and postulates. Though Freud was certainly not primarily interested in the philosophy of science, it is still true, and it has often been said by psychoanalysts and recently also by others (Frenkel-Brunswik, 1954), that his "sophistication" in this respect was much greater than early reactions to his work would let one realize. But we have to consider that logical clarification is not usually found in the early development of a science and is often not the work of the great explorers (Hartmann, Kris, Loewenstein, 1946). It is only more recently that it has become, in the case of analysis, a subject of particular interest to a great number of workers.

Psychoanalysis was, of course, "new" not only because of its conceptual language, its method, and the methodological problems it posed, but "new" also as to content. The reorganization of commonly accepted knowledge, as a consequence of new data having been found and new modes of thinking having been introduced, and of the replacement of old scientific, or old common-sense, or socialized, "truths" by the new ones, is mostly a slow and often a difficult process. In analysis, such new insights, which do not only add to our knowledge but also force upon us a revision of old ways of thinking, abound. There is also the additional difficulty that some (not all) of its discoveries could be made only under specific conditions (the analytic situations); and known facts often appeared in confrontation with such discoveries in a different light. On the other hand, looking at these discoveries from outside analysis, it seemed difficult to "place," if I may say so, these unexpected and apparently improbable insights, their real connections with other factors being hardly understood. Attitudes toward demands for reconsideration of what had appeared to be safely anchored knowledge do not of course always observe the lines of logical thinking. Psychoanalysis has systematically studied—has, indeed, to study in every single clinical case—this problem, that is, the conditions for the capacity or incapacity to observe new phenomena in the realm of psychology and to think rationally about them. At any rate, once the shock the content of Freud's discoveries had represented to his contemporaries had somewhat subsided, people started to take them more seriously and even to attribute to them a certain amount of scientific standing. This process of rehabilitation of analysis was then fortified by the confirmation of psychoanalytic findings in medicine and child psychology, and through the proven usefulness of analytic hypotheses in these fields, as well as in anthropology, and in other social sciences. This naturally led to a different evaluation of the psychoanalytic method, too, which was at the origin of these discoveries, and of the psychoanalytic theories of which these hypotheses were a part.

It is not surprising that the newness and the scope of the psychoanalytic findings made changes of concepts and the introduction of new hypotheses imperative. In his tentative formulations, Freud cccasionally did not even disdain to take models of motivation from common-sense psychology. But to these common-sense elements, confronted with new facts and subjected to analytic conceptualization, mostly rather uncommon sense has accrued. It also seems, from the perspective of a few decades of empirical work, that quite a few methodologically questionable formulations have proved their heuristic value. Given the state of the psychology of personality, risks as to the development of the method as well as of hypothesis formation had to be taken. One could not limit the field to those parts that could already be handled in an unobjectionable way. Knowing the inherent difficulties of the subject matter, one may well be inclined to postdict that without the courage and impetus of a genius this most comprehensive attack on the explanation of human behavior that we call analysis could hardly have come about.

I said before that even today some logical uncertainties persist. The methodological demands made on science, the signposts which indicate which routes are open and which prohibited, which ways are likely to lead to dead ends, are generally geared to the logically best-developed branches of science. These we rightly admire as models of methodological clarity (which is not to deny that even there methodological controversies arise). Progress in physics, or in biology, has repeatedly led to demands on psychoanalysis for reformulation of its theories in accordance with these developments in other sciences. In principle there is no reason why such borrowings could not enrich the tools or the clarity of analytic thinking, as has happened with other models. But this question is less one of the theory of science than of the, we could say, "practical" needs of a specific science—the empirical question of the fitness of certain elements of logically well-structured sciences for other less developed fields. There is also, of course, the question of the necessarily different conditions in different fields. There is the need to outline a fruitful methodological approach to the less systematized sciences, to allow maximal productivity on a given level of insight into the relations between fact and hypothesis and according to the degrees of formal organization.

Before discussing in a more general way the relations between data and theories in psychoanalysis, I next shall speak of one of the inherent difficulties of our field. Every psychologist is confronted with the problem of how knowledge of the mental processes of others can be achieved. (I am not speaking here of the possibility of knowing another person's subjective experience.) As to our own mental processes some do—and some don't—refer to "self-experience." For those who do, a further difficulty is introduced if, as is the case in psychoanalysis, self-experience is accepted in principle, but its cognitive value remains in doubt. That is, it is a question of further investigation as to what is the indicative value of a given element of self-perception in terms of mental process. Looked at from this angle, analysis can be termed a systematic study of self-deception and its motivations. This implies that thinking about our own mental processes can be found to be true or false. There is in analysis, as you know, the concept of "rationalization," to give you an example. While self-experience is obviously an important element in analysis, its theories, as I said before, transcend this level of discourse.

The lawlike propositions of metapsychology are not formulated on the level of self-experience. Generally, Freud's views on introspection have not always been clearly appreciated. They are, though, evident already in the kind of psychoanalytic thinking that is comparatively close to observational data, as in Freud's ideas on the psychopathology of everyday life (1901). In a slip of the tongue, for instance, when, in place of a word we consciously intended to use, another one, not consciously intended, appears, we use the behavioral aspect in evaluating the psychological situation—we use it, that is, in taking the word actually spoken as an indication of an unconscious motivation that takes precedence over the conscious one.

The data gathered in the psychoanalytic situation with the help of the psychoanalytic method are primarily behavioral data; and the aim is clearly the exploration of human behavior. The data are mostly the patient's verbal behavior, but include other kinds of action. They include his silences, his postures (F. Deutsch, 1952), and his movements in general, more specifically his expressive movements. While analysis aims at an explanation of human behavior, those data, however, are interpreted in analysis in terms of mental processes, of motivation, of "meaning"; there is, then, a clear-cut difference between this approach and the one usually called "behavioristic," and this difference is even more marked if we consider the beginnings of behaviorism rather than its more recent formulations.

As to the data, it is hard to give, outside the analytic process itself, an impression of the wealth of observational data collected in even one single "case." One frequently refers to the comparatively small number of cases studied in analysis and tends to forget the very great number of actual observations on which we base, in every individual case, the interpretations of an aspect of a person's character, symptoms, and so on.[1]

By keeping certain variables in the analytic situation, if not constant, as close to constancy as the situation allows, it becomes easier to evaluate the significance of other variables that enter the picture. The best-studied example of this is what is called the "passivity" of the analyst, in contradistinction to the considerably more pronounced activity of the psychotherapist. This is not to claim that psychoanalysis

---

1. Thus every single clinical "case" represents, for research, hundreds of data of observed regularities, and in hundreds of respects.

is an experimental discipline. However, there are situations where it comes close to it. At any rate, there is sufficient evidence for the statement that our observations in the psychoanalytic situation, set in the context of psychoanalytic experience and hypotheses, make predictions possible—predictions of various degrees of precision or reliability, but as a rule superior to any others that have been attempted in the psychology of personality. Due to the emphasis on the genetic viewpoint, many predictions are what has been called "predictions of the past" (Hartmann and Kris, 1945), that is, reconstructions of the past which can often be confirmed in astonishing detail (Bonaparte, 1945). One obvious limitation of our predictive potential is, of course, the great number of factors determining, according to psychoanalytic theory, every single element of behavior—what Freud has termed "overdetermination." Still, our technique is constantly directed by tentative predictions of the patient's reactions. Also, studies in developmental psychology by means of direct child observation, such as have been conducted by E. Kris and other psychoanalysts (M. Kris, 1957), are guided by the formulation of expectations and their checking in individual cases. Here I just want to point to one way in which psychoanalytic hypotheses can be used vis-à-vis individual cases and how they may be confirmed in experience. I may mention here that problems of validation of psychoanalytic hypotheses ought not to be equated, as has too often been done, with the problem of therapeutic success.

A further difficulty results from the fact that psychoanalytic theory must also deal with the relation between observer and observed in the analytic situation. There are personality layers, if you will excuse this term, that in the average case the observed cannot reach without the help of the observer and his method of observation. But the insight of the observer ought not to be confused with the insight of the observed. Some of these problems belong in a theory of psychoanalytic technique. But there is also the problem of the "personal equation" (see chapter 6, *Psychoanalysis: A general psychology;* E. Kris, 1950b). The field of observation includes not only the patient but also the observer who interacts with the former ("participant observation"). The interaction of analyst and analysand is accounted for in the theories of transference and countertransference. As to the potential handicaps of observations traceable to the mental processes of the observer, they are subject to the constant scrutiny of the analyst. Some such handicaps of psychological observation can certainly be eliminated by the personal analysis of the observer, and this is one of the reasons that a didactic analysis is an essential element in the training of our students of analysis. Thus, what I want to say here is not that in the psychology of personality objectivity is impossible. It is rather that psychoanalysis has discovered potential sources of error and found a way to combat them.

Distortions of self-observation as well as of observations of others that occur as consequences of instinctual pressure are clinically easily traceable, and can be accounted for by analytic theory. To one aspect of this problem we find a close analogy in the behavior of animals: the "world" of the hungry animal is different from the "world" of the same animal in heat. In man, following structure formation, the situation is more complex. How much we can perceive psychologically with respect to ourselves and others, and how we perceive it, is also determined by defensive and other functions we attribute to the ego; and the superego, too, can influence our perceptive range and lead to distortions. The influence of central personality factors—needs, desires, affective states— on perception in general (nòt just of the psychological field) has also been experimentally demonstrated; and how, despite this, "objective" perception is possible is an object of special study (G. Klein, 1958). The questions of objectivation and of "testing of reality," as Freud called it, are also accounted for in psychoanalytic theory and lead again to the concept of degrees of ego autonomy that I mentioned before.

The body of analytic theories on the "mental apparatus" must include, as an essential sector, hypotheses fit to explain the distortions of psychological observation. No doubt this involvement of the observer and the potential sources of error of his perception and judgment represent an added difficulty in analytic clinical practice and research. But it is well known that even in other fields, and often to a troubling degree, this problem plays a role. However, this complication we are confronted with in analysis is an essential feature of certain aspects of human behavior rather than a result of imperfections of the state of psychoanalytic theory. There is, as I have said, also a psychologically fruitful side to these same complexities that have led to some methodological discontent. Corrections of at least some distortions of psychological observation and thinking are within the reach of our method. In the so far most comprehensive study of Freud's development, his biography by Ernest Jones, the role of his self-analysis in the unfolding of his thought has been emphasized. Now, self-analysis has this function only in exceptional cases; but we have similar experiences in great numbers from the analysis of others. In a more diluted way, this correction of blind spots can occasionally even be achieved outside analysis, as a consequence of changing attitudes toward certain factors that are essential for a psychology of personality.

It is very likely that in the work of Freud and other analysts so-called "intuitions" have played a role. But it is clear that, certainly in Freud, his striving for scientific discipline, his patient accumulation of observational data, and his search for conceptual tools to account for them have reduced their importance to a stimulus factor in the formation of psychoanalytic theories. Many subjects approached in analysis had before Freud been studied by so-called intuitive psychology only. But he was wont to oppose psychoanalytic psychology to intuitive psychology, and the development psychoanalysis has taken bears out this point. Still the relation between data and theory is no doubt a rather complex one in psychoanalysis. There are the cases in which, mostly in the beginning, he approached a problem with what he called "a few psychological formulae," that is, tentative hypotheses, whose heuritic value must be determined. To give you one example: certain clinical observations on hysterical patients had been made by Breuer before Freud, and also by Janet. But these discoveries were viewed from the angle of dynamic unconscious processes of conflict and defense only by Freud. It was with him and not with the others who had made similar observations that they opened the way to the understanding of mental conflict in general, which was later found to be an essential factor in normal and abnormal development. Here the introduction of fruitful hypotheses was decisive for the scientific momentum of a discovery. It led to an integration of the observed facts and also to the discovery of new facts. It is true in psychoanalysis as elsewhere that theories cannot be considered as mere summaries of observations. Actually, "the storehouse of pre-existing knowledge influences our expectations" and often "preconscious expectations . . . direct the selection of what is to be registered as observation and what seems to require explanation" (Hartmann, Kris, Loewenstein, 1953, p. 16). It is also obvious in psychoanalysis that the psychological investigator "must know that every step of his progress depends on his advances in the sphere of *theory*, and on the conceptual consistency, breadth and depth reached therein" (K. Lewin, 1926, p. 78).

In dealing with new observations and often new hypotheses it has become unavoidable to redefine the meaning of many concepts in analysis and to add new ones. Some concepts that have meaningfully been used, e.g., in studying the psychology of lower animals in experimental situations, are less fit if we deal with human behavior. Also, concepts common in everyday usage, in medicine, in philosophy, had to be redefined for psychoanalytic purposes. I mention this here, because it has sometimes made interdisciplinary communication more difficult. Thus, as I said before, the concept of instinctual drives has been radically modified. And there are redefinitions, in analysis, also of the concepts of libido, of anxiety, and others. To this, I may quote W. Heisenberg's statement (1952) that "the transition . . . from previously investigated fields to new ones will never consist simply of the application of already known laws to these new fields. On the contrary, a really new field of experience will always lead to the crystallization of a new system of scientific concepts and laws."

The analyst's observations are made in a clinical setting. The psychological object is studied in a real-life situation: the patient comes to another person, the analyst, in the hope of being freed from limitations of his capacity for work and his enjoyment of life, imposed by changes in his personality that are considered pathological but remediable. This means readiness for hundreds of hours of work and for being confronted with his life history, with parts of his personality that have been repressed, and, generally, with many surprising and often unpleasant insights into his mental processes. In the therapeutic situation, motivations are mobilized that help to combat the natural resistance against objective scrutiny of one's self. Such motivations can hardly be expected to be available outside a real-life situation; actually the many attempts outside of analysis to create, for purposes of investigation, situations meant to mimic situations of real life have not led very far. This point, then, refers chiefly to the superiority of analysis in making data available and creating a readiness for their observation.

On the other hand, it is good to remember Freud's reactions when after years of experimental work he decided to follow his research interests in the clinical field (and the quite similar reactions we meet today in young scientists turning to psychoanalysis). "He [Freud] confessed to a feeling of *discomfort*. He who had been trained in the school of experimental sciences was writing what read like a novel. Not personal preferences, he said, but the subject matter forced such a presentation on him" (Kris, 1947). He was confronted with a mostly unexplored field, with human motivations, human needs and conflicts. "Everywhere," he said later, "I seemed to discern motives and tendencies analogous to those of everyday life." Some concepts of common-sense psychology, which, as I said before, were tentatively applied, had to be redefined, though the terms were sometimes retained. Thus common-sense psychology soon proved insufficient; nor could the scientific psychology of his day and its methodology be of great help. Freud had only what he called a "few formulae," or hypotheses, to guide him. But it was only after the special and the more general theories of analysis had been developed that the full meaning could be extracted from the clinical data he had gathered.

There is always something ambiguous about the meaning of "clinical research" in general. There exists, so far as I know, no really satisfactory presentation of the subject in terms of the philosophy of science. I just want to say here a word about Freud's case histories. Every one of his comprehensive case histories is at the same time a study in psychoanalytic theory. I mention them at this point because they show the constant mutual promotion of observation and hypothesis formation, the formation of definite propositions which make our knowledge testable, and the attempts to validate or invalidate them.

Another aspect of the clinical origins of psychoanalytic theory is the fact that more was found, in the beginning, about pathological than about normal behavior. The etiology of neurosis was studied before the etiology of health, though psychoanalysis has, in principle, always aimed at a comprehensive general psychology. Also, as I mentioned, more became known, in the first attempts to deal with the field, about the instinctual drives, especially about sexuality and its development, than about the forces opposing the drives in the typical ego-id conflicts. This, however, has changed in the last two or three decades, and thus analysis has today come closer to what it always was intended to be, though not every aspect and not every implication of its very comprehensive conceptual frame have so far been actually developed.

In clinical work, one is used to being guided by signs and symptoms in forming an opinion concerning the presence or absence of a pathological process. But the question of the significance and the use of signs for purposes of explanation is, of course, logically of much wider relevance. Different meanings can be attributed to the terms sign, signal, expressive sign, symbol, and so on, and these differences are important also in psychoanalysis. However, I do not propose to deal with this problem here. Suffice it to say that a considerable part of psychoanalytic work can be described as the use of signs—a series of associations, a dream, an affect vis-à-vis the analyst—as indications of mental processes. In this sense one speaks of the psychoanalytic method as a method of interpretation (Hartmann, 1927; Bernfeld, 1932; Loewenstein, 1957). This has both a cognitive and a therapeutic aspect. They partly coincide, that is, in so far as a therapeutic agent of foremost significance in analysis is making the patient aware of, and capable of integrating, previously unconscious and, through defense, split-off processes. Some of those signs, for example, some of the symbols we find in dreams, have a rather ubiquitous meaning, while the interpretation of others requires a closer scrutiny of the individual under observation. At any rate, there are many situations in which the relation between a sign and what it signifies becomes easily recognizable, for instance, in the associations immediately following the observation of some detail of behavior. In others, various levels of theory have to be introduced to explain the connection. Such sign systems are used today not only in the psychoanalytic situation but also in the study by analysts, by means of direct observation, of child development. Many childhood situations of incisive significance for the formation of the adult personality have a low probability of direct manifestation. One tries to learn about the sign function of data of child behavior for a recognition of the central, and often unconscious, development that we know from the psychoanalytic interview. At this point it is possible, or even likely, that a misunderstanding may occur of what I have said about a low probability of manifestation outside analysis of certain processes investigated in analysis. I want, then, to add explicitly that this was not meant to be a general statement. Many phenomena first studied in the analytic situation could later be studied also in the direct observation of psychotics, in so-called applied psychoanalysis, or in the direct observation of children. What I want to emphasize in this context is that the comparative study of reconstructive data and data of direct observation of children can, on the one hand, lead to the confirmation of analytic propositions; on the other hand it can lead to the formulation of more specific hypotheses.

The essential importance of constructs for the coherence of the psychoanalytic system (or whatever we choose to call it) can be gathered already from the brief outline I have given in the first part of this discussion. Theories, or hypotheses of a different order, connect them with observational data. That these constructs, which are introduced because of their explanatory value, cannot be directly defined in terms of observational data, but that inferences from the constructs can be tested by observation, has long been known in psychoanalysis (Hartmann, 1927). Still, some of these constructs seem particularly suspect to many critics of analysis. An occasional lack of caution in the formulation of its propositions, or Freud's liking for occasional striking metaphors, has led to the accusation against analysis of an anthropomorphization of its concepts. But in all those cases a more careful formulation can be substituted which will dispel this impression.

There is, then, the question whether and in what sense such constructs are considered "real"; and, more specifically, the question has often been asked whether and in what sense Freud considered constructs like libido, the "system unconscious," and the substructures of personality in the sense of structural psychology, as real. He said that the basic concepts of science form the roof rather than the foundation of science and ought to be changed when they no longer seem able to account for experience; also that they have the character of conventions. But he certainly thought that what he meant to cover by these basic concepts had effects which could be observed. He was in no danger of confusing concepts with realities; he was a "realist" in a different sense. He does not seem to have thought that "real" means just "the simplest theoretical presentation of our experiences," but rather that those basic concepts pointed to something real in the ordinary sense of the word.

It is quite possible that Freud, as Frenkel-Brunswik (1954) has said of "scientists of great ingenuity," sometimes proceeded "from observation directly to hypothetical constructs and . . . derived the intervening variables later." But it is also evident from Freud's work that he by no means always spelled out the ways in which he had arrived at the formulation of his constructs. It is hard to say in a general way under what conditions a direct transition from data to constructs would seem legitimate or fruitful. It has been suggested by Ellis (1950) that "where intervening variables are of a limited usefulness in scientific theorizing, hypothetical constructs take in the widest range of relevant phenomena, and lead to a maximum success in the prediction and explanation of behavior."

It is obvious that among the intervening variables "dispositional concepts" play a significant role in analysis. The term "mental disposition" has actually been used in analysis, but the same kind of concept is often also covered by different terms. It has been pointed out (Hartmann, 1927) that the concept of "latent attitudes" used by Koffka and others comes rather close to psychoanalytic thinking. The term mental tendency is ubiquitous in psychoanalysis, and many of these tendencies, as mentioned before, are understood to be not manifest but in the nature of a disposition.

Speaking now of the series independent–intervening–dependent variable, I want to quote a passage from Rapaport (1958) about a significant aspect of intervening variables in analysis. He clearly states the point I have in mind: "Let us assume that an aggressive drive is our independent variable and overt behavior toward an (actual or thought) object our dependent variable. It will be noted that in a certain subject at certain intensities of the drive we will observe aggressive behavior (in deed or thought) toward the object, at other intensities we will observe no overtly aggressive behavior but rather excessive kindness (reaction formation). In other subjects at certain intensities the aggressive behavior will be diverted from the object to other objects (displacement) or upon their own self (turning round upon the subject), or will be replaced by ideas and feelings of being aggressed by the other (projection). In these observations the defense of reaction formation, displacement, turning round upon the subject, projection, etc., will be conceptualized as intervening variables."[2] Here let me remind you of what I said before, that the explanation of manifest behavior presupposes in every single

---

2. This passage is quoted from the original draft of this paper, and was slightly altered in the published version.

case the consideration of a great number of variables. The statement, current in analysis, that the same manifest action, attitude, fantasy may have different "meanings" (that is, may be the result of the interaction of different tendencies) has often been misunderstood. It has been said that it opens the door to bias or arbitrary interpretation. This argument seems to neglect the point I have just made. What the psychoanalytic approach has shown is a complex interdependence of a variety of factors, and of patterns of factors. I may mention too, in this context, that working with unilinear causal relations alone has not always proved satisfactory. The essential fact of interdependence of mental functions does not always allow a clear-cut answer to the question of which variable has to be considered as independent and which one as an intervening variable. A stimulus from the outside world will sometimes be considered an independent variable, but in another context also an instinctual tendency or an autonomous tendency of the ego (Rapaport, 1958). We came across this problem of relative independence in speaking of the secondary autonomy of the ego, but it has a much wider significance in psychoanalytic psychology.

Turning now to the validation of psychoanalytic hypotheses, I shall follow Kris (1947) in distinguishing validations in analysis from validations outside of it. To begin with the former, I may repeat that the amount of time spent in the study of any single individual is vastly greater, and the wealth of data considerably richer, than in any other clinical set-up. This alone would make the use of the analytic method in the analytic situation the *via regia* to the psychology of personality. In this setting, data do appear which are not, or not easily, accessible to other methods. This asset as to fact finding has, of course, a disadvantage in another respect: an observation an analyst makes may seem entirely credible to another analyst who possesses the necessary experience, an interpretation quite convincing, while the same observation may appear hardly credible, the same interpretation highly improbable or artificial, to one who approaches the field with a different method and in a different setting. For the analyst, one constant angle of his work is the observation of data and of sequences of data, the tentative interpretations (in search of the common elements in such sequences), and the checking of his interpretations against the subsequent (and past) material. It is safe to say that the greater part of evidence for the psychoanalytic proposition still lies with this work.

To broaden the reach of intersubjective validation beyond the relatively small group of workers in psychoanalysis, and also for teaching purposes and for comparing different techniques, the recording of interviews has been recommended by many (Kubie, 1952) and practiced by some. More recently, records of analytic interviews were submitted to other analysts, who were asked to predict the developments in subsequent sessions (Bellak, 1956). Such studies are likely gradually to attract a greater number of research workers, but, for the present, their potential contribution to the scientific status of analysis cannot yet be estimated.

As to the genetic propositions of analysis, the direct observation of children not only has become a rich source of information, but has also given us the possibility to make our hypotheses more specific and to check their validity. A great number of Freud's hypotheses on childhood could be confirmed by direct observation of children. But to validate more completely our genetic propositions, "systematic observations of life histories from birth on" are necessary. "If the longitudinal observation in our own civilization were to be systematized and the study of life histories were to be combined with that of the crucial situations in Freud's sense, many hunches might be formulated as propositions, and others might be discarded" (Hartmann and Kris, 1945).

The literature on experimental research, both in animals and in man, devised for the purpose of testing propositions derived from psychoanalysis has become very extensive. It has been repeatedly reviewed (Sears, 1943; Kris, 1947; Benjamin, 1950; Frenkel-Brunswik, 1954; and others), and I do not think I should go into it in any detail here. The following remarks are, then, random remarks and do not attempt to be in any way systematic. The classical animal experiments of Hunt, Levy, Miller, Masserman are probably known to many of you. Many of the animal experiments were conducted with considerable insight and great skill. Where the experimental set-up is adequate, the frequency of "confirmation" is impressive. Or, as Hilgard (1952) states, "It has been possible to parallel many psychoanalytic phenomena in the laboratory. When this is done, the correspondence between predictions according to psychoanalytic theory and what is found is on the whole very satisfactory."

Of course, we would not expect that every psychoanalytic proposition can be tested in animal experiments (Frenkel-Brunswik, 1954). But there are also definite limitations to so-called "experimental psychoanalysis" in the human. It appears difficult (though it has been attempted occasionally) to study "real" conflicts with the tools that "experimental psychoanalysis" has at its disposal (Hartmann and Kris, 1945; Kris, 1950b). And I may insert here that even experimentation that tends to remain close to "life situations," as does the work of K. Lewin, Dembo, Zeigarnik and others, is not quite free from those limitations.

A rather harsh criticism of Sears' "Survey" has been voiced by Wisdom (1953). But also with others who do not share his point of view, a certain amount of dissatisfaction has become apparent (A. Freud, 1951b; Rapaport, 1958; Kubie, 1952). Sometimes in those experiments the hypotheses tested were not psychoanalytic propositions at all, though the author had meant them to be. Sometimes they were taken over literally from psychoanalytic writings, but the context in which they appear in analysis, and thus their function, were not sufficiently considered; thus the results had to be ambiguous. It also happened that, looked at from the vantage point of analysis, experiments could be considered as validations of certain points of analysis, though not of those the author had in mind. In evaluating the results of "experimental analysis," there is, in addition, the perspectival character of every method to be considered, highlighting certain aspects and throwing others into the shade. Every method implies a selection, and data are being centered in different ways, depending on our approach (Rapaport, 1958). That is, an analysis of the methods used, and an attempt to correlate them, becomes of prime importance.

On the whole, this field of research has not so far decisively contributed toward a clarification or systematization of psychoanalytic theory. As a rule, these studies do not go beyond what has been demonstrated in analysis before (Hilgard, 1952; Kubie, 1952); they have often neither achieved new insights nor stimulated research. But, at their best, they have a value as confirmatory (or nonconfirmatory) evidence. Apart from this, they have greatly contributed to bridging the gap between psychoanalysis and other psychological disciplines. Also, "experimental psychoanalysis" continues to expand, and there is the possibility that certain drawbacks of its beginnings will be overcome.

Another source of potentially fruitful contacts is the confrontation of psychoanalysis with learning theory. Thus Dollard and Miller (1950) have attempted "to give a systematic analysis of neurosis and psychotherapy in terms of the psychological principles and social conditions of learning." They concentrate their study on Freudian principles, and the theorist of analysis, though often disagreeing, will profit from this and similar ventures.

This review of experimental checking of psychoanalytic hypotheses is admittedly a sketch only. But even if it were not, even if I had given the full picture, it would remain beyond doubt that the main body of evidence rests not on these studies but on the wealth of empirical data gathered by the analytic method in the analytic situation. The task better to define his concepts, to work toward a higher level of clarification and systematization of his hypotheses, rests, in the main, still with the analyst. This is, of course, far from saying that attempts at validation using extra-analytical methods, or criticisms originating in points of view different from those of analysis, are not to be welcomed by analysts. It is to be hoped, though, in the interest of sound interdisciplinary communication, that these criticisms, more than has often been the case in the past, will be based on a close familiarity with the methods of analysis, with the special nature of its subject matter, and with the role theorizing has played and plays in its development.

REFERENCES

ADRIAN, E. D. (1946), The Mental and the Physical Origins of Behaviour. *Int. J. Psycho-Anal.*, 28.

ALLPÖRT, G. (1937), *Personality*. New York: Henry Holt.

BELLAK, L. & SMITH, B. (1956), An Experimental Exploration of the Psychoanalytic Process. *Psychoanal. Quart.*, 25.

BENJAMIN, J. (1950), Methodological Considerations in the Validation and Elaboration of Psychoanalytical Personality Theory. *Amer. J. Orthopsychiat.*, 20.

BERNFELD, S. (   ), Der Begriff der Deutung in der Psychoanalyse. *Z. angew. Psychol.*, 52.

———— (1944), Freud's Earliest Theories and the School of Helmholtz. *Psychoanal. Quart.*, 13.

BONAPARTE, M. (1945), Notes on the Analytical Discovery of a Primal Scene. *The Psychoanalytic Study of the Child*, 1.

DEUTSCH, F. (1952), Analytic Posturology. *Psychoanal. Quart.*, 21.

DOLLARD, J. & MILLER, N. E. (1950), *Personality and Psychotherapy*. New York: McGraw-Hill.

ELLIS, A. (1950), An Introduction to the Principles of Scientific Psychoanalysis. *Genet. Psychol. Monogr.*, 41.

FRENKEL-BRUNSWIK, E. (1949), Intolerance and Ambiguity as an Emotional and Cognitive Personality Variable. *J. Personal.*, 18.

———— (1954), Psychoanalysis and the Unity of Science. *Proc. Amer. Acad. Sci.*, 53.

FREUD, A. (1951b), The Contributions of Psychoanalysis to Genetic Psychology. *Amer. J. Orthopsychiat.*, 21.

FREUD, S. (1895), Project for a Scientific Psychology. *The Origins of Psychoanalysis, Letters to W. Fliess* (1887-1902). New York: Basic Books, 1954.

———— (1901), The Psychopathology of Everyday Life. *Standard Edition*, 6.

———— (1913), The Claims of Psycho-Analysis to Scientific Interest. *Standard Edition*, 13.

———— (1923b), Psycho-Analysis. *Standard Edition*, 18.

HARTMANN, H. (1927), *Die Grundlagen der Psychoanalyse*. Leipzig: Thieme.

Psychoanalysis as a Scientific Theory 343

———— (1939a), *Ego Psychology and the Problem of Adaptation.* New York: International Universities Press, 1958.

———— & Kris, E. (1945), The Genetic Approach in Psychoanalysis. *The Psychoanalytic Study of the Child,* 1.

———— ———— & Loewenstein, R. M. (1946), Comments on the Formation of Psychic Structure. *The Psychoanalytic Study of the Child,* 2.

———— ———— ———— (1953), The Function of Theory in Psychoanalysis. In: *Drives, Affects, Behaviour,* ed. R. M. Loewenstein. New York: International Universities Press.

Heisenberg, W. (1952), *Philosophic Problems of Nuclear Science.* New York: Pantheon.

Hilgard, E. (1952), Experimental Approaches to Psychoanalysis. In: *Psychoanalysis as Science,* ed. E. Pumpian-Mindlin. Palo Alto: Stanford University Press.

Klein, G. (1958), Cognitive Control and Motivation. In: *Assessment of Human Motives,* ed. G. Lindzey. New York: Rinehart.

Kris, E. (1947), The Nature of Psychoanalytic Propositions and Their Validation. In: *Freedom and Experience,* ed. S. K. Hook & M. R. Konwitz. Ithaca, N.Y.: Cornell University Press.

———— (1950b), Notes on the Development and on Some Current Problems of Psychoanalytic Child Psychology. *The Psychoanalytic Study of the Child,* 5.

Kris, M. (1957), The Use of Prediction in a Longitudinal Study. *The Psychoanalytic Study of the Child,* 12.

Kubie, L. (1948), Instinct and Homoeostasis. *Psychosom. Med.,* 10.

———— (1952), Problems and Techniques of Psychoanalytic Validation.

———— (1953), Some Implications for Psychoanalysis of Modern Concepts of the Organization of the Brain. *Psychoanal. Quart.,* 22.

Lampl-de Groot, J. (1947), Development of the Ego and Superego. *Int. J. Psycho-Anal.,* 28.

Lewin, K. (1926), Comments Concerning Psychological Forces and Energies, and the Structure of the Psyche. In: *Organization and Pathology of Thought,* ed. & tr. D. Rapaport. New York: Columbia University Press, 1951.

Loewenstein, R. M. (1957), Some Thoughts on Interpretation in the Theory and Practice of Psychoanalysis. *The Psychoanalytic Study of the Child,* 12.

Lottig, H. (1931a), *Hamburger Zwillingsstudien.* Leipzig: Barth.

Rapaport, D. (1958), *The Structure of Psychoanalytic Theory: A Systematizing Attempt. Psychological Issues,* Monogr. 6. New York: International Universities Press, 1960.

Sears, R. (1943), Survey of Objective Studies of Psychoanalytic Concepts. *Soc. Sci. Res. Council Bull.,* 51.

VON MISES, R. (1939), *Kleines Lehrbuch des Positivismus.* The Hague: van Stockum & Zoon.

WISDOM, J. (1953), *Philosophy and Psycho-Analysis.* New York: Philosophical Library.

21

Psychoanalysis as Scientific Method *

Jacob A. Arlow

An interdisciplinary consideration of problems of methodology in psychoanalysis presumes that a knowledge of the psychoanalytic method is shared in common among the discussants. However, from the manner in which the discussion has developed it seems clear that any such presumption was unfounded. Since it is impossible to assess the levels of validity of various psychoanalytic hypotheses or operational concepts without first knowing just what method of investigation psychoanalysis employs, a few simple, yet fundamental, observations, relative to the basis of the psychoanalytic method, are offered in this contribution.

In his presentation Dr. Hartmann mentioned that the psychoanalytic situation is central to the problem of the psychoanalytic method of investigation. The psychoanalytic situation consists of the following: the patient (or subject) lies on a couch not facing the analyst (or experimenter). In accordance with a previously established understanding the subject proceeds to report verbally, as far as he is able, all thoughts, ideas or sensations which occur to him during the session. The subject is expected to report these data of consciousness in an indiscriminate manner, leaving aside all considerations of value judgments. This applies equally to considerations of judgment based on

I am indebted to Dr. Charles Brenner for certain suggestions and criticisms. —J.A.A.

*Reprinted by permission of the New York University Press from *Psychoanalysis, Scientific Method and Philosophy*, edited by Sidney Hook. Copyright © 1959 by New York University.

moral standards, the significance of the data for the therapy, the personal nature of the thoughts and even the seeming irrelevance of what is experienced. To the extent that he finds it possible, the subject is expected to act in the role of an uncritical reporter.

A complementarily objective and uncritical attitude on the part of the analyst towards the productions of the subject is the other major component of the analytic situation. The function of the analyst is to listen in an unbiased, unprejudiced way without introducing any predetermined concept of the origin or meaning of the phenomena under investigation. Every aspect of his manner and the procedure must reflect that his only interest is to help the patient to analyze and understand his thoughts and behavior. This is one of the reasons that the subject lies on a couch facing away from the analyst. This part of technique aims towards eliminating any additional source of possible ambiguity in communication. The analyst may betray a thought process of his own through some physiognomic change, or at least the subject may think he has. An intrusion of this sort constitutes a source of contamination of the field of observation. These are the very same considerations that form the basis for another fundamental aspect of the analytic situation, namely, the anonymity of the analyst. The personal life of the analyst, his private likes and dislikes, his professional, moral, esthetic or political predilections should not be permitted to enter into the analytic situation. By minimizing external sources of mental stimulation the psychoanalytic situation brings under survey data whose appearance is determined primarily or almost exclusively by the mental activity of the subject. This principle would be undermined if the analyst as a personality were permitted to enter the analytic situation, if his values, prejudices, etc., were permitted to operate as stimuli to the subject's thinking. It would be very difficult under such circumstances to know whether we were dealing with some response to the analyst or whether we were dealing with the proper area of psychoanalytic scrutiny, namely, the repetitive behavior patterns of the patient which are autogenously determined. The goal of the analytic situation is to create a set of conditions in the field of observation in which the data are supplied by the subject exclusively. All events, verbal or motor, which transpire in the analytic situation constitute the data of observation.

The fact that many people can report that Analyst A, B or C did not behave in the manner just described or did not set the conditions in the field as indicated is totally irrelevant to our problem, which is to study the validity of the psychoanalytic method of investigation. Reports of breaches of psychoanalytic technique cannot be used in evaluating the psychoanalytic method any more than reports of contamination or sloppy technique in bacteriology can be used to invalidate the findings of that science.

To permit ourselves a brief digression at this point we may exploit the analogy further. In bacteriological investigation contaminants introduce dynamic changes into the experimental situation. When understood through the appropriate technique such "accidents" may yield valuable data leading to further knowledge and development. The discovery of penicillin may be cited as an obvious example of this type of event. Similar situations supervene in analysis. Life provides the contaminations of the field of observation. By accident the patient may come upon some knowledge concerning the analyst, his family or his background. Such events introduce dynamic changes into the analytic situation. To these events, again, the analyst must maintain a detached and observing attitude. He does not respond to the realistic aspects of the material but studies instead the proper area of observation, namely, the patient's reactions, the effects of the intrusion of this foreign body into the analytic situation. Properly studied, this type of accidental contamination of the field of operation yields valuable data and insight.

These are the main outlines of the analytic situation. Every aspect of psychoanalytic technique is oriented towards preserving the objective, neutral, uncontaminated relationship of the field of observation. The very definite understanding concerning the practical arrangements of time, of appointments, of duration of session, fee for treatment, buttress the atmosphere of the analytic situation.

Psychoanalysts recognize that psychoanalysis is certainly not the only form of psychotherapy, nor does it have to be considered the most efficacious form of treatment of mental illness. Therapeutic efficacy is a related but not a central aspect of the problem of psychoanalytic methodology. Many forms of psychotherapy and other experiences may affect mental illness in a beneficent way, but only psychoanalysis has the methodological tools to investigate and attempt to explain these effects.

Because of the principles that underlie psychoanalytic technique, those who are acquainted in a practical way with the psychoanalytic method are convinced that it constitutes by far the closest approach to a controlled experimental situation that has as yet been devised to study the total functioning of the human mind. Indubitably, it is far from a perfect investigative technique. The context of therapy is a formidable but inevitable hazard. In addition, in common with the study of all dynamic situations, especially biological systems, psychoanalysis suffers from certain very definite methodological disadvantages. Some of these are: incomplete control over many of the factors in the field of observation, the impossibility of reduplicating precisely the events and situations studied, etc.

Although the analytic situation corresponds most closely to the experimental laboratory of other sciences, psychoanalytic methodology is hardly comparable to that of chemistry or physics (perhaps with the exclusion of physiological chemistry). On the other hand, because it considers the unconscious motivations and the genetic background that the subject brings into the experimental situation psychoanalysis has been able to indicate various sources of error in the "laboratory" technique of experimental psychology, a technique which, in academic circles, is apparently held in higher scientific esteem than psychoanalysis.

There is a basic principle or assumption that underlies the technique which has been devised and called the analytic situation. This is the principle of psychic determinism, the assumption that there is causality in the functioning of the human mind. Without such an assumption, psychological investigation of any sort would be meaningless—unless one would be willing to accept as the basis of mental life the crudest type of response to stimuli or the random, though unknown, fluctuation of the metabolic processes in the brain. In any event, such an approach flies in the face of common sense.

Essentially psychic determinism implies the application to the phenomena of mental life of the same criteria for causality and relatedness that apply to the phenomena of nature in other sciences. Once the data of observation have been gathered, the process of correlation and interpretation proceeds as in other fields of science, taking into account consistency of hypotheses, repetitive patterns of sequential relationships, the ability to predict certain phenomena on the basis of a knowledge of these patterns, etc. These principles need no repetition. It seems, however, that there is little conviction that the method of observation and procedure outlined above is actually followed in psychoanalysis. To become convinced of this, one has to observe the psychoanalytic process at first hand or else study detailed expositions of correlation and interpretation of data as utilized in psychoanalysis. Expositions of this sort appear in Freud's *Interpretation of Dreams*, in *The Psychopathology of Everyday Life*, in *Wit and its Relation to the Unconscious*, in the *General Introduction to Psychoanalysis*, and in some of the classic case histories by Freud. It is true, unfortunately, that in many psychoanalytic writings authors have not been as precise in the exposition of their methodology as was Freud in his pioneering work. There are many reasons for this, but perhaps the main one is the fact that in writing for a group of colleagues, analysts assume that the method employed is well known, and for purposes of convenience employ a "shorthand" of exposition which does away with the necessity of detailing elaborate reports at great length.

What was, and perhaps still is, one of the most controversial of psychoanalytic concepts, namely, the notion of mental functioning occurring outside of the scope of consciousness, becomes a necessary and inevitable conclusion if the principle of psychic determinism is applied to the phenomena of mental life in an unbiased and objective fashion. The study of slips of the tongue constitutes perhaps the easiest and most convincing method of demonstrating this principle. It does not require too much effort to demonstrate that slips of the tongue are motivated, and that sometimes the person who makes the slip is perfectly aware of the motive at the time he makes the slip; or that the person was not aware of the motive at the time that he made the slip of the tongue but after some reflection could understand that such motivation could actually exist; and finally there are those instances where the motivation for the slip of the tongue remains completely unknown to the person who made the slip and he resists any implication of motivation, although the motivation appears quite clear to others who heard the slip of the tongue in the context in which it happened. For illustrations of this point one is referred to the works mentioned above.

The regular and consistent patterning of the data of observation permits the analyst to make predictions which can be confirmed by further observation. In his discussion Dr. Loewenstein described how a supervising analyst is in a position to make and, in fact, does make many predictions on the development of the case and on the appearance of certain specific material. It should be noted that these predictions are made on the record of a patient whom the supervising analyst has not even seen. The frequency and specificity of predictions is far beyond chance relationship. Phenomena of this sort must be observed at first hand by critics of analytic methodology. It is possible that a fruitful interdisciplinary study of psychoanalytic methodology might be developed by having a student of methodology sit in on a supervised psychoanalytic case.

The fact is that analysts are always making predictions, which they submit to confirmation or invalidation by the further study of their data. A simple clinical illustration may be introduced at this point to illustrate this method of operation. During an initial interview I asked a patient how long he had been married. He answered, "Sixteen months, three weeks." The overly exact quality of this response aroused in me the suspicion that I was dealing with a person whose character structure was

colored by obsessional thinking and compulsive traits. To confirm my
suspicion I asked further, "How long did you know your wife before you
married her?" He answered, "Two years, three months." At this point,
inwardly, I made a further set of predictions concerning this individual's
mental traits. I guessed that he would be especially concerned with
money, that he would have a passion for accumulating it, keeping
meticulous records of his financial transactions, and that he would be
most reluctant to spend it. A further set of predictions concerned his relationship to cleanliness. I could guess that he would be excessively neat
regarding his person and his clothes, tidy in his surroundings, orderly in
his manner, and vigorously punctual regarding appointments and the
fulfillment of financial obligations. Questioning confirmed each of these
predictions in minute detail. But even further predictions can be made
on the basis of the minimal hints given by this patient. In the course of
detailed psychoanalytic investigation it could be predicted that a specific
type of childhood experience regarding bowel training and interest in
excrement would emerge. Such predictions in psychoanalysis are beyond the probability of a guess. These are predictions that have been
validated regularly, hundreds of times in psychoanalytic investigations.
Thus, we can see how a pathognomonic detail may enable the trained
and experienced psychoanalyst not only to predict a whole set of
correlative conditions but to hypothesize correctly concerning the
genesis and development of certain mental characteristics. Naturally,
there is a hierarchy in the predictability of phenomena in psychoanalysis just as there is in the phenomena of other sciences. The example
given above is one of the best known and best validated relationships
observed in psychoanalysis.

     An historical note might be of interest here. The correlation
between certain traits of the individual's character and a specific set of
childhood experiences was hypothesized by Freud on the basis of data
obtained from the anlaysis of adult patients. Utilizing this data, he was
able to hypothesize the genetic elements in the individual's early
childhood which were related to these character traits. Subsequently,
these retrospective reconstructions were substantially validated by direct
observation of the behavior of children. Direct observation on children
confirmed the hypotheses concerning the age at which the characteristic
conflict concerning bowel training and excremental play took place. In
addition, the quality of the relationships, exactly as predicted from the
data of the analyses of adults, could be observed in statu nascendi.

     The distinction between data of observation and hypotheses should
be kept in mind in connection with the so-called Oedipus complex. It is
by no means a matter of chance that precisely this aspect of psychoana-

lytic theory aroused the interest of the group—but this is not the time to discuss this special interest. To begin with, a distinction should be made between the oedipal phase and the "Oedipus complex." The reason for placing the phrase "Oedipus complex" in quotes will be discussed later.

The oedipal phase refers to the period of the child's life which falls roughly between the ages of three and six years. The significant characteristic of this period, so far as certain aspects of the emotional development of the individual are concerned, relates to sexual and aggressive feelings towards the parents or towards those who fulfill the corresponding role for the child. Sexual and aggressive feelings are directed toward both parents. The quality of these relationships differs in the little boy and in the little girl. Little girls undergo a longer and more complex set of oedipal reactions. Also, the oedipal reaction differs from one boy to another depending upon the specific structuring of his life situation and all of the antecedent vicissitudes of his development. The *most frequent* pattern for the usual kind of boy during this period consists of *predominantly* tender sexual feelings towards the mother and rivalrous feelings of hostility towards the father. The word "predominantly" must be emphasized and underlined because we are dealing here with a phase of development in which both tender and hostile feelings are felt for both parents. In unusual situations, which may develop for a variety of reasons, the predominant pattern described above may be reversed. The little boy may prefer his father and have tender sexual wishes directed toward him, feeling at the same time hostile rivalry toward his mother.

The term "oedipal phase" rather than "complex" is used here because what is being discussed is a regular developmental phase to be observed in children reared in family patterns in civilized society. The existence of the relationships which give the characteristic quality to this phase is not a matter of conjecture or reconstruction. It is a matter of observation. If one listens to children, watches them, plays with them and studies them, one will be able to hear expressed in various forms— directly, through play activity, through fantasy, through the dreams which may be told—precisely those wishes which are characteristic of the oedipal phase. (Why these observations were not made or understood before Freud is another problem, irrelevant to the methodology of psychoanalysis but pertinent to the resistance to psychoanalytic findings.)

Thus, psychoanalytic concepts concerning the existence of the oedipal phase are of one order of validity. It corresponds to a description, a summary of observed data, not to any reconstruction or hypothesis. It is quite a different matter, however, when one turns to the "Oedipus complex." An entirely different order of methodology is involved at this point. In effect, an hypothesis is advanced concerning the significance, the interpretation of data acquired during psychoanalytic investigation of adults. In a condensed and simplified form, the hypothesis may be put into the following words: "In his current life the subject (or patient) is behaving in response to the sexual and aggressive wishes which he felt towards his parents during the ages of three to six, i.e., during the early oedipal phase." The subject is usually unaware of any such processes occurring in his mental life. He may have substituted other figures for his parents and his expression of the sexual and aggressive feelings may have undergone certain distortions, disguises and transformations. One can see at a glance that the validation of such an hypothesis involves methodological considerations and problems of quite a different nature from the observation of children during the oedipal phase. A host of data has to be interpreted, integrated and correlated before the reconstruction and the validation of the specific features of the Oedipus complex in the adult subject are possible. This is accomplished within the analytic situation following the principles of psychic determinism and the available canons of causality as outlined at the beginning of this contribution.

Professor Sidney Hook raised the following question: "On what specific evidence would a psychoanalyst decide that a child did not go through the oedipal phase?" In response to this question we may say that such cases have been described. From what has been said above it is possible to understand that in such an instance we would be dealing with an anomaly of emotional and mental development. Phenomenologically, the little boy who does not achieve the oedipal phase of development would express no tender or romantic feelings or fantasies regarding his mother. He would not express any wish to grow up and marry her, nor try to oust his father as the rival from the marriage bed. Manifestations of a wish to exhibit his penis to the mother, to press his penis against her, to have her admire and fondle his penis would not appear. Evidence of pleasurable manipulation of the penis and concomitant fantasy as observed in normal development would be minimal in such a case. Such a child would hardly regard the other individuals in his environment as distinct entities or personalities. They would be important to him only in so far as they could grant immediate satisfaction of his bodily wants or needs. Once they had fulfilled these functions he would lose interest in his parents or nurses. He would hardly refer to them, conjure up few images or memories concerning them, and have no concern about their personal feelings or individuality. Considerations of masculinity or femininity would be minimal and completely subordinate to preoccupation over dependency, passivity, sleeping, eating and bowel function. We would anticipate in such a child impulsive emotionality and very meager identification with the standards, the ideals and behavior of his human environment. These are only a few features of the picture of a child who does not develop an oedipal phase, but sufficient features have been mentioned to indicate that the concept of an oedipal phase is not a procrustean bed into which psychoanalysts wish to force all the data of observation. The existence of an oedipal phase in the development of the young child is based upon definite, observable patterns of behavior, upon a concrete set of interpersonal relations and upon a host of other mental phenomena. Definite criteria of a positive and negative nature must be available before one can say whether a child has or has not achieved the oedipal phase of development.

In summary, it should be acknowledged that psychoanalysis is not an esoteric cult in which the analyst foists upon gullible neurotic patients a preconceived mumbo-jumbo inherited from Freud. Psychoanalytic therapy is a meticulously painstaking investigation into human mental processes. It is by no means a perfect experimental tool, but it is, nevertheless, a rational and objective procedure, governed by strict methodological considerations and operating within accepted canons of the scientific method.

22

Psychoanalysis as a Unified Science*

Gardner Murphy

I shall begin by asking two psychoanalytically oriented questions: first, why does anyone *want* psychoanalysis to be, or to become, a *unified theory* of behavior; and secondly, if anyone wants this, how is he going to get it? Specifically, to what needs is psychoanalysis a response? What cultural and personal needs are served by it: conscious, preconscious and unconscious? What were the occasioning circumstances for its birth? Why was Freud the first major respondent? How did his personality and outlook interact with the biocultural demands? The cultural epoch of the late nineteenth century witnessed a deep need to see both abnormal and normal adjustments in terms of new cosmic dimensions, such as those given by evolution; new cultural dimensions, such as those given by the new anthropology; and new scientific and philosophic dimensions as given by the methods of reduction, analysis, element finding, and system construction, already exemplified in physics, chemistry and the biology of the cell. From this viewpoint Freud's training in histology, as seen in the new evolutionary terms, becomes not so much an organic bias from which he drifted away as a consummation of many other nineteenth century trends and a preparation for psychoanalysis.

But at a deeper level, why the craving for system, for order? Partly because living things are organized. Disturb their symmetry, their hierarchic organization, and they rebuild. The central nervous system

*Reprinted from *Psychoanalysis and Human Values*, edited by J. H. Masserman, 1960. Reprinted by permission of Grune & Stratton, Inc. and the author.

lives, as our phrase for it shows, on system. Any system requires component parts, requires structural and dynamic modes of interrelating; these must embody an integration and must come to terms with the world which lies outside the system.

Any scientific or philosophic system must therefore note the following four steps. (1) It must specify the elements which can be found through analysis; (2) it must show how the elements are interrelated; (3) it must solve the problem of the character of the resulting functional integrations; and (4) it must specify how the resulting system interacts with the environment. As pointed out by E. B. Holt, Freud's first step was to find his basic elements not in states of awareness, but in energies, in drives, thus solving simultaneously the problem of the nature of the elements and laying the foundation for the problem of the ways in which they may become articulated. Of course, Freud's restlessness about his solution is evident in his recurrent preoccupation with instinct, with various reformulations of the libido theory, the later struggle with dual instinct proposals, and the obviously unfinished character of these first speculations regarding the nature of the drive. Moreover, Freud's earlier and also his later ego psychology, insofar as it transcended the original theory of instinct, remained rooted in the conception of energies rather than in the traditional sensations, ideas and motor acts of earlier psychologies; for psychoanalysis the component elements have been and remain *energy components, dynamic components*. He was working here with a fundamental biological issue. As exemplified in *Beyond the Pleasure Principle*, he made clear that the resulting physiologic problems could only be solved by exacting and sustained physiologic research, much of which has in recent years been undertaken. His effort to reconcile the strictly physiologic definition of drive with the classical problems of hedonism, the search for pleasure and the avoidance of pain, articulates with his conception of the unconscious, in which there may be, for example, the unconscious pursuit of a goal, not acknowledged by the individual as being desired.

Now we must consider the mode of combining the drives. The drives were connected early in Freud's schema, both with specific objects, as in the theory of cathexis, and with one another, as in the transformation of instinctual energies into the dynamics of the ego, and later the superego, held at bay the instinctual forces of the id. He saw, moreover, that there is facilitation as well as conflict between life tendencies, as in the process of overdetermination and as in the structuring and creative process of the dream work. His conception of well defined component parts and the mode of their interrelation paid relatively little attention to the contemporary studies of conflict and integration by other investigators, as for example, in the physiology of the sympathetic and parasympathetic systems, the studies of facilitating and inhibiting effects of the endocrine organs, and especially competition and cooperation among action tendencies, as studied by the Russian school under the general head of the dominance relations of reflex systems.

Summarizing up to this point: Freud saw both of the first main issues for a system, namely, the need for elements, which he defined in terms of instinct, and the need for stating the mode of their interconnection, which he defined mainly as their tendency to crowd upon or block one another. In both instances, however, he made limited use of the contemporary concepts so similar to his own, which could well have served to make his ideas more easily understood and could well have given a larger framework within which systems stated in somewhat different ways could have been reconciled.

Now as to the third issue, the way in which the conflict or mutual facilitation of elements can lead into the formation of a true structural whole; Freud's metapsychology contained several brilliant features involving both topographic, dynamic and economic modes of synthesis, and phrases such as "the mental apparatus" indicate clearly that he saw that there were problems much larger than those of the concatenation of elements into a network. He saw problems of stable and unstable equilibrium, problems of viable and nonviable integration. It may appear odd in this connection to note that he appears to have been uninterested in the problem of specifying what modes of articulation may become maximally stable (ultra-stable, Ashby would say) and the question of whether such ultra-stability should be conceived in terms of healthy adjustment or in terms of the rigidities which belong to psychopathology.

In the same vein he appears to have been relatively uninterested in the fourth problem which the modern system builder raises, namely, the sociocultural question of the articulation between the system which one individual personality presents to us and the equally rich systems presented by the other personalities which compose a group in a society. At least if we may take our cue from the *Group Psychology and Analysis of the Ego,* while conceiving of individuals as entering into the group or crowd situation, he was not interested in problems of the different structural composition of groups from which a social psychology could have arisen. Nor, *a fortiori,* was he aware of the varying cultural contexts within which groups carry on such different lives and sustain such different functional relations between one individual and another. I suggest, then, that while Freud, in reference to the first two major issues, namely the elements and the mode of their articulation, saw the

problems which the era demanded, he failed mainly in not seeing that
others were working on very similar problems of system building; while
with the third issue, the nature of integrated wholes, he made a brilliant
beginning; and with the fourth, the relation of these personal wholes to
society at large, he appears to have been only slightly concerned.

At this point it would be easy for the man of 1958 to introduce a
derogatory note as if the early Freud had perversely missed points that he
was extensively seeking. This, however, itself misses the point. Freud, in
the last years of the nineteenth century, and in the beginning years of the
twentieth, was seeing issues as an extraordinarily perceptive student of
human pathology and psychopathology *had* to see them. In other
words, the needs which were being satisfied were those of a wise
psychopathologist who was already taking on as much as he could
handle; and the medical men who followed him were already taking on
as much as they could in accepting and applying what Freud had to
teach. The defects of the system as seen from the point of view of 1958 are
in many ways comparable to the defects of Darwinism as seen likewise
from the point of view of 1958. No one today berates Charles Darwin for
his lack of perception of many issues, such as those relating to the
continuity of the germ plasm as seen by Weisman and those relating to
the frequently supportive, rather than competitive, relations of members
of a species, as demonstrated by the life work of Allee. These were issues
which at the time were not yet ready for focus.

The danger to science today lies not in making too much use of
Freud, but in failing to use him as we use Darwin. Often we insist, I
might say, upon freezing or encapsulating Freud within a period—as if
his words, having become holy writ or his perspectives ossified, could
offer more to contemporary humanity than those of a living figure,
changing with the new biological and cultural perspectives, changing
above all in terms of the new needs—individual and social—which the
era presents. The needs of a systematic theory are not fixed solely by the
internal structure of a coherent system of ideas. Even Euclidean geometry, even Newtonian physics, turned out to be less self contained than
that. One way of formulating the issue is to say that every doctrine
belongs to a time, place and culture; or, as Karl Mannheim would put it,
in terms of the "sociology of knowledge," every thought pattern is
relative to the capacity of the men of a given era for perception,
generalization, reflection, interpretation.

As students of Freud, however, we must push considerably further
than this. The relevance of Aristotle, Galileo or Darwin is not limited
solely to the Greek, the sixteenth century Italian, or the nineteenth
century British definition of science. There are some permanent and

universal, because they are "common human," issues. There are certain cultural discoveries channeled through individual discoverers, but becoming universal, because they are common human. To these one refers when one develops concepts of unconscious motivation, unacknowledged goals, conflict, the never completely uprooted force of infantile experience in adult character structure, and many other components which we believe, as of 1958, are likely to be permanently assimilated in some recognizable form, as permanent contributions to a theory of human behavior.

We have tried to understand why a unified theory of human behavior was wanted, and why Freud built it as he did. But there are further questions: By whom are the theories needed; who responds to the Freudian challenge; why are the resulting theories so different; how do the theories fare with others who have different needs? This means that we must ask why it is that those living and working with human beings vary so widely as to what they believe to be the needs, and as to the character of their own evaluation of the response to these needs. Quite aside from the easy parlor game of taking one another apart and finding all sorts of infantile residues and adult paranoid or compulsive traits which prevent them from agreeing with us, and quite aside from the mildly amusing "standard operating procedure" of showing that each of us exemplifies the best reality testing functions, it would be proper, I think, to say that one man's need to understand may be focused at a more intuitive level, another's at a more verbal and analytical level; that a man's way of looking for the elements or components required by a system may be more microscopic in one case, more a matter of naked-eye-sweeping-the-field in another; that sensitivity to large interpersonal issues may take the form of very intense study of intrapersonal conflicts in one case, of sociocultural conflicts in another. One man may think, as George Klein would say, as a "leveler," finding a place for everything in a sort of peer group of many realities, while another, called a "sharpener," may quickly establish a hierarchy of realities from a central one down to supposedly trivial ones. There are, in other words, cognitive as well as affective, differences among the observers. Interacting with this is the fact that each analyst in his training and experience has actually encountered somewhat different kinds of phenomena among different samples of his patients. He has, moreover, formed friendships and professional relationships which make certain classes of work more satisfying to him. As Skinner would say, he has been rewarded or reinforced for one way of looking at the nature of man; another man has been reinforced for another way. The same goes, I believe, for the laboratory investigator, the field anthropologist and the social philosopher. They are all human, they all seek the fulfillment of their needs, they all belong in an ultimate orchestration of what can be described as human need-fulfillment. There are many kinds of psychoanalysis struggling to be useful, and struggling for cultural survival, jsut as there are many kinds of psychological systems, old ones dying, new ones being born, all the time.

Now, if in this perspective you ask me how well has psychoanalysis succeeded in doing the things which Freud set out to do over sixty years ago, I would have to reply, "Succeeded *for whom?* Succeeded *in what ways?*" In the same breath it must be acknowledged that psychoanalysis has certainly not achieved that kind of orderly and convincing structure which, let us say, geology or astronomy has succeeded in achieving, though these latter sciences make scarcely more use of experimental method than psychoanalysis does. Why has psychoanalysis not achieved a compellingly ordered system—I mean compellingly ordered for all who seek to find such order? I believe largely for two reasons. First, because the needs which have just been described have not been so explicitly acknowledged and are so difficult to acknowledge. In other words, there are psychoanalytic reasons, or reasons intelligible in psychoanalytic terms, why psychoanalysis itself has not been capable of consistent and rigorous reality testing in the face of the half-acknowledged differences in needs between different persons who use it. I would plead for a much more radical psychoanalytic study of the reasons for the successes and failures of the psychoanalytic system. I advisedly use the word *reasons*, having in mind both reason as it belongs to the reality testing structure of science and reason as it belongs to the world of rationalization with which we are all so familiar. It is a genuine psychoanalytic test that is to be carried out; it will deal with reason at both these levels, indeed at all levels of the rational and the irrational.

A second reason for failure to complete a unified system: Psychoanalysis has not achieved a form of realization which the sciences always need, namely, semantic clarification, the consistent and clear use of terms; and with them, the development of objectivity, that is, the definition of events in such fashion that they depend relatively little upon the subjective or autistic interpretations of individual observers. These steps might at first seem to suggest the need of what Sears called, fifteen years ago, "the objective study of psychoanalytic concepts." But Sears was primarily concerned with experimentation. I believe, however, that the science of geology and astronomy are closer counterparts for psychoanalysis as a system. They have sought and achieved a rigorous and systematic use of terms and modes of observation and cross checking of widely different kinds of observation with one another.

While it is doubtful whether an era of experimental investigation is as yet opening up for psychoanalysis, there is no doubt that genetic and comparative methods are yielding a great deal. The sister sciences of child psychology, comparative psychology and cultural anthropology have already made headway along this road, using the method of experiment here and there but not relying primarily upon it. These sister sciences, indeed, are so close to psychoanalysis, learn so much from it and give so much to it that they may act as catalytic agents in accelerating this kind of systematic development in psychoanalysis and at times merge with it.

One thing, however, that stands in the way of this massively structured, broadly articulated psychoanalytic conception is a literal adherence to the verbal formulations used by Freud. The observed clinical phenomena are forever precious; but the words used to describe them are socioculturally stained in the time-space realities of another way of thinking. To carry out the figures of speech, a fresh histologic staining job and a fresh in vivo orientation will have to be carried out before the work can be fully fruitful.

Until such an integration is achieved, I believe we must acknowledge a certain narrowness among many of the devotees of each of the various human sciences, including the analysts. Many of the profoundest discoveries of psychoanalysis were likewise being made during the same years, perhaps in less adequate form, but still being made, by other modes of investigation. Just as it does not subtract from the importance of the Freudian discoveries if we quote the Athenian or Shakespearean plays in which many of these same dynamic principles are formulated, it does nothing to weaken Freudian theory if we note that in physiologic and psychological laboratories similar proposals have been emerging in recent decades. The psychoanalytic system will be strengthened, not weakened, by recognizing that others have independently established many of the same principles.

If it is true then we *can* get what we want, namely, a psychoanalysis which is a unified theory of human behavior, just *how* can we get it? I have hinted that we can get it in a more generous glory-sharing conception of research to which all the human sciences contribute, one to another. But what precisely are the other more orderly systems with which the psychoanalytic system must today share its glory? I believe that there are at least five of them, not all of them as comprehensive as psychoanalysis, but all of them striving, as psychoanalysis strives, toward achieving a unified theory of human behavior.

1. The phenomenologic-existential systems, though frequently unresponsive to the vertical or depth dimension with which most of us

here would be concerned, are concerned with the fullest possible
appreciation of the complexities, subtleties, inherent reconciliations
and conflicts within the experience world of an individual and also with
the mode of transition from this experience world to that of another in
the course of time, providing data without which no comprehensive
psychology can afford to try to live.

2. Gestalt, or organismic psychology, premised upon the conception of structural wholeness not based solely upon the juxtaposition of
component elements, but upon lawful and orderly modes of articulation
given in the living system itself or given in the very nature of the universe
of nature of which human life is an expression.

3. The Pavlovian system, now enriched by the systems of Hull,
Skinner and others who have markedly extended the area of behavior
envisaged as understandable in terms of the dynamics of the process of
conditioning.

4. The biochemical systems, such as those of von Bertalanffy,
Weiss, and recently Williams, in which the rich individuality of the
system-building function within each living individual has been brilli-
antly and systematically developed; and finally

5. The sociocultural system which has, despite the huge human
difficulties, learned in recent years the necessary humility to define
component parts in culture, the modes of their interrelation, the
character of the structural wholes, and in particular the interpersonal
integrations so essential to the understanding of self realization and self
defeat and without which we could scarcely deal at all with the large
problems of the dependence of the individual man or woman upon the
fantastic complexities of cultural demands upon the adjustment potential of his or her own organic, biologic nature.

Do we mean then to suggest that psychoanalysis as a theoretical
system must somehow sit side by side with these other five systems in a
huge battle of wits to determine ultimately in the court of fresh evidence
who has the best formulation? Far from it. Ultimately, the same living
individual is a biochemical system, a Pavlovian physiologic system, a
Gestalt system, a sociocultural system, a phenomenal system, and a
psychoanalytic system. One system may be richer than another, but all
share greatly, overlap greatly with others. This prompts me to comment
on Dr. Mohr's challenging notes relating to interdisciplinary thinking
and to eclecticism. You can build two utterly different kinds of eclectic
systems. One of these wrenches a piece from biochemistry, and tries to
wedge it, so to speak, between a repression and a reaction formation;
another tries to drive three conditioned responses and a socially defined
value conflict between two phenomenalist experiences. This kind of

eclecticism is made of pieces that won't fit, nonviable grafts, essentially foreign bodies. But the kind of eclecticism that consists of using different glasses, different ways of looking at the same one unified living style, is one which can use all the six languages that I have tried to describe. We may strive to see the process of repression in phenomenalist terms, in physiologic terms, as for example, conditioned response terms, or as aspects of imbalanced Gestalten, or in terms of sociocultural conflict or all these together. Sometimes only one of our six systems has clearly seen an issue; often two or three have seen and struggled with it; occasionally, as in the modern psychology of self and ego, all six have something vital to say. Let us consider the possibility that they are not saying six contradictory things, but saying one thing in six languages. The efforts of linguists, or logicians, and of general systems theory, and of men and women trained in several disciplines, can all help to develop that comprehensive system which, because it is most open to all of human nature, may ultimately be the most coherent and most useful. Psychoanalysis need have no fear that any other system will steal its thunder, or run off with its priceless booty; for it is as close to man himself as are any, and can in time assimilate its message to all of them, as they, in turn—if they are productive enough and generous enough—can achieve a richer life by the fullest utilization of psychoanalysis. The suggestion is that as time sweeps over the heads of individual explorers and they are submerged in the larger ocean of common human knowledge, a hidden archipelago of their various forms, all in intimate articulation, all in one structured system, will *ultimately* be achieved. So it will be not only with the least, but also with the greatest:

> Of his bones are coral made.
> These are pearls that were his eyes;
> Nothing of him that doth fade,
> But doth suffer a sea-change
> Into something rich and strange.
> —Shakespeare: *The Tempest*

23

Assessments and Applications *

James A.C. Brown

Once it is realized that acceptance of the general standpoint of psychoanalysis no more commits us to Freud's philosophy or the commonly held assumption of his time than acceptance of Newton's theory commits us to his peculiar theological doctrines or his views on alchemy, the way is opened to a consideration of psychoanalytic theory as both a theoretical and an applied approach in psychology. Science is a hard discipline and necessitates an attitude that nobody is capable of maintaining all the time, nor would it be desirable if they could, and Freud's impeccable approach to fact-finding is not invalidated by demonstrating that he was also a man of his time with strong personal convictions of his own. When in his later years he became interested in telepathy, and, in fact, published some papers on the subject, Freud wrote in reply to a letter from Jones inquiring whether telepathy would now be included as part of psychoanalysis: 'When anyone adduces my fall into sin, just answer him calmly that conversion to telepathy is my private affair like my Jewishness, my passion for smoking, and many other things and that the theme of telepathy is in essence alien to psychoanalysis.' The real criticism of psychoanalytic orthodoxy is not that there was anything wrong with Freud's methods or observations but that there was something very far wrong indeed with the attitude of the group which kept his *explanations* fixated at the level of Herbert

*Reprinted by permission of Penguin Books Ltd. from *Freud and the Post-Freudians*, by James A. C. Brown. Copyright © the estate of J. A. C. Brown, 1961, 1964.

Spencer's sociology, an anthropology which was half speculative, half travellers' tales, and an extremely naive moral and political philosophy; that there was an arrogance bordering on dottiness in the assertion that only members of this body were qualified to criticize its theories, when we know that hardly one trusted the insight of another or was capable of distinguishing between personal feelings of loyalty and devotion to scientific truth. In fact, in terms of generally accepted criteria Freud's is an extremely good theory which explains an immense number of facts with a minimum number of assumptions, and on the whole does so both economically and convincingly. It poses many new questions, invites further applications, and in this way differs from an open-and-shut theory such as Adler's, which has no further applications outside the clinical sphere for which it was designed and is economical at the expense of adequate detail. Whatever criticisms may be made of Freud's theories the fact remains (and this is perhaps the supreme instance of his tremendous genius) that, whilst making no claim to know all the answers, he was well aware of the right questions psychology should ask. By the single assumption of psychic determinism Freud brought every manifestation of the irrational into the sphere of scientific investigation, showing that no matter what an individual said or did was always the truth—not necessarily about reality but about the individual himself. Sane or insane, drunk or sober, literate or illiterate, genius or idiot, rational or irrational, sick or healthy, the invidual's projections or the projections of social groups are scientific facts capable of being interpreted. The old criticism that Freud took his material from a relatively small group of Viennese neurotics who were not only unstable in their judgements but were discussing events or alleged events which had supposedly happened many years earlier and did not seem even at the time of recounting to be inherently likely ones, shows a complete misunderstanding of his approach. Thus, when it was found that the sexual seductions in early life reported by his patients had never in fact occurred, Freud, after an initial period of frustration, came to realize that the fact that the patients felt *as if* they had occurred was equally significant. Individuals and groups give themselves away by the material they project upon external reality, and of course the fact that they do so is the basis of projective techniques in the personality tests which are widely used by psychologists today. Myths, fairy-tales, literature, political and religious beliefs, or art, become scientifically meaningful to the psychologist precisely to the degree that they do *not* correspond with the facts of external reality, and from this there follows the converse proposition that to the extent they do so correspond they are none of the psychologist's business. Unfortunately this has not always been realized by psychoanalysts, and we have seen how Rank and others made the most far-fetched interpretations of cultural objects such as jugs and bowls, spears and swords, whose significance is adequately accounted for purely in terms of utility. That such objects may *come to assume* a different significance from the original one is self-evident, but it is difficult to imagine a container with any shape that does not betray the fact that, like the womb, it is intended to contain, and if swords and spears were designed *because* they are phallic symbols we shall have a good deal of strain put upon our ingenuity when we are expected to find a sexual significance in stones, bombs, or poison gas. The fact that objects with a similar function tend to possess a similar form does not entitle us to assume with the Freudians that the chronologically earliest example of the object *caused* the development of subsequent examples, or with Jung that they are all imitations of an archetypal object or idea. Generally speaking, physicians make poor scientists because a scientist must be a good theoretician, a physician a good practitioner and empiricist, and the fact that an explanation or method works in practice has not the slightest bearing on its scientific truth. In an address to the British Medical Association in 1959 the eminent neurologist Lord Adrian described the immense revolution Freudian theory had brought about in the field of medicine, but pointed out that its therapeutic results could not be adduced as evidence for its truth since the whole history of medicine shows that the scientific validity of a particular line of treatment has not always much to do with its success. 'In the past, success in the treatment of neurotic complaints has been claimed for methods as different as the removal of the colon, the anchoring of a wandering kidney, and the laying on of hands,' he asserted, and it is impossible to deny that this is so, since even orthodox psychoanalysts have been vociferous in claiming that the successes claimed by other schools are due to nothing but the patient's suggestibility. Nevertheless a major reason why psychoanalysis proved acceptable to the man in the street, to the artist and novelist (who could not conceive of an Adlerian theory of art), to the social worker or the psychiatrist (who realized that the content of schizophrenic phantasies could be understood in Freudian or even Jungian terms but never in Adlerian ones), is precisely the fact that it can be applied to real situations whereas the undoubtedly important results obtained by experimental psychologists in general cannot. They can of course be applied in very many situations—in testing and selection for jobs, in industry, in education, and so on—but in few that press closely upon the individual as a person. The adolescent with sexual problems, the psychiatrist who needs to understand his patient, the novelist, or for that matter the advertising firm making use of motivational research, would get cold comfort from a text-book of psychology, but Freud showed how many forms of behaviour, ranging from the home life of the ordinary man or woman to the lives of the gods, from an isolated act of assault to general warfare involving millions, could be fitted together within a common frame of reference that made some sort of sense. The pattern was found satisfying (a) because it had an inner consistency, (b) because it seemed to explain behaviour adequately, and (c) because, once one had got used to the unfamiliar jargon, Freudian theory appeared to be saying things that one had vaguely known all along. Professor Notcutt (Psychology of Personality) points out that even those who regard dream symbolism as far-fetched or ridiculous often know perfectly well what symbolism means. A man dreamt that he came into the kitchen and, on opening the electric oven, saw that there was a bun inside on the tray; on waking up the dream seemed to him to be completely meaningless; yet, when at the local bar a soldier said to him, 'My wife has a bun in the oven,' he had no difficulty whatever in knowing what he meant. As Notcutt says, 'anyone who has spent a few hours leaning on a bar counter listening to dirty jokes will have heard in conscious form all the sexual symbols that Freud "discovered" in *The Interpretation of Dreams*. With the leer in the voice and the gleam of glasses to define the context, it is not difficult to interpret most of the symbols which at other times would be deeply hidden.' Many of the Freudian mechanisms of defence are so familiar to us that they have for long been enshrined in everyday speech: 'There are none so blind as those who don't want to see' (repression or dissociation), 'kicking the cat' (displacement), or the man who sees the mote in his brother's eye when he cannot see the beam in his own (projection), are examples. The ordinary man or woman *knows* that from an early age the child is interested in the mystery of birth, in its genitals and bowel motions, that one commonly refers to 'daddy's little girl' or 'mummy's little boy' rather than the reverse, that dreams mean something (although exactly what is another matter), that people frequently make mistakes 'on purpose', that protestations of sexual innocence or pacific propensities are most frequently made by those in whom one suspects the reverse, and no amount of criticism from the scientific psychologist is going to make him think otherwise. If psychology cannot encompass such everyday observations, so much the worse for psychology. Nor does it take a great effort of imagination to see that the children of fervent atheists or agnostics are as likely to become fervent Catholics as to adopt the views of their parents but are unlikely to be indifferent to religious issues, or to note that their attitude is likely to depend more on their basic filial attitude than their intellect. That such conclusions are intuitively arrived at and are therefore not always expressed in a form that appeals to the scientist or put forward with what he would regard as adequate supporting evidence may be granted; that adequate supporting evidence is provided by Freud may be denied; but that they are to be rejected as inherently non-scientific because of their nature is peculiarly a conception of the experimental psychologist. Professor H. J. Eysenck, in an essay entitled 'What is wrong with Psychoanalysis?' *(Uses and Abuses of Psychology)*, supports this view and notes the distinction made by German philosophers between *verstehende* psychology (i.e. a commonsense psychology which tries to *understand* human beings) and *erklarende* psychology (which tries to describe and *explain* their behaviour on a scientific basis), pointing out that the former category is the one to which psychoanalysis rightly belongs. He then states 'quite briefly and dogmatically' that consequently 'it is essentially non-scientific and to be judged in terms of belief and faith rather than in terms of proof and verification; and that lastly its great popularity among non-scientists derives precisely from its non-scientific nature, which makes it intelligible and immediately applicable to problems of "understanding" other people. This judgement I believe to be a statement of fact, rather than a value judgement.' This point of view is worthy of note but it must be said equally dogmatically that it is not one which is widely held by psychologists in general, that the contrast between *verstehende* and *erklarende* psychology is inapplicable to the present issue, since Freud's methods were entirely in accord with the ordinary scientific approach, and that if Freud introduced an irrelevant metapsychology it would be equally easy to show that strict use of the scientific method by psychologists has frequently led to results which vie for absurdity with any conclusions of the psychoanalytic schools, although for precisely the opposite reason: that not enough attention was paid to the wider context of the object of study. The contrast between *verstehende* and *erklarende* in German is not that between mere understanding and explaining, which in English signify pretty much the same process in the sense that when something is properly *explained* it is reasonable to say that it has been *understood;* the implied contrast in German is between *intuitive understanding* (as when one says, 'I understand how you feel') and *scientific explaining in terms of 'laws'*—which are not, of course, laws in the usual sense but statements of probability arrived at by a process of induction from a large number of individual observations. When confirmation of many such observations leads to a high degree of probability we speak of a scientific law, when it is of a lower degree we speak of a theory, and when it is lower still we speak of a hypothesis; between the extremes of law and hypothesis there is a quantitative, not a qualitative difference. This is so (1) because it is never possible to test all cases that would validate a law, and (2) because it is never possible to investigate every hypothesis that would explain a given phenomenon and therefore, other things being equal, a hypothesis is likely to be preferred in so far as it complies with the criteria already mentioned. Nor is any law universally 'true' regardless of circumstances, for even physical laws such as Boyle's or Charles's equations dealing with the interrelationships between volume, temperature, and pressure of gases are true only within a quite narrow range of temperature or pressure; in the same way the Oedipus complex as described by Freud was the one he observed in bourgeois Vienna at the turn of the century, and as Fenichel points out, Malinowski's findings in the Trobriand Islands do not show that there are places where the Oedipus complex does not exist, but rather that the form taken by the complex varies from one culture to another. Circumstances alter cases in both physics and psychology, and it is one of the commonest failings of the strict experimental scientist to ignore the fact that they do or to ignore how widely 'circumstances' may be spread. For example there has been, and perhaps still is, an extraordinary inability on the part of some psychologists to see that where human beings are concerned the very fact that they are being experimented upon becomes an additional factor which inevitably affects the result; so, prior to Mayo, industrial psychologists simply assumed (wrongly, as he was able to show) that any change in the physical environment of the workshop which was followed by alterations in mood or productivity on the part of the workers must be the sole cause of the alteration. Early studies of perception were carried out on the fallacious assumption that perceptions exist uninfluenced by expectations, social norms, needs, complexes, and other emotional factors which form an important circumstance of any experiment. In place of the psychoanalyst's frequently inaccurate and inexact mode of expressing himself, his bad logic and worse metaphysics, the psychologist often presents us with a view of the scientific method so naive as to confound the critic who wants to reject what is unscientific in Freudian theory. That two American psychologists would ask college students to recall at random pleasant and unpleasant experiences on the assumption that, if repression were a fact, more of the former than the latter would be recalled is bad enough; that, as Professor Eysenck assures us, a group of strong and presumably normal individuals were persuaded to starve themselves for an appreciable period in order to prove that Freud's theory of dreams as wish-fulfillments was false because they did not dream of food, strains one's credibility; but that an eminent educational psychologist should solemnly 'prove' the Oedipus complex to be a myth by the simple expedient of asking a number of other professional psychologists about the preferences of their own children towards one parent or the other baffles comprehension. Freud at no time said that unpleasant experiences as such were likely to be forgotten he said that experiences which might conflict with other dominant tendencies of the personality were likely to be repressed whether as experiences they were pleasant or not; he did not say that for any appreciable period a child showed overt preference for the parent of the opposite sex, because the very word 'complex' refers to *unconscious* attitudes which are unconscious precisely because they are forbidden; he did not assert that hunger made one dream of food, although explorers and others subjected involuntarily to hunger have said that it did, and he would certainly have seen through the fallacy of supposing that voluntary and experimental subjection to starvation bears any resemblance in its emotional significance to the involuntary situation in which the basic issue is not primarily lack of food but imminent proximity of death. 'Do you think that I am easier to be played on than a pipe?' asked Hamlet, and apparently some psychologists believe that the answer to what was intended as a rhetorical question is in the affirmative. Without any further nonsense Hamlet should be asked the simple question: 'Do you, or do you not, have an Oedipus complex?' (Perhaps, on second thoughts, it would be more scientific to ask his mother the Queen, who was naturally in a better position to observe Hamlet's childhood reactions and is clearly an intelligent and unbiased witness.) Dr Eysenck rejects the psychoanalytic concept of reaction-formation which, as he says, allows a person who theoretically should show behaviour pattern A to react away from this pattern to such an extent that he shows the opposite pattern Z (as violent aggressiveness leading to compulsive gentleness by a process of repression). This, he complains, allows the hypothesis to be verified regardless of whether the individual is timorous or aggressive. Possibly the hypothesis is badly expressed in terms of Aristotelian logic, although entirely in conformity with Hegelian dialectic, but the fallacy lies in supposing that compulsive gentleness and aggressiveness are opposites rather than variations along a scale of 'conflict about aggression' which in a truly gentle person is poorly represented. What the proposition says is that conflict over authority in early life predisposes to conflict over authority in later life—that there is a type of 'pseudo-gentleness' recognized by most people without psychological theorizing and sharply distinguishable from the genuine article which is the result of absence of such conflict. The attitude of the experimental psychologist to the measurement of personality traits is incomprehensible to those whose approach is fundamentally a dynamic one. For instance the supposed 'trait' of suggestibility is investigated by observing the reaction of an individual when, with eyes shut and feet together, it is suggested to him that he is swaying, the degree of sway being measured although there seems to be not the slightest *a priori* reason to suppose that suggestibility is a unitary trait that some people have a lot of and others just a little, still less reason to suppose that if there were it could be correlated with sway, and no reason at all to think that suggestibility is independent of who is doing the suggesting, what is suggested, or the mental and physical state of the subject at the time of the test. Here again it is assumed that a subject *pretending* to do something in an experiment responds in the same way as in a real situation, and it is far from clear what the psychologist proposes to do with his results once he has succeeded in plastering a framework of personality with all its traits in specified amounts, like the numbered areas on the head of a phrenologist's dummy. What happens then? One must be forgiven for supposing that the answer appears to be that, so long as the traits never interact, nobody cares very much what they do. Dr Raymond Cattell of the University of Illinois is another eminent psychologist who is dazzled at the prospect of founding psychology on a basis of measurement, since nothing, it appears, is truly scientific unless it makes use of mathematics. But our initial enthusiasm—unless we are exceptionally credulous—is quickly damped by the discovery that although figures and symbols appear in plenty of his works they are based on the answers to such questions as the following: 'Are you attentive in keeping appointments?', 'Would you feel embarrassed on joining a nudist colony?', 'Have people called you a proud, stuck-up, self-willed person?', 'Do you think people should observe moral laws more strictly?', 'Do you crave travel?' Surely the compiler of such a questionnaire must be aware that anybody who answered these questions truthfully (except in the interests of pure research) conveys to the tester one single piece of information: that the testee ought to see a psychiatrist. For the questions imply value judgements and nowhere more so than in the United States where they are in use, and nobody but a fool would do other than answer them in the way that revealed himself in the best possible light. Furthermore they refer to subjects about which most people are a great deal more touchy than the most intimate details of their sexual life, because they feel greater responsibility for them. Many people would admit to perverse sexual practices sooner than admit that others regard them as proud and stuck-up or that they are careless about appointments, and any American male who admitted failure to live up to the national stereotype of 'maleness' of the red-blooded rather than the blue-blooded variety, extreme sociability and distaste for being alone, punctuality, broadmindedness except about 'homosexualists' and Communists, generosity, and support for the Church 'or some other worth-while-cause'—which, incredible as it may seem, is one of the questions asked of him in the name of science—would already be under psychoanalytic treatment.

These views are by no means typical of psychology as a whole, and it is broadly true to say that, although psychologists do not ordinarily deal with the sort of material which concerns the psychoanalyst and are likely to leave the whole subject of personality severely alone, their reaction to Freudian theory has been favourable if not uncritical. One thing however is certain, and that is that few text-books of psychology ignore Freud and many are built around his theories, whereas none have ever been built around Adlerian or Jungian theory, and the other schools are rarely even mentioned. Adler is likely to be mentioned in connexion with the mechanism of compensation and Jung in connexion with the word-association test or the introversion-extraversion dimension of personality, but their theories as such are not recognized as serious contributions to scientific knowledge. The reason for this discimination is clear. It is that Freud alone amongst the founders of analytic schools understood and made thorough use of the scientific method in his investigations. Freud's approach was as logical and his findings as carefully tested as Pavlov's but he was able to deal successfully with phenomena inaccessible to Pavlov; for in spite of denials the fact remains that the foundations of his method—psychic determinism and the relentless logic of free association—are scientific, and are so over a wider area of experience than anything before or since. It is worth while repeating that, so far from implying intuition, Freud's method was to take everything anybody said at any time or place regardless of truth or falsity in terms of external reality to be used as basic data in revealing the dynamics of the personality in precisely the same way that meteorological data might be used to chart the weather map of a geographical area. Since the data are subsequently referred back to fundamental mental processes, it is beside the point to say that they were initially obtained from Austrian middle-class Jews suffering from hysteria (if, in fact, this is true), because even at that time it was clear that they were equally applicable to British working-class Gentiles or Andaman Islanders. It is curious that those who would not be prepared to assert that the physiology of digestion or respiration recognizes national, religious, or class boundaries are prepared to make an exception in the case of the fundamental dynamics of the mind. The differences noted by the cultural schools are variations which do not affect the basic issues, and if we wish to reject Freudian theory we must either reject determinism and the validity of the technique of free association, thereby admitting that there exists an area of experience to which the rules of science do not

apply, or else—and this attitude rests on firmer ground—we may deny
the validity of Freud's interpretation of the data. Freud's work does not
represent a limited theory of the type beloved by experimental scientists
and cannot therefore be compared with the laws of Boyle and Charles, of
Ohm, or of Weber and Fechner, which deal mathematically with the
relationships between a small number of data within a narrow range of
observations; it is a hypothesis covering a wide range of facts with
correspondingly less overall accuracy in matters of detail. In this respect
it is comparable in form to Newton's hypotheses which made an
imaginative leap into space on the basis of a few observations of the
behaviour of falling objects on earth—although fortunately for Newton
nobody was foolish enough to complain that he had not tested out his
hypothesis on the extragalactic nebulae. Newton's and Freud's propositions were inadequate to explain every phenomenon, which is why they
are described as hypotheses, but Freud still awaits his Einstein. The
relative status of Freud in the eyes of the world is significantly shown in
the number of books written by orthodox psychoanalysts or written
about his work by non-psychoanalysts. The number, of course, is legion.
Yet from a reasonably wide acquaintance with the literature of the other
analytic schools it would be difficult to think of even half a dozen significant commentators on Adler in the last twenty years, and although
Jung himself has been a most prolific writer his commentators in
English and German over the same period have been only slightly more
numerous, even if his work has frequently been discussed in articles and
to some extent in books by intellectuals who were not psychologists.
British or American psychiatrists make no mention of Jung in standard
text-books except for the now historical work on schizophrenia contained in his earliest publications long before his break with Freud. In
fact, of all those discussed here only Freud (including Anna Freud and
Melanie Klein) and Jung have any considerable influence in Europe so
far as theory and psychotherapeutic practice is concerned, and the Neo-
Freudians have had as little influence here as Klein in America. Perhaps
the clearest picture of their relative significance, if not necessarily of their
scientific validity, can be obtained from a brief account of the distribution of the schools in Europe and America which as we have seen are the
main centres. Neo-Freudianism in America is centered in New York,
where Horney formed a group known as the Society for the Advancement of Psychoanalysis, which has its own Institute for training.
Sullivan's group began in Washington and Baltimore and is known as
the William Alanson White Foundation, which also has an Institute in
New York with which Fromm has been associated although most of his
work has been in the direction of teaching and writing. Nevertheless by

far the greatest number of analysts in the United States remain more or less orthodox Freudians, as is the important Institute in Chicago under Franz Alexander, and excluding the Neo-Freudians, most of the other schools have a relatively insignificant following. There are small Adlerian and Jungian groups scattered throughout the country,but practically speaking Adlerian psychology as a system is dying out, not so much by rejection as by absorption, so far as medically-trained analysts are concerned. It is, however, still in use by lay workers in education, child guidance, and counselling. The strongest Jungian groups are in England and Switzerland, but by reason of its larger population America possibly possesses a greater total number of Jungian analysts than either of these two countries. Almost alone among non-Freudian groups the Jungians have maintained their position and may even in recent years have improved it, particularly outside the medical and scientific spheres. Jung has come to be regarded by many as a sage or a prophet of our times, particularly by those whose real aim is to discover some sort of religious viewpoint and find Freud too materialistic. A few analysts in both Europe and America still make use of the methods of Rank, Reich, and Stekel, but these schools have never had the slightest appeal to the scientific psychologist.

In considering the various schools discussed here, the following points have to be borne in mind if we wish to avoid the mistake of assessing all by the same standards: (1) all took their origin largely from Freud and frequently begin their exposition with a criticism of the orthodox viewpoint; (2) there is little—indeed surprisingly little—divergence of opinion about actual clinical observations and the main disagreements occur in relation to their immediate interpretation, their relative importance, the framework of reference into which they are fitted, and their significance for psychotherapy; (3) they do not in all cases cover the same group of phenomena (e.g. Jung, Rank, and Freud discuss cultural phenomena at length, Adler and Horney concentrate on the individual ego); (4) not all set out to present a scientifically coherent account of personality but rather those aspects of personality relevant to a method and theory of psychotherapy as practised by the school; this in turn is not unrelated to such factors as the temperament of the founder, the type of patients treated, and the therapeutic limits he has set himself. Clearly, when a theory is of this nature it would be futile to criticize it in terms of scientific personality theory when it can only be counted 'wrong' if it fails therapeutically or if it bases itself on assumptions which the psychologist has good reason for believing to be false. For the most part psychologists have recognized this significant distinction. They have taken Freud's theories on his own estimate of them as serious

contributions to scientific psychology, and tney have largely ignored
Jung, because, whatever Jung's intentions, his theories are not expressed
scientifically nor are they subject to scientific proof or disproof. This is
not a value judgement and it is not in the least inconsistent with the
conviction held by many people that Jung is a great and profound
thinker; it is merely an admission that his work can no more be
scientifically assessed than that of Kierkegaard or Sartre, Nietzsche or
Pascal. So far as the other schools are concerned, the psychologist
concerned with personality theory has been prepared to accept, or at any
rate to take note of the criticisms of Freudian theory by the Neo-
Freudians; he is interested in Jung's theory of personality types (which
can theoretically be tested), in Adler's account of certain ego defence
mechanisms, and perhaps in Suttie's or Klein's accounts of the origins of
love and hate in early life, because unlike the psychoanalyst he is not
committed to an almost total acceptance of Freudian orthodoxy. Generally he is prepared to take psychoanalytic theory as a useful frame of
reference, to be modified or corrected on scientific grounds, because there
actually exists a Freudian *normal* psychology, social psychology, and
anthropology represented today by such authorities as Anna Freud,
Melanie Klein, Roheim, and Kardiner. Again, this is not a value
judgement and interest in their works is not inconsistent with believing
that the views expressed are largely mistaken, but it is a fact that no child
psychologist today ignores the theories of Freud and Klein and no
anthropologist ignores Roheim or Kardiner however much he may
disagree with them. Yet although there exist Neo-Freudian schools in
America described as Horneyian, Frommian, and Sullivanian, it is not
easy to see wherein their specificity lies or on the basis of what new and
objective clinical data their divergence from Freud or from each other
rests. No systematic account amounting to a new theory has been
presented by any of the three, and one is left with the general impression
that Fromm is a man of broad if not particularly original learning who
disagrees with Freud in numerous respects and, reasonably enough,
attempts to bring his thought into closer alignment with modern views;
that Horney disagrees with Freud on similar grounds and produces an
Adlerian-type theory which does not deny the unconscious but largely
ignores it in favour of an analysis of the patient's interpersonal relationships; that Sullivan says little in criticism of Freud, who, in any case, was
not a fundamental influence—or at any rate *the* fundamental one—in
the development of his psychology, but that he too is mainly concerned
with distortions of personal relationships, judgements, and behaviour
as revealed in the transference situation. What we do not know is what
parts of Freudian theory Fromm *does* accept since, had we not been

informed to the contrary, we should have thought that he was an ordinary Freudian who saw that Freud's cultural outlook was outdated or at least not universally applicable. Nor do we know very much about Horney outside the consulting-room except what most people would be prepared to accept as an interesting and illuminating account of what goes on in interpersonal relationships at a fairly superficial level, described as it might be by a sensitive behaviourist observing the reactions of individuals without any sort of analysis whatever. Of other forms of behaviour she tells us nothing. Sullivan is even more puzzling because, while he apparently feels dissatisfied with Freudian mechanistic modes of description, his own in terms of 'dynamisms' is expressed in an excruciatingly tortuous language, which is the more irritating in that it complicates rather than simplifies and even gives the impression that the complexity is a deliberate 'show-off'. At one moment he is expressing himself with all the directness of a quaintish old-timer leaning over the bar of a saloon—no nonsense about 'libido', it must be 'lusts', and *they* come into action as everybody knows at puberty not with earlier oral or anal stages—the next moment he is inventing neologisms with all the aplomb of a Mid-West vendor of patent medicines whose classical education began and ended with a year's study of dispensing to enable him to write and read prescriptions. In this respect he goes one better than other American scientific text-books which tend to be either out-and-out 'folksy' or so full of detail and novel words and phrases as to be downright incomprehensible (in fact, the works of one eminent sociologist have been hailed with respect here largely because, although it would be difficult to find many who understand even a single page, the general feeling has been that anyone who takes so much trouble to invent a new language must have something to say). Sullivan uses both methods, from the archaic 'middling example' and the wrong use of ordinarily used words such as 'euphoria' to the half-pompous, half-popular definition of dynamisms as 'relatively enduring configurations of energy which manifest themselves in characterizable processes in interpersonal relations' and are not 'some fanciful substantial engines, regional organizations, or peculiar more or less physiological apparatus about which our present knowledge is nil'. The realization that Sullivan's style is peculiar is not a purely personal one; it is commented upon by many critics, and another American, Ruth Munroe, finds in it 'the precarious summit of a brilliant display of fireworks', which, however, has not been the general impression it has made on others.

What is obvious about these three schools is that they are socially rather than biologically oriented, that they overtly or by implication criticize Freud's metapsychology and social psychology, and that Horney and Sullivan are almost entirely concerned with clinical problems, Fromm with sociological ones. It is, in fact, impossible on the basis of his major works to discover where Fromm's analytic followers obtain their specifically Frommian clinical data, since even in earlier papers published in German his main concern seems to have been with moral and social issues of the kind already described rather than with patients. A characteristic feature is their emphasis on the ego and its relationships in a social background, while the unconscious is proportionately disregarded save as a means of explaining how distortions of relationships and reality sense arose in early experiences. Analysis of the transference as a sample interpersonal situation is a logical consequence of this attitude. It is noteworthy, too, that there is less emphasis on biological factors and that the personality is regarded—particularly by Sullivan— as the resultant of social relationships, although Fromm pays some attention to temperament and Horney rather vaguely speaks of a 'real' self in spite of the fact that on any interpersonal theory of personality the 'neurotic' self must have started to develop from the earliest days. From a practical point of view the main failing of these schools is their lack of system and detail, in which they stand in direct contrast to Freud's unremitting attention to both or even to Adler's logic, which simply ignored aspects of behaviour which did not fit the pattern or were regarded by him as irrelevant. Those who like clear-cut logical statements are likely to feel irritated when Sullivan, having presented a perfectly reasonable if limited theory, proceeds to throw in other concepts which are outside the mainstream of his argument—for example, the vaguely-defined 'power dynamism', and his appeal to 'empathy' which apparently lacks any analysable sensory foundations and has been found unnecessary by every other school save that of Jung. The Neo-Freudians all too frequently attack an orthodoxy which no longer exists, and so far as analytic procedure is concerned we are never told wherein their attitude to the ego differs from that of Anna Freud, save that she thinks in terms of analysis of the defence mechanisms and resistances which keep repressed unconscious attitudes of sexualized hostility and distort personal relationships in the process. Most European analysts, however, would agree with Miss Freud that defence mechanisms or parataxic distortions cannot be dealt with without investigation of the unconscious roots. Similarly, although Sullivan's concept of parataxic distortion possibly gives a clearer picture of a process which *distorts* contemporary relationships as a result of unsatisfactory early ones, it is fully comprehended in Sigmund Freud's concept of projection, which in its wider connotation is used to explain the same observations; the sole difference is that Freud is concerned about causes, Sullivan about results.

The divergences of opinion between all the schools represented here are perhaps more apparent than real because they are based on clinical material accepted by all. In the early days Freud did not disagree with Rank's concept of the birth trauma but with its application in the form of separation anxiety as an explanation of psychic phenomena in general; he did not disagree with Adler's theory as applied to ego psychology but with its over-enthusiastic use outside this sphere; he did not disagree with Jung's group unconscious or interest in mythology but appears to have become rather impatient when Jung's concern with these subjects seemed to interfere with the more practical issues of therapy and with his preparation for assuming the role of Joshua to Freud's Moses within the psychoanalytic movement. In the case of Ferenczi, Freud was furious as one might expect him to be over Ferenczi's convictions that the analyst should show a human and loving attitude towards the patient in place of the orthodox impersonal and mirror-like one, and Stekel's active therapy had a familiar reception. But in all these cases the initial clash was one between personalities rather than any direct clash of ideas. We have seen that a theory of psychotherapy must to some extent reflect the temperament of the person who devises it, the type of patient he most frequently sees, and the more material issues such as time and money. Stekel, Rank, and Ferenzci were in part trying to solve the ever-pressing problem of how to shorten the course of analysis without reducing its effectiveness, Stekel by direct attack on the neurotic system, Ferenzci by cooperation and sympathy, and Rank by setting a time limit from the start. The temperamental factor which influences the individual's approach to reality particularly impressed Jung, who has said that his theory of types originated from his observations of the reactions of Freud, Adler, and himself in the days of the early dissensions, and he has even asserted that some patients are best treated along Freudian lines, some along Adlerian lines, and others by his own method. No doubt the fact that Jung's patients have been predominantly schizophrenics whose condition in former times was likely to prove static for long periods, or older people whose mental dynamics are likely to be set, has some connexion with the generally static impression conveyed by the Jungian system, which Glover does not even regard as a dynamic psychology but rather as a derivative of the old faculty school on which a mystical philosophy has been superimposed. From personal observation it would appear that even those who describe themselves as Jungians or Adlerians make very considerable use of Freudian concepts when it suits their convenience. Jung shares with Rank the disconcerting attitude towards scientific truth and reality noted earlier; for example, a Jungian analyst will refer to witches or other entities ordinarily regarded as supernatural or pure superstition, and it is not always easy to discover just what is meant when they are said to be 'real'. Is a 'witch' 'real' (a) in the straightforward medieval sense when both the individual claiming the title and the rest of society accepted it, (b) as a member of some modern sects who claim to practice witchcraft but are not believed by society in general to be other than foolish exhibitionists, (c) in the sense of a patient who claims the title but in fact is deluded and requires psychiatric treatment? Since the first category no longer exists in civilized communities, the second is no concern of the psychiatrist, and the third, one might suppose, would be better explained in other and simpler terms and better treated than by agreeing with the patient's own diagnosis, it would appear to be confusing the issue to use the word witch to describe her or him (since witches, it seems, are of both sexes) save in a highly metaphorical sense. This would still be true if, as a Jungian would probably say, the concept refers to an archetype which is by definition real; for as Roheim has pointed out similarities in thought and belief are quite adequately explained in terms of shared experience and tradition, and to describe an idea as real is misleading even to a Platonist outside his study. Rank's contribution to this confusion—and his distinction, shared with Sullivan, of being the other worst writer in the analytic field—is revealed in the following quotation from the last page of *Will Therapy, Truth and Reality:* 'Questions which originate from the division of will into guilt consciousness and self-consciousness cannot be answered through any psychological or philosophical theory for the answer is the more disillusioning the more correct it is. For happiness can only be found in reality, not in truth, and redemption never in reality and from reality, but only in itself and from itself.'

Other differences between the schools arise because of differing ways of describing the same observations or from semantic confusions. The former is a problem common to all psychologists and arises in part from the fact that the more complex forms of behaviour can be described either from a determinist and behaviourist point of view, which emphasizes drives or conditioned reflexes, or from a hormic and striving point of view, which emphasizes aims, goals, and purpose. From the one standpoint the organism is seen as being pushed from behind, from the other as being drawn from in front, and whether or not this leads to any significant difference in ultimate conclusions, it obviously leads to considerable differences in the way the situation is described. The semantic problem in psychology is that the psychologist has inevitably to make use of many words in everyday use which have widely divergent meanings and frequently emotional overtones which are liable to be ignored. Thus all that the general public knew of Freud in the early years was that he was the man who said that everything was sex—a statement which at that time was not entirely untrue but which disregarded Freud's special use of the word and seriously underestimated the emotional overtones the word held (guilt, 'rudeness', etc.) for the ordinary man. Now the most obvious difference between Adler's and Freud's theories is that the former describes in terms of goals and sees neurosis in terms of fictive goals, whilst the latter describes in terms of *Triebe* or drives seeking satisfactions which, when blocked, seek substitute satisfactions or produce neurotic symptoms. A swimmer returning to the beach who makes use of a large wave to be swept in quickly and without exertion behaves in a way which can be described scientifically by the laws of physics and hydrodynamics and psychologically in terms of psychic structure and dynamics; but Adler admitted the concept of purpose regarded with suspicion by scientists and saw the swimmer making use of external circumstances to attain a deliberately-sought end. The neurotic is distinguished from the normal person in seeking unrealistic goals which, however, are not unconscious in the Freudian sense but disregarded as reflecting little credit on himself (cf. Sullivan's 'selective inattention' and Stekel's 'life-lie'). The facts are not at issue, the interpretations are, and there is no means available to science save the criteria already mentioned of proving one interpretation right and the other wrong. Nor are Adler and the more superficial analytic schools necessarily contradicting the massive body of Freudian data relating to early experiences; what in effect they are doing is declaring them unnecessary to the psycho-therapist. Because Freud does not think in terms of conscious or subconscious purpose he attaches relatively little significance to secondary gains, regarding them simply as superficial adjustments the patient makes on the basis of his neurosis to the problems set by his environment; because Adler does, the concept of secondary gains is broadened and becomes the major issue in treatment. Both are right within their own limits because as every psychiatrist knows the more superficial neuroses are 'cured', in the sense that their symptoms disappear, either when their obvious purpose is pointed out to the patient or when the environment is so altered that it is no longer possible to gain advantage from them. This of course is not a cure from the Freudian standpoint nor indeed from that of the psychiatrist, who would agree that a normal person does not resort under stress to hysterical symptoms or become anxious in the face of what are not generally regarded as anxiety-producing situations, but it is a social cure; and he is apt to become impatient with the perfectionism of the psychoanalyst when it is suggested that, for a patient who has lived in what his associates and himself regard as 'normal' health for twenty or thirty years before developing overt symptoms, the only cure is a complete Freudian analysis. It is impossible to doubt that of the soldiers one saw during the war with neuroses a very large number would not have broken down had it not been for what, after all, were not ordinary circumstances. Were they neurotic before? Were they prone to wet the bed at a late stage of childhood, recognized as mummy's boys, afraid of enclosed spaces, worried about exams or teacher, shy with girls? Or were they rather bombastic and boastful, liable to get drunk more often than is thought usual, given to telling tall stories, or getting in trouble with the law? Perhaps they were, and so perhaps in many of these respects were the psychiatrists who treated them or the commanding officers who wanted to have them court-martialled. But whereas we laboriously investigated the past of our patients we were not so quick to investigate our own or that of the men who did not develop an overt neurosis as a basis for comparison. Nor did we investigate the characters of that deservedly honoured group which superficial inspection would suggest to contain a very high percentage of psychopaths and neurotics—the men who won decorations for bravery or for undertaking dangerous exploits, or the not inconsiderable number of men who positively enjoyed war. Neurosis is in part socially defined, so neurotic character traits which prove socially useful are not often regarded as abnormalities and even the more irritating ones such as dependency, fussiness, or mild hypochondria are not looked on as anything more than ordinary idiosyncrasies. It is not unreasonable for the individual who has broken down in later life or after being exposed to stress of a more or less severe nature to say in effect: 'Take away my symptoms and leave my traits alone, because if I was not always happy or always as competent as I might have been I nevertheless got on quite well; other people thought me normal and I thought so too.' The mild chronic neurotic often does not think of himself as such and in the course of time develops a regime suited to his problems; he does not worry because he is claustrophobic in the underground, he takes the bus instead; he does not worry about his occasional attacks of functional dyspepsia, he takes a dose of baking soda and forgets about it; his periods of depression or anxiety are interpreted as signs of being run-down, and he takes a pharmacologically inert 'nerve tonic' to 'build himself up', as of course it frequently does. If he is asked about his symptoms, he will expatiate about them at length, because after all he has 'studied himself', but if he is told of their psychological significance he will become really worried, and if psychoanalysis is suggested he will think his adviser unreasonable—and many psychiatrists would agree with him. As a rule the psychiatrist does not see this type of patient, although it is far commoner than the more florid case he may come to regard as typical; but the family doctor does and, thinking along Adlerian lines without necessarily having heard of Adler's name, will ask himself: 'What's old Jones's problem now? The factory? No, everything seems all right there. His home? Well, it has been quite happy lately and there has never been any serious difficulty anyhow—except . . . of course, this is the beginning of the fortnight when his mother-in-law comes for her yearly visit—he had the same symptoms this time last year!' So Jones is given a nerve tonic in which he has great faith, although the doctor almost blushes to sign a prescription for it, and is advised to 'get out a bit more for a couple of weeks or so', which is the official authorization for being out more often than not during the critical period. This is successful psycho-therapy for this case and it would be unsuccessful or at the least unhelpful to attempt to bring Jones's guilt-laden incestuous longings for his mother-in-law and his earlier incestuous longings for his own mother as a child into consciousness, even if they existed. The vast majority of people in the world are not rootless intellectuals free to range about in the realm of ideas at will and tied to no particular social norms; they are ordinary individuals living in communities with very strict social and religious codes of behaviour which are highly resistant to novel ideas. Their churches teach that incestuous and other forbidden desires are a grave sin, and their laws that, no matter what a man may feel or think, there are certain things he must not do, and to cause anyone to think otherwise will result in maladaptation to his community whatever it may do to his mind. Psychoanalytic theories are the most useful device for understanding the human personality we possess, and so far as detail is concerned they are really the only one; psychoanalysis is a valuable method of treating the type of case so carefully specified by Freud himself, the fairly severe and persistent neurosis which proves disabling to a youngish individual of high intelligence and otherwise strong character—in fact, a rather small proportion of all neuroses; the psychoanalytic approach is a helpful one in understanding the dynamics of social movements and planning social schemes and policies, provided the actual planning is not left to those whose proper concern is treating the abnormal rather than advising the normal. Repression and the irrational lie at the very foundations of society and the wise policy may sometimes be to play along with them, lightening the burden they may cause here, supporting their edicts there, because no psychologist or psychoanalyst, much less psychiatrist, can give a better reason for *not* stealing, *not* killing, *not* committing incest (all antisocial acts in any society) than the ingrained belief that in the beginning it was said, 'Thou shalt not'. It may be possible to explain in psychological terminology why this was said, but such an explanation is unlikely to convince simple people or children or have the same prohibitive power. Those who deal with the mentally sick are not always realistic in their appraisal of social realities; both by reason of their work itself and sometimes by reason of that law of compensation which, as Adler showed, attracts people to employments which have a morbid personal interest, their views may be narrow and emotionally biased. The employer may be very sorry to hear that his factory manager suffers from an anxiety neurosis, but what he really wants to know is why it should be that this man's symptoms demand rest at home specifically at times when important problems are cropping up, and why he remained at work without absence for nearly a whole year when a rumour was going about that the new trainee might fill his place—the rumor was incorrect but it nevertheless seemed to have an effect on what the psychiatrist had assured the employer was 'an illness, just like other illnesses'. The magistrate or judge may understand perfectly when he is told by a psychiatrist that the men arrested for importuning have always been practising homsexuals, that the respectable lady found stealing pencils was symbolically stealing love (or even something more concrete if the psychiatrist has strong Freudian leanings), that the man who attacked a policeman was in effect attacking the drunken father who beat his mother each Saturday evening, but he is unlikely to see what all this has to do with breaking the law, because in the eyes of most people explaining is not the same as condoning, and the fact that one has a desire for a thousand pounds is not ordinarily regarded as a reason for stealing it no matter how easy it would be to do so. In cases such as these it is sometimes the psychiatrist or the psychoanalyst who is wrong, because he does not realize that one cannot apply conclusions derived from a quasi-scientific discipline concerned only with describing objectively, explaining objectively, and treating scientifically *without reference to personal responsibility or guilt or appeal to 'will-power'* to a totally different sphere which, except in unusual individual cases, accepts these concepts as forming the very foundations of human society. Of course he would be entirely within his rights and perhaps logically justified if he explained that he could conceive of a society where employers thought not in terms of laziness or incompetence but in practical ones of suitability or unsuitability for a particular job; where judges thought, not in terms of crime and punishment, but of maladaptation to social demands and its treatment; but he does not explain whether or not this is his position and therefore necessarily limits himself to a kind of double-talk which makes the worst of both worlds. Any moderately educated person without a specialist axe to grind can see for himself that mental illness is not 'just like other

depression', impossible for a wealthy embezzler to be worried about the prospect of appearing in court without the authorities being informed that he is suffering from 'severe nervous shock', and difficult for the pacifist called up for military service to avoid being described as an 'inadequate psychopath'. But the psychiatrist's real position is that he judges nobody, because it is not his business to attach medical tags where they do not properly belong and by so doing decrease the area within which people are to be regarded as fully responsible for their behaviour. It is equally dangerous, one might think, that so many people have been led to believe that the ordinary emotions of worry, anxiety, depression, boredom, and tiredness in normal degree or in situations to which they would appear, a natural response, should require, not that problems should be actively dealt with or some discomfort tolerated, but some form of medical treatment, with the result that a large proportion of the population is more or less constantly under the influence of stimulating or·sedative drugs. Freud devised a means of diagnosing man's troubles, not of suppressing them, and the emotions we are so desirous of suppressing are the mental equivalents of body symptoms which may give warning that all is not well. Obviously there is a gap somewhere between the important knowledge of man and society we already possess and the ignorant and half-baked way in which we apply it. But the way of dealing with this situation is not that we should wait until one-half of the world's population, looking back sadly to the good old days when their ancestors were worried about where the next meal would come from, sits in marvellously-equipped clinics waiting for the other half to come and treat it, but rather that we should set about wondering what is wrong with our outlook and what is wrong with our way of life that we should have need of so much psychiatry and often-misapplied psychology. It took the best part of forty years for industrial psychologists to make the staggering discovery that the best way to get people to do a good day's work is not some special technique of applied science but simply to treat them as responsible individuals whose group life at their job is an important aspect of their life as a whole. We spend heaven knows how much on treating delinquency as an individual problem when research has shown that, as common sense would suggest, it is frequently a function of the group which has to be treated *as* a group rather than a function of the individual requiring individual therapy. Psychologists conspire to produce tests for the selection of officers in the services or managers in industry, and, while nobody who knew the amount of scientific forethought lavished upon them would wish to deny that they test *something,* many of us are still wondering what that something is; for there is not much use in testing people to find out if

illnesses', that in fact with the exception of cases which are in effec
organic diseases with psychic complications it is not an illness at all bu
a form of social maladjustment; he can see that serious forms of madnes
or insanity are frightening to all of us (regardless of whether or not the
can be cured or whether they are more scientifically or considerate l
described as psychoses) because they change the personality and the suf
ferer becomes a different person in a way that does not happen if, fo
instance, he loses both legs. Intelligent people in positions of authority
can observe that aspect of a neurosis which leads the individual to evade
responsibilities and behave in a way which his associates may interpre
as malingering, and they may note too the equally significant fact that
when evasion is not permitted the individual's condition may even in
some cases improve; the apparent failure of some psychiatrists to note
the same facts or to draw logical conclusions from them is likely to result
in their being regarded as simpletons. Those connected with the law are
often well aware when the accused pleads loss of memory that what
people forget is what it suits them to forget and that there are degrees of
loss of memory right up to that experienced by the ordinary man, but in
court the psychiatrist frequently speaks of it as if it were a brain tumour,
something that is just there, a fixed and circumscribed disease rather
than a self-protective mechanism. Having taken up a rather foolish
position, he is asked foolish questions—does the accused recall the name
of his school, does he remember how to tie his bootlaces, if he does not
know he is married why did he after the crime go to collect his family
allowance—which are all based on the assumption that a large block of
'memory' has been destroyed by a pathological condition which has
little to do with the person himself. The psychiatrist does not always
admit that there are no means available to him which are not equally
available to the ordinary man by which he can tell whether the loss of
memory is genuine and is quite likely to suffer the indignity of finding
himself confronted by one of his colleagues who will swear precisely the
opposite of all that he has given in evidence. These examples are not
given in order to discredit the psychiatrist who, according to his own
lights, is behaving quite correctly and arguing perfectly rationally, but
to show once more the dangers of arguing from a discipline which
eschews moral judgements and responsibility to circumstances where
they are assumed to be valid. In such circumstances his refusal to
consider them may be accepted as a value judgement in itself, as indeed it
sometimes is when the official nomenclature is strained to br. aking-
point in order to bring into the category of sick those who are simply sad,
worried, or bad. In some circles it is almost impossible to mourn the loss
of a loved one without being labelled as suffering from 'reactive

they will make good officers or managers unless we know what it is that makes the good ones good. Of this we may be quite sure: that they would exclude from the service, let alone a commission, every single military or naval leader of note in the whole of British history, not only such noted eccentrics as Lawrence and Wingate but also Nelson, Marlborough, Wolfe, and Montgomery, that they would exclude from industry every important leader from Ford, Hearst, and Morgan right up to the present day. Psychoanalysts and psychologists are at one in supposing that it is a good thing to be normal, in spite of the fact that it is almost as difficult to discover a 'normal' genius as it is to discover a 'Nordic' blonde one, that it is a good thing to be happy and contented, although probably the largest number of happy and contented people are either in mental hospitals or in institutions for the mentally defective—Dr Jones indeed expresses regret that Oscar Wilde, Dr Johnson, Schopenhauer, and Swift were unable to resort to medical treatment for their mental conditions. They would, he says, have had happier lives had they done so. But neither in the history of psychoanalysis nor today is there any evidence whatever to suggest that psychoanalysts are happier, more normal, or more free from prejudice than other men and quite a lot of evidence that might suggest the contrary—which would be no great matter were it not for their own claims. The sort of questions one has asked psychiatric patients and the conclusions one has drawn from the answers are almost embarrassing to recollect; for what useful conclusions is one to draw from the knowledge that X did not do well at school where he was lazy and indifferent, that he was inhibited about sex, that he was shy and ordinarily solitary, that his father was an alcoholic and he is still over-attached to his mother on whom he continually sponges, that he has never settled down to a steady job although now over thirty? That X is an inadequate psychopath, a case of schizophrenia simplex, or that in less than ten years his name, George Bernard Shaw, will be world-famous? Yet had even one of these facts been known to a psychological tester or a psychiatrist, very considerable significance would have been attached to it and subsequent revelations—save the last—would have been seen in the light of the earlier ones. Freudians are perhaps less likely than non-Freudian psychiatrists to attach weight to facts taken in isolation, but this has to be counterbalanced by their extraordinary lack of any sense of reality shown, for example, in a document intended for official consumption where it is stated that unrest in the coal-fields must have some connexion with the miner's unconscious conflicts aroused by the fact that he has to use his phallic pick on 'mother earth', thus committing symbolic incest! As in the case of an earlier example, the question is not whether this astonishing statement is true or false as a statement, but

whether anyone could seriously believe it to have the slightest relevance
in the circumstances and how anyone could expect it to be accepted by
management. On the other hand it is not necessarily more peculiar than
the picture of the 'normal' Britisher arising from the conspiracy between
psychologists and psychiatrists and deducible from the stock questions
of their clinical examinations and personality tests. This paragon, we
are led to suppose, is hale in body and limb and never gave his parents a
moment's anxiety during childhood years; he loved them both equally
(but not excessively) and was liked (but not too much) by both brothers
and sisters. His ability to get on with people was shown at school, where
he was a conscientious if not brilliant scholar, and on the playing field,
where his prowess on the football—i.e. Rugby football—field and at
cricket led to his captaincy of both First Fifteen and First Eleven in his
final year; he was *never* interested in politics nor, although a regular
attender at church, was he 'morbid' about religion. Taking a good First
in Modern History at Oxford, he has fulfilled his early promise both in
military and civil life, is popular amongst his many friends and full of
sympathy for the underdog in a non-political way, since as a moderate
member of the Conservative Party he naturally remains politically
unbiased. This account, if exaggerated, is not wholly a parody, because
it is undoubtedly the case that definite views on political or religious
subjects or unconventional views about anything, strong emotions
generally, anything suggesting conflict in early life or later, a tendency
to shyness or unsociability, excessive studiousness, and any interest at all
in sex or 'culture' incur the suspicions of both the clinician and the
psychological tester in Britain and America, although in America the
suspicion of studiousness or culture is perhaps greater. Since this
conception of normality is consciously or unconsciously present in the
minds of those who wish to get on, many of the questions in personality
tests answer themselves, so that 'do you read many books?' does not mean
what it says but, according to one's outlook, either 'are you one of the
ignorant and semiliterate masses who never opens a book?' or 'are you
one of those unsociable so-and-sos who never takes his nose from a book
and thinks he is an intellectual?' The trouble is not that psychologists
and psychiatrists in practice make value judgments, but that they are not
aware they are doing so. Psychoanalysts again are much less prone to
this danger, but this is at least partly due to the fact that their opinion in
matters involving such issues is less frequently sought, and they cannot
be absolved from spreading by implication a view of man's nature which
to the intelligent outsider seems to infer that all problems are individual
problems which are not only individual but infantile. Hence battle
neuroses are caused, and industrial unrest is initiated, by the Oedipus

complex and have really little to do with war or fear of unemployment, and the world of experience is not simply liable to emotional distortion but is actually a completely individual creation. All these eccentricities arise from the 'tunnel vision' which so many specialists sooner or later seem to develop, by becoming so intent on their special fraction of a special subject that they cannot see the obvious or their own observations in proper perspective in a wider context—no doubt much of the popular success of writers such as Fromm, Horney, and Riesman, or, to a lesser extent, Jung, arises from the fact that successfully or otherwise they try to avoid this danger. It is true that orthodox Freudians have also written on the wider implications of Freudian theory, but to the lay mind their contributions are more likely to cloud than to clarify the issue; analytic theory can hardly probe deeper into the past than Klein has done and is unlikely to go beyond Jung in search of man's superstructure of myths and archetypes; so unless we are to be restricted to the mere filling-in of details, any future advance must be in the direction of the analysis of social and cultural phenomena and its application in the light of modern knowledge from related fields. The general acceptability of a scientific theory is not wholly dependent upon its validity as science, because history shows that its relevance to the contemporary situation and the degree to which it conforms to the contemporary approach are equally important. In a world which increasingly sees all human problems as social problems, psychoanalysis as a method of treatment may well fall into desuetude, not because it does not work, but simply because it is inapplicable to the problems of the day. Even now, the knowledge that thousands of citizens of New York or London are being analysed by hundreds of psychoanalysts begins to seem more incongruous than sad, as we are likely to argue that lying individually on a thousand individual couches talking in the presence of a thousand individual analysts seems a peculiar method of attacking a social problem. This is not a criticism of psychoanalytic theory, which is likely to become increasingly recognized as the greatest single advance in our understanding of the human personality so far conceived, but it is an expression of doubt whether under changing conditions it will continue to be important in its original form as a therapy. It was Freud, after all, who showed that neurosis is not an illness in the classical sense but a form of social maladaptation, that it is not either present or absent in a given individual but present in varying degrees, and that psychoanalysis as a treatment is applicable to a relatively small proportion of the population; but his followers have failed to draw the logical conclusions that, if this is so, it must be dealt with socially on the basis of a psychoanalytic understanding of personality and the nature of society, and that on the same basis it must be treated in individual patients when this is necessary by methods which are brief and do not strive for perfectionist goals. There is no logical contradiction involved in seeing that, although every neurosis has deep-seated roots, its immediate causes are often superficial and environmental, and when these are dealt with the symptoms disappear. The very real danger today is that neuroses may cease to be dealt with by psychological methods based on understanding at all, and that with new pharmacological and medical or surgical methods we shall be 'cured' by being made insensible to conflicts rather than facing up to them and trying to understand what is wrong with our way of life. Instead of realizing that there are circumstances which justify attitudes of guilt, remorse, shame, anxiety, or injustice, we shall treat them as inconvenient 'symptoms' to be dispelled by a tranquilizer or thymoleptic drug. Freud's work will make an even greater impact in the future when it is removed from the category of an expensive and prolonged method of treatment for a minute portion of the population carried out by practitioners who often have very little interest outside their own specialty and sometimes adopt a paranoid and contemptuous attitude towards the rest of the world. It is a scientific anomaly that it should be possible for a psychoanalyst to have his own private social psychology which never comes into contact with ordinary social theory because those to whom the truth has already been revealed have no need of such trivialities. Psychoanalysis has so much to offer that it is absurd that it should be restricted in this way, and it is to the credit of the Americans, whether we agree with their conclusions or not, that they should have been the first to make the attempt to break down the barriers. For the explanation of the irrational is a special task of the twentieth century.

24

Conclusions*

David Shakow
David Rapaport

Freud, after a period of intensive work in various fields of medicine and physiology, turned his attention to problems more directly related to the understanding of human nature. He saw psychological phenomena differently from both his predecessors and contemporaries. When he reported what he saw, he was generally greeted with skepticism. Thereafter, through his long, active, and markedly productive life he developed his ideas in isolation, assisted only by a group who identified strongly with him. In such circumstances, how did his vast influence on the psychology of which he had never been a part come about?

Using a broad definition of influence as a guide in our attempt to answer this question, we found that ideas which demonstrably originated in the Freudian body of theory and observation have indeed permeated virtually the whole range of psychology. In fact, we have seen that with the cumulative growth of this influence, Freud has become the most prominent name in the history of psychology. Nevertheless, this growth in influence has not, at least so far as psychology is concerned, been continuous: it has had its ebbs and flows, its enhancements and abatements, its leaps and halts.

A separation existed between psychoanalysis and psychology in spite of their common heritage from the Helmholtz tradition—a

*Reprinted from *The Influence of Freud on American Psychology*, by David Shakow and David Rapaport, by permission of International Universities Press, Inc. Copyright © 1964 by International Universities Press, Inc.

tradition which permeated the biological and physiological sciences when Freud started his work. It would seem that this gulf actually arose out of the different way in which each viewed its commitment to the Helmholtz program. Psychology did not recognize Freud's serious commitment to the "forces equal in dignity" part of the Helmholtz school oath as parallel to their own concern with the first part of this oath, the part which called for a "reduction to physical-chemical forces." Its own early focus on the "rigor" demanded by the latter led psychology to skip almost entirely the naturalistic stage usual in the development of a science and to identify itself with the "exact" of a hypothetical Science, rather than with the "meaningful" that psychoanalysis had chosen. Since psychology had not come to terms with defining the proper place and time for exact measurement and quantification, there arose confusion in the use and meaning of the terms "good" and "bad" science—"bad" science being taken to be that which characterized psychoanalysis. The "naturalistic" method which fitted psychoanalysis so well was derogated as "unscientific."

Despite superficial indications to the contrary, Freud, in his broad philosophic orientation, appears to have gone back to the spirit of the Enlightenment with its integration of intellect and affect, rather than adhering to either the Romantic Period's marked overemphasis on affect or to the later nineteenth century's heavy emphasis on intellect alone. It was inevitable that some vestigal aspects of the Romantic Period in which he grew up remained. However, these aspects were not intrinsic. It is only those persons identified with that movement, and those who are the strongest and most rigid exponents of the narrower Helmholtz view, who emphasize the Romantic trend in Freud. In contrast to the Romantic approach, Freud's was introspective rather than intuitive, deterministic rather than indeterministic, based on observation rather than on speculation, empirical rather than deductive. Although his approach substituted the consulting room for the laboratory, his data came from the *analyst's* chair rather than from the *arm*chair.

Pressures from the twentieth century *Zeitgeist*, both the "direct" pressures of the views expressed by psychoanalysts in their writings, and the "indirect" pressures of students, colleagues in other fields, and the popular and semipopular literature on psychoanalysis, forced psychologists to establish contact with psychoanalysis. Their initial responses ranged from complete rejection to complete acceptance, and at practically all levels were accompanied by conflict and hesitancy. Psychologists' reactions to Freud certainly in part were based on weaknesses in psychoanalysis: the lack of theoretical systematization, the poor translations of Freud's works, the inadequacy of the secondary sources, and the tone of presentation of psychoanalysis by Freudian students. But psychology had its own weaknesses, many of which grew out of its self-consciousness as a young discipline attempting to take its place among the established sciences. Academic psychology, having patterned itself after these sciences, had turned prematurely to rigorous experiment, and in the process had artificially restricted its content.

Nonetheless, our general discussion and our closer examination of the special areas of the unconscious and motivation revealed considerable evidence of accumulating Freudian influence. In this we professed to see a pattern. That Freud introduced important new areas and a new view of man to psychology has been almost universally accepted. In indirect, and at times even devious, ways, psychology has become pervaded by Freud's ideas of the role of the unconscious and its manifestations, of motivation (particularly its goal-directedness), his idea of the genetic approach, and his principle of psychological determinism. It has, however, most frequently been his conceptions, rather than his concepts and theories, that have received attention. His concepts have usually been modified, often into "common-sense" versions, and too often without awareness that a modification had been made.

Freud's methods—those developed in the process of working out his theories—have been rejected by psychologists. For a long time psychology had few alternative methods available for testing his concepts. Consequently, acceptance of Freud's conceptions has been essentially based on a sort of "psychologist-as-clinician" knowledge, rather than on the rigorous criteria prevalent in experimental psychology.

While Freud's influence on psychology has become increasingly great, it has not been accompanied by proportionate conversance; acceptance of his conception of man has been accompanied by relatively less acceptance of the means by which it was derived, its concepts, or its complexities. In sum, Freud has had great impact, but not an influence that has been accompanied by true understanding.

It was for these reasons, as well as those we presented in the comparison of Darwin and Freud with which we opened our essay, that we were compelled to conclude that Freud had a more difficult time in being accepted. Nevertheless, in the view of some, Freud has still left us with "The most important body of thought committed to paper in the twentieth century" (Rieff, 1959, p. x). This view appears to be valid if we have reference to the life sciences. It has even been suggested that the twentieth century may go down in history as the "Freudian Century" (Nelson, 1957, p. 9). It would perhaps be more nearly correct if only the first half of the century were so characterized. We must not forget the cataclysmic importance achieved by nuclear physics in the latter half of the century.

In which areas of psychology has Freud's influence been greatest? If we were to use the most convenient categorical system at hand, the one recently adopted by *Psychological Abstracts*, we might list the following fields of psychology as most markedly affected: abnormal, personality, developmental, industrial and social, and psychotherapy. Some areas of experimental psychology (motivation, emotion, memory, and imagination) have also been substantially affected, and others (learning, thinking, and perception) have obviously been at least "touched." For a more graphic representation of these evaluations, we might apply the rating system Murphy used in his presentation to the Division of Clinical Psychology, on the occasion of the Freud Centennial in 1956 (Murphy, 1956). According to this system, our ratings are: Experimental—learning 2, thinking 2, perception 2, imagination 4, motivation and emotion 4, memory 4; Physiological 0;[1] Animal 2; Developmental 4; Social 3; Personality 5; Therapy 4-5; Abnormal 5; and Industrial 4. It will be noted that our list and ratings do not differ substantially from Murphy's.

Having looked at the historical background of the present position of psychoanalysis, it remains for us to examine briefly some of the problems and prospects for the future, as psychoanalysis takes its place as part of psychology. One of us, in attempting a systematization of psychoanalytic theory, has presented the main lines of the problems that lie ahead (Rapaport, 1959, pp. 155–167). We shall outline some of these arguments, adding relevant points where appropriate. We urge the reader to refer to the original for a detailed discussion.

The obstacles to the integration of psychoanalysis with psychology are of two types: practical obstacles that lie in both psychology and psychoanalysis, and certain theoretical obstacles that arise from the nature of their common field of study.

The practical obstacles lying within psychology are various. We have already noted some of the problems arising from psychology's self-consciousness,[2] a self-consciousness which was reflected in a preoccupation with "*the* scientific method" and experimental design at the cost of substantive concern. There has been, too, a tendency in psychology toward addiction to a "single theory" or to a "single method," a trend closely associated to the prevalence of "schools." Another obstacle is the

1. Pribram's (1962) recent article examining Freud's "Project" is, however, an especially promising study relating present-day neuropsychological thinking to Freudian ideas.

2. For earlier discussions of these points, see Shakow (1953, 1956).

extension to problems in psychology of what Adelson (1956) has called the notion of "perfectibility"—the natural American propensity to be optimistic (see Shakow, 1960b). Although this attitude of optimism has become most obviously involved in problems in therapy, it can also be seen in theories about the basic nature of man (for instance, Maslow, 1962).[3] These theories have developed largely in reaction to an exaggerated concern with the pathological, but tend to neglect the negative forces with which individuals must contend. Psychoanalytic ego psychology appears to have dealt with this area in a much more realistic fashion.

Psychoanalysis, too, has its practical obstacles. The first of these is a problem which we considered earlier: the lack of a systematic theoretical literature, especially on the general psychoanalytic theory. Although this situation is to some extent being alleviated by the work of persons like Rapaport (1955, 1959) and Gill (1963), it still remains an obstacle to theoretical progress. Another handicap is the training offered by psychoanalytic institutes. Its almost exclusive limitation to physicians, its essentially "night school"[4] character, its emphasis on private practice which does not foster theoretical interest[5] and development, and results in a limited number and kind of patient, are all handicaps to theoretical progress. It is not surprising, therefore, that some demand has grown up in recent years for relatively independent institutes to be associated with both medical schools and with graduate departments of psychology (Shakow, 1962).

In addition to the two kinds of practical problems we have considered, there are a number of theoretical obstacles arising from the very nature of the subject matter and the field which psychoanalysis and psychology have in common. Regard for the individual's legal and moral rights is a major empirical barrier to the observation and manipulation of behavior inside and outside the laboratory. This problem also has important theoretical aspects: the effects of such trespass upon the subject, the observer, and the observation.[6] There is, too, the "hierarchy" problem. Much experimentation lies ahead before

3. It is surprising that in this work Maslow makes no reference to psychoanalytic ego psychology or ego psychologists.

4. With some exceptions, such as the Chicago Psychoanalytic Institute and the Boston Psychoanalytic Institute, which have weekend classes. But all institutes have the disadvantage of being part-time and do not afford the opportunity for serious full-time concentration.

5. As Boring said about his analyst: "He was, moreover, dealing solely and particularly with ME and not with the human mind in general. It was I, not he, who wanted to make the generalizations" (Boring, 1940, p. 6).

6. See Sternberg, Chapman, and Shakow (1958), Shakow (1960a), and Cohen and Cohen (1961) for a detailed discussion of some aspects of this problem.

laws of hierarchic transformation are developed which will permit adequate handling of field problems taken into the laboratory. Still another problem grows out of the fact that a large proportion of psychological phenomena occur only in the contact of one person with one or more others. The method of participant observation has been developed to deal with this problem, but the implications of this method have not yet been theoretically formulated,[7] and the lack of such systematization has in turn retarded the theory's development.[8] A final obstacle is that of mathematization, including quantification.

Some progress has been made in the attempt to deal with these various problems. First efforts are being made toward handling the difficulties created by participant observation through the development of alternative techniques. Knowledge of dyadic and other social situations is being advanced by the use of techniques for studying "organized complexity," interdisciplinary teams, and modern computational devices (Weaver, 1948). The "hierarchy" problem has offered more difficulties because the theoretical aspects of hierarchic transformation have not been developed. This difficulty is, of course, somewhat alleviated by the fact that not all problems need to be taken to the laboratory. Although as many problems as possible should be brought under laboratory control, efforts to deal rigorously with field situations should be continued and increased.[9] A start toward dealing with quantification would be a survey of "objective studies" of psychoanalysis. Instead of centering on the *results* of these studies, however, such a survey would give special attention to the *methods*, the *target variables*, and the *techniques* by which these variables were quantified.

Over a decade ago one of us had the opportunity to take stock of mid-century trends in what was broadly defined as the area of experimental psychology (Shakow, 1953). At that time a number of trends appeared conspicuous. One of these was the growing awareness by psychology of its own overconcern with its formal disciplinary aspects, and the resultant ego-[10] rather than task-orientation.[11] Together with this awareness were noted early signs of revolt against this

---

7. See, however, S. Bernfeld (1941), and Gross (1951).

8. This problem is considered in Sternberg, Chapman, and Shakow (1958) and in Shakow (1960a) in the context of a discussion of sound-film recording, which does not involve participant observation. Another variant, involving the use of closed-circuit television as a possible way to circumvent some of the problems of participation, is considered in Shakow (1959b).

9. See Barker (1963). Also see the discussion of Soskin's paper in "Proceedings of the Twenty-Fifth Anniversary Meeting of the Society for Research in Child Development" (1960, pp. 216–217). See also Hilgard, Gill, and Shakow (1953).

10. One view of some of the results of this ego-orientation is revealed in Broad's (1933, p. 476) extreme statement: "Poor dear Psychology, of course, never got far beyond

preoccupation with our neighbors' presumed interest in our affairs. Another important trend noted was the growing interest in Jamesian "more nutritious objects of study," reflected in increasing attention to molar studies, accompanied by a diligent search for methods to handle the "organized complexity" involved.

Rapaport (1959) has made some important complementary points. More recently, Koch, in his Epilogue to the third volume of *Psychology: A Study of a Science* (Koch, 1959, pp. 729-788), has presented a more systematic statement of a similar point of view. In his "concluding perspective," based on his review of the formulations made by the thirty-four contributors to the first three volumes of the *Study*, Koch says:

> It can in summary be said that the results of Study I set up a vast attrition against virtually all elements of the Age of Theory [approximately the 1930-1955 period] code. . . . [None of the contributors] is prepared to retreat one jot from the objectives and disciplines of scientific inquiry, but are inclined to re-examine reigning stereotypes about the *character* of such objectives and disciplines. There is a longing, bred on perception of the limits of recent history and nourished by boredom, for psychology to embrace . . . problems over which it is possible to feel intellectual passion. . . .
> *For the first time in its history, psychology seems ready—or almost ready—to assess its goals and instrumentalities with primary reference to its own indigenous problems.* . . .
> This preparedness to face the indigenous must be seen as no trivial deflection in the line of history. . . .
> . . . at the time of *its* inception, *psychology was unique in the extent to which its institutionalization preceded its content and its methods preceded its problems.* If there are keys to history, this statement is surely a key to the brief history of our science. . . . Never had inquiring men been so harried by social need, cultural optimism, extrinsic prescription, the advance scheduling of ways and means, the shining success story of the older sciences.
> The "scientism" that many see and some decry in recent psychology was thus with it from the start. It was conferred by the timing of its institutionalization. If psychology had been born a century, three centuries earlier, it would have been less "scientistic." There would have been that much less science, and science-of-science to emulate. Those who use the term "scientism" dismissively are sensing a problem but decrying the inevitable. Yet, few who fairly look at the brief history of our science could agree that the *balance* between

---

the stage of mediaeval physics, except in its statistical developments, where the labours of the mathematicians have enabled it to spin out the correlation of trivialities into endless refinements. For the rest it is only too obvious that, up to the present, a great deal of Psychology consists mainly of muddle, twaddle, and quacksalving, trying to impose itself as science by the elaborateness of its technical terminology and the confidence of its assertions."

11. This theme is also considered in Shakow (1949, pp. 203-204) in terms of "purity."

extrinsically defined tradition and creative innovation—prescription
and production—has for any sizeable interval been optimal. From the
earliest days of the experimental pioneers, man's stipulation that
psychology be adequate to *science* outweighed his commitment that it
be adequate to man. . . . It is, for instance, significant that a Freud,
when he arrived, did not emerge from the laboratories of 19th century
experimental psychology; nor was the ensuing tradition of work
particularly hospitable to his ideas until rendered desperate by the
human vacuum in its own content.

. . . There is a new contextualism abroad, a new readiness to
consider problem-centered curiosity a sufficient justification of
inquiry, but much effort is still invested in apologetically reconciling
such impulses with Age of Theory code. . . .

. . . What emerges from the critique of Age of Theory ideology
made by our authors is a far more open and liberated conception of the
task of psychology, the role of its investigators and systematists, than
we have enjoyed in recent history [Koch, 1959, pp. 783–786].

Why do we make so much of these developments? Because they have
direct reference to a central aspect of Freud's influence: the long delay in
integration of his ideas and the many vicissitudes hindering the
achievement of their appropriate place in psychology. But in making
these points about the past, are we not, as Koch says, "decrying the
inevitable"? Are we not trying to "hurry history," questioning the
relentless march of historical forces, the forces of the dominant aspects of
the *Zeitgeist*, which nothing could have changed? Those of us who have
wished that the integration of Freud into psychochology had been more
rapid recognize that it would have required psychologists who were
objective and task-oriented; who saw their central concern as the
understanding of human nature; who reacted to Freud as a colleague
(rather than as an outsider) equally interested in achieving this
understanding; who accepted Freud as bringing to the field an insight
into areas of crucial importance for psychology; who did their utmost to
understand the theories and the methods which were being proposed;
who marshaled the forces necessary for developing topics in these areas
further, expanding the methods to make them more searching. In fact,
earlier integration of psychoanalysis into psychology would have
demanded that the psychologists of the period disregard both internal
pressures and social pressures, would have demanded that they disregard
both their own values and prejudices and those facets of the scientific
Zeitgeist that impinged on them most closely. But, of course, it was the
Zeitgeist, as could have been predicted, that disposed otherwise.[12]

___

12. We are placing the "responsibility" here primarily on the *Zeitgeist*. We have a
sneaking notion that many more psychologists would have allied themselves with the
aspect of the *Zeitgeist* which emphasized the "meaningful" if they had not been so
overwhelmed by the "scientific" *Zeitgesit*.

It may be, of course, that just as the attainment of hybrid vigor requires different combinations of periods of inbreeding and outbreeding, so the optimal development of a science requires different concentrations of attitudes at different periods in its development. If this is so, then psychology has certainly gone through its period of "inbreeding." We have been through a period which has been weighted heavily with the strongly held narrownesses and limited commitments we have described, as well as with the "negatives" which Boring discusses with such tolerance (Boring, 1942, p. 613). Perhaps these were inevitable for the period.

Can it be, however, that an atmosphere favorable for the "outbreeding" which some wished for this earlier period, but which the meainstream of the *Zeitgeist* was not ready to support, is now in the process of developing? Can it be that we, with Koch, are correct in our judgment that now the main force of the scientific *Zeitgeist* is changing and asserting itself in an emphasis on meaningfulness, even though the new atmosphere is still permeated with the smog of tradition, the heritage of an irreversible history?

As the effects of its early negative characteristics—which we, however, cannot help believing any science needs in at least some degree during all phases of its growth—subside, psychology seems to be developing more positive qualities. These include a readiness to face substantive aspects of problems, with insistence upon only the degree of rigor necessary to protect the substance; an appreciation of the psychologist's personal motivations for entering the field (see Roe, 1953), and an appreciation of the stage of psychology's scientific development (see, for example, Adrian, 1946, and R. C. Tolman, 1947); a readiness to participate in a group commitment to a field where tolerance for tentativeness needs to be great; above all, an ability to recognize the value of a variety of approaches to psychology,[13] even if one's personal commitment is to one particular approach. These are the qualities of mature psychologists who have to work with an inevitably adolescent psychology.

Freud has at times been compared with various great "idea" men— Anaximander, Confucius, Jesus, Leonardo, Newton, Kierkegaard, Kant, Darwin, Marx, Pasteur, Einstein; with great *"conquistadores"*—

13. See R. B. Perry (1938, p. 79). Speaking of James, he said: "Had he known the psychology of today, he would have said, 'The tent of psychology should be large enough to provide a place for the bohemian and clinical speculations of a Freud, or the rigorous physiological methods of a Lashley, or the bold theoretical generalizations of a Köhler, or the useful statistical technique of a Spearman. Only time will tell which of these, or whether any of these, will yield the master hypothesis which will give to psychology that explanatory and predictive power, that control of the forces of nature, which has been achieved by the older sciences.'"

Moses, Hannibal, Columbus, Magellan, Captain Cook; and with great "methods" men such as Socrates. It is actually not surprising that the number and range, indeed, even the exaltedness, of the comparisons are so great. Besides' the difficulty of categorizing great men simply by finding their counterparts, there is the difficulty of keeping individual emotions out of the situation. From one point of view, Freud *was*, despite his own denials, a great "idea" man, whose ideas revolutionized[14] not only psychology but a large part of twentieth century thought. From another point of view, Freud *was* a *conquistador*, a great discoverer who opened up and explored hitherto unprobed areas in man. And again, Freud *was* a great "methods" man (see S. Bernfeld, 1949, pp. 183-184), as the "free association" method attests.[15]

But one thing characterized Freud above all: the constantly changing, developing nature of his theoretical system. He continually checked his hypotheses and theories against his observations, always ready to adjust them in reply to the demands of new facts. (There was, of course, an element of natural reluctance about revising his views, particularly in cases where new data originated outside of his own experience.) In all his correcting and revising he was constantly building, basing new ideas on new or old theories and hypotheses, even going back to long abandoned ideas if new data warranted.

Should we not try to emulate him by avoiding the extremes of either accepting his theories as dogma merely because they are his, or rejecting these same theories merely to indicate our independence from him? Can we not follow his own essential concern for congruence between fact and theory, building in part on what he has already given us, examining his

14. In line with Kuhn's (1962) discussion of paradigms, Freud may be said to have been truly a "revolutionist," for he replaced an older paradigm with a newer one. Those who do so are the persons who are called "great men." Also see Boring's (1963) Presidential Address, "Eponym as Placebo," at the XVII International Congress of Psychology.

15. And we would be negligent in not adding that Freud was a great "faults" man as well. That Freud had a number of traits that might be considered negative needs pointing out for the implications they may—or may not—have for the evaluation of his theories. Jones (1955, Chapter XVI) discusses most of them, including his preoccupation with personal secrecy, his indiscreetness, his tendency to make black-and-white judgments of people, his dependence upon and overestimation of others. The last was, not surprisingly, accompanied by "defensive" imperviousness to their views.

In quite another class of "faults" lie Freud's presumed or actual personal problems (about many of which Puner [1947] speaks), and the "subjective prejudices" which led to his overemphasis on sex (about which Jung [1962] reminisced toward the end of his life). Taken at one level, whatever the retrospective falsification involved in Jung's memories after some half a century, we must admit that no matter how necessary the emphasis on sex may have been to compensate for its previous neglect, and how much of this can be explained by the broad definition given sex in Freud's system, the early overemphasis cannot be denied. It led to many perhaps unnecessary misunderstandings which only later

views and testing them to the fullest, and developing new theories as needed?

What use are *psychologists*—all those professionally involved with human nature—to make of Freudian thinking? The answer lies essentially in the recognition that Freudian thinking is part of man's conquest of nature—the understanding of human nature. Psychoanalysis, like psychology of which it is a part, is not the possession of any group, not the property of the members of any organized association; it belongs to man. Being an "early Freudian" or a "trained Freudian" may carry certain rewards and certain claims in other settings, but has no relevance here. For psychoanalysis is part of the heritage which great men provide. As the discipline most directly involved, it is up to psychology to understand, develop, and build on this heritage, making the changes that imagination coupled with careful observation and experiment indicate.

REFERENCES

ADELSON, J. (1956), Freud in America: Some Observations. *Amer. Psychologist*, 11:467-470.

ADRIAN, E. D. (1946), The Mental and the Physical Origins of Behaviour. *Int. J. Psycho-Anal.*, 27:1-6.

BERNFELD, S. (1949), Freud's Scientific Beginnings. *Amer. Imago*, 6:163-196.

BORING, E. G. (1942), *Sensation and Perception in the History of Experimental Psychology*. New York: Appleton-Century.

———— (1948), Book Review: W. Dennis, ed., "Current Trends in Psychology." *Psychol. Bull.*, 45:75-84.

———— (1963), Eponym as Placebo. In *History, Psychology, and*

developments, particularly the more recent emphases in ego psychochology and the efforts of the neo-Freudians, are helping to correct. This particular problem is a most complicated one which we cannot enter into here.

But taken at another level, most of these arguments are essentially puerile, and relevant at only a minor level of discourse. They are obviously irrelevant at the crucial level with which we are concerned, the one dealing with the fundamental importance and soundness of theories. Theories in psychology, especially motivational theories, *must* come out of man's struggle with himself. They are too near the center of man's being to be developed "objectively," without regard for content, and divorced from living. Theories in the biological and natural sciences, though equally subject to determination by generalized needs, are much less likely to be contentually affected by the personalities of their originators. But psychology's subject matter is by its very nature associated with the "muck"—the repository of needs, memories, perceptions, feelings—that constitutes the history of our being. By their objective examination, however, psychologists compare and transform this muck, and from such processes general theories develop.

Science: Selected Papers, ed. R. I. Watson & D. T. Campbell. New York: Wiley, pp. 5-25.

GILL, M. M. (1963), Topography and Systems in Psychoanalytic Theory. *Psychological Issues*, 3(2). New York: International Universities Press.

JONES, E. (1955), *The Life and Work of Sigmund Freud*. Vol. 2: Years of Maturity, 1901-1919. New York: Basic Books.

JUNG, C.G. (1962), Jung on Freud. *Atlant. Monthly*. 210:47-58.

KOCH, S. (1959), Epïlogue. In *Psychology: A Study of a Science*. Vol. 3: Formulations of the Person and the Social Context, ed. S. Koch. New York: McGraw-Hill, pp. 729-788.

KUHN, T. S. (1962), *The Structure of Scientific Revolutions*. Chicago: University of Chicago Press.

MASLOW, A. H. (1962), *Toward a Psychology of Being*. Princeton, N. J.: Van Nostrand.

MURPHY, G. (1956), The Current Impact of Freud upon Psychology. *Amer. Psychologist*, 11:663-672.

NELSON, B., ed. (1957), *Freud and the 20th Century*. New York: Meridian Books.

PERRY, R. B. (1938), *In the Spirit of William James*. New Haven: Yale University Press.

PUNER, H. W. (1947), *Freud: His Life and His Mind*. New York: Dell, 1961.

RAPAPORT, D. (1955), *The Development and the Concepts of Psychoanalytic Ego Psychology*. Twelve seminars given at the Western New England Institute for Psychoanalysis. Multilithed.

———— (1959), The Structure of Psychoanalytic Theory: A Systematizing Attempt. In *Psychology: A Study of a Science*. Vol. 3: Formulations of the Person and the Social Context, ed. S. Koch. New York: McGraw-Hill, pp. 55-183. Also in *Psychological Issues*, 2(2). New York: International Universities Press, 1960.

RIEFF, P. (1959), *Freud: The Mind of the Moralist*. New York: Viking Press.

ROE, A. (1953), A Psychological Study of Eminent Psychologists and Anthropologists, and a Comparison with Biological and Physical Scientists. *Psychol. Monogr.*, 67(2): Whole No. 352.

SHAKOW, D. (1953), Some Aspects of Mid-Century Psychiatry: Experimental Psychology. In *Mid-Century Psychiatry*, ed. R. R. Grinker. Springfield, Ill.: Thomas, pp. 76-103.

———— (1960U), Psicopatologia y Psicologia: Nota Sobre Tendencias. *Rev. Psicol. Gen. Apl., Madrid*. 15:835-837.

———— (1962), Psychoanalytic Education of Behavioral and Social Scientists for Research. In *Science and Psychoanalysis*. Vol. 5: Psychoanalytic Education, ed. J. H. Masserman. New York: Grune & Stratton, pp. 146-161.

TOLMAN, R. C. (1947), A Survey of the Sciences. *Science*, 106:135-140.

WEAVER, W. (1948), Science and Complexity. *Amer. Scientist*, 36:536-544.

Mohammed Mujeeb-ur-Rahman received his Ph.D. in psychology from the University of New Mexico where he served for a time as assistant professor of psychology. He has lectured in psychology at Osmanian University, India, has held an appointment at St. Francis Xavier University in Nova Scotia, and has served as a consultant to the Stanford Research Institute. At the present time, he is a member of the psychology department at the University of Prince Edward Island, Canada.

2295-3-SB
5-45